R307.77

Utopias in American History

Utopias in American History

JYOTSNA SREENIVASAN

A B C · C L I O

Santa Barbara, California   Denver, Colorado   Oxford, England

Library of Congress Cataloging-in-Publication Data

Sreenivasan, Jyotsna.
Utopias in American history / Jyotsna Sreenivasan.
p.   cm.
Includes bibliographical references and index.
ISBN 978-1-59884-052-0 (hard copy : alk. paper)—ISBN 978-1-59884-053-7 (ebook : alk. paper)   1. Utopias—United States—History.   I. Title.
HX653.S64 2008
307.770973—dc22   2008027051

12 11 10 09 08   1 2 3 4 5 6 7 8 9 10

Editorial Manager: James P. Sherman
Submission Editor: Alex Mikaberidze
Production Editors: Anna A. Moore/Christian Green
Production Manager: Don Schmidt
Media Editor: Jason Kniser
Media Resources Manager: Caroline Price
File Manager: Paula Gerard

ABC-CLIO, Inc.
130 Cremona Drive, P.O. Box 1911
Santa Barbara, California 93116–1911

This book is also available on the World Wide Web as an ebook.
Visit www.abc-clio.com for details.

This book is printed on acid-free paper. ∞
Manufactured in the United States of America

Contents

Acknowledgments

I would like to thank my editors at ABC-CLIO for their enthusiasm, insights, and help with this book: Steven Danver and Alexander Mikaberidze. I would also like to thank Betsy Bybell at the Latah County Public Library in Moscow, Idaho, for going beyond the call of duty to procure stacks of obscure books on long-forgotten communities through the Inter-Library Loan system. I couldn't have written this book without all of you!

Introduction

What Is a Utopian Community?

Utopia is a word coined by Thomas More, a 16th-century English writer, from two Greek words. It literally means "nowhere." More imagined and wrote about an ideal country where citizens lived in harmony and prosperity. He called his ideal country "Utopia."

Today, a "utopian community" refers to a group of people trying to live according to their highest values. Utopian communities are communities in which unrelated people live together by choice and that are designed to foster values that the members think are important, such as spirituality, cooperation, economic equality, or a simple lifestyle. These communities are formed to offer what are seen as better alternatives, a better way of life, than what can be found in the larger society. These kinds of communities are also called communes, collective settlements, or intentional communities.

Members of utopian communities generally share resources and labor. In other words, the members of the community live together, work together, and share their money, food, and other belongings, to a greater or lesser degree. Some communities go as far as sharing things like child care, with the entire community involved in caring for the children. In other communities, families have their own houses and their own belongings, but they may share strict spiritual beliefs, rules about living, and some work and property.

All societies—including the one you live in now—are designed with some values and foster some values. But utopian communities are very aware of how their values differ from those of the larger world. They are proactive in promoting their own values and trying to create structures that foster them.

The Beginnings of Utopian Communal Life

Communal living may have begun with human evolution. Historian Donald Pitzer points out that early humans banded into kinship groups and tribes. These cooperative groups helped individual members to survive and thrive (1997, 3).

As human society developed, so too did the urge for some groups to withdraw from the mainstream of society and create their own idealistic, utopian communities. The earliest utopian communes that scholars are aware of may have been self-sufficient Taoist communes in China in the fifth century BCE. In the Western world, the earliest utopian communities that we have evidence of are the Jewish Essenes, who attempted to create their own communities in the face of the imposition of Greek values upon their culture. About 4,000 Essenes lived communally in Palestine (now

Israel) from 150 BCE to 68 CE. The early Christians also lived communally, according to the New Testament Book of Acts (Zablocki 1980, 25–26).

Throughout most of history, the vast majority of utopian communities had a religious or spiritual basis. In fact, some of the most widespread and enduring types of utopian communities are monasteries and nunneries, where men and women live separately and carry out religious duties. We will not discuss these in this book, but will concentrate on communities that include women, men, and children.

Why Study Utopias in American History?

You might ask, Why study communal utopias in America? After all, America is the land of individualism, of personal freedom. The "American Dream" is the idea that any individual, with hard work and determination, can achieve success and prosperity. Communal sharing has nothing to do with American values—does it?

Yet the freedom experienced by those who live in the United States has also led in a different direction. A 1998 article in the *Washington Post* about a modern socialist commune, Twin Oaks, is entitled "The Other American Dream." And in many ways starting a utopian community is in fact an alternative American dream.

Utopian communities among the Europeans in the New World began soon after the Pilgrims arrived. Starting in the 17th century, persecuted religious sects fled Europe for North America, and some of them set themselves up communally in the land that would become the United States. The first communal society in the New World is believed to have been the Valley of the Swans, an extraordinary group founded in Delaware in 1663, which espoused freedom of thought and religion, and separation of church and state. Unfortunately this fledgling community was destroyed by the English in 1664.

An Israeli scholar who has studied American communes, Yaacov Oved, points out that "since 1735 there has been a continuous and unbroken existence of communes in the United States. There is no equivalent in any of the other countries of the modern world" (1988, 3). Oved gives several reasons for this phenomenon, including the availability of land (albeit land taken from the American Indians) and a tradition of liberty and religious tolerance. Paul Boyer suggests that "American society, with its comparative lack of hierarchy, freedom from the weight of tradition, and openness to social innovation, has historically provided a particularly congenial environment in which communal experimentation could flourish" (1997, xi).

A number of religious groups, persecuted for their beliefs in Europe, fled to the New World and later the United States in order to live in peace, and some of them formed communal societies. Such groups include the Society of the Woman in the Wilderness, the Amish, the Shakers, the Harmony Society, the Zoar Society, the Amana Colonies, and Bishop Hill.

In addition to religious tolerance, the U.S. political system was inspiring to others. According to Oved, the United States itself was designed to "set an example of a perfect society. . . . The United States, being independent of the old system, would carry the message of a social experiment for all of humanity. It would be the place where those social and political ideals, which European thinkers had cogitated but which could not be carried out there, might materialize" (1988, 5). Robert Owen (founder of New Harmony), Etienne Cabet (founder of the Icarian movement), Thomas Hughes (founder of Rugby), and other European social reformers looked to the United States as a place where their ideal society might take root and flourish.

According to Arthur Bestor, "of all the freedoms for which America stood, none was more significant for history than the freedom to experiment with new practices and new institutions" (1950, 1). Bestor sees communal living as one of four ways of reforming society. The other three are the individual thinker who influences others; revolution; and gradualistic reform movements targeting certain conditions (such as alcoholism or poverty). "Communitarianism does not correspond to any of these [other three]. It is collectivistic not individualistic, it is resolutely opposed to revolution, and it is impatient with gradualism" (1950, 3–4).

Another reason to study utopian communities, besides their significance in American history, is that such communities can give us insights into new ways of solving problems. According to sociologist Rosabeth Moss Kanter:

> Social science has rarely had "laboratories" of the scale and scope of utopian communities. Contemporary social systems, from schools to families to businesses, are founded on many assumptions about human needs and the requirements of social life, which communities challenge. Confronting the "givens" of American life with data from communal orders poses interesting questions. For example, can commitment and collective feeling replace individual, material rewards as a source of motivation? Is the nuclear family in its present, isolated form a necessary ingredient in emotional satisfaction? Could productive work be reorganized, perhaps in terms of rotating shared jobs rather than individual careers? . . . As America's problems grow, so does the need for conceiving new ways of being and doing, and hence for a return of the utopian imagination (1972, viii).

Overview of Utopian Communities in America

Over the history of the United States, there have been a number of "peaks" of commune building—times when more communal societies started. The first of these peaks occurred in the late 1700s (when the Shakers were newly active). The first part of the 1800s saw several waves of Christian and socialist community building, including the Christian communal societies of Harmony, Zoar, Bishop Hill, and Oneida; the socialist communities New Harmony, the Icarian movement, and the Fourierist phalanxes; and the antislavery communities. Toward the end of the 1800s, the Christian Hutterites arrived in the United States, and have since grown into one of the largest utopian communal movements in the country. The end of the 1800s was also an active period for communities based on socialism and other new economic and political theories: the socialist Kaweah Cooperative Commonwealth began, as well as Fairhope, based on the single-tax theory, and Home, an anarchist community. The Theosophical Point Loma also started at this time.

The years of the Great Depression, the 1930s, saw a flurry of cooperative and communal activity sponsored by the U.S. government: the New Deal communities, which involved about 50,000 people. Also starting at this time was the Catholic Worker Movement, an anarchist and socialist movement to help the needy. The Peace Mission Movement experienced incredible growth during the Great Depression. During the late

1960s and 1970s, the hippie-inspired communes took off, including communities based on Eastern religions and the "Jesus Freak" communities (Zablocki 1980, 31–32).

The latest major American utopian communal movement, the cohousing movement, which began in 1991 in the United States, had grown to over 2,000 households as of 2007 and is poised for even greater growth.

Kanter divides utopian communities into three categories: those with a desire to live according to spiritual values; those that hoped to reform society through political or economic means; and those that wanted to promote personal growth by connecting people on a deeper level. Kanter suggests that these three categories correspond in a general way with three historical periods of American communities. Spiritual communities predominated until 1845; communities based on socialism, anarchism, or other political or economic ideals flourished from 1820 to 1930 or so; and communities that promoted personal growth became important after World War II, and especially in the 1960s. However, she points out that communities can belong to more than one category. For example, Oneida was a Christian community, yet was also interested in socialism and personal growth (1972, 8–9).

Some utopian communities of the past have left a lasting impression, even after the community itself has folded. The Moravian movement founded the towns of Bethlehem, Pennsylvania, and Winston-Salem, North Carolina. The Shakers pioneered a unique, simple style of furniture that is still in high demand today. They are also credited with inventing many tools still in use; for example, the flat broom, clothespin, and circular saw. The members of the many short-lived Fourierist communities were involved with starting the cooperative movement in the United States, as were members of the Jewish agricultural communities. Out of the Oneida community grew one of the world's largest manufacturers of silverware. A business started by Amana members has become one of the world's largest manufacturers of refrigerators. Synanon pioneered a self-help approach to treating drug addicts.

There are many utopian or intentional communities around the world today. The Fellowship for Intentional Community estimates that there are several thousand such communities, including the more than 900 listed in its *2007 Communities Directory*. Many of these communities are small or in the formative stages.

In this book, we examine only a small number of the many utopian communities that have formed and dissolved over the history of the United States. This book concentrates on communities that are (or have been) exceptionally large, long-lived, influential, or unique. I have tried to cover the important communities in the history of the United States through the early years of the 21st century, but I know I may have overlooked communities that others might consider important.

Why Form a Utopian Community?

Some communities were formed in order to separate their members from the outside world, which was seen as sinful. These communities did not want to influence or interact with the outside world—they simply wanted to be left alone to live their own separate lifestyle. Often, these communities had to flee persecution in Europe. The Amana Colonies, the Amish, the Harmony Society, the Hutterites, the Zoar Society, the Bruderhof, and the Love Family are examples of such separatist communities.

Other religious communities, while believing the outside world to be sinful, interacted extensively with outsiders. They wanted to influence outsiders to join with them and be "saved." Such communities included the Davidian and Branch Davidian movements and the House of David movement. The International Society for Krishna Consciousness (Hare Krishnas) also believed the outside world to be sinful, yet actively sought converts in the outside world: they believed that chanting the Hare Krishna mantra (prayer) would lead to spiritual awakening, peace, and unity.

Some communities—particularly socialist communities—were formed in order to influence and transform the outside world into adopting the lifestyle and values of the communal experiment. These communities hoped that their shining example would influence others to form similar communities. New Harmony, the first secular, socialist community in the United States, founded in 1825, was meant to be a model for a plan to be adopted all over the industrialized world. The Icarians, a socialist community of French immigrants founded in 1848, hoped to set up a huge community with as many as a million people, which would be the envy of the rest of the world. The Llano colonies, socialist communities founded in 1914, thought they had a solution to the widespread poverty of the Great Depression. In 1933, the Llano leader worked with a Texas senator to introduce national legislation that would have replicated the Llano colony around the country as a way to solve unemployment.

Some nonsocialist communities also hoped to transform the outside world. The founder of the Brotherhood of the New Life (1861–1900), Thomas Lake Harris, wrote that he and his followers believed their community to be "a germ of the Kingdom of Heaven, dropped from upper space and implanted in the bosom of the earthly humanity—in fine, the seed of a new order; the initial point for a loftier and sweeter evolution of man" (Hinds 1961, 143). The Fairhope community, founded in 1894, hoped that its example of single-tax economics would convince the rest of the country to adopt the single tax. The leader of Point Loma, a Theosophical community founded in 1897, hoped to set up a series of "Raja Yoga" schools around the world, modeled on the one at Point Loma. The Ananda Colonies, founded in 1968, hope to "usher in a new spiritual renaissance" around the world, according to their Web site.

Although no single community movement succeeded in transforming the outside world to the extent that they envisioned, together they offer a real alternative to mainstream American society, based as it is on private ownership, nuclear families, and materialism. The communities showed Americans (who were often intensely curious about communal experiments) that there were other ways of living a happy, productive life.

Why Live in a Utopian Community?

Why do people choose to leave their familiar ways of life and join with other people to follow unfamiliar rules and live in a way that might be considered unusual?

People join for practical as well as idealistic reasons. During times of economic hardship, people might join a communal society if they believe that it will help them provide for their families, or provide a way out of an intolerable living situation. People also join a community because they want to live with others who share their religious beliefs, or their beliefs in other values such as economic equality. They might join because they want to become part of a small, close-knit community, or to live with a friend or family member who is already part of that community (Zablocki 1980, 105).

The Shakers, a Christian sect that split from the Quakers, are one of the most famous of the American utopian communities. Thousands of people joined the Shakers from the time they landed in the American colonies in 1774 through the early 1900s, when they became largely defunct. One estimate suggests that at least 20,000 people lived part of their lives as a Shaker (Brewer 1997, 37). Why were people attracted to this religion that required them to give up marriage, childbearing, and personal property?

William Kephart suggests that some of the reasons may have been practical. In the 18th and 19th centuries, divorce was illegal or, at best, difficult to obtain. A woman or man in an unhappy marriage could join the Shakers and be separated from her or his spouse, since the women and men lived separately (1978).

Another practical reason for joining may have been economic. A person who was having trouble making enough money—such as a widow with young children—could join the Shakers and receive adequate food, clothing, and child care in exchange for working within the community. During the 18th and 19th centuries, there was no life insurance and jobs for women were limited.

However, not everyone who joined the Shakers came from an unhappy marriage, or was having trouble making ends meet. Many people were truly attracted to the Shaker religion—the combination of order and simplicity in daily life and the frenzied dancing and singing on Sundays. Some people believed that Mother Ann (the Shakers' first leader) was indeed the female incarnation of Christ (Kephart 1978 164–166).

In times of economic trouble, there is great advantage to pooling resources and living communally. The Zoar Society, a Christian sect that fled Germany, originally adopted communal living, because, upon arriving in the United States, it realized that some of its members were too old or sick to farm their own private land. A member of the Zoar Society describes the benefits of communal living:

> The advantages are many and great. All distinctions of rich and poor are abolished. The members have no care except for their own spiritual culture. Communism provides for the sick, the weak, the unfortunate, all alike, which makes their life comparatively easy and pleasant. In case of great loss by fire or flood or other cause, the burden that would be ruinous to one is easily borne by the many. Charity and genuine love to one another, which are the foundations of true Christianity, can be more readily cultivated and practiced in Communism than in common, isolated society. Finally, a Community is the best place in which to get rid of selfishness, willfulness, and bad habits and vices generally; for we are subject to the constant surveillance and reproof of others, which, rightly taken, will go far toward preparing us for the large Community above (Hinds 1961, 38).

In addition to the economic benefits, the Zoar member quoted above emphasized the spiritual benefits of communal living: that charity and love for one another can be better fostered in a communal setting. Indeed, the spiritual aspect of communal living was often of primary importance. A number of Christian communities adopted communal living because they believed in following the example of the early Christian church as described in the New Testament Book of Acts of the Apostles. After the death of Jesus, the early Christians shared all their wealth and resources with each other, and no one was to own any private property. American communities influenced by the Book of Acts include Bishop Hill, Bohemia Manor, The Family/Children of God, The Farm, Harmony Society, the House of David movement, Jesus People USA, the Shakers, and the Zoar Society.

Even if a community did not take its inspiration from the Book of Acts, the members might still choose communal living for spiritual reasons. The Moravians, who began settling in the United States in 1741, were a branch of an Eastern European Protestant sect. They discovered that members of a similar age and life situation encouraged each others' spiritual growth, so in some of their communities, they organized their living arrangements into "choirs"—single women lived communally with other single women, single men lived with other single men, and married people lived in their own choirs.

The Hutterites, a Christian Anabaptist sect (those who believe in adult baptism), fled Germany for the United States in 1874. For them, communal living is intimately tied to their spiritual beliefs. They believe that in order to return to God (from whom we were separated because of Adam and Eve's fall from grace), one should live communally, share income and property, and remain separate from the rest of the world. Hutterites believe that the individual "self" must be broken, and that every person should work and live for the sake of the entire community.

The Catholic Worker Movement, a socialist and anarchist spiritual movement founded in 1933 to serve the poor and needy, believes that its communal homes are a way "to live in accordance with the justice and charity of Jesus Christ," according to its Web site.

During the 1960s and 1970s, when the hippie youth movement led to the formation of perhaps a thousand utopian communities, young people joined such communities because of distrust with mainstream society and of the belief in the idea that by creating a new kind of society, they could create a new kind of human: one who is unselfish and free (Kephart 1978, 284–287).

Why Do Some Utopian Communities Endure while Many Others Fail after a Few Years?

There have been perhaps thousands of utopian communities formed throughout the history of the United States. Most were very small and/or very short-lived. Are there certain qualities or practices that help some communities to survive longer than a few years?

In order to answer this question, Kanter compared 30 19th-century American communities: nine that lasted at least 33 years and 21 that lasted 15 years or less. The successful communities included the Shakers, the Harmony Society, Amana, Zoar, the Keil communities, Oneida, and Jerusalem. The unsuccessful communities included Brook Farm and other Fourierist phalanxes, Bishop Hill, and New Harmony and other Owenite communities (1972).

Kanter concluded that the successful communities included more "commitment mechanisms" than the unsuccessful ones. In other words, the successful communities included more ways to cause members to be fully committed to the community. These commitment mechanisms allowed the communities to survive challenges such as poverty, illness, fire, persecution, and natural disasters. Without many commitment mechanisms, the unsuccessful communities tended to disband in the face of challenges (1972).

Kanter identifies six commitment mechanisms that communities use. "Sacrifice" means that members must give up something in order to join. Members might commit to giving up alcohol, tobacco, rich foods, meat, fashionable dress, luxurious living arrangements, or sexual relations. Although one might expect that sacrifices would discourage people from remaining in a community, Kanter says the opposite occurs. "Once members have agreed to make the 'sacrifices,' their motivation to remain participants increases" (1972, 76). "Investment" is the idea that members must contribute property and/or labor to the community, and they may not be reimbursed for these when they leave. "Renunciation" involves giving up relationships outside of the community, and also weakening exclusive relationships within the community (such as couple or family relationships), so that members are connected strongly to the group as a whole, and not to individuals within or outside the community. "Communion," the feeling of connectedness and belonging within the whole group, is fostered when members share work, meals, property, meetings, and celebrations. "Mortification" occurs when communities have practices to help members change their behavior to fit with the ideals of the community. For example, some communities used regular confession or public punishment of people who deviated from community rules. They might honor certain spiritually advanced people with leadership positions. "Transcendence," the feeling of being part of something meaningful and awe-inspiring, can be fostered with a group ideology or philosophy that explains important aspects of humanity and the world and a leader who is seen as having spiritual or magical powers (1972, 75–125).

These commitment mechanisms helped members to be more committed to the group as a whole, and to its survival, than to themselves or their biological families.

How This Book Is Organized

This book is organized to allow you to easily compare and contrast the utopian communities. For each community, information about when the community began and ended, the religious or other belief system, how the community earns money, how the leaders are chosen, how children are cared for and educated, and so forth are included.

Separate entries are included on the philosophies and ideologies that influenced the formation of communal utopias, such as anarchism and socialism. Historic events of importance to communal utopias have separate entries as well, including the Industrial Revolution and the Great Depression.

The book also covers topics of general concern, such as child rearing, education, leadership, the status of women, and pacifism. These topics will help you understand how different communities throughout history have dealt with these important issues.

The chronology that follows this introduction will help you to put the various communal movements in perspective with other events in American history.

You will notice that, while each community believes that it is doing things in order to live the best possible life, each has different views as to what that life should be like, and how to achieve it.

References

Bestor, Arthur Eugene. *Backwoods Utopias: The Sectarian and Owenite Phases of Communitarian Socialism in America: 1663–1829*. Philadelphia: University of Pennsylvania Press, 1950.

Boyer, Paul. "Foreword," in *America's Communal Utopias*, edited by Donald Pitzer. Chapel Hill: University of North Carolina Press, 1997, ix–xiii.

Brewer, Priscilla. "The Shakers of Mother Ann Lee," in *America's Communal Utopias*, edited by Donald Pitzer. Chapel Hill: University of North Carolina Press, 1997, 37–56.

Hinds, William Alfred. *American Communities*. New York: Corinth Books, 1961.

Kanter, Rosabeth Moss. *Commitment and Community: Communes and Utopias in Sociological Perspective*. Cambridge, MA: Harvard University Press, 1972.

Kephart, William. *Extraordinary Groups: The Sociology of Unconventional Life-Styles*. New York: St. Martin's Press, 1978.

Oved, Yaacov. *Two Hundred Years of American Communes*. New Brunswick, NJ: Transaction Books, 1988.

Pitzer, Donald. "Introduction," in *America's Communal Utopias*, edited by Donald Pitzer. Chapel Hill: University of North Carolina Press, 1997, 3–13.

Zablocki, Benjamin. *Alienation and Charisma: A Study of Contemporary American Communes*. New York: The Free Press, 1980.

Chronology

1492 Christopher Columbus sails from Spain and lands in North America. His goal is to find gold and slaves to enrich Spanish coffers. His voyage marks the beginning of exploration by Europeans of the Americas and the beginning of the genocide that killed millions of Native Americans.

1500s The first black slaves are believed to have traveled to North and South America with French, Spanish, and Portuguese explorers.

1565 Spaniards found St. Augustine, Florida—the first permanent European settlement in what is now the United States.

1607 About 100 colonists from England found Jamestown in present-day Virginia, on land that was part of an Indian confederacy led by Chief Powhatan.

1619 The first black slaves begin to arrive in the American colonies.

1620 Puritans from England establish Plymouth Colony in present-day Massachusetts, on land inhabited by the Wampanoag Indians.

1636 Harvard College is founded.

1647 Massachusetts establishes the first public school system in the American colonies.

1663 Valley of the Swans, a liberal Christian community based on freedom of religion, speech, and thought, is founded in Delaware by Dutch settlers. The community is destroyed by English forces in 1664.

1684 Bohemia Manor, a branch of the Protestant Dutch Labadist community, starts in Maryland.

1694 The Society of the Woman in the Wilderness, a celibate millennialist Christian community, is begun in Pennsylvania after members flee Germany. The community ends in 1708.

1727 Bohemia Manor in Maryland ends.
   The Amish, who are Christian Anabaptists, begin fleeing to the United States from Switzerland. They settle first in Pennsylvania.

1732 The Ephrata Cloister, a Christian Pietist community, is started in Pennsylvania with a leader from Germany.

1741 The Moravian movement, a Protestant sect from Eastern Europe, starts its first American settlement in Pennsylvania. In 1753, members start a second major settlement in North Carolina.

1752 The first cooperative-type business in the American colonies, a fire insurance company, is started in Philadelphia by Benjamin Franklin.

1754 The French and Indian War starts over which country—France or Great Britain—would control eastern North America.

1763 The French and Indian War ends with Great Britain as the winner.

In an effort to control the colonies and enrich its treasury (depleted from the French and Indian War), Great Britain stations a standing army in North America and begins passing laws taxing the colonists for molasses, newspapers, tea, paint, and other goods.

1770 The Boston Massacre occurs, during which British troops kill three civilians and wound eight others after civilians taunt the troops.

1773 The Boston Tea Party takes places to protest the tax on tea; colonists dump British tea into Boston Harbor.

1774 The Shakers, a Christian offshoot of the Quakers, starts in New York when their leader and a handful of followers flee England.

The First Continental Congress meets to discuss actions against the British.

1775 The Revolutionary War begins between American colonists and the British government.

1776 The Second Continental Congress declares the colonies to be independent of the British, writes the Declaration of Independence, and forms the United States of America.

1783 The Revolutionary War ends with the Treaty of Paris, giving the United States control over all of North America from the Atlantic Ocean to the Mississippi River.

1786 The Ephrata Cloister ends its fully communal economy.

1787 The U.S. Constitution is written and ratified the following year. The Bill of Rights is added in 1791.

1788 Jerusalem, a communal society associated with the Society of Universal Friends, the first religious group to be founded by a native-born American woman, is started in New York.

1800 Washington, D.C., becomes the nation's capital.

Early 1800s Industrialization begins slowly in the United States.

1803 The Harmony Society, a Separatist Christian sect, starts in Pennsylvania when its leader and his followers flee Germany.

The Louisiana Purchase is finalized. President Thomas Jefferson buys the land between the Mississippi River and the Rocky Mountains from France for $15 million and the size of the United States almost doubles.

1804 Meriwether Lewis and William Clark leave St. Louis to begin their exploration of the Louisiana Territory and the Oregon region, reaching the Oregon coast in 1805 and returning to St. Louis in 1806.

1812 The U.S. Congress declares war on Great Britain for allegedly interfering in American shipping and encouraging Indians to attack pioneers. During this War of 1812, British troops capture Washington, D.C., in 1814 and burn the Capitol. The Treaty of Ghent ends the war in 1815, with neither side winning.

1814 The Harmony Society moves to Indiana.

1817 The Zoar Society, a Christian Pietist sect, is founded in Ohio when members flee Germany.

1819 The first antislavery communities begin, which were largely unplanned and very informal.

1820 The Missouri Compromise calls for Missouri to be admitted to the union as a slave state (in which slave-owning is allowed) and Maine to enter as a free state (in which slavery is not allowed).

Jerusalem in New York ends.

1824 The Harmony Society moves back to Pennsylvania.

1825 New Harmony, the first nonreligious, socialist community in the United States, begins on Harmony Society land in Indiana. The community, spearheaded by Robert Owen, lasts only until 1827. However, Owen inspires the formation of a number of other socialist communities through the 1860s.

The Erie Canal, the most important American canal, is completed, connecting the Hudson River in New York with the Great Lakes.

1825 to 1835 Over 1,300 religious revivals take place in western New York, giving this region the name "Burned-Over District," from the religious fervor burning in people. The Burned-Over District gives rise to a number of utopian communal movements.

1826 Nashoba, one of the first planned antislavery communities, begins in Tennessee and ends four years later, in 1830.

1829 Wilberforce, one of the first antislavery communities to be formed by African Americans, is started in Ontario, Canada, and ends in 1836.

1830 The Church of Jesus Christ of Latter-day Saints (Mormons) is founded by Joseph Smith in New York. Mormons value economic cooperation.

Congress passes the Indian Removal Act, which forces the eastern Indian tribes to move west in order to make room for white settlers.

1830s and 1840s The antislavery movement gains momentum and attention. Harriet Tubman leads 300 slaves to freedom through the Underground Railroad.

1831 Equity, an anarchist community, is started in Ohio. This short-lived community ends in 1835.

1836 The American Transcendentalist movement starts with the publication of the book-length poetic essay *Nature* by Ralph Waldo Emerson and the formation of the Transcendental Club in Boston.

1841 Brook Farm, a community founded on principles of American Transcendentalism, starts in Massachusetts.

1842 Dawn, an antislavery community featuring a school for former slaves called the British-American Institute, is founded in Ontario, Canada, and ends in 1868.

1843 The Amana Colonies, a Christian Pietist community, starts when members flee Germany and settle on land in upstate New York.

The North American Phalanx, a major community based on the ideas of French socialist Charles Fourier, starts in New Jersey.

1844 Brook Farm converts to a Fourierist phalanx.

The Wisconsin Phalanx, a major Fourierist phalanx, begins and ends in 1850.

The Keil community, a Christian sect, starts in Missouri. A second branch is begun in 1856 in Oregon.

1846 By this year, 24 Fourierist phalanxes had begun in the eastern and midwestern states, and also by this year about 15 of them had already folded.

Bishop Hill members, persecuted for their Pietist Christian beliefs, flee Sweden and settle in Illinois.

1847 Brook Farm ends.

Utopia, an anarchist community, is started in Ohio and ends in 1865.

1848 The Icarian movement, a socialist community, attempts a beginning in Texas, and settles in 1849 in Illinois. It starts branches in Missouri in 1856, in Iowa in 1860, and in California in 1881.

The Oneida community, a Christian Perfectionist sect, begins in New York.

The first American women's rights convention is organized in Seneca Falls, New York. The convention adopts a Declaration of Sentiments asking for equal rights for women, including the right to vote.

Gold is discovered in California, triggering the "gold rush" (people rushing to California to find gold).

1849 Elgin, the most successful of the antislavery communities, is started in Ontario, Canada.

Mid-1800s The Moravian movement abandons its communal economy.

1850 The Fugitive Slave Act is passed to make it easier for southern slave owners to recapture escaped slaves.

Congress issues the first land grants to develop the U.S. railroad system.

1851 Modern Times, an anarchist community, starts in New York and continues until 1863.

1854 The Amana Colonies buys land in Iowa and begins a 10-year process of moving its entire membership to Iowa.

1855 The North American Phalanx, one of the largest of the Fourierist phalanxes, ends.

1860 The Shakers reach their largest membership of 5,000 in about two dozen communities spread over the eastern part of the United States.

By this time, about 4 million black slaves live in the United States.

1861 Bishop Hill ends.

The Brotherhood of the New Life, a mystical Christian community, starts in New York and moves to California in 1875.

The Civil War begins; it was fought over several issues, chief among them slavery.

1862 The Port Royal antislavery community begins in South Carolina and ends in 1866.

1863 The Emancipation Proclamation is issued by President Abraham Lincoln, freeing all slaves.

1865 President Lincoln is assassinated.

The American Civil War ends.

Congress ratifies the Thirteenth Amendment to the U.S. Constitution, officially ending slavery.

Late 1800s Industrialization proceeds rapidly. Machines replace hand labor, and communities that made a living from handmade goods suffer.

1869 The Koreshan Unity, a Christian community based on a belief that Earth is hollow, starts in New York. The community moves to Illinois in the late 1880s and then to Florida in 1894.

The first railroad line across the United States is completed—the world's first "transcontinental" rail line.

1873 The Elgin antislavery community ends.

1874 The first Hutterite colonies start in South Dakota when members flee Europe because of persecution.

1875 Orderville, the most successful and longest-lived of the Mormon communal experiments, is started in Utah, and ends in 1885.

1878 The first telephone exchange opens in Connecticut and is soon followed by exchanges throughout the United States and Canada. The telephone had been patented by Alexander Graham Bell in 1876.

1879 Henry George's book on single-tax economics, *Progress and Poverty*, is published and becomes a best seller. "Single taxers" advocated a tax on land only.

1880 Rugby, a cooperative community designed for the "younger sons" of British aristocracy, starts in Tennessee.

1880s Jewish agricultural communities are started across the country to help Russian Jews enter farming.

1881 The Keil community ends.
The Oneida community ends.

1884 *Cooperative Commonwealth* by Laurence Gronlund is published. This is the first attempt to explain Marxism and socialism to the American public.

1885 Kaweah Cooperative Commonwealth, a socialist community, is started in California and lasts until 1892.

1886 The American Federation of Labor (AFL) is started by a group of skilled laborers in order to gain better pay and working conditions.

1887 Congress passes the Dawes Act, breaking up Indian land into plots, giving Indian households some of the plots and selling the rest to whites.

1888 The novel *Looking Backward 2000–1887* by Edward Bellamy is published, becomes a best seller, and leads to the formation of Nationalist clubs and socialist communities.

1894 Fairhope, based on socialist and single-tax ideas, is founded in Alabama.
Ruskin, a socialist community, starts in Tennessee and moves to Georgia in 1899.

1896 Home Colony, an anarchist community, starts in Washington State.

1897 Point Loma, a Theosophical community built around a boarding school for children, starts in California.

1898 The last Icarian community, in Iowa, ends.
The Zoar Society ends.

1900 The Brotherhood of the New Life ends.
The first of the "three Ardens" starts in Delaware. These communities are based on the single-tax theory (taxing land only).

1901 The Ruskin community ends.
The Oldsmobile becomes the first mass-produced automobile.

Early 1900s Rugby ends.
Most Shaker groups have ended.

1903 The House of David movement, a Christian millennialist community, starts in Michigan.
President Theodore Roosevelt begins creating wildlife refuges, national parks, and national forests. By 1909, the Roosevelt administration had set aside 42 million acres of national forests, 53 national wildlife refuges, and 18 areas of "special interest," such as the Grand Canyon.

1905 The Harmony Society ends.
The Industrial Workers of the World, a working-class trade union, is formed in Chicago. Its goal is to organize all workers in any industry into a union, and members do not believe in excluding women, people of color, or unskilled workers (as the AFL did).

1910 The Modern School Movement, an anarchist movement to reform children's education, begins in the United States.

1914 Llano del Rio, a socialist community, is founded in California. The community moves to Louisiana in 1918 and renames itself "New Llano."

1915 The Ferrer Colony, an anarchist community built around a Modern School for children, starts in New Jersey.

1916 The building of a nationwide road system is begun.

1917 The Peace Mission Movement, a Christian sect based on racial equality and positive thinking, starts in New York and eventually spreads across the country.

1917 to 1918 The United States fights in World War I.

Hutterite young men refuse to fight in World War I because of their pacifist beliefs. They are drafted, mistreated, and even tortured within the military. Two Hutterite men die as a result of this treatment. In response, all the Hutterites in the United States flee to Canada.

1920 The United States adopts the Nineteenth Amendment to the Constitution, specifying that women have the right to vote.

For the first time, the majority of Americans are living in urban areas.

1921 Home Colony ends as an anarchist community.

1923 Mohegan, an anarchist community built around a Modern School, starts in New York.

1929 A huge stock market crash leads to the Great Depression.

1930s The Great Depression, a time of poverty and hardship, is experienced in the United States and around the world.

Many Hutterite colonies are re-established in the United States; the nation is eager to woo back these valuable farmers during the Great Depression.

1932 The Amana Colonies decide to stop living communally and reorganize their businesses as a corporation.

1933 President Franklin D. Roosevelt starts the New Deal program to help end the Great Depression.

The New Deal communities program begins nationwide, with the goals of helping people out of poverty and educating people in cooperative ideas. The first community is Arthurdale in West Virginia. Other prominent colonies are Dyess in Arkansas (started in 1934) and Jersey Homesteads in New Jersey (started in 1936). About 50,000 people participate in the New Deal communities.

Sunrise, an anarchist community, starts in Michigan and later moves to Virginia, where the community ends in 1939.

The Catholic Worker Movement—based on Catholicism, socialism, and anarchism— begins in New York City. Its goal is to serve the needy.

1934 Congress passes the Indian Reorganization Act, which restores tribal ownership of reservation land.

1935 The Davidian movement, an offshoot of the Seventh-Day Adventists, begins communal living in Waco, Texas.

1937 New Llano ends in Louisiana.

The first "Greenbelt" city, a New Deal planned cooperative city, is completed in Maryland. Greenhills in Ohio and Greendale in Wisconsin are founded in 1938.

1941 Woodbine, one of the most successful of the Jewish agricultural communities, ends in New Jersey.

1941 to 1945 The United States fights in World War II.

1942 The U.S. government sets up the Manhattan Project to develop the first nuclear weapons.

The Point Loma community ends.

Koinonia Farm, a Christian community dedicated to racial equality, starts in Georgia.

1944 to early 1950s The U.S. government sells the New Deal houses and businesses to private owners.

1945 The United States drops two nuclear bombs on Japan, killing an estimated 140,000 people.

The United States joins the United Nations as a charter member.

The Cold War begins with the United States and the Communist Soviet Union building stockpiles of nuclear weapons.

1948 The novel *Walden Two* by B. F. Skinner is published. It describes a utopian community in which negative behaviors and emotions are limited through behavioral conditioning.

1950 to 1953 The United States fights in the Korean War, in order to prevent Communist North Korea from taking over South Korea.

1950s Television grows in popularity, and by the end of the decade TV sets are found in most American homes.

Communists are targeted for persecution in the United States. Sen. Joseph McCarthy is a leader of this movement, accusing hundreds of government employees of being Communist sympathizers. Union organizers and nonprofit organizations are also suspect.

1950s and 1960s The civil rights movement takes place all over the United States, with the goal of equal rights for African Americans.

1954 The Bruderhof, an Anabaptist Christian community that was founded in Germany in 1920, starts its first U.S. branch in New York.

The Supreme Court rules in *Brown v. Board of Education of Topeka* that the common southern system of separate public schools for black and white children is inherently unequal and thus against the law.

1956 The Ferrer Colony ends.

1958 The first passenger airplane service begins between the United States and Europe.
Synanon, a community dedicated to drug-addict rehabilitation, starts in California.

1959 The first Camphill community, which provides innovative education for the mentally disabled, is started in the United States. The movement is begun in 1939 in Scotland by refugees fleeing the Nazi invasion of Austria.

1961 The Modern School Movement ends.
The United States and the Soviet Union begin a "space race," with both nations launching spacecraft to orbit Earth.

1963 Congress passes the Equal Pay Act, requiring equal pay for men and women doing the same work.

1964 to 1974 The Bruderhof reconcile with the Hutterite movement and become a fourth "leut" within the Hutterites.

1964 Congress passes the Civil Rights Act, which prohibits racial discrimination in employment, education, and public facilities. It also prohibits sex discrimination in employment.

1965 Congress passes the Voting Rights Act, which helps southern blacks exercise their right to vote by banning poll taxes and providing for federal supervision of voter registration.

Mid-1960s The women's movement begins a second wave of organizing, spurred by Betty Friedan's book *The Feminine Mystique,* published in 1963. The women's movement calls for equal rights for women, including equal pay and legal abortion, among other rights.

Mid-1960s to early 1970s The hippie youth movement begins and spreads. In general, the movement stands for peace, environmental protection, personal freedom, spiritually intense experiences, and economic sharing. Several long-lasting utopian communities grow out of this movement.

1965 The International Society for Krishna Consciousness, a movement based on Hindu teachings, begins in California.
The United States enters the Vietnam War, allegedly to prevent Communist North Vietnam from taking over South Vietnam. The atrocities of this war touch off the largest antiwar movement in the history of the United States.

1966 Tassajara Zen Mountain Center, a Buddhist retreat and residential facility, starts in California.

1967 The Zen Center of Los Angeles starts.

Twin Oaks, based on socialism and equality, starts in Virginia.

1968 The Ananda Colonies, based on the teachings of Hindu saint Paramhansa Yogananda, begins the first colony, Ananda Village, in Nevada City, California.

The Family/Children of God, an evangelical Christian group, starts in California and soon begins traveling around the country.

The Renaissance Community/Brotherhood of the Spirit, a "New Age" spiritual group, starts in Massachusetts.

1969 The San Francisco Zen Center starts.

The Love Family, a controversial Christian community, starts in Washington State.

The United States launches the *Apollo 11* spacecraft to the moon. Neil Armstrong and Buzz Aldrin become the first people to set foot on the moon's surface.

1970 Vajradhatu, a Tibetan Buddhist organization, starts with one community in Vermont. Later it changes its name to Shambhala and starts a number of residential communities.

1971 The Farm, based on an eclectic spirituality, starts in Tennessee.

1972 The first anticult organization, Parents Committee to Free Our Sons and Daughters from the Children of God, starts in California.

Jesus People USA, an evangelical Christian community, starts as a traveling group and eventually settles in Illinois.

The Rainbow Family of Living Light, a temporary anarchist community based on an eclectic spirituality, starts with its first Rainbow Gathering in Colorado.

Congress passes Title IX of the Education Amendments, banning gender discrimination in schools and colleges.

1973 The Supreme Court decision in *Roe v. Wade* establishes women's access to legal abortion.

The United States removes its last ground troops from Vietnam.

1974 The term *Internet* begins to be used to refer to a global system of computer networks.

1980 The Mountains and Rivers Order of Zen Buddhism starts, which includes the Zen Mountain Monastery and Zen Center of New York City.

1981 Rajneeshpuram, based on the teachings of the Indian swami Bhagwan Shree Rajneesh, starts in Oregon.

1982 The Koreshan Unity ends.

1987 Rajneeshpuram ends.

1988 The Renaissance Community/Brotherhood of the Spirit ends.

1989 The World Wide Web, a system of interlinked documents available via the Internet, is created by Englishman Tim Berners-Lee.
    Synanon ends.

1990 The Fellowship for Intentional Community publishes its first directory of communities in the United States and the world, with 300 listings.
    Scientists begin publicizing the threat of "global warming," the projected increase in the temperature of Earth's oceans and surface air, which is predicted to cause extreme weather conditions and rising sea levels as polar ice melts.

1991 The first cohousing development in the United States is built in California.
    The Soviet Union is dissolved, breaking up into Russia and other countries and ending the Cold War.

1993 The Branch Davidians are confronted by armed U.S. government officials in Waco, Texas. The resulting standoff and fire kills over 70 Branch Davidians.

1995 The Bruderhof and Hutterites break off all ties with each other.
    The Global Ecovillage Network is founded to encourage communities to incorporate environmentally sound design and a low-impact lifestyle.

1998 The United States and Russia launch the first two modules of the International Space Station.

2001 The September 11 terrorist attacks, the worst in the history of the United States, kill 3,000 people and destroy the two towers of the World Trade Center in New York City.

2007 The Fellowship for Intentional Community directory of communities lists 900 communities in the United States and the world.

Amana Colonies

At a Glance

Dates of existence in North America: 1843 to 1932
Locations: New York, Iowa, Ontario (Canada)
Peak membership: 1,800
Religious or other belief: Christianity, Pietism, Community of True
Inspiration

History

The Amana Colonies were one of the longest-lived, most successful utopian communities in the United States.

The community began when about 700 members of the "Community of True Inspiration," as they called their religion, fled to the United States between 1843 and 1844 because of religious persecution in their native Germany. These "Inspirationists" bought land near Buffalo, New York, and named this first settlement "Ebenezer."

In Germany, they had not been living communally, but they decided to do so in the United States. For one thing, they felt it would be easier to live together since they did not know English. In addition, they wanted to separate themselves from the bad influences of the outside world. Some members were also influenced by the description of the early Christian church, which held all things in common. One of their leaders, Christian Metz, visited another Christian communal society, Zoar Society in Ohio, and was convinced that his church should adopt a similar way of living.

They adopted a constitution stating that land and other means of production were owned by the community, but that furniture and other household goods were owned privately. The community provided food, housing, health care, and a spending allowance for personal items.

In New York, they built four separate villages (named Middle Ebenezer, Lower Ebenezer, Upper Ebenezer, and New Ebenezer). Each had its own church, dining hall, workshops, and farms. The community was doing well, but as more and more of their church members arrived from Europe and their population grew to more than a thousand, they found it difficult to acquire enough land at a good price. Also, they felt they were too close to the sinful influences of the city of Buffalo.

They then bought land in Iowa and named their new settlement "Amana." Between 1854 and 1864, the entire population of Ebenezer moved to Amana. Again, they established a number of different villages (named Amana, East Amana, Middle

Amana, High Amana, West Amana, South Amana, and Homestead), each with its own communal kitchen facilities, workshops, and farms.

The community reached its peak membership—about 1,800—in 1881. Membership declined gradually until, by 1932, its population was at about 1,300. In that year, the group decided to stop living communally. The main reasons for this included the fact that many of the community's businesses were not producing enough income, due in part to the Great Depression, and also because a majority of the members voted to end the communal aspects of their society.

The society was reorganized into two parts: a joint-stock corporation that controlled the businesses, and the Amana Church Society, which was in charge of the religious life of the community. The businesses that were not making money were closed, and the others were run more efficiently. This reorganization was called the Great Change.

In the 1930s, two Amana members started a company to manufacture refrigerators and freezers. This business grew so large that the Amana Society sold it in 1950. Today, the company continues to manufacture refrigerators and freezers for home use under the Amana name.

Many members continued to live on Amana land and work in Amana businesses, but now that they owned their own homes, they modernized and made changes. They could buy what they wanted with their money, and they could dress however they liked. They held one church service per week, instead of 11, as was the case during their communal phase.

Today, the Amana Church congregation is made up of about 500 people and holds services in both German and English.

Beliefs and Practices

Members of the Amana Society call themselves the Community of True Inspiration. This form of Christianity grew out of another form, called Pietism, which arose in the early 1700s in Germany. Pietism was opposed to the established Lutheran Church, which had grown less concerned with the religious well-being of the common people and more concerned with intellectual debate. A number of Pietists began to believe that God could speak directly to humans through inspired individuals, who were called *Werkzeuge,* or "instruments." The Community of True Inspiration was so named to distinguish between inspiration from God (true inspiration) and inspiration from Satan (false inspiration).

The need to live communally is not a part of this religion. The Amana Society adopted communal living for practical reasons as well as spiritual reasons (to separate themselves from the influences of the outside world, for example), but there was nothing originally in the religion that dictated that its followers must live communally (as the Hutterite and Bruderhof religions do, for example). As a result, even after they decided to share their property and income, some members continued to be unhappy with the system. In 1854, their leader, Christian Metz, received an "inspiration" from God condemning anyone who was opposed to communal living and apparently this satisfied most of the members.

A former member recalls, "The pattern of communal living was established purely as an economic measure and not primarily as a religious practice. Unlike Marxist communism, the system of the Inspirationists was controlled by religion. The purpose of the communal system was to simplify the business of living so that members might have more free time for their larger calling of serving the Lord" (quoted in Yambura 1960, 29).

The two Werkzeuge of the Amana community were Christian Metz and Barbara Heinemann Landmann. Their words, along with the words of earlier Werkzeuge in Germany, have been written down and serve as religious texts for the community. Since the last Werkzeuge, Landmann, passed away in 1883, the words of these Werkzeuge have been used for the Sunday sermons.

From some of the German Werkzeuge's revelations, the community gained its "Twenty-One Rules for the Examination of our Daily Lives" and the "Twenty-Four Rules for True Godliness." These rules instruct them to obey God and their superiors; to avoid laughter and levity; to maintain inner and outer calmness; to bear all inner and outer sufferings in silence; and to keep separate from the outside world. One of the rules warns against the company of women and another directs followers to avoid weddings and other feasts. In spite of these rules, however, members of the Amana society were not celibate. They valued celibacy, but they permitted marriage. However, when a couple married they were "demoted" in rank (in terms of seating in the church service) temporarily. They were also temporarily demoted every time they had a child. Small families were favored over large families.

Church services were held 11 times per week, with men, women, and children sitting separately. The community celebrated the usual Christian holidays as well as two unique holidays. The Unterredung was a spiritual self-examination held yearly. Members were to search themselves for sins and confess these sins to the elders. Every few years, following the Unterredung, a Liebesmahl (Lord's Supper) celebration was held, which was a time of rejoicing and festivity.

During church services, the members were seated according to a specific order, based on age and status in the community. There were three different groupings, or congregations: the older members, the middle-aged members, and the children and young married people. Within these groupings, those with higher status sat farther back. A person could be demoted—made to sit closer toward the front, or made to sit with a lower congregation—for misdemeanors such as breaking community rules, or for marriage or the birth of children (which were considered weaknesses—celibacy being the ideal). A person could also be promoted to a higher status with good behavior. The women and men entered church through separate doors and sat on separate sides of the room.

Their clothing was made of dull colors—blacks and grays. Bright colors were discouraged, as were ornaments, cutting a woman's hair, or anything that would suggest fashion. Various consumer items and celebrations were banned, such as greeting cards, outside newspapers, birthday and wedding celebrations, card playing, tricycles, bicycles, and drinking parties.

The Inspirationists were pacifists and paid others to replace any of their young men who were called to war. However, after the Great Change, when the Inspirationists were no longer living communally, the church left the question of military service up to the individual, and many did participate in World War II.

In keeping with their goal of separating themselves from the world, the Amana members were not allowed to vote.

Daily Life

The seven Amana villages were about a mile and a half from each other, laid out on either side of the Iowa River. "The main street of each village was nothing but a country road bordered by deep open ditches and narrow wooden sidewalks," recalled a former member. "Along this street were our homes, schools, churches and shops, though you might have had some trouble identifying them. There were no conventional store fronts, but you could find the post office or the general store or the pharmacy by the large lettered signs on the various buildings" (quoted in Yambura 1960, 18).

The Amana members spoke a unique form of German that they called Kolonie-Deutsch. They learned English in school.

The Amana Colony members lived as family units in apartments (usually there were four apartments per building). Often, grandparents or other family members lived in the same building or nearby. The buildings were generally unpainted. Charles Nordhoff, who visited Amana in the late 1800s, noted that the style of living was adequate but simple. "The table is clean but has no cloth. The dishes are coarse but neat; and the houses, while well built, and possessing all that is absolutely essential to comfort according to the German peasants' idea, have not always carpets, and have often a bed in what New-Englanders would call the parlor; and in general are for use and not ornament" (Nordhoff reprinted 1960, 33).

The members ate their meals at their village dining hall, with the men, women, and children sitting separately. As was (and is) common with other communities of Germanic origin (such as the Hutterites), the Amana members ate often: breakfast, lunch, an afternoon snack, and supper.

The Amana members were encouraged to be productive and useful even during leisure hours. Sports were discouraged. Instead, when they had time to themselves, members made furniture, clocks, toys, rugs, quilts, and lace. There was not much reading material to be found in the colonies.

How They Made Their Living

The community met almost all of its own needs. Its members grew their own food, raised their own animals, and had their own carpenters, masons, blacksmiths, saddlers, soap makers, shoemakers, watchmakers, and so forth. The men worked on the farm or in the workshops. The women worked in the kitchens and gardens.

The community earned money through a combination of farming and industry. In both Ebenezer and Amana, it had cloth mills, sawmills, and flourmills. The group sold the products from their mills nationally. These included wool blankets, flannel cloth, socks, gloves, yarn, and patterned cotton cloth. Locally, its members sold products from their farm, as well as soap and lumber.

People of Amana Colony, Iowa, gather for prayer before a meal, ca. 1875. (Library of Congress)

Leadership and Decision Making

The Werkzeuge, or inspired religious leader, was the head of the community. Under the Werkzeuge was a 13-member Great Council, elected every year by the men over 21 and single women over 30. This Great Council made decisions about practical matters that affected all the villages, such as new businesses and construction, members' spending allowances, admission of new members, moving members from one village to another, and so forth. The Great Council appointed three to six elders to serve each village on a local council, which assigned housing and employment to members and helped the local business managers with their business decisions.

Women could not assume any leadership position except that of "kitchen boss." However, the community had one married woman Werkzeuge, Barbara Heinemann Landmann.

How New Members Were Recruited or Chosen

Prospective members were required to live in the community for two years. If admitted as a full member, the member had to turn over all personal property to the community.

Children and Youth

New mothers were granted two years of maternity leave from community work. At age two, the child was sent to the Kinderschule run by a few older women who could no longer work in the kitchens or gardens. There was no attempt to teach the children anything academic in this preschool—it was simply a place for them to play. Even at this young age, the children were taught to knit and crochet and contribute to the work of the community. According to Madeline Roemig, the children made "thumbs and fingers" for gloves (1987, 318).

At age five, the children began elementary school. The Amana elementary school was a public school that received state funds and taught the state-required curriculum. The teachers were college-educated men from Amana. Girls and boys received the same education. The school also included time for learning crafts and manual trades. Boys as well as girls learned to knit and crochet. The teacher also taught the history of the community and hymns.

The children helped out with communal work: harvesting vegetables and fruits, haymaking, threshing, and assisting with the younger children in school.

Young people finished school and began to work at age 14. The boys could try out various crafts and trades. The girls worked in the community kitchens and gardens. Some of the boys were sent for further schooling outside the community, when the community foresaw the need for a doctor, pharmacist, or teacher, for example.

Marriage was not allowed until a young woman was 20 and a young man was 24. The couple had to get the approval of the elders and had to live in separate villages for one or two years during their engagement.

Relationship with the Outside World

The Amana members strove to keep themselves separate from the outside world. They interacted with outsiders when they sold their products. They also fed and sometimes took in traveling hoboes and gypsies who needed help. Moreover, Amana members often hired outside help as needed for their businesses. They seem to have had few problems with the outside world.

Reasons for Ending the Communal Aspect

The main reason for ending the communal, separatist aspect was that the members voted not to continue it. Although many of their businesses were not showing a profit at the time they reorganized, they could probably have restructured the businesses while still living communally. But the members chose not to.

Even before the 1932 Great Change that ended communalism, the Amana members had begun to do things to challenge their communal lifestyle. For example, in the early 1900s, if members were needed to work overtime, they demanded overtime pay. Some members sold products—such as canned goods, needlework, and crafts—to the outside world, and kept the profits. In addition, apparently many members would take money out of the communal coffers for their own use.

Influence on the Outside World

The community had no interest in influencing the outside world, preferring to keep themselves separate from what they considered to be the sinful influences of the world. Yet the Amana community remains a fascinating part of American history.

The Amana Colonies were designated a National Historic Landmark in 1965 and are today a tourist attraction. Visitors can purchase goods from Amana businesses, such as the woolen mill, furniture shop, and general store, and learn about the history of the community.

References

Andelson, Jonathan. "The Community of True Inspiration from Germany to the Amana Colonies," in *America's Communal Utopias*, edited by Donald Pitzer. Chapel Hill: University of North Carolina Press, 1997, 181–203.

Barthel, Diane. *Amana: From Pietist Sect to American Community*. Lincoln: University of Nebraska Press, 1984.

Nordhoff, Charles. *The Communistic Societies of the United States: From Personal Visit and Observation*. New York: Hillary House Publishers, 1960 (first published 1875).

Roemig, Madeline. "The Individual and the Community: Education in Communal Amana," in *Communal Life: An International Perspective*, edited by Yosef Gorni, Yaacov Oved, and Idit Paz. New Brunswick, NJ: Transaction Books, 1987.

Yambura, Barbara, with Eunice Willis Bodine. *A Change and a Parting: My Story of Amana*. Ames: Iowa State University Press, 1960.

WEB SITES

Amana Church Society: http://amanachurch.org/ (accessed April 4, 2008).

Amana Colonies: www.amanacolonies.org/ (accessed April 4, 2008).

Amana Heritage Society: www.amanaheritage.org/ (accessed April 4, 2008).

Amana Society: www.amanasociety.com/ (accessed April 4, 2008).

Amish

At a Glance

Dates of existence in North America: 1727 to present
Locations: most are located in Ohio, Pennsylvania, and Indiana; there are also settlements in New York, Michigan, Illinois, Missouri, Iowa, Wisconsin, Minnesota, Kentucky, Tennessee, Virginia, North Carolina, Delaware, Georgia, Oklahoma, Montana, Florida, Texas, and Canada
Peak membership: over 100,000 and growing (U.S. and Canada)
Religious or other belief: Anabaptist Christianity

History

The Amish are a different kind of utopian community than many in this book. They share very little property and income, and each family lives in its own separate, privately owned house. However, they live together in mutually supportive communities and share a way of life and a culture. They are "utopian" in the sense that they believe their way of life is better than that of the surrounding mainstream culture, and they take care to separate themselves from that outside culture. They are more than a religion, because you cannot be Amish without living in an Amish community. For that reason, they are included in this book.

The Amish religion began in 17th-century Switzerland. It is a branch of the Mennonites, an Anabaptist sect (believers in adult baptism). A Mennonite spokesman, Jacob Amman, began to advocate for a stricter adherence to religious practices. He wanted the Mennonites to practice "shunning" (social avoidance of those who are excommunicated from the church), and foot-washing, among other things. Followers of Amman split from the Mennonites and began calling themselves "Amish."

All Anabaptist sects were subject to persecution in Europe, and many followers fled to the United States. The Amish began immigrating to the United States in the 18th century, settling at first in Pennsylvania. A second wave of Amish immigrated in the 19th century, settling in Ohio, Illinois, Iowa, New York, Maryland, and Canada. Since then they have spread to several states.

Beliefs and Practices

The Amish are Anabaptists, like the Bruderhof and the Hutterites. As an Anabaptist group, the Amish believe that people should be baptized as adults, when they can fully understand and accept their religion. They believe in separating themselves from the world, which they view as sinful.

The Amish way of life has many prohibitions that are designed to keep the Amish separate from the outside world. There are a number of different branches of Amish that vary in the strictness of their prohibitions, their specific religious practices, and style of dress. In general, the Amish do not use tractors in their fields, but pull their plows with horses. Some mechanized farm machinery is allowed, such as milking machines, but other machinery is banned. The goal is to keep the farm small and modest.

Amish clothes are made of dark cloth, with no patterns. The men must grow a beard once they get married. The women and girls wear ankle-length dresses with long sleeves and high necks, and caps or bonnets over their hair, which they are not allowed to cut. Anything not considered functional is banned, including jewelry, cosmetics, belts, and neckties.

Most Amish are not allowed to own cars—they travel by horse and buggy. Telephones in the home are not allowed. Electricity is banned, because with it might come too much materialism in the form of electrical gadgets. Musical instruments, radios, television, and computers are banned, as is travel by airplane, central heating in homes, and wall-to-wall carpeting.

In addition to the prohibitions on dress and modern conveniences, the Amish are not allowed to marry non-Amish people or to enter into business partnerships with them.

The Amish are pacifists: they do not engage in violence or warfare. They do not even believe in violence for the purpose of self-defense.

The Amish believe that men are to rule over women, just as Christ is the head of the church. However, an Amish woman's first loyalty is to God, and not to her husband. Divorce and birth control are not allowed.

The Amish value humility, simplicity, and tidiness. They try to steer clear of pride, personal power, wealth, and status. They value working with the soil and with nature.

They hold worship services every other Sunday in a member's home. The entire church district helps the host family get ready for the service: cleaning house and barn, cooking, moving aside furniture, and arranging the church benches. The service is about three hours long, followed by a meal. The non-service Sundays are given over to relaxing, Bible reading, and visiting.

The Amish celebrate the usual Christian holidays, although without the display and materialism of the outside world. Santa Claus and the Easter Bunny do not visit Amish homes. In addition, the Amish hold "communion" services twice a year. During this time, the baptized Amish members confess their sins and attend an all-day service. The members are paired off by gender and they wash each other's feet, after which they clasp hands and kiss each other. This ritual symbolizes humility and fellowship.

If a baptized member of the Amish church strays from the rules, he or she is warned; if the person continues to stray, "shunning" can follow. The shunned member cannot eat at the same table with baptized adults, nor can he or she sell goods or services to or perform favors for baptized members. The shunned member can, however, eat at the same table with the young people who are not yet baptized and can attend church services. Shunning ends when the member mends his or her ways and accepts the teachings of the Amish church.

Daily Life

The Amish are also called the "Pennsylvania Dutch," with "Dutch" being a corrupted form of *Deitsch* (German). They speak three languages: at home and with each other, the Amish speak a German dialect, called Pennsylvania German; they learn English in school; and their Bible is printed in High German, which they can read and understand.

The Amish live in "settlements"—groups of families who reside near each other in a rural area. There may be non-Amish families living among the Amish as well. Within each settlement is one or more church districts. Since worship services are held in a private home, the church district must be small enough so that all families can be accommodated in a home (about 30 to 40 families). Because of this need to accommodate the congregation and because Amish couples generally have many children, Amish homes tend to be large.

While the men do the farmwork or the income-generating work, the women are in charge of the house, the children, and the vegetable garden. In addition, an Amish woman makes all the clothes for her family and sometimes helps with farm chores. Amish couples have an average of seven children.

Amish food is rich and plentiful, and includes meat, eggs, dairy products, pickles, vegetables, and fruits. Fried foods and desserts are favorites. The Amish pray silently before and after meals.

In their free time, Amish enjoy singing, visiting relatives, hunting, sports, hiking, and needlework. Amish quilts have become collectors' items and sometimes command prices of $10,000 or more. In some Amish settlements, smoking or chewing tobacco is common and accepted among men; in other settlements, it is frowned upon.

Amish people "retire" between the ages of 50 and 70. The farm or family business is turned over to one or more children, and the parents move into a nearby small house called the "grandfather house."

How They Make Their Living

About half of Amish families make a living by farming. Others make a living by manufacturing items or providing services needed within Amish society, such as furniture, buggies, blacksmithing, harness making, or owning a store catering to the Amish.

While the Amish do not share most of their income—each family makes its living independently—they do pool their money and run their own "insurance plans" in case of property damage or hospitalization. They do not participate in outside insurance plans.

They also share work at times, such as a barn raising: when a new barn (or other building) needs to be built, Amish people from the entire community donate their labor. The Amish also help each other with quilting, housecleaning, baking, and preparing the house and barn for a preaching service. Members help each other when someone is sick or otherwise in need.

While most property is not shared, Amish communities collectively build their own school buildings on land often donated by an Amish farmer and pay for the teacher.

Leadership and Decision Making

An Amish leader is expected to be humble and to serve the community. The leaders are chosen by voting and are called *Diener,* which means "servants." There are three or more leaders within each church district. Women are not allowed to hold these positions, but baptized women are allowed to vote, along with the baptized men. The Diener are religious as well as community leaders: they preach during worship services, perform baptisms and weddings, and also make sure their congregation is following the Amish way of life. The leaders are chosen for life and are not paid for their services.

How New Communities Form

The Amish do not engage in active missionary work, although outsiders are welcome to become baptized as Amish.

However, because Amish people generally have large families, Amish communities continue to grow and expand. Amish families might choose to move to another Amish settlement, or to start a new settlement, for a variety of reasons: to find cheaper land or a better way to make a living; to join or form a more conservative or more liberal branch of Amish; to escape from conflicts or disagreements within their church district; or to escape a section of the country that has become overcrowded.

Children and Youth

Amish babies sleep with their parents and are almost never left alone. As young children, they are encouraged to be helpful. At age six, the Amish child is sent to school.

The Amish educate their children in one- or two-room schools through eighth grade within their own communities. This is another way in which they separate themselves from the outside world. The Amish school teaches the basics of reading, writing, and arithmetic, in addition to hymns and prayers. The school emphasizes accuracy rather than speed and group achievement rather than individual competition.

Amish children are not allowed to attend high school or college. The Amish believe that higher education is not necessary for the Amish way of life. They also equate more education with more sinfulness: they see that the outside world is highly educated, but also highly corrupt.

After eighth grade, the young people begin to work in their family's business or around the house. The unbaptized youth are expected to deviate somewhat from Amish rules in order to get a taste of the outside world before committing to the Amish way of life. For example, some young people are allowed to work at a nearby factory or at the home of a non-Amish family. A young man might acquire a driver's license and even buy a car, which he would park away from his home. A young person might acquire a radio, attend a movie, or wear clothing that is forbidden. Because youth are not yet baptized, the community leaders do not take action against these transgressions, as long as they are discreet.

At about age 16, Amish youth begin to look for a mate. They meet other young Amish at Sunday evening singing groups and at weddings and work parties. This time of life is called *rum springa,* or "running around." An Amish young person must marry someone from a church district whose beliefs are in agreement with their home church district but must avoid marrying a close relative.

If an Amish-raised youth decides not to become baptized, he or she is not shunned but is welcome to participate in all family gatherings. However, without being baptized, an Amish person cannot marry another Amish person or enter into a business partnership with an Amish person.

Relationship with the Outside World

The Amish interact with the outside world through their non-Amish neighbors, through tourists who want to see what Amish life is like, and sometimes by providing goods and services to the non-Amish. While the Amish are not allowed to run for public office, they are allowed to vote for public officials.

Because they keep to themselves and are honest and hard working, the Amish generally have good relationships with the outside world. However, conflicts have arisen over several issues: public schooling, Social Security payments, and military service.

When public schools were first established, the Amish were supportive, but only sent their children to school through fourth grade. These public schools were often one-room rural schools, similar to the Amish-run schools of today. As states required parents to send their children to school for more and more years, the Amish compromised and agreed to school attendance through eighth grade.

However, as the one-room community schools were consolidated into larger, more centrally located schools, the Amish feared that their children would become too influenced by the outside world if they continued to attend public school. In the 1930s, the Amish began building and running their own private schools.

During the first half of the 20th century, states tried to force Amish parents to send their children to high school. In Pennsylvania, for example, some parents were arrested numerous times. The parents generally refused to pay the required fine and so were often sent to jail until a friend or supporter paid the fine. In 1955, a compromise was reached in Pennsylvania: Amish youth who have completed eighth grade can attend "Amish vocational school"—they perform household and business duties under parental supervision, keep a daily journal, and attend classes three hours per week. Other states followed Pennsylvania's model.

But the problem was not over. In the 1960s, in one Iowa county, school authorities began fining Amish parents for sending their children to a substandard school (the Amish schoolteacher was not state-certified). At one point, school authorities came to the Amish school and tried to forcibly take the children to public school. Finally in 1967, the Iowa state legislature passed a law allowing religious schools to apply for an exemption from the state educational standards.

Also in the 1960s, officials from a Wisconsin county arrested three Amish fathers for refusing to send their children to public school. The case made it all the way to

Poster promoting Pennsylvania showing an Amish family. (Library of Congress)

the U.S. Supreme Court, where in a 1972 unanimous ruling the justices stated that it was unconstitutional to compel the Amish to attend high school, since it conflicted with their religious beliefs.

Another conflict with the outside world arose over the question of Social Security payments, which in 1955 were extended to cover self-employed people, including farmers. The Amish did not want to receive the benefits, because they believe in self-sufficiency and they believe it is the responsibility of their community to care of the elderly. In 1965, a federal law was passed allowing members of religious groups to seek exemption from Social Security taxes and payments.

Yet another conflict with the outside world revolved around military service. The Amish are pacifists, so when they were called for military service, they generally elected to pay fines, hire substitutes, or perform a civilian assignment. During World War I, the Amish conscientious objectors were sent to military camp for training, and if they refused to put on a military uniform or participate in drills, they were subjected to punishment such as solitary confinement and physical abuse.

During World War II, a number of pacifist churches (Mennonites, Quakers, and Brethren) succeeded in getting a law passed that allowed conscientious objectors to bypass military training and instead perform service projects with government agencies or nonprofit organizations. Amish leaders were leery of this program because it required young men to move away from their community, often to an urban area, and allowed them the freedom to dress and act in non-Amish ways. The Amish negotiated with the government to gain "farm deferments" for baptized Amish young men, which would allow them to work on a farm away from their home community. Some Amish chose to serve a prison term rather than do any kind of alternative service.

Influence on the Outside World

The Amish have no interest in influencing the outside world, preferring instead to keep themselves separate from it. However, by insisting on their religious rights, they expanded religious freedom for everyone in the United States. In addition, the unique Amish way of life is fascinating to many and provides a window into another viable way of living.

The Future of Amish Society

The Amish have changed slowly to allow families to make a living and handle the demands of life, yet also to preserve their separate, modest, plain way of life. For example, while the Old Order Amish do not own cars, they are allowed to accept rides in cars driven by others. Amish are not allowed to have telephones in their homes, but they can make a telephone call on a pay phone. Amish cannot have an electric freezer in the home, but they can rent one in a store, or buy one and keep it at a non-Amish neighbor's house. While electricity is banned, the Amish can use power from propane gas or batteries.

The Amish continue to wrestle with the issue of technology and modern gadgets (Stein 2005). How much of this should they prohibit? Are cell phones allowed? What about rollerblades?

Until the 1970s, most Amish made a living by farming. But the explosive growth of Amish communities and the dearth of farmland at a reasonable price caused many Amish to seek other work. However, they decided not to seek employment in the outside world but instead to set up small businesses within the community. Some Amish businesses now cater to non-Amish customers, selling furniture, camping gear, vegetables, or building supplies, or capitalizing on the many tourists who come to see the Amish by offering buggy tours and selling Amish quilts, crafts, and food.

Since the 1970s, the number of Amish small enterprises has skyrocketed. For example, within 13 church districts in Lancaster County, Pennsylvania, the number of Amish businesses grew from a handful in 1960 to over 100 in 1992. However, the Amish are unlikely to produce the next multimillionaire business owner, because they aim to keep their businesses small. If an enterprise begins growing too large for one family to handle, they often prefer to sell off portions of it, rather than to hire a lot of outsiders (Kraybill 1995).

See also: Bruderhof; Hutterites

References

Hostetler, John. *Amish Society,* 4th ed. Baltimore, MD: The Johns Hopkins University Press, 1993.

Hostetler, John, and Gertrude Enders Huntington. *Children in Amish Society.* New York: Holt, Rinehart and Winston, 1971.

Kephart, William. *Extraordinary Groups: The Sociology of Unconventional Life-Styles.* New York: St. Martin's Press, 1976.

Kraybill, Donald. *The Riddle of Amish Culture.* Baltimore, MD: The Johns Hopkins University Press, 1989.

Kraybill, Donald, ed. *The Amish and the State.* Baltimore, MD: The Johns Hopkins University Press, 1993.

Kraybill, Donald. *Amish Enterprise: From Plows to Profits.* Baltimore, MD: The Johns Hopkins University Press, 1995.

Stein, Joel. "What's Next . . . with the Amish." *Time* 166 (2005): 124.

Ananda Colonies

At a Glance

Dates of existence in North America: 1968 to present
Locations: California, Oregon, Rhode Island, Washington State
Peak membership: 1,000
Religious or other belief: spiritual teachings of Paramhansa Yogananda, a Hindu saint

History

The Ananda Colonies are a group of seven residential communities: five in the United States, one in Italy, and one in India. They are an outgrowth of Ananda Village, which was founded in 1968 in Nevada City, California, by J. Donald Walters, a disciple of Paramhansa Yogananda, a Hindu saint from India.

Yogananda was born Mukunda Lal Ghosh in 1893 in northern India. From a young age he was interested in knowing God and sought out spiritual teachers. At the age of 17, he found his "guru" (teacher), Swami Sri Yukteswar Giri, and became his disciple. During this time, he continued his education, graduated from Calcutta University, then took vows as a monk and received the name Yogananda.

Yogananda came to the United States in 1920, where he lectured and formed the Self-Realization Fellowship in 1925 in Los Angeles to spread his message, namely, that there is an underlying unity in all religions and that a person can have a direct experience of God. He taught a form of yoga called Kriya Yoga, which involves pranayama (breath control) and meditation to help people become more aware of the divine. He published several editions of *Autobiography of a Yogi*, which tells the story of his search for God and a guru, his coming to the United States, and the founding of the Self-Realization Fellowship.

Walters became a disciple of Yogananda in 1948. Yogananda died in 1952, when Walters was 25 years old. A top staff member with the Self-Realization Fellowship, Walters received full ordination as a monk and took the name Swami Kriyananda. In 1962, Kriyananda was asked, because of internal conflicts, to leave the Self-Realization Fellowship. Kriyananda believed that Yogananda had asked him to spread the fellowship's message as widely as possible and to start World Brotherhood Colonies. Yogananda had mentioned such colonies in one of the last chapters of his autobiography. The first World Brotherhood Colony was established during Yogananda's lifetime in Encinitas, California, in 1947, on 30 acres, with hermitages, a café, a hotel, and a swimming pool. The colony offered spiritual classes and grew

*Portrait of Swami
Kriyananda, formerly
J. Donald Walters, founder of
the Ananda Colonies.*
(Courtesy of Ananda Village)

vegetables for residents of the Self-Realization Centers in Encinitas and Los Angeles (Yogananda 1951, 480). This colony was later converted into a hermitage for un-married people only.

Between 1967 and 1969, Kriyananda bought land in the Sierra Nevada foothills, near Nevada City, California. The community was named *Ananda* (meaning "bliss" in Sanskrit).

The community was started in the era of the hippie movement and hundreds of young people began arriving to see what was going on. "Many of this horde were dropouts, seeking an easy life rather than spiritual one," wrote Oliver and Cris Pope-noe. "They ate the fledgling community's food, ran up its phone bill, and told the members how they ought to be living" (1984, 7).

These young people often took drugs, even though they had promised to abide by the community's "no drugs" rule. Many of them did not want to help Kriyananda build a spiritual village and many were not willing to work hard. Kriyananda did not want to be the manager of the community—only its spiritual leader—and he made an effort to put the responsibility for meeting the mortgage payments on the members of the community. He did not want the community to share income, because he believed that the most efficient way to manage the community's finances was to make individuals and families responsible for their own income and expenses. People who did not wish to work eventually left the community (Popenoe 1984, 7–8; Gardner 1978, 154–158).

In 1976, a forest fire destroyed many of the community's homes, although most public buildings were spared. This fire, while financially difficult for the community, had the positive effect of weeding out people who were not committed to Ananda.

By soliciting donations, Ananda was able to rebuild the homes. By the early 1980s, the community had 250 adults and 70 children.

In 1980, Ananda decided to try to incorporate as a town. It dropped this idea two years later because the surrounding community was against it. At about this time, another spiritual community led by an Indian swami, Rajneeshpuram, was also trying to incorporate as a town (in Oregon) and the bad publicity surrounding Rajneeshpuram may have also caused the Ananda community to reconsider.

In the 1980s, the community opened a meditation training center and yoga retreat for the public called "Expanding Light." Also in the 1980s, other Ananda colonies started in Seattle; Sacramento and Palo Alto, California; and Portland, Oregon.

In 1990, Ananda decided to add the words "self-realization" to its name. This sparked a lawsuit from the Self-Realization Fellowship in Los Angeles, which claimed it owned the term *self-realization*, as well as the writings, photos, and sound recordings of Paramhansa Yogananda and sought $6 million in damages from Ananda. The lawsuit dragged on for 12 years. Finally, the courts decided that while the term *self-realization* could not be trademarked, and while Ananda was allowed to use Yogananda's writings for religious purposes, Ananda had infringed on the Self-Realization Fellowship's ownership of sound recordings of Yogananda and ordered Ananda to pay $29,000.

During the time of this lawsuit, Ananda had to deal with another lawsuit—from a former woman member, Anne-Marie Bertolucci, who in 1997 accused Kriyananda of sexually harassing her. Ananda believed that the Self-Realization Fellowship was behind this lawsuit as well, because Bertolucci and witnesses in her favor were involved with the Self-Realization Fellowship; however, Ananda was not allowed to introduce evidence to that effect. The jury found Kriyananda and Ananda guilty and ordered Ananda to pay over a million dollars. Ananda filed for bankruptcy but did manage to pay the required amount.

Despite these challenges, Ananda continued as an organization. Kriyananda continued to lead the worldwide movement until 1998, when he left the United States to start communities in Italy and then in India in 2004.

As of 2007, there were about 1,000 people living in Ananda colonies around the world, according to the Ananda Web site.

Beliefs and Practices

According to Yogananda, the World Brotherhoood colonies were to be a vehicle toward world peace. In his autobiography, Yogananda wrote: "An urgent need on this war-torn earth is the founding, on a spiritual basis, of numerous world-brotherhood colonies. 'World brotherhood' is a large term, but man must enlarge his sympathies, considering himself in the light of a world citizen" (1951, 480).

In a 1932 article in his magazine *East-West,* Yogananda described how these colonies should be formed. He recommended that each community be formed by 25 married couples and their children. Each family would put in $10,000, and together, they would buy land, build homes, and grow their own food. The children were to be educated at community schools. He further recommended that parents have only one child. The children, when grown up, should go out into the world to earn their $10,000 with which to start a new community. The communities should be based on simple living and "fellowship of all religions," said Yogananda. Such communities would "establish absolute universal peace and harmony" (Yogananda 1932).

At Ananda, members believe there are many spiritual masters who can lead a person to divine consciousness, including Paramhansa Yogananda, Jesus, and Buddha. Meditation and Kriya Yoga are believed to help people reach "communion with God [through] an awareness of the deeper, higher self," according to Kriyananda (Chandler 1988).

Communities hold regular morning meditation. At the Nevada City community, Sunday services are held that are open to the public. The services include meditation, chanting, and a sermon by an Ananda minister.

At Ananda Village, residents must be disciples of Paramhansa Yogananda. The other Ananda communities are organized around the teachings of Yogananda, but residents are not required to be his disciples.

Members who want to take spiritual vows can participate in a training program of several years and join the Ananda Monastic Order, which is open to single and married people who dedicate themselves to living by the teachings of Yogananda, and who take vows of simplicity and self-control.

At the Ananda communities, sexuality is considered a private matter. Living together while not married, as well as divorce, are both acceptable, as are celibacy, marriage, and homosexuality. Swami Kriyananda was married from 1985 to 1994. New members are asked to refrain from having a romantic relationship with another member for at least one year from the time they join.

Daily Life

The living arrangements vary depending on the community. In Nevada City, residents live in a variety of houses. The Crystal Hermitage includes a main building with communal kitchen and dining facilities, library, and room for special events. The backyard has a community swimming pool. A shrine to the community's gurus (including Yogananda and his gurus), a Christian-style chapel, and terraced gardens surround the main building.

In Palo Alto and Portland, the residents live in apartments and share common areas such as kitchen and dining facilities, a swimming pool, and a meditation room.

While diet is up to each individual, the food served at Ananda is vegetarian. Alcohol and recreational drugs are not allowed.

Gardens of the Crystal Hermitage at the Ananda Colony, California. The Crystal Hermitage is considered the spiritual heart of Ananda Village. (Courtesy of Ananda Village)

How They Make Their Living

Ananda members are responsible for their own finances. Some members work for community-owned businesses and receive wages, out of which they pay a monthly fee for community services. Members are not required to turn over personal wealth to the community, but they are encouraged to make voluntary donations to the community.

Ananda-controlled businesses have included meditation centers, health food stores and restaurants, general contracting, publishing, and a health clinic.

Leadership and Decision Making

Kriyananda was the community's spiritual director until 1998, when he left for Italy to start a community there. He appointed Jyotish and Devi Novak as the spiritual directors of Ananda Worldwide. They help the Ananda centers and communities adhere to the teachings of Paramhansa Yogananda.

Each Ananda community is incorporated separately. Ananda Village in Nevada City has a village council to deal with practical matters such as membership, infrastructure, and finances. This village council is made up of some elected members and some appointed members. The appointed members include the general manager, village manager, and other representatives of major areas of the community. The elected members are voted in by the Ananda monastic order (Warner 2007; Powers 2007).

How New Members Are Recruited or Chosen

Potential members of Ananda Village are invited to apply for a Karma Yoga program of two weeks to three months, during which time they work six hours per day within the community and learn meditation, yoga, chanting, and prayer. They can then become disciples of Yogananda and receive initiation into Kriya Yoga meditation. If they continue to want to pursue membership at Ananda, they can apply for the one-month Living Discipleship program, an immersion into the practice and teachings of the community. After this, they can join the first-year residency program that includes classes and guided spiritual practices. The potential member may then be accepted as a member of Ananda Village or may move to another Ananda community.

Children and Youth

Children live with their parents. While some Ananda communities have schools, called Living Wisdom schools, families can also choose to send their children to public or private schools outside the community. The Living Wisdom schools are open to students outside the Ananda communities. The Nevada City community has a Living Wisdom high school that accepts boarding students from all over the world.

The goal of the Living Wisdom schools is to help students become more balanced, mature, and harmonious in mind, body, and spirit. The curriculum involves the usual academic subjects, as well as art, theater, music, computers, and physical education. Hands-on learning and service projects are emphasized, as is participation in spiritual ceremonies.

Relationship with the Outside World

Most of Ananda's conflict with the outside world has come from the Self-Realization Fellowship, which carried on a 12-year lawsuit against Ananda.

Ananda's relationship with the local community is generally good. Members of the Nevada City community have been involved with the local volunteer fire department as firefighters and staff members. Community members also volunteer at local nursing homes and animal shelters and are involved with the local chamber of commerce.

See also: Hippies; Rajneeshpuram

References

"Ananda Journal; Commune Flourishes, As Does Neighborliness." *New York Times,* September 1, 1988. http://query.nytimes.com/gst/fullpage.html?res=940DE6D9103CF932A3575AC0A96E9 48260.

Chandler, Russell. "Twenty Years of 'Divine Joy.'" *Los Angeles Times,* August 7, 1988, 3.

Gardner, Hugh. *The Children of Prosperity: Thirteen Modern American Communes.* New York: St. Martin's Press, 1978.

Popenoe, Oliver, and Cris Popenoe. *Seeds of Tomorrow: New Age Communities That Work.* San Francisco: Harper and Row, 1984.

Powers, Lisa, director of member services, Ananda Village. Phone conversation with author, August 6, 2007; e-mail correspondence, October 1, 2007.

Warner, Maria, Ananda Sangha, USA. E-mail correspondence with author, July 25, 2007.

Yogananda, Paramhansa. *Autobiography of a Yogi.* New York: Philosophical Library, 1951.

Yogananda, Paramhansa. "How to Burn Out the Roots of Depression by Divine Methods." *East-West,* April 1932, www.mysticalportal.net/ (accessed July 2007).

WEB SITES

Ananda Village: www.ananda.org/ananda/village/index.html (accessed July 2007).

Ananda Village Entry in Fellowship for Intentional Community: http://directory.ic.org/records/?action=view&page=view&record_id=43 (accessed July 2007).

"Frequently Asked Questions" about Ananda: www.anandaanswers.com/test.html (accessed July 2007).

Living Wisdom Schools: www.livingwisdom.org/ (accessed July 2007).

Self-Realization Fellowship: www.yogananda-srf.org/ (accessed July 2007).

Swami Kriyananda: www.swamikriyananda.org/ (accessed July 2007).

Anarchism

The word *anarchism* means "no government." Anarchists see central government as both harmful and unnecessary. They believe that power corrupts society, that private property is not compatible with human freedom, and that governmental authority and private property lead to crime. Anarchists believe that humans can achieve freedom and happiness in a society without central rulers—a society in which work and products are shared.

Anarchism is similar to socialism in that both systems hold that workers should own the means of production—in other words, that workers should own their own businesses or tools of their trade. But anarchism sees individual freedom as the highest goal and views the government as the main obstacle to this freedom. Socialism sees economic equality as the highest goal and sees capitalist corporations as the main obstacle to attaining this goal. Advocates of socialism have no problem with a central government run on socialist principles, while advocates of anarchism do not advocate any central government at all.

Several utopian communities have been based on anarchist principles, including the Catholic Worker Movement, the Ferrer Colony, Home Colony, and Rainbow Family of Living Light. All are profiled elsewhere in this book.

Although the idea of living without government is an ancient one, the modern anarchist movement started in the 19th century with a French socialist and writer, Pierre-Joseph Proudhon (1809–1865). He was born into a lower-middle-class family: his father was an innkeeper and brewer. Proudhon was trained as a printer and earned a scholarship to study in Paris. He believed in reason and scientific progress, and supported the notion of human liberty from government authority and religious superstition. Furthermore, he attacked capitalists, who owned property without having worked for it.

Proudhon's key principles were "mutualism"—a system of independent peasants and artisans who would own their own land and tools, and a system of factories run by associations of workers; "federalism"—local communities and industrial associations working together on the basis of contracts, instead of laws; and "direct action"—the idea that the workers should liberate themselves and organize into industrial associations. While Proudhon called himself an anarchist, his followers called themselves mutualists.

Another important anarchist was Mikhail Bakunin (1814–1876), a Russian nobleman. He was friends with Proudhon and influenced by Proudhon's thinking, but he promoted the idea of a violent revolution to overthrow the existing social structure, whereas Proudhon believed the transition to an anarchist system should happen peacefully. Bakunin also recommended that the means of production be owned collectively, although he thought workers should be paid based on how much they worked. Bakunin's followers began calling themselves anarchists in the 1870s. Bakunin and his followers participated in meetings of the International Working Men's Association, a socialist organization founded by Karl Marx. The anarchists were vying for control of this organization, but the socialists ended up ousting the anarchists in 1872.

Peter Kropotkin (1842–1921), another Russian nobleman, agreed with Bakunin that the means of production should be owned collectively, but he went further, stating that the products should be distributed according to need and not according to how much people worked.

In the 1880s and 1890s, anarchism became associated with violence and terrorism. Anarchist leaders argued that "propaganda by the deed" (a dramatic rebellious act) was more effective at spreading anarchist ideas than books and pamphlets. In 1881, Czar Alexander II of Russia was assassinated. Although the killers were not anarchists, the anarchists were so impressed with the power and effectiveness of the action that, at their Congress of London, they advocated the idea of propaganda by the deed.

Anarchists in various countries assassinated government leaders, including King Umberto I of Italy, Empress Elizabeth of Austria, President Sadi Carnot of France, President William McKinley of the United States, and Antonio Canovas del Castillo, prime minister of Spain. These assassinations were typically carried out by individuals, not by organized groups of anarchists.

Not all anarchists supported this kind of violence. Many anarchists promoted their views through song and poetry, and by setting up libraries and experimental schools. "For every attention-getting deed, there were dozens of anarchist schools, cafes and cabarets, libraries and theater groups," explains Richard Sonn (1992, 50).

During the 19th century, nonviolent anarchist ideas developed in the United States. Important proponents of this system of thought included Josiah Warren, who founded several utopian communities (see below), and Henry David Thoreau, author of *Walden* and an advocate of individual conscience over government law.

Anarchists value human freedom over any kind of authority. Because of this distrust of authority, it has been difficult for anarchists to form strong national or international organizations. Nevertheless, anarchists have had a lasting influence on liberal movements. The movement for African American civil rights used the principles of civil disobedience to protest laws that they considered unjust. Environmental groups such as Earth First! have used nonviolent and violent tactics to stop actions that are legal but that harm the environment. The feminist movement argues that governments have been patriarchal and oppressive to women. In 1999, anarchists led massive demonstrations in Seattle against the World Trade Organization, which is not a government yet wields power over individual lives all over the world.

Throughout the 1800s and 1900s, many anarchist groups in the United States set up experimental schools and communities in which to demonstrate and live out their principles. The largest and longest-lived of these were the Home Colony in Washington and the Ferrer Colony in New Jersey. These are profiled elsewhere in this book.

The Modern School Movement, active from 1910 to 1961, was an anarchist attempt to change the way children are educated. Anarchists believed that children learned best by doing, and so the Modern Schools emphasized crafts and exploration, rather than memorization. The movement started at 30 or so schools around the country, most of which were short-lived. Among the longest-lived of the Modern Schools were the ones at Ferrer Colony and its sister settlement, Mohegan.

Two major communities based on anarchist ideals continue to flourish to the present day. The Catholic Worker Movement is unique in that it combines Catholicism, socialism, and anarchism in its communities. The Rainbow Family of Living Light is a temporary community that does not believe in designating leaders. Both are profiled in this book.

Other important anarchist communities are detailed below.

Equity (1831–1835) and **Utopia** (1847–1865): Both of these were started in Ohio by Josiah Warren, a follower of Robert Owen. When Owen's New Harmony community failed, Warren set out to create his own communities, which were among the earliest American attempts at anarchist communities. Equity had six families; each owned their own land and home, but they ran a sawmill communally. In Utopia, as in Equity, the dozen families each owned their own land and homes, and cooperatively ran a sawmill and printing shop. There were no rules or leadership, although they did hold public meetings. After Warren left in 1848, Utopia gradually lost its anarchist features.

Modern Times (1851–1863): This community was also founded by Josiah Warren and at its height had about 200 members living on Long Island, New York. As in the aforementioned communities, families owned their own land and homes, and there were no rules or constitution. They ran an orchard and vegetable garden communally and had a communal cafeteria. They set up their own schools for children as well as adults, where students could learn practical skills such as carpentry and typesetting, along with reading, writing, arithmetic, dancing, history, music, and languages. Members were allowed almost complete freedom regarding their personal lives, in terms of whom they chose to live with and whether or not they practiced any form of religion.

Within the community, members exchanged community money, called "labor notes," to pay for services offered by other members, such as shoemaking and sign-painting. Nevertheless, the community was not able to be self-sufficient—many members earned their living by working in New York City, 40 miles away.

In 1864, the community decided to become the village of Brentwood, New York. Members no longer wished to live by anarchist ideals. They wanted to benefit from the outside economy (note that land prices on Long Island had risen). Many members also fought on the Union side during the Civil War.

Sunrise (1933–1939): This community was started by Joseph Cohen and other Jewish anarchists. Cohen had lived in the Ferrer Colony, another anarchist community. The group bought a farm in Michigan and lived communally in apartments for families and dormitories for single people. They prepared and ate meals in a common kitchen and dining room. They established an elementary school for their children. At its height, the community had about 200 people.

As in other anarchist communities, Sunrise had no formal constitution. Followers had trouble deciding how to allocate the work of the community. As anarchists, they did not believe in forcing anyone to work, but the fact remained that the work needed to be done. They experimented with a number of systems, including allowing workers to choose their own tasks, and dividing members into work groups that would arrange their own work schedule.

In addition to their problems with leadership, the people of Sunrise suffered through drought, floods, pests, and fire. The community was in debt, and it sold its land to the government in 1936. About 20 families from Sunrise went to Virginia to begin their community anew in a warmer climate. They bought a farm in 1937. As before, the group suffered from disagreements. Members began to leave, and in 1939, the group decided to end the community.

See also: Catholic Worker Movement; Ferrer Colony (Stelton); Home Colony; Owen, Robert; Rainbow Family of Living Light; Socialism

References

Oved, Yaacov. *Two Hundred Years of American Communes.* New Brunswick, NJ: Transaction Books, 1988, 311–331.

"Socio-Economic Doctrines and Reform Movements." *The New Encyclopedia Britannica,* 2005 ed., volume 27, 409–413.

Sonn, Richard D. *Anarchism.* New York: Twayne Publishers, 1992.

Wunderlich, Roger. *Low Living and High Thinking at Modern Times, New York.* Syracuse, NY: Syracuse University Press, 1992.

Antislavery Communities

At a Glance

Dates of existence in North America: 1819 to 1860s
Locations: Ohio, Indiana, Illinois, Michigan, Pennsylvania, South
  Carolina, Tennessee, and Ontario
Peak membership: 3,500 to 5,000, plus 10,000 in Port Royal, South
  Carolina
Religious or other belief: secularism

History

In the decades before the Civil War, one of the most perplexing issues among anti-slavery activists was what to do with former slaves once they were free. Many people did not believe that blacks could integrate successfully with mainstream white society. One group of activists proposed sending freed slaves to Africa, and accordingly the American Colonization Society acquired land along that continent's west coast. Between 1821 and 1867, 10,000 African Americans went to live there, and the country was eventually named Liberia, or "free land."

However, many African Americans objected to being sent to what they saw as a foreign land. They wanted to stay in the land of their birth. A number of people, both white and black, proposed the idea of planned communities in North America for former slaves. In the 40 years before the Civil War, at least 20 different communities were attempted or formed. The most ambitious and successful of them are profiled in detail below.

Unlike many of the other utopian communities in this book, the antislavery communities were not meant to be permanent. In fact, although the members lived in community, often sharing work and income, the purpose of the communities was to teach these former slaves how to be prosperous and self-reliant in American society. The communities were seen as "way-stations" on the way to true freedom. They provided job training in agriculture or a mechanical trade. They also provided a way for members to "learn to be free, learn how to earn their way in a free American society, and learn the virtues and morals as well as the customs and mores of American society" (Pease and Pease 1963, 19).

The first of these kinds of communities began with very little planning. For example, a handful of white slave owners freed their slaves and bought land for them in northern states. Later activists put more thought and planning into the antislavery communities.

Although slavery was a problem of the United States, many of the antislavery communities were started in Canada. Former slaves often fled to Canada to escape slave catchers who were active in the United States and also because Canada generally had no discriminatory laws against blacks. Even in America's northern "free" states, there were often laws that, for example, prohibited blacks from testifying in court, or that required blacks to produce a certificate of freedom before being hired. In Canada, on the other hand, blacks were entitled to full citizenship and voting rights—although socially and economically, blacks often suffered discrimination there, as well.

Nashoba (Tennessee, 1826–1830): This community is notable for being one of the first planned, well-organized attempts in the United States to answer the question of where former slaves should live. It was started by British philanthropist and activist Fanny Wright. She was inspired by Robert Owen and his community of New Harmony, and by the Harmonist Society of George Rapp.

Wright wanted to form a community that would allow slaves to buy their freedom and that would provide education and training to blacks. She proposed to buy land on which to grow cotton and to provide employment for 50 to 100 slaves in a cooperative labor system like that of Rapp's Harmonists. Wright calculated that the slaves could buy their own freedom with five years of labor. During this time, black families would have access to educational opportunities. Wright hoped that her experiment would be a model that every state could follow.

In 1825, Wright bought land near Memphis and named her community "Nashoba"—the local Native American name for the Wolf River that ran through the land. She advertised for the help of carpenters, bricklayers, and other laborers, and invited anyone, black or white, who wished to work for the community to join. In February 1826, a South Carolina slaveholder sent a female slave and her six children to Nashoba, and Wright herself bought about 10 slaves for her community. The community built cabins, dug a well, cleared ground, planted potatoes and cotton, and fenced an apple orchard. They started a store and built a dance hall.

By the end of the year, Wright was exhausted and ill from malaria. She appointed a 10-member board of trustees for the community, including Robert Owen and his son, Robert Dale Owen, and deeded the community to them. By the beginning of 1827, the community still had not attracted the blacksmith, carpenter, or bricklayer they desired. They had no sawmill or dairy, and the school had not yet been started.

To recover her health, Wright sailed for Europe in May 1827, leaving the community in the hands of the board of trustees (only three of whom actually lived on site). Wright did not believe in punishing the slaves, but after she left, one of the trustees, James Richardson, began flogging the slaves. New rules were instituted curtailing the slaves' right to see their children, to eat whenever they pleased, or to receive gifts from outsiders. The community that hoped to train blacks for freedom was deteriorating into an oppressive prison.

In addition, Richardson publicized the fact that he was living, without the benefit of marriage, with a free woman who was one-fourth black. Wright herself did not believe in marriage and had no problem with interracial relationships, but this revelation shocked the outside world.

Wright returned to Nashoba in January 1828. When she got there, she found that Richardson had left. The people of the community were subsisting on an unbalanced diet that lacked milk and vegetables—corn bread, pork, and rice were the only foods available to the adults and their growing children. Soon after her arrival, Wright published a piece she had written in favor of sexual freedom, against marriage, and in favor of complete mixing of the races. This also shocked the outside world and turned public opinion against her.

Because of the community's financial difficulties, Wright and the trustees decided to end the communal aspect of Nashoba and instead declared that residents were to pay $100 per year and provide for their own expenses and housing. Wright left once more, and in 1830, Nashoba ended. Wright freed the slaves and found them a place to live in Haiti.

Nashoba was a noble idea that failed because too few people believed in it enough to join or to send their slaves there and because there was not enough competent leadership to guide it to success.

Wilberforce (Ontario, Canada, 1829–1836): This was one of the first communities to be formed by African Americans (as opposed to being formed for African Americans by whites). A group of blacks in Cincinnati, hoping to escape race riots and restrictive laws in Ohio, appointed a committee to find land for a settlement. In October 1829, land was bought in western Ontario and the first settlers began to arrive. Quakers in Ohio and Indiana helped to pay for this land. At its height, about 200 African Americans settled in Wilberforce.

Reports of the community are contradictory: One observer noted that the community had a temperance group, a Sunday school, a day school, timber lands, 100 head of cattle, as well as horses and pigs, a sawmill, a flour mill, and a general store. Another observer reported that the houses were "wretched, badly built and very small" (quoted in Pease and Pease 1963, 51). What is known for certain is that the community was beset by leadership and financial problems from the beginning. The leaders quarreled among themselves over money, and the school that was to be established may never have gotten off the ground.

Dawn and the British-American Institute (Ontario, Canada, 1842–1868): This community formed around a school for African Americans called the British-American Institute, which was started by three antislavery activists. One of these activists was an escaped slave named Josiah Henson and the other two were white men.

Because education was key to prosperity, and because African Americans were often denied access to education, these activists wanted to establish an institution that catered to the educational needs of former slaves. The British-American Institute provided basic elementary education and vocational training to both children and adults.

Around this school arose the community of Dawn, which consisted of about 500 blacks on 1,500 acres, surrounding the 300 acres owned by the school. The settlers raised corn, wheat, oats, and tobacco. They also ran a sawmill, a gristmill, a rope factory, and a brickyard.

Apparently none of the school's leaders was a competent money manager, and the community was constantly in debt. Henson and other leaders often traveled to solicit funds for the school. A Boston philanthropist and former trustee of the institute wrote that "the Manual Training Institute here ran well for a season, and accomplished much good; but . . . it has run down, and can hardly be resuscitated without a miracle. The property connected with it is deeply encumbered. . . . The steam saw mill is doing no good. It has not paid the cost since it commenced running, and had better never been built" (quoted in Pease and Pease 1963, 68).

In 1850, the school was transferred to the American Baptist Free Mission Society, and it flourished for a few years before faltering again. A British antislavery leader, John Scoble, arrived in 1852 to take charge. But he seemed to make no difference. The school and its leaders continued to be the subjects of a long series of financial investigations. No actual wrongdoing was found, but it was clear that the school was not doing well financially. The institute was finally abandoned in 1868. The land was sold and the profits were given to the Wilberforce Educational Institute for the Negro in the nearby town of Chatham, Ontario.

Elgin (Buxton) (Ontario, Canada, 1849–1873): This was the most successful of the antislavery communities. It was begun by an Irish-born minister, William King. He moved to the United States, married a Louisiana plantation owner's daughter, and found himself the owner of slaves. He was uncomfortable with slavery, and after his wife and child died, he decided to form a community for his slaves and other former slaves. He chose Ontario as the location for his community, because he was working there as a missionary.

King formed the Elgin Association, which purchased land south of Chatham, Ontario. He was quite particular about who lived in his community. Those who wished to be admitted had to produce "certificates of good moral character" (Pease and Pease 1963, 99). Each black family was required to buy at least 50 acres of land, payable over 10 years. King also specified minimum requirements for housing: each family had to build a house measuring at least 24 feet by 18 feet and divided into at least four rooms. He even required that families erect picket fences and plant flower gardens. Alcoholic beverages were not allowed at Elgin.

Families helped each other with building, clearing land, and planting. The community planted corn, wheat, tobacco, hemp, and oats and raised milk cows, sheep, hogs, and horses. Elgin had a sawmill, a brickyard, and a potash factory (potash is a kind of fertilizer), as well as carpenters, cobblers, blacksmiths, and other craftspeople. By the late 1850s, about 1,000 people lived in the community.

Within a year of its founding, the community had started a school. Local white children also attended the school, making it the first integrated public school in all of North America. Unlike other schools of that time for black children, the Elgin school did not emphasize vocational training at the expense of academic subjects. The students at Elgin learned Latin, Greek, and algebra in addition to the basic subjects. Some students from the Elgin school went on to college.

Although King was a Presbyterian minister, members of the community were not required to attend his church—or any church at all.

The community suffered some setbacks—the potash factory burned down, for example—but on the whole it prospered and grew. One settler encouraged others to "come to a land of liberty and freedom, where the coloured man is not despised nor a deaf ear turned to them. This is the place to live in peace and to enjoy the comforts of life" (quoted in Pease and Pease 1963, 96). Perhaps the biggest reason for the prosperity was the work to be found nearby with the Canadian railroad, which paid such good wages that, for a few months of work, a man could pay off his yearly mortgage.

SEA ISLAND SCHOOL, No. 1.—ST. HELENA ISLAND. ESTABLISHED APRIL, 1862.

TEACHERS { MISS LAURA M. TOWNE,
ELLEN MURRAY.
MRS. HARRIET W. RUGGLES.   Supported by the Pennsylvania Branch.

EDUCATION AMONG THE FREEDMEN.

Pennsylvania Branch of the American Freedman's Union Commission.

PENNSYLVANIA FREEDMEN'S RELIEF ASSOCIATION.
No. 711 Sansom Street.

TO THE FRIENDS OF EDUCATION AMONG THE FREEDMEN.

As we enter upon our work for another year, we wish to present a statement of our plans and wants to the people.

The various organizations throughout the country having the education of the Freedmen in charge, have provided schools for 150,000 persons, in care of fourteen hundred teachers. The expense of supporting these schools has been borne by voluntary contributions.

It is frequently asked, Does not the Government accomplish this work through the "Freedmen's Bureau?" The simple answer is, No! The "Bureau" has no authority to employ teachers. The representatives of the "Bureau," from the honored Commissioner

The Port Royal Experiment was an effort to demonstrate that freedmen could be converted from slave labor to free labor. It was also a way to prepare for the upcoming emancipation of the slaves and to deal with the numerous slaves who had attached themselves to advancing Union forces during the Civil War. (Library of Congress)

King encouraged the community members to vote. They defeated a racist politician in a local election and helped to elect a sympathetic member of Parliament. He also asked the members to elect a Court of Arbitration that would settle community disagreements. King continued to be the director of the Elgin Association, and he decided who would be admitted to the community. But the Court of Arbitration gradually took over the management of the community.

After the Civil War, many people from the Elgin community returned to the United States. Two doctors from Elgin helped set up the first public hospital for blacks in the United States. Another Elgin man, James Rapier, went on to serve in the U.S. Congress.

Even today, descendants of the Elgin community continue to live nearby in North Buxton, Ontario. The community has been preserved as a historic site under the name of Buxton National Historic Site and Museum.

Port Royal (South Carolina, 1862–1866): Although this is often included among lists of antislavery communities, it was not really a voluntary community at all, but more like a benevolent company town.

It started during the Civil War, when northern (Union) troops invaded Port Royal Island in South Carolina. The white landowners fled, leaving behind about 10,000 slaves. The army put these former slaves to work at wages, picking cotton. A number of philanthropists also arrived to provide humanitarian help to the blacks. They provided schools and care for the elderly and ill.

After the army left, a white man, Edward Philbrick, bought several plantations and hired former slaves to work for him. He hoped to show that nonslave labor could produce a greater profit than slave labor. He also provided schools on his planta-tions. He did manage to make a handsome profit on his land. Philbrick sold his land at below-market cost to some of his workers in 1866.

Influence on the Outside World

Only a small minority of African Americans participated in the antislavery commu-nities. About 500,000 blacks were free by 1860 and at most, 5,000 spent any time liv-ing in a community.

Although the idea behind these communities was noble, the communities them-selves were generally unsuccessful in achieving their goals. William and Jane Pease suggest that the antislavery communities missed the point: "They trained the Negro to live in white society—trained the Negro, that is, to adjust. It never occurred to these communitarians, it seems, that the issue involved all of American society, that to solve it meant changing white attitudes as well as black" (1963, 162).

See also: Civil War; Harmony Society; New Harmony and Owenite Movement;
   Owen, Robert

References

Eckhardt, Celia Morris. *Fanny Wright: Rebel in America.* Cambridge, MA: Harvard University Press, 1984.
Pease, William, and Jane Pease. *Black Utopia: Negro Communal Experiments in America.* Madison: State Historical Society of Wisconsin, 1963.
Ullman, Victor. *Look to the North Star: A Life of William King.* Boston: Beacon Press, 1969.

WEB SITES
Buxton National Historic Site and Museum (Elgin): http://www.buxtonmuseum.com/ (accessed June 2006).
U.S. Department of State, Bureau of African Affairs, Background Note—Liberia: www.state.gov/r/pa/ei/bgn/6618.htm (updated December 2007).

Bellamy, Edward

Edward Bellamy (1850–1898) was a Massachusetts lawyer and journalist whose novel *Looking Backward 2000–1887* inspired the formation of a number of utopian communities.

Bellamy became aware of the suffering of the urban poor while studying in Germany. He was also influenced by Laurence Gronlund, author of *Cooperative Commonwealth* and the first writer to try to explain socialism to Americans. After practicing law for a short time, Bellamy became an editor for the *Springfield Union* in Massachusetts and then an editorial writer for the *New York Evening Post*. He wrote several novels.

Looking Backward 2000–1887 was published in 1888 and sold over a million copies. The novel is about a man, Julian West, who is transported from Boston in

Edward Bellamy attracted a huge following with his 1888 utopian novel, Looking Backward, *which predicted what life would be like in the United States in 2000.* (Library of Congress)

1887 to Boston in the year 2000, where he encounters a utopian city. The pressing issue of West's era had been labor unrest. His host in 2000 explains that the labor problem was solved when all industries were taken over by the government. In this society, there are no wars, and instead of military service, all citizens between the ages of 21 and 55 perform "industrial service" according to ability and interest. Each worker receives an equal credit to be used for purchasing goods and services.

Before writing the novel, Bellamy was not associated with any socialist groups. However, socialists were very inspired by the ideal world depicted in the novel. After its publication, Bellamy began speaking publicly about his ideas. Over 150 Nationalist Clubs formed all over the country to promote the idea that industries should be owned and operated by the government.

Bellamy's novel influenced the formation of Theosophical utopian communities such as Point Loma, and of socialist communities such as Llano del Rio and Ruskin.

See also: Gronlund, Laurence; Llano del Rio and New Llano; Point Loma and Theosophical Communities; Ruskin; Socialism

Reference

Bellamy, Edward. *Looking Backward, 2000–1887.* New York: Grosset and Dunlap, 1888.

Bible Communism

Many of the communal Christian utopias have been influenced by descriptions in the New Testament of how the early Christians lived communally.

Christian teachings state that after the death and resurrection of Jesus, the apostles converted about 3,000 people in Jerusalem to Christianity. Acts 2 (44–45) describes the living arrangements of these new Christians: "All the believers were together and had everything in common. Selling their possessions and goods, they gave to anyone as he had need" (*New International Version of the New Testament;* hereafter cited as NIV).

Two of the apostles, Peter and John, are said to have performed the miracle of healing a crippled man. In response, the number of believers rose to 5,000. They all continued to live communally, as described in Acts 4 (32–37): "All the believers were one in heart and mind. No one claimed that any of his possessions was his own, but they shared everything they had. With great power the apostles continued to testify to the resurrection of the Lord Jesus and much grace was upon them all. There were no needy persons among them. For from time to time those who owned lands or houses sold them, brought the money from the sales and put it at the apostles' feet, and it was distributed to anyone as he had need. Joseph, a Levite from Cyprus, whom the apostles called Barnabas (which means Son of Encouragement), sold a field he owned and brought the money and put it at the apostles' feet" (NIV).

This book of the Bible also tells the story of a married couple who sold land and gave only a portion to the apostles, secretly keeping the rest for their own use. Because of their deceit, they both fell down dead (Acts 5:1–10).

See also: Bishop Hill; Bohemia Manor; The Family/Children of God; The Farm; Harmony Society; House of David Movement; Jesus People USA; Shakers; Zoar Society

Reference

New International Version of the New Testament, International Bible Society, 1973.

Bishop Hill

At a Glance

Dates of existence in United States: 1846 to 1861
Location: Illinois
Peak membership: about 700
Religious or other belief: Christianity, Pietism, Separatism, Perfectionism

History

Bishop Hill was a promising utopian community, similar to the Amana, Harmony, and Zoar communities. However, despite its early economic prosperity, the community disbanded just 15 years after it started.

Bishop Hill was started by Swedish lay preacher Eric Jansson and his followers. At the age of 22, Jansson experienced a miracle in which he was healed of the rheumatism from which he had suffered for many years. At the same time, he had a vision that he had been deceived by the Lutheran Church and that the true source of spiritual knowledge was the Bible and Jesus Christ. Jansson became a Pietist—he believed that personal religious devotion was more important than ritual, and he rejected the rituals and clergy of the established Lutheran Church. He began to preach while selling wheat flour door-to-door (Elmen 1976, 3–4, 25).

Jansson also preached the idea of perfectionism—the idea that humans are not inherently sinful and that those who truly believe could lead sinless lives. The Janssonists compared the Swedish Lutheran Church to Satan and in 1844 publicly burned Lutheran hymnbooks and other church literature. Jansson was arrested and tested for insanity, and his followers were harassed (Elmen 1976, 60–91).

The Janssonists had heard from earlier Swedish settlers in the United States that it was a land of religious freedom, and they sent one of their members to the United States to find a place for them to settle. This member chose land in Illinois, near a small Swedish Methodist congregation.

In 1846, over 1,000 Janssonists sailed for the United States. The Janssonists pooled their wealth in order to buy passage on the ship, since not everyone was able to afford the trip. They were also inspired by the example of the early Christians, who pooled their wealth and lived communally (Wagner 1997, 300).

Many Janssonists died on the ship and others left the group when they landed in New York. When Jansson and about 400 of his followers reached their land in Illinois, they named it "Bishop Hill" in honor of Jansson's birthplace in Sweden. They built 30 semi-underground log cabins for the first settlers. Many of them died of star-

Steeple building in Bishop Hill, Illinois. Bishop Hill was a Janssonist colony established during the 1840s. (Library of Congress)

vation during their first winter. Although they had money, there was almost no place to buy food nearby.

As soon as the weather grew warm in 1847, the members began to build their community. By June they had a flourmill, sawmills, brickworks, a tannery, a roofing shake factory, and shops. They also began to build frame and brick buildings, including a huge apartment building called "Big Brick" to house 72 families. Completed by 1850, at that time Big Brick was reportedly the largest building in the United States west of Chicago (Wagner 1997, 305).

In 1848, a man named John Root joined the community and married Jansson's cousin, Charlotta. Root proceeded to mistreat his wife and forced her to leave the community. She was rescued by community members. Jansson, Charlotta, and other community members fled to St. Louis for three weeks, because Root had organized a mob and was threatening to attack the community. After Jansson's return to the colony, he traveled to Cambridge, Illinois, to take care of legal business. There, Root, who was also at the courthouse on business, shot and killed Jansson in May 1850.

After Jansson's funeral, the community chose seven trustees as leaders. They prospered economically for many years. According to the Bishop Hill Web site, "In the period 1848 to 1861, Bishop Hill was the major center of commerce between Rock Island and Peoria" (http://www.bishophillartscouncil.com/History/).

In 1858, as the United States experienced financial troubles, 250 banks in Illinois closed. The Bishop Hill community went into debt, and members were upset because they thought the trustees were not telling them the whole truth about their finances. Many members wanted to end the communal system. In 1861, the community was dissolved and the property divided among the members (Wagner 1997, 310).

Beliefs and Practices

Members of Bishop Hill attended two services daily and three on Sundays. At first they worshiped in a log church with a canvas roof and later in a brick church (Elmen 1976, 125). While Jansson was alive, he was the main preacher. After his death, apparently community members took turns preaching.

Charles Nordhoff, who visited a number of communities in the late 1800s, states that "their religious life was very simple. They had no paid preacher, but expected their leaders to labor during the week with the rest. At [their services], after singing and prayer, the preacher read the Bible, and commented on what he had read. . . . They had no library, and encouraged no reading except in the Bible. . . . They discouraged amusements, as tending to worldliness" (1965, 346–347).

During the early years of the colony, when food was scarce, Jansson sometimes ordered the community to fast for as many as several days. He also ordered the community to adopt celibacy during this time, probably to discourage the birth of more children as the community was just getting started. In 1848, when the community had adequate money and housing, Jansson paired couples off and married them (Wagner 1997, 303–304).

Jansson preached that members could overcome illness through faith. Despite this, the community suffered from fatal illnesses such as an epidemic of cholera in 1849, which killed about 200 members, including Jansson's wife and two of his children (Elmen 1976, 141–142).

The Bishop Hill members visited other religious communities, including the Shakers. In fact, some members were so influenced by the Shakers that they wanted to institute celibacy at Bishop Hill. Some Bishop Hill members went to live in the Shaker community of Pleasant Hill, Kentucky, after the Bishop Hill community was dissolved.

Daily Life

While many American utopian communities of European origin tried to maintain the language and customs of their home country, Bishop Hill residents tried to "Americanize" themselves as soon as possible. Jansson had promised his followers that, as soon as they landed in the United States, they would automatically be able to speak English. Although this miracle did not materialize, members began to study English as soon as they arrived. Jansson preached his first sermon in English in June 1847, about a year after landing in the United States.

Families lived in rooms in one of several communal buildings. Members ate in one of three communal dining halls: the men ate at separate tables from the women, and the children dined in a different room (Sutton 2003, 58).

Women and men generally performed tasks traditional to their gender. In Sweden, women performed a wider variety of tasks than was common in the United States, so the women at Bishop Hill made bricks, built bridges, and planted crops in addition to the traditional female work of cooking and sewing (Wagner 1997, 304).

How They Made Their Living

The people of Bishop Hill farmed Indian corn, broom corn, wheat, barley, oats, potatoes, and flax. They wove the flax into linen and carpeting, and this was one of their most important sources of income. They raised hogs, cattle, sheep, chickens, turkeys, and geese. Their flour mill was the only one within 30 miles. They also ran sawmills, a tannery, and various shops, and manufactured wagons and carriages for sale outside the community. In addition, Bishop Hill ran a hotel for stagecoach travelers going to or from St. Louis.

Nordhoff remarks that Bishop Hill "had the finest cattle in the state; and their shops and mills earned money from the neighboring farmers." He also reports that the community had a contract to grade part of the Chicago, Burlington, and Quincy railroad line (1965, 345–346).

Leadership and Decision Making

Eric Jansson was the community's leader. After he died, the community chose seven trustees as leaders.

How New Members Were Recruited or Chosen

Although the community tried to learn English and intended to spread its message throughout the United States, most new members came from Sweden.

Children and Youth

Children lived with their parents. The community hired an American to teach English to the children and also made sure the children memorized the names of American presidents and counties in Illinois. Women of the community taught the children arithmetic and writing. At the age of 14, the children were finished with school and began to work in the community (Sutton 2003, 58).

Relationship with the Outside World

Bishop Hill wanted to be both separate from the outside world and engaged in converting those in the outside world to its faith. Almost as soon as he arrived in Illinois, Jansson appointed a group of 12 "apostles" to learn English so as to spread the community's message in the United States. However, apparently few if any conversions took place (Elmen 1976, 133).

Reasons for Ending the Community

The murder of Eric Jansson was a serious blow to the members of Bishop Hill, although they recovered and prospered for some years after.

Jon Wagner suggests that one reason Bishop Hill ended so soon, after such a promising beginning, might be that the members began to be more interested in their businesses and less interested in religion (1997, 313). Paul Elmen, in his biography of Eric Jansson, noted that as the community matured, "the character of the community began slowly to change from that of poor and pious settlers to reasonably well off burghers" (1976, 127). Wagner also suggests that, because Bishop Hill members tried to Americanize themselves, they had more trouble maintaining their separateness from the outside world (1997, 313).

Influence on the Outside World

The Bishop Hill colony has probably been more influential in Sweden than in the United States. The community was one of the first large groups of Swedes to immigrate to the United States and led the way toward more Swedish emigration. The community is so well known in Sweden that the king and queen of Sweden have paid visits to its historic site, and the government of Sweden has issued a postage stamp commemorating the site (Wagner 1997, 314). According to the Bishop Hill Web site, the royal family of Sweden continues to support its preservation.

In 1984, Bishop Hill was recognized as a National Historic Landmark. About 125 residents live in the village, including some descendants of the original settlers. The site remains a tourist attraction.

See also: Amana Colonies; Harmony Society; Shakers; Zoar Society

References

Elmen, Paul. *Wheat Flour Messiah: Eric Jansson of Bishop Hill*. Carbondale: Southern Illinois University Press, 1976.

Nordhoff, Charles. *The Communistic Societies of the United States*. New York: Schocken Books, 1965.

Sutton, Robert. *Communal Utopias and the American Experience: Religious Communities, 1732–2000*. Westport, CT: Praeger, 2003.

Wagner, Jon. "Eric Jansson and the Bishop Hill Colony," in *America's Communal Utopias*, edited by Donald Pitzer. Chapel Hill: University of North Carolina Press, 1997, 297–318.

WEB SITES
Bishop Hill, Illinois: www.bishophill.com/ (accessed October 2006).

Bishop Hill Arts Council—Bishop Hill Colony State Historic Site: http://bishophillartscouncil.com/History/ (accessed May 2008).

Bohemia Manor

At a Glance

Dates of existence in United States: 1684 to 1727
Location: Maryland
Peak membership: 100
Religious or other belief: Labadist Christianity

History

Bohemia Manor was one of the earliest utopian communities in the United States. It was an outgrowth of a Dutch community started by Jean de Labadie, who was born in France in 1610 and started his career there as a Catholic priest. He became a Protestant in 1650 and was expelled from France by Catholic authorities. Labadie spent several years in Geneva and then settled in the Netherlands, where he tried to reform the Dutch Reformed Church. He was suspended from this church in 1668.

Labadie continued his preaching and attracted followers in the Netherlands. One of his most famous converts was Anna Maria van Schurman, a celebrated scholar and artist. Another prominent convert was Maria Sybilla Merian, an artist who is famous for her drawings of insects and plants (Saxby 1987, 117, 264).

The Labadists began to live communally, holding all their goods in common. When the Dutch government started to restrict the activities of his church, Labadie and his followers moved to Westphalia and then to Altona (both in present-day Germany). Labadie died there in 1674. Pierre Yvon succeeded him as the leader of the community.

Yvon and his followers returned to settle in the Netherlands. William Penn, the founder of Pennsylvania and a Quaker leader, visited them there in 1677. He found them to be similar to Quakers: "They are a serious, plain people, and are coming nearer to Friends [Quakers], as in silence in meetings, women speaking, preaching by the Spirit, plainness in garb, and furniture in their houses" (quoted in Saxby 1987, 253–254).

The Labadist community grew and found it difficult to support all their new members with their existing businesses. They decided to start new communities and looked to the New World. They first tried setting up a community in Suriname, South America, which was a Dutch colony. This community was stricken by insects, snakes, tropical diseases, failed harvests, and pirate attacks (Saxby 1987, 277–279).

The Labadists were at first reluctant to consider North America as a site for a new community, because they objected to the fact that they might have to raise tobacco to earn a living (tobacco was a major cash crop). They also objected to the use of slave labor. Nevertheless, in 1679 two Labadists traveled to North America and arranged to buy a tract of land in Maryland from Augustine Hermann, who had named the land "Bohemia Manor" after his own birthplace. The sale was finalized in 1684 and the Labadists began settling in.

In 1692, the Labadists still in the Netherlands ended the practice of holding property in common. Although Pierre Yvon stressed that the community itself would continue, many members left. Within a decade, the community in the Netherlands had shrunk from 300 members to 30 members. The members left, grew older, and died, until the community dwindled to a close (Saxby 1987, 315–328).

In 1698, the Labadists at Bohemia Manor divided up some of their land among the individual families. The reason for this is unclear, but some historians theorize that they were having trouble making a living by owning everything in common (Saxby 1987, 305–306).

In 1721, the declining Labadist community was visited by Conrad Beissel, who later started the Ephrata Cloister. Over the next two years, the leaders of the community died, including Peter Sluyter, leader of the Maryland branch. Members began dispersing, and by 1727 the community had ended (Saxby 1987, 308–309).

Beliefs and Practices

Bartlett James describes Labadism as an effort to "reform the established church, to infuse a sentiment of deeper fervor in its formal administrations, and to awaken in the believer devoutness of spirit by enjoining austerities of life, abnegation of the flesh, and renunciation of the world" (1899, 9).

In a letter to a follower, Labadie explained: "We are to deny ourselves, be not of this world, flee evil, do good, mortify the flesh by the Spirit, crucifying it with its appetites and lusts, leave the things that are behind and of earth; seek and find things that are from above; to be sober, patient, modest; to watch, pray and bear our cross, and finally produce the fruits of true repentance" (quoted in Saxby 1987, 155). Labadie was influenced by the communal living of the early Christian church as described in the Acts of the Apostles (155).

Although William Penn found that their practices were similar to Quaker practices, and although outsiders sometimes confused the two religions, the Labadists were not eager to join with the Quakers. In fact, Penn first visited the Labadists while Labadie was still alive, and Labadie refused to meet with him. Later, when two members of the Labadists were touring North America seeking a place for a community, they stayed for times with Quakers, and declared that "these people are still covetous, and . . . almost all of them are attached to the world and to themselves" (quoted in Saxby 1987, 208–210, 295).

Bohemia Manor members prayed silently before meals, beginning and ending their prayers as the spirit moved them. A visitor to the community was informed that "secret prayer was more acceptable than to utter words; and that it was most proper for every one to pray as moved thereto by the Spirit in their own minds" (quoted in Saxby 1987, 307).

Daily Life

Although celibacy was valued, many Labadists were married. Families were assigned rooms together. Women and men ate separately. Each member was assigned work, and "degrading tasks were assigned those suspected of pride" (James 1899, 16–17).

In the Netherlands, the community had not heated their bedrooms even in the winter, partly because firewood was scarce. In Bohemia Manor, the leader, Peter Sluyter, outlawed fires "as a mortification of the flesh," although wood was abundant in the area (Saxby 1987, 303).

The Labadists dressed plainly and ate meagerly. "If a particular foodstuff was especially distasteful to members, as a discipline it was made a steady diet" (Durnbaugh 1997, 18).

How They Made Their Living

According to Bartlett James, the Labadists cultivated tobacco "extensively" and used slave labor for this purpose, although they were originally reluctant to do both. They also raised corn, flax, hemp, and cattle (1899, 39).

Leadership and Decision Making

The Labadists in Maryland looked to their home community in the Netherlands for final leadership. Pierre Yvon, who succeeded Jean de Labadie as the leader of the Labadists, "was regarded as the Supreme Father of the whole Church." Yvon was assisted by a group of "superintendents," which included men and women. These superintendents were in charge of advising Yvon, raising new members from the status of "novice" to full membership, and teaching the children (James 1899, 15).

The Maryland branch was headed by Sluyter, who was one of the two Labadists who had originally traveled to America to find land. A former member claims that Sluyter and his wife exercised "absolute authority" over Bohemia Manor (quoted in James 1899, 15).

How New Members Were Recruited or Chosen

While Labadie was alive, new members were attracted by his preaching. Apparently Bohemia Manor was not particularly successful at attracting new members from among the local people.

In the Netherlands, there were three classes of membership: visitors, who lived in cottages just outside the gate of the community; probationers, who were expected to participate fully in communal life but who were still considered to be holding on to their self-love and self-interest; and the "elect," or first class, who addressed each other as "sister" and "brother" (Saxby 1987, 246).

Children and Youth

Although celibacy was valued, children were seen as a blessing from God, and married couples often had large families. Children were the responsibility of the entire community. Parents were not supposed to be overly affectionate with their own children. Children were assigned a tutor or governess to oversee their education and upbringing. A former member accused the community of instilling fear in the children through corporal punishment (Saxby 1987, 248, 303–304).

Relationship with the Outside World

The Labadists were among the first white settlers in Maryland. They took part in local politics: two members were justices of the peace in 1702 (Saxby 1987, 307).

Reasons for Ending the Community

After the communities in the Netherlands and Bohemia Manor ended full communalism and introduced private property, the membership dwindled until the communities ended.

Influence on the Outside World

Bohemia Manor was a branch of a larger movement and on its own seems to have made very little impact on the outside world. Few converts were gained to the Maryland community. However, according to James, the Labadist movement as a whole "is recognized by Dutch writers as one of the most significant developments in the Reformed Church of the Netherlands" (1899, 26).

T. J. Saxby states that Labadist literature influenced Quakers and Mennonites and that some of Labadie's hymns were printed in German hymnals. "In their day [the Labadist] message was electric" (1987, 333–334).

See also: Bible Communism; Ephrata Cloister

References

Durnbaugh, Donald F. "Communitarian Societies in Colonial America," in *America's Communal Utopias*, edited by Donald Pitzer. Chapel Hill: University of North Carolina Press, 1997, 17–19.

James, Bartlett. *The Labadist Colony in Maryland*. Johns Hopkins University Studies in Historical and Political Science, Series 17, Number 6. Baltimore, MD: The Johns Hopkins University Press, June 1899.

Saxby, T. J. *The Quest for the New Jerusalem, Jean de Labadie and the Labadists, 1610–1744*. Dordrecht, Netherlands: Martinus Nijhoff Publishers, 1987.

Brook Farm and Fourierist Phalanxes

At a Glance

Dates of existence in North America: 1841 to 1892
Locations: Illinois, Indiana, Iowa, Kansas, Massachusetts, Michigan, New
    Jersey, New York, Ohio, Pennsylvania, Texas, Wisconsin, and
    Ontario
Peak membership: approaching 4,000
Religious or other belief: secularism, socialism

History

The Fourierist phalanxes represented the most widespread movement for secular, socialist utopias in 19th-century America. Most were short-lived (lasting from one to
three years), but 29 of them were formed over the course of 50 years. Furthermore,
supporters of the communities went on to found the cooperative movement in the
United States.

Brook Farm did not start out as a Fourierist phalanx but converted to one after a
few years. It is the most famous phalanx, and despite its short duration (1841 to 1847),
much has been written about it. Brook Farm was started by several well-known
Americans, including author Nathaniel Hawthorne and journalist Charles Dana.
Hawthorne even wrote a novel, *The Blithedale Romance,* based on his experiences
at Brook Farm.

The Fourierist phalanxes began in the mind of French socialist Charles Fourier.
He was a salesman who deplored the capitalist economic system's failings, such as
the creation of artificial food shortages and the poverty of factory workers. He wanted
to form a society based on cooperation, peace, and class harmony.

Starting in 1808, Fourier came up with his system of *phalanges* (phalanxes in English), which is explained below. Fourier's writings were difficult to understand, and
few people took interest until an American, Albert Brisbane, traveled to France and
became a disciple of Fourier. Brisbane returned to the United States in 1834, attempted to raise the huge amount of money necessary to build a phalanx, and failed
to do so. He then translated a version of Fourier's work and this book, *Social Des-
tiny of Man*, was published in 1840.

Meanwhile, in March 1841, a group of ministers and intellectuals near Boston
started a community they called Brook Farm, based on Transcendentalist principles.
They wanted to "insure a more natural union between intellectual and manual labor," according to founder George Ripley (quoted in Delano 2004, 34), so that there

would be no separate intellectual class and labor class. Brook Farmers began working in agriculture and started a school for children as well as adults.

In 1842, Brisbane began publishing a column in the *New York Tribune* about Fourierism. Ripley and the Brook Farmers read the column with interest. In 1844, encouraged by Brisbane, the Brook Farmers decided to become a Fourierist phalanx. They were already following many of the Fourierist ideas, and they hoped that by joining the Fourierist movement, they could attract more members and more financing.

Thousands of other Americans read the column as well, and Brisbane attracted large audiences at lectures. At a time of economic depression, Americans were drawn to the idea that, working together, they could create a society of equality and plenty. The name of the movement was pronounced "*foor*-yer-ism" in the United States.

By 1846, 24 phalanxes had begun in the eastern and midwestern states and about 15 of them had already folded. None of them had the money to construct the kind of buildings envisioned by Fourier and Brisbane, but most bought a lot of land in anticipation of such building. Unfortunately, the land was often unsuitable for farming or was far from the cities where they could sell their products. Many members of the phalanxes had very little idea of how they would earn a living and many of them admitted members indiscriminately. Most of the phalanxes went under after just one or two years due to debts and internal bickering. The more successful and long-lasting phalanxes are described below.

By 1846, as many phalanxes collapsed, the Fourierists realized that they needed a way to control the movement and spread its ideas in a more orderly way. They formed a national association in order to create a true Fourierist community. Fourierist leaders began a lecture tour in the eastern states and organized local clubs. Some of these clubs started cooperative stores or insurance plans.

In 1847, Brook Farm folded. The headquarters of the movement moved to the North American Phalanx. The Fourierists decided that, instead of trying to salvage the existing phalanxes, they would attempt to raise the money for a true model phalanx. However, a year later they decided that they would not be able to fund such a venture. Working with the money they had, the Fourierists instead transformed the North American Phalanx into a model community. Unfortunately, the modest phalanstery built at the North American Phalanx did not satisfy the dreams of some of the movement leaders, who still hoped to build the grand edifice described by Fourier.

By this time, the public's interest in Fourierism had declined, perhaps because prosperity had returned to the country. The national organization and its newspaper, *The Harbinger*, ended in about 1851. At this point, only one phalanx was in existence, the North American Phalanx. It too ended, in 1855, as a result of an internal split and a fire.

However, even after this, two more Fourierist-inspired communities tried to make a go of it in the United States. By 1855, a Frenchman had raised $250,000 to set up a Fourierist colony in Texas. The community bought over 2,000 acres of land, but it proved to be unsuitable for farming and infested with rattlesnakes. At its height, 250 people lived in La Reunion, most of whom were French-speaking. Financial mismanagement and lack of leadership led to the end of the community in 1859.

A silk farm was started in Kansas in 1869, inspired by Fourierism. Although its founder, who was from France, hoped to make the farm into a cooperative venture, with workers sharing the profits, for the most part it was simply a successful model factory town with nice working and living conditions, and possibly some profit-sharing. Silkville ended in 1892.

Beliefs and Practices

Fourier's plan for a community was grandiose. He declared that a phalanx should contain 1,620 people living in a building, called a *phalanstere* (phalanstery in English), surrounding a courtyard, with workshops nearby. Fourier came up with the number 1,620 because he theorized that all humans are composed of 12 basic passions, in different proportions, resulting in 810 different personality types. His community would include two of each type: one male and one female. The grounds of each phalanstery would include 6,000 acres of gardens, orchards, and forests. Fourier believed that members would naturally gravitate toward the work they liked best, and that because of the workers' happiness they would be so productive as to have ample leisure time.

Fourier predicted that, because of the happiness engendered by the phalanxes, humans would undergo a physical evolution: they would grow to seven feet tall, live for 144 years, acquire replaceable teeth, and be able to withstand intense pain. After 16 generations in the phalanxes, humans would even develop long, useful tails, at the end of which would be found a small, strong hand (Beecher 1986, 340).

Fourier also included in his community a plan for a "new amorous world" in which sexuality would be freed from societal constraint and would operate as a force for harmony.

Brisbane was a little more practical. In his version of Fourier's work, he deleted any mention of the amorous world and of the physical evolution of humans and recommended phalanxes of about 400 people located near major cities, for easy access to markets that could buy phalanx products. Such a phalanx would cost $400,000 to start. All the land and property was to be owned communally.

Brisbane and Fourier insisted that once a phalanx was created whole in this way, its members would naturally form themselves into working groups that would satisfy each worker's abilities and interests. Workers were to spend only two hours per day on a task before rotating to another job, in order to avoid boredom. More menial, unpleasant tasks were to be rewarded with a higher share of the community surplus than more attractive work.

There was very little thought or planning given to how the phalanxes were to be governed. "Fourier conceived the phalanx as a self-operating mechanism run by 'attraction' without legislation and supervised by a tiny and largely honorific corps of officers . . . that would merely advise members on the scheduling of tasks" (Guarneri 1991, 129–130).

Another important Fourierist principle was the "right to labor"—everyone should be provided with work and there should be no unemployment, and everyone was to be guaranteed a place to live, along with sufficient food, clothing, and medical care.

Fourierists believed that women should be free from economic dependence and should be allowed the same education as men. The Fourierists also relied on communal child care.

Fourier envisioned that an ideal world would be composed of 2 million phalanxes. Fourierists believed that once the first phalanx was established, the rest of the world would peacefully and easily transform itself into phalanxes.

The Major Phalanxes

None of the phalanxes was able to raise the kind of money to build the ideal society proposed by Brisbane and Fourier. While most were disorganized and short-lived, some of them managed to last for more than a few years. A description of the more successful phalanxes follows.

Brook Farm (1841–1847): Brook Farm was founded in 1841 by a Unitarian minister named George Ripley, who was a member of the "Transcendental Club" started by Ralph Waldo Emerson. As noted, Ripley wanted to foster a union between intellectual and manual labor at his community. As he wrote in a letter to Emerson, he wanted "to combine the thinker and the worker, as far as possible, in the same individual; to guarantee the highest mental freedom, by providing all with labor, adapted to their tastes and talents, and securing to them the fruits of their industry; to do away with the necessity of menial services, by opening the benefits of education and the products of labor to all; and thus to prepare a society of liberal, intelligent and cultivated persons, whose relations with each other would permit a more simple and wholesome life than can be led amidst the pressure of our competitive institutions" (quoted in Francis 1997, 42).

Although few of the other members of the Transcendental Club joined the community, within 18 months of its founding, Brook Farm had grown from a handful of people to 70 members. Most of them were boarders who paid for their lodging and food or students who paid tuition and worked for their board. This was one of the few sources of income for the community, which was on shaky financial footing.

The Brook Farmers worked hard: 10 hours per day, six days per week, during the warmer months, and eight hours per day during the colder months. In exchange for this work, members received a room, meals, medical care, education, and other necessities. One member, Mary Ann Dwight, enjoyed the work but observed that "we need more leisure, or rather, we should like it" (quoted in Delano 2004, 170). The members did find time for picnics, boat rides on the Charles River, walks in the woods, and singing.

Brook Farmers made some attempt at mixing the genders in work, although many of the chores were often actually divided along traditional gender lines. The men performed the heavy farm work and the women cleaned, cooked, and tended the flower and fruit gardens. However, a man did all the community's baking and both genders taught in the school. In addition to farming and running the school, Brook Farmers also tried to make money through manufacturing pewter ware, shoes, and sashes and blinds.

After three years of existence, the Brook Farmers were proud of the fact that they had "abolished domestic servitude," in the words of member Charles Dana (quoted in Delano 2004, 161). Members worked for each other. They were also proud of the fact that their school was open to both girls and boys and was not restricted only to

George Ripley first gained recognition as a literary critic for the New York Tribune *in the 1830s. Ripley was a noted Transcendentalist and a Unitarian minister who founded Brook Farm, a utopian community in West Roxbury, Massachusetts. Brook Farm survived from 1841 to 1847, when financial problems forced its closure.* (Cirker, Hayward and Blanche Cirker)

the upper classes. The school at Brook Farm was innovative: instructors held classes outdoors and emphasized literature, drawing, music, and dancing.

After converting itself to a Fourierist phalanx in 1844, Brook Farm became the headquarters of the movement and began publishing the Fourierist newspaper, *The Harbinger*. Brook Farm also began construction of a phalanstery to house its members.

However, troubles soon arose. An outbreak of smallpox spread throughout the community in November 1845. Parents pulled their children out of the Brook Farm school. The epidemic caused so much financial trouble that the Brook Farmers did not have money for a Thanksgiving dinner. Their neighbors supplied them with turkeys and other food.

The community, beset by debts, was then struck by a fire in March 1846 that destroyed the partly built, three-story phalanstery. The phalanstery was to have been the centerpiece of the community, containing a dining hall for 400 people, a lecture hall, and 100 sleeping rooms and suites. The building was not insured. Community members began to leave, and by 1847 the community had ended.

North American Phalanx (1843–1855): This phalanx was located in Red Bank, New Jersey, about 40 miles from New York City. At its height, it had 120 members.

The North American Phalanx lasted longer than other phalanxes for a number of reasons: members bought less land initially than some others did and so had less debt; they constructed temporary dwellings at first, instead of trying to build a grand phalanstery; and members carefully screened those who wanted to live in the community. The North American Phalanx accepted only about a third of those who applied, preferring people who were committed to Fourierist ideals and who had some capital or work skill to contribute. Prospective members also had to go through a 10-month probationary period before being admitted to full membership.

Because it was near New York City, the community was able to make money by selling fruits, vegetables, and flour in the city. It prospered but did not grow much. Perhaps its admissions policy was too strict. The community actually had to hire outside laborers at times.

With support from the national organization of Fourierists, the North American Phalanx built a modest phalanstery with a library, offices, space for 200 in the dining room, and sleeping rooms for 100 upstairs. By the early 1850s, it appeared that the North American Phalanx might be a model Fourierist community. A visitor in 1851 saw members dancing in the dining hall to violin music. Some of the women wore bloomers (knee-length dresses over full pants). He also described "excellent, wholesome food" and good accommodations (quoted in Noyes reprinted 1961, 474–477).

Despite the apparent success of the community, internal disagreements arose. Some members and supporters wanted to make the North American Phalanx more religious. In 1852, this group left and set up another phalanx a few miles away.

Two years later, disaster struck: the North American Phalanx's flour mill burned down. Although it was insured, the insurance company went bankrupt. Fourierist supporters offered loans for rebuilding, but the disillusioned members voted not to rebuild it. The community closed in 1855.

Wisconsin Phalanx (1844–1850): This phalanx was located in Fond du Lac County and had 180 members at its height. It was unusual in that it had no debt and was the most productive farm of all the phalanxes. It produced wheat, corn, potatoes, hay, and vegetables. Families could choose to eat in the central dining hall or cook their own meals. Although the community was financially successful, some members left when the community decided to build a phalanstery to house members, rather than to provide individual homes.

Eventually, many members stopped believing in Fourierism and decided to sell the land for a profit, which they did in 1850. A former member remarked that the community folded because of "the love of money and the want of love for the Association [Fourierism]. Their property became valuable, they sold it for the purpose of making money out of it" (quoted in Noyes 1961, 448).

Reasons for Decline of the Communities

Carl Guarneri summarizes the demise of Fourierism: "For all their problems of leadership, membership, and organization, at the bottom the collapse of the American phalanxes was an ideological one. Beyond and beneath the specific ills of the communities lay the more general problem of a utopian creed that promised too much and required too little of its adherents. American Fourierism was literally too good to be true. . . . When American reformers adopted Fourier's imaginings as the basis for a practical social movement, they promised a combination of instant social transformation and magnificent economic abundance that no society could have fulfilled" (Guarneri 1991, 175).

Influence on the Outside World

The phalanxes welcomed visitors. The idea was to transform the world, after all. And the outside world was curious. In a single year, Brook Farm may have received 1,000 or more visitors (Delano 2004, 53). One scholar estimates that at least 15,000 Americans were involved at one time or another in a Fourierist phalanx or a Fourierist organization (Guarneri 1997, 167).

Although Fourierism did not manage to transform the world into phalanxes, people who were influenced by Fourierist thought went on to form cooperative stores, workshops, households, and insurance plans. Guarneri credits the Fourierists with founding America's cooperative movement: "Whereas in England it was Owenite ideas that stimulated working-class cooperatives . . . in the United States the Fourierists virtually founded the movement" (1997, 174). Fourierist ideas helped people to see how they could benefit by cooperating with each other.

See also: Socialism; Transcendentalism

References

Beecher, Jonathan. *Charles Fourier: The Visionary and His World*. Berkeley: University of California Press, 1986.

Delano, Sterling. *Brook Farm: The Dark Side of Utopia*. Cambridge, MA: Belknap Press of Harvard University Press, 2004.

Francis, Richard. *Transcendental Utopias: Individual and Community at Brook Farm, Fruitlands, and Walden*. Ithaca, NY: Cornell University Press, 1997.

Guarneri, Carl. "Brook Farm and the Fourierist Phalanxes," in *America's Communal Utopias*, edited by Donald Pitzer. Chapel Hill: University of North Carolina Press, 1997, 159–180.

Guarneri, Carl. *The Utopian Alternative: Fourierism in Nineteenth-Century America*. Ithaca, NY: Cornell University Press, 1991.

Noyes, John Humphrey. *History of American Socialisms*. New York: Hilary House Publishers, 1961 (first published 1870).

Oved, Yaacov. *Two Hundred Years of American Communes*. New Brunswick, NJ: Transaction Books, 1988.

Pitzer, Donald. "Patterns of Education in American Communal Societies," in *Communal Life: An International Perspective,* edited by Yosef Gorni, Yaacov Oved, and Idit Paz. New Brunswick, NJ: Transaction Books, 1987.

WEB SITE

Brook Farm Historic Site: www.newtonconservators.org/26brookfarm.htm (accessed April 7, 2008).

Brotherhood of the New Life

At a Glance

Dates of existence in United States: 1861 to 1900
Locations: California, New York
Peak membership: 75
Religious or other belief: Christianity, mysticism

History

The Brotherhood of the New Life was founded by Thomas Lake Harris, a poet and spiritual seeker who was raised Baptist in upstate New York, became a Universalist minister, dabbled in spiritualism (communication with spirits, including people who have died), studied the teachings of the 18th-century Swedish philosopher Emanuel Swedenborg and became a Swedenborgian minister, and finally created his own theology and a community to go with it.

Harris was first involved with founding a community in 1850, at a time when he was involved in spiritualism. He and a few others led a group of spiritualists to Mountain Cove, Virginia, where they set up a communal farm. This community ended in 1853.

Harris's own theology, the Brotherhood of the New Life, developed around 1857. At that time, he was a Swedenborgian minister. He reportedly received visitations from spirits during that year and wrote about his revelations. However, the Swedenborgian Church (called the New Church) condemned these writings. In 1859, Harris went to Great Britain to preach, and there he gathered his first followers for the Brotherhood of the New Life.

In 1861, he and his followers began living communally in New York. As it grew, the community bought more land and eventually settled in Brocton, New York. By 1868, there were 75 people living in the community. Seven years later, in 1875, Harris moved with a few of his followers to Santa Rosa, California. Harris claimed that he was spiritually guided to move to California and await further revelations. The community in Brocton remained until 1881, when all its members moved to California. The community there was named Fountain Grove.

Trouble arrived for the community in 1891. Margaret Oliphant wrote a biography of her cousin, Laurence Oliphant, who was a wealthy supporter of Harris's and one of the more prominent members of the community (he had forsaken his seat in the British Parliament to join with Harris). Laurence Oliphant had left the community in 1881. Margaret Oliphant's book painted a picture of Harris as an immoral man who cheated members financially. In addition to this negative publicity, a visitor, Alzire

Thomas Lake Harris was a spiritualist who founded the utopian society Brotherhood of the New Life. (Cirker, Hayward and Blanche Cirker)

Chevaillier, claimed that Harris had made sexual advances toward her, and that the members of the community were Harris's slaves. Chevaillier lectured in Santa Rosa and spread her views, leading local outsiders to become hostile toward Harris.

In 1892, Harris left Fountain Grove. Eight years later, he sold his property in Fountain Grove to five members of the community. This marked the formal end of the Brotherhood of the New Life community, although it had begun to decline and many members had begun to leave years before, just after Harris's departure. The property was to revert to the member who lived the longest, which was a man of Japanese descent, Kanaye Nagasawa. He became the sole owner in the 1920s and continued managing the Fountain Grove winery until he died in 1934.

Beliefs and Practices

The Brotherhood of the New Life was a Christian community. Harris preached that he—Thomas Lake Harris—would be the one to announce Christ's second appearance on Earth. According to Harris, God combined both genders and Christ was a man-woman. Humans could come close to God by practicing something called "divine breathing" or "internal respiration" (quoted in Hine 1953, 16).

The sexual practices in the community were misunderstood. Harris preached that, because God was both male and female, humans could approach union with God by seeking "conjugial love," that is, a spiritual union between a human and his or her heavenly counterpart of the other gender. These ideas gave rise to rumors of sexual license within the community. In fact, community members seemed to have been mostly celibate. After his first wife died, Harris married twice more and both times the union was said to be celibate. Very few children were born within the Brotherhood of the New Life communities (Hine 1953, 23–26).

Work was very important to the community. Its members called themselves "The Use," which referred to the emphasis they put on the usefulness of each community member's work. This was not just material usefulness but spiritual as well—members served humanity through their work, and the community believed that outsiders would be inspired by the "inner light" of the products of this work (Hine 1953, 19–20).

Each member was given a name to be used within the group. Harris's name was "Faithful," for example. The names were chosen as a way to encourage a person's spiritual growth (Schneider and Lawton 1942, 155).

Although Harris formed a community that shared labor, income, and living quarters, he did not see his experiment as "communism." He preferred to call it "theosocialism." He believed that all people are free and equal because of the "Divine immanence" within them. Harris felt that secular socialism was flawed because it was not based on religion (quoted in Hine 1953, 28–29).

Daily Life

In New York, the community lived much like other people in the surrounding areas: they lived in farmhouses without a common dining room, although groups of people ate together. Harris decided where members were to live. Community members enjoyed a band, music lessons, and lectures on such topics as natural history and geography (Schneider and Lawton 1942, 158–159, 163–164).

The Fountain Grove community was situated about two miles north of Santa Rosa, California, on rolling hills. The community built a two-story mansion with sitting rooms, a library, a huge dining room, a kitchen, multiple bedrooms, indoor plumbing, and bathrooms. Harris and several community members lived in this house, which was surrounded by gardens, lawns, and ponds.

Other members lived in a nearby two-story redwood building and another small house. A quarter mile from these three buildings were the winery and other outbuildings. The community was built around a barn with a conical roof that still stands today.

Members ate together in the communal dining hall. Harris often wrote poems to read at breakfast time. Singing and dancing were considered important. Harris played piano and the members sang hymns he had written (Hine 1953, 21–23).

Harris sometimes separated family members in order to promote communal harmony, or to encourage love for all humankind. For example, one of the most well-known members, Laurence Oliphant, was not allowed to see his mother for months. Harris also separated Oliphant from his wife for years, rarely allowing the two to see each other (Hine 1953, 25–26).

How They Made Their Living

Members were encouraged to donate wealth to the community, and Harris attracted a number of wealthy members, including Laurence Oliphant, a former member of

the British Parliament, and Oliphant's mother. Outside supporters also gave donations to the community.

In California, members of the Fountain Grove community planted grapes and made
wines that were popular in the eastern United States and beyond. According to the history section of the Santa Rosa, California, Web site, the winery shipped 200,000 gallons
of wine per year around the world. Harris believed that the wine from his community
contained within it the love and fraternity of the community itself, and so was a way
to convey divine love to anyone who drank it. The Fountain Grove winery continued
operating until 1934, long after the community itself disbanded (Hine 1953, 19).

The members of Fountain Grove also farmed, operated a flour mill, and opened
a restaurant, a hotel, and a general store at the nearby railroad station. Many of these
enterprises were not run well, partly because Harris believed in assigning people to
work in areas with which they were not familiar in order to promote spiritual growth
(Schneider and Lawton 1942, 160–163).

Leadership and Decision Making

Harris was the leader of the community. According to members and ex-members,
those who did not choose to obey Harris's decisions were forced to leave. Harris
himself described the community's leadership differently, however. He stated that
there was a council of directors consisting of 19 members who made decisions by
consensus: "If any one of them fails to perceive the propriety of a course or plan
agreed upon by the other eighteen, it is accepted as an indication of Providence that
the time for carrying out the course or plan has not yet come; and they patiently wait
until the entire Council becomes 'of one heart and one mind' as to the matter proposed" (quoted in Schneider and Lawton 1942, 157–158).

How New Members Were Recruited or Chosen

Harris's speeches and philosophy attracted new members, which included a few former Shakers, Americans from all over the country, people from Great Britain, and a
few from Japan. These Japanese members came from a group of 20 Japanese guests
who stayed in Brocton, New York, to study with Harris. Members were asked to promise obedience to Harris. They were not required to turn over their personal wealth to
the community, but were encouraged to do so (Schneider and Lawton 1942, 148–154).

Children and Youth

Children often lived separately from their parents, especially if Harris felt the parents
were selfishly attached to their own biological offspring. The children were cared for
by selected community members (Schneider and Lawton 1942, 159; Hine, 1953, 24).

Relationship with the Outside World

Until about 1891, the outside world seemed to ignore the Brotherhood of the New
Life. During the 1870s and 1880s, the local California newspapers portrayed Harris

as a wealthy man who had created a country estate for himself. With the publication of Margaret Oliphant's biography of Laurence Oliphant, the outside world began to view the community with suspicion (Hine 1953, 30).

Reasons for Ending the Community

After the departure of their founder and leader, Thomas Lake Harris, members began drifting away and the community dwindled and died.

Influence on the Outside World

Fountain Grove was an important part of Santa Rosa history. The community eventually owned 1,500 acres and ran an extremely successful winery.

See also: Burned-Over District; Shakers

References

Hine, Robert V. *California's Utopian Colonies*. New Haven, CT: Yale University Press, 1953.
Schneider, Herbert W., and George Lawton. *A Prophet and a Pilgrim*. New York: Columbia University Press, 1942.
Taylor, Anne. *Laurence Oliphant, 1829–1888*. Oxford, U.K.: Oxford University Press, 1982.

Web site
History of Santa Rosa, California: http://ci.santa-rosa.ca.us/VISITORS/HISTORY/Pages/fountaingrove.aspx (accessed April 7, 2008).

Bruderhof

At a Glance

Dates of existence: 1954 to present (since 1920 outside of the United States)

Locations: Connecticut, New York, Pennsylvania, as well as England, Paraguay, Uruguay, Germany, and Australia

Peak membership: 3,000 worldwide

Religious or other belief: Anabaptist Christianity

History

The Bruderhof movement began in Germany when a group of young adults, disillusioned by World War I, wanted to find a way to bring Christianity into everyday life. Influenced by the New Testament passage in Acts that describes how the early Christians lived communally, a handful of young men and women, led by Eberhard Arnold, rented a farm and farmhouse in 1920. The movement grew, and in 1930, Arnold visited the Hutterites in Canada for a year, hoping to join with their movement. Although Hutterite rules differed somewhat from Bruderhof rules—the Hutterites do not allow instrumental music or dancing, for example—Arnold's group felt it would be a good idea to join with them.

Arnold was ordained as a Hutterite minister in 1931. He returned to Germany and his group adopted Hutterite dress: the men grew beards and the women wore long skirts and a head scarf.

When the Nazis came to power in Germany in 1933, the Bruderhof young men were threatened with military service. The Bruderhof, who are pacifists, gradually left Germany, settling in England by 1938. Arnold had died in late 1935. In 1940, the British government, which was at war with Germany, threatened to intern the German-speaking Bruderhof members. The group decided to flee England and hoped to join the Hutterites in North America; however, they were denied entry to both Canada and the United States. Subsequently, they fled to Paraguay.

When World War II ended in 1945, the Bruderhof again sought to enter North America. The Hutterites in North America sent over $50,000 in money, clothing, and tools to help the Bruderhof but soon learned that the Bruderhof were not following all of their rules: The Bruderhof continued to smoke, dance, watch movies, and play musical instruments. At this point, the Hutterites for the most part ended their association with the Bruderhof.

In 1954, a group of Bruderhof journeyed to the United States and formed their first U.S. community in Woodcrest, New York. A number of members of a community in Georgia called Macedonia joined with the Bruderhof, moved to New York, and brought along their successful wooden toy business, Community Playthings.

By the late 1950s, the Bruderhof membership worldwide consisted of about 1,500 people, with communities in Paraguay, Uruguay, Germany, and England, as well as the United States. Its members hailed from an even wider variety of countries. The various Bruderhof communities were run by Arnold's sons and sons-in-law.

Between 1959 and 1962, the community underwent a crisis, during which about 600 people were expelled or left, and almost all the "hofs" (the name given to the communal villages of the Bruderhof) outside of North America were closed. Experts are at a loss to definitively explain the reasons for the upheaval, but some speculate that it was prompted by (1) a leadership struggle among Arnold's descendants and the various hofs they led; (2) a conflict over whether the Bruderhof should be most concerned with missionary activity, or with their own internal spiritual growth; or (3) economic issues (the Woodcrest branch was self-sufficient economically, while some of the other branches were not).

A few years later, about 200 of the exiled members rejoined the Bruderhof. The movement continued to grow and started new colonies in the United States, England, Germany, and Australia. The Bruderhof continued their engagement with the outside world, marching for civil rights with Dr. Martin Luther King Jr., and protesting capital punishment. They visited kibbutzim in Israel (the Israeli communal movement), and helped set up a (short-lived) Bruderhof in Nigeria.

Between 1964 and 1974, the Bruderhof attempted a somewhat successful reconciliation with the Hutterites and were again welcomed as a fourth leut, the "Arnoldleut," of the Hutterites. However, in 1990, two of the three Hutterite leuts stopped recognizing the Arnoldleut as part of the Hutterian Brethren. The Hutterites continued to be dismayed at the Bruderhof's use of musical instruments and candles at worship services and their marches and protests on behalf of social issues, among other things. The third Hutterite leut ended ties with the Bruderhof in 1995. Today, the Bruderhof are not considered part of the Hutterian Brethren.

Beliefs and Practices

The Bruderhof are Anabaptists, like the Amish and the Hutterites. They believe that people should not become baptized until they are adults and have the capacity to understand and freely choose their faith.

In the Bruderhof view of the world, humans are caught in a struggle between good and evil. Humans can help God to win the world over for good. The Bruderhof believe that by living in community, they can empty themselves of ego and allow themselves to be filled with the Holy Spirit. In this way, they can pattern their lives after the will of God.

Joy and euphoria are important to the Bruderhof. They believe that joy is the natural state of humans when filled with the Holy Spirit. Another way of describing this would be peace or fulfillment. A sense of playfulness is also valued. Both adults and children enjoy games and pranks.

The Bruderhof love celebrations. In addition to the Christian holidays, they celebrate individual birthdays (adults included). In order to commemorate something special such as a wedding or to welcome a member of another hof, the Bruderhof hold "love meals," during which they prepare festive foods, decorate the dining room, sing, and emphasize the joy of the occasion.

The Bruderhof hold spiritual meetings on Sunday evenings and sometimes on a weekday evening as well. During these meetings, after a reading of an inspirational text and a period of silence, the Servant of the Word, which is each hof's highest leadership position, seeks to discern and speak the common prayer in the hearts of all present.

There are not many prohibitions in Bruderhof life, although there are preferred ways of behaving. Members own cars, but they share them within the community. They own two planes so members can travel to other hofs. Watching television or going to movies is not prohibited, but the Bruderhof members prefer to create their own dance, music, and theater performances. Divorce, birth control, and extramarital sexual activity are all prohibited.

Another strong prohibition is gossip. The no-gossip rule is called "The First Law of Sannerz" (Sannerz being the first German community of the Bruderhof), and copies of this rule are posted throughout each hof. If someone has a problem with someone else, they must talk directly to each other to resolve it. If it cannot be resolved in this way, they must bring in a trusted third person to help them.

The Bruderhof are pacifists; they do not believe in violence, even for self-defense.

The Bruderhof do not believe that men and women are equal. They claim that women are meant to do the nurturing work, and men are meant to do the work of leading. The work of women and men is seen as equally important, but women, while encouraged to offer their thoughts about decisions, must ultimately give way to male authority. Women are not allowed to hold the position of Servant of the Word.

Daily Life

The Bruderhof membership is divided into hofs. Each hof might have 300 or more people living in it. The hofs are all under central Bruderhof leadership, and people can be moved from one to another as needed.

The village is organized around a central dining hall and kitchen, with living quarters, school buildings, and workshops arranged around it. Sometimes Bruderhof members move into existing buildings: one American hof took over a former hotel, for example, and an English hof now lives in a former tuberculosis sanatorium.

Each family is assigned a set of rooms in which to sleep and socialize. Families also eat breakfast and weekly family meals together in their apartments. All other meals are eaten in the central dining hall.

The Bruderhof men are expected to begin work in the workshops at around 7:30 in the morning. The women spend less time on communal work and more time—about two to three hours per day—on work in their own apartments. A midmorning snack is served, and then lunch, after which people have some time to themselves before going back to work. There is a break for a midafternoon snack, and after the evening meal, people might engage in meetings, sports, play rehearsals, or music practice.

While the men generally perform the income-generating work, the women clean, cook, wash and mend clothes, and care for children. Men and women do work together sometimes: the men serve the food and wash the dishes, and the genders work together in the school, the community office, and sometimes in the workshops. The Bruderhof work six days per week and rest on Sundays.

Meals begin with a song and prayer, and while people are eating, one brother reads out loud. Although radios, television, and newspapers are not common, the Bruderhof might learn, while eating, about that week's world affairs as reported in the *New York Times*. Meals might consist of meat or fish, eggs, dairy products, vegetables, bread, fruit, and dessert. Wine and coffee are also consumed.

Bruderhof men wear beards and dark pants. Women wear calf-length dresses in a variety of colors, and head scarves.

How They Make Their Living

The Bruderhof make their own clothing and shoes, and they grow or raise much of their own food. With their move to the United States, the Bruderhof inherited a successful wooden toy business, Community Playthings, from an American sister community that joined with them. Nowadays, this business manufactures high-quality wood furniture and supplies for day care facilities and classrooms. The Bruderhof have also started Rifton Equipment, featuring adaptive products for people with disabilities, and Spring Valley Signs, which makes wooden signs.

Leadership and Decision Making

The Bruderhof was first led by Eberhard Arnold, and then by his male descendants. The Bruderhof as a whole has one elder, and each community has a minister, who is called the Servant of the Word. The leaders are seen as people who serve the community, rather than lead it. Under the Servant of the Word are several witness brothers, stewards, and housemothers who oversee the various work departments on the hof. The leaders are not chosen for life and can be replaced as necessary.

The Bruderhof do not operate based on democracy but on unanimity. In a democracy, the idea is that everyone has different opinions and different needs, and that by voting, the decision that is favored by the majority will win. However, this often means that a large minority of people will not be happy with the decision or that the decision will not be right for a large minority.

The Bruderhof, in contrast, believe that the right decision for any problem exists and that decision will be suitable and good for everyone and for the group as a whole. This right decision can also be described as "God's will." It is the job of the Bruderhof members to listen and look in order to figure out this correct decision. Sociologist Benjamin Zablocki describes the decision-making process in this way: "No person acting alone can ever find this right decision. For this reason, everyone in the Bruderhof has a duty to become involved in every decision and to speak his mind if any relevant thought occurs to him, even if it contradicts the entire rest of the Bruderhof. . . . When the decision is fairly clear, someone who disagrees in an angry or resentful way is often said to be 'bringing in a disturbance.' In order to differentiate this from performing one's proper duty of speaking out, the attitude, not the objective content, is the focus of attention. The proper way to dissent is never to say, 'I object,' but rather, in a tentative voice, 'I have a question'" (1971, 155). The Servant of the Word is the person who puts into words the decision that is felt to be right by the entire group.

The Bruderhof makes decisions at meetings of full (baptized) adult members. These meetings take place several times a week.

While women are not eligible to be the Servant of the Word, they can exercise leadership as one of the housemothers, older women who supervise the women's work and are in charge of distributing things like cloth, needles, school supplies, and toys.

How New Members Are Recruited or Chosen

Visitors are always welcome at Bruderhofs. If a person wants to join, he or she is asked to live and work in the Bruderhof for six months to a year. After this, he or she can ask to become a novice member of the community, and then after a time as a novice, he or she can ask to be baptized. Upon formally joining the community, the member must give all money and property to the community. About 30 percent of Bruderhof membership is made up of converts—people who did not grow up in the faith.

Children and Youth

When a baby is born, the mother and father retreat with the baby to the "Mother House" for six weeks. After that time, the baby is cared for during much of the day in the Baby House. Because she must be on call to nurse the baby, the mother is given tasks that are easily interruptible. After age three, the children move to the preschool building and then on to the school on the hof property, where they are educated through grade eight.

The Bruderhof schools are influenced by the philosophies of Friedrich Froebel, who started the first kindergarten in Germany, and by Maria Montessori, originator of the Montessori method of education, which stresses the importance of the environment, natural discovery, and self-direction in children's learning. In addition to the basics of reading, writing, and arithmetic, the schools emphasize drama, music, arts and crafts, Spanish, and exploring natural surroundings. There is no homework until fifth grade. The children begin to work around the community when they are in upper elementary school (Spielhagen and Cooper 2002).

After eighth grade, the Bruderhof children attend local public high schools and then often go on to college or vocational school, if they desire further education. The young people are encouraged to live for a year or more in the outside world, so they can make an informed decision about whether or not they want to become baptized members of the Bruderhof and dedicate their lives to the community.

Young people do not date but socialize together in groups. The "singles," as they are called, live in their own separate rooming houses: one for women and one for men. They generally eat breakfast and other meals together and go on outings together.

When a woman or man wants to marry, she or he tells the Servant of the Word or a housemother. These elders counsel the young people and help them to decide whether they are called to be husband and wife. The baptized members of the hof must approve of the engagement. During the marriage ceremony, the couple is asked to agree that their marriage is subordinate to the community, and that if one spouse were to leave the community, the other would not follow just for the sake of family unity.

Relationship with the Outside World

Most people living on the hof are discouraged from interacting with outsiders. However, the high school students and young adults are encouraged to mix with outsiders and to live in the outside world for a time. The Bruderhof also relate with the outside world through their businesses, through visitors to the hofs, through their activism on behalf of social issues, such as an end to capital punishment, and through community service projects. In addition, sometimes parents from the outside enroll their children in a Bruderhof elementary school.

While the Bruderhof generally enjoy good relationships with the outside world, a vocal group of ex-members has criticized the communities for such practices as preventing former members from seeing family who are still living on a hof.

Influence on the Outside World

Many people who buy Bruderhof products are probably unaware that these products are made within a Christian utopian communal society. The Web sites for the main Bruderhof businesses, Community Playthings and Rifton Equipment, do not even mention the Bruderhof name. In the early years of the 21st century, the Bruderhof kept a low profile and did very little outreach to attract new members.

However, other communitarians who come into contact with members of the community are often profoundly affected by the experience. For example, after visiting with the Bruderhof, some members of the Koinonia Farm Christian community encouraged Koinonia to merge with the Bruderhof. Koinonia ended up remaining independent, but some Koinonia members joined the Bruderhof individually.

A founder of the cohousing movement in the United States, Chuck Durrett worked with the Bruderhof in 1995 and noticed their signs against gossip. He was so impressed with this idea that he urged his own cohousing community, Doyle Street Cohousing in California, to adopt a similar philosophy, which it did.

See also: Amish; Cohousing; Hutterites; Koinonia Farm/Koinonia Partners

References

Durrett, Chuck. "An Open Letter about Gossip." December 2006, http://www.cohousing.org/cm/article/gossip (accessed April 7, 2008).
Haavie, Erikah. "Bruderhof Live, Work in Shared Simplicity: Group Believes Lifestyle Actualizes Bible's Teachings." *Poughkeepsie Journal,* August 9, 2003, www.poughkeepsiejournal.com/projects/cultures/lo080903s4.shtml (accessed June 2006).

Mitchell, Alex. "Amish 'Cousins' Fight for Right to Stay in Australia." *The Sun-Herald* (Sydney), March 6, 2005, www.smh.com.au/news/National/Amish-cousins-fight-for-right-to-stay-in-Australia/2005/03/05/1109958158819.html (accessed June 2006).

Oved, Yaacov. *The Witness of the Brothers: A History of the Bruderhof.* New Brunswick, NJ: Transaction Publishers, 1996.

Spielhagen, Frances R., and Bruce S. Cooper. "Forming Social Capital: The Bruderhof Schools." *Journal of Education* 18 (2002): 49–53.

"Teen Considers Future at Religious Commune." *New York Amsterdam News* 96 (2005): 20.

Tyldesley, Michael. *No Heavenly Delusion? A Comparative Study of Three Communal Movements.* Liverpool, U.K.: Liverpool University Press, 2003.

Zablocki, Benjamin. *The Joyful Community: An Account of the Bruderhof, a Communal Movement Now in Its Third Generation.* Baltimore, MD: Penguin Books, 1971.

WEB SITE

Community Playthings: www.communityplaythings.com/ (accessed June 2006).

Buddhist Communities

At a Glance

Dates of existence in United States: 1966 to present
Locations: California, Colorado, New York, Vermont
Peak membership: 65 (San Francisco Zen Center); 150 (Zen Center of Los Angeles)
Religious or other belief: Buddhism

Buddhism first came to the United States in the mid-1800s, when large numbers of Chinese and Japanese immigrants arrived in the United States. However, it was not until the 1950s and 1960s that large numbers of native-born Americans began turning to Buddhism.

While the vast majority of Buddhist practitioners in the United States do not live communally, a small number of American Buddhists have formed residential communities in which men and women, families and single people, live and work together and meditate together. These communities typically host meditation practices and retreats for the general public.

Living together in a Buddhist community is a way of deepening one's practice in Buddhism and meditation. According to the Zen Center of New York's Web site, "Spending a period of time in residential training at the center is a powerful way of concentrating all one's daily activities into a single stream of awareness. Residency can provide support, structure and stability, which in time, become deeply internalized and integrated into one's own experience of the spiritual path. At the same time, residential training offers flexibility to allow one to live and practice within an intimate sangha, or spiritual community, while tending to the everyday needs of one's life" (http://www.mro.org/zmm/residential.php).

The major residential communities follow either a Zen Buddhist (Japanese) tradition or Tibetan Buddhist tradition. However, the residential aspect of the communities is perhaps uniquely American. Rick Fields, in his history of Buddhism in America, comments that Japanese Buddhists who visit the Zen Center of Los Angeles "have never seen anything like it." The spiritual leader of the Zen Center of Los Angeles, Taizan Maezumi-Roshi, explains it this way: "Buddhism in the East has traditionally emphasized the enlightened one and his teachings, while American practice seems to express itself especially in community, in which we manifest the enlightened life" (quoted in Fields 1981, 363).

Starting in the early 1900s, Zen Buddhist masters from Japan traveled to the United States, lecturing and teaching. Some of these teachers felt that Zen Buddhism in Japan had become too tradition-bound, and saw the United States as a fresh, new place in which to explore Buddhism. They encountered Americans who were tired of institutional religion and who sought spiritual experiences outside of the traditions they were familiar with. By the 1950s, more and more young people were attracted to this new spiritual tradition, causing what one historian describes as a "Zen boom." During the 1960s and 1970s, as hippies became increasingly interested in alternative religions, the boom continued, becoming a "mass religious movement" (Seager 1999, 40, 91).

Zen Buddhism has become very popular in the United States. "Zen, while only one Buddhist sect among many in Japan (and not even the most popular of them), has in the United States achieved a degree of recognition unrivaled by any other Buddhist group until the recent emergence of Tibetan Buddhism," writes Diane Morgan (2004, 147).

In general, Buddhism relies heavily on meditation and/or chanting as a way to achieve a state of "nirvana"—a state of release from the sufferings of the world, which are caused by worldly desires and attachments. Buddhists do not have to give up other religious traditions in order to practice Buddhism. In fact, one prominent Zen leader, Bernard Glassman, continued to follow Jewish traditions as well, celebrating the traditional Jewish Friday night Shabbat meal with his family (Popenoe and Popenoe 1984, 22–23).

The first residential American Buddhist community was the **Tassajara Zen Mountain Center** near Carmel-by-the-Sea, California, started in 1966. The spiritual leader of the San Francisco Zen Center wanted a mountain retreat center to help deepen the meditation practice of his students. Supporters contributed money to buy the Tassajara Hot Springs, located in a remote canyon and featuring hot springs, guest cabins, and kitchen facilities.

The Tassajara Center opened its doors with a three-month retreat. Each day began with a wake-up bell at four in the morning. The students meditated and chanted throughout the day, with breaks for meals. They listened to lectures by the roshi (spiritual leader). They also performed manual labor within the center. This manual labor is considered an essential part of Zen training. The food was vegetarian and included brown rice, cheese, eggs, Japanese miso soup (a soybean-based soup), and bread.

After the initial three-month retreat at the Tassajara Center, students returned to San Francisco and wanted to continue living together. They moved in together in row houses near the San Francisco Zen Center. In 1969, the Zen Center bought a large building with rooms for 70 people and a communal kitchen and dining room. This was the beginning of the residential aspect of the **San Francisco Zen Center**. Some residents worked for the center, while others held outside jobs. The center started businesses making and selling zafus and zabutons (the cushions people sit on during meditation) and clothing. "Within a short time [the San Francisco Zen Center] had become a kind of showcase or pilot project of the emerging American Buddhism," writes Rick Fields (1981, 268).

As of 2007, there were between 45 and 65 permanent residents of the San Francisco Zen Center. They live in single and shared rooms in the City Center building or in nearby apartments. Residents participate in daily meditation sessions and attend classes. The group also has Green Gulch Farm, started in 1972, which grows organic vegetables for the San Francisco Zen Center.

Meanwhile in Los Angeles, Zen students bought a home in 1967 that could house several students. More and more people wanted to live there, and the **Zen Center of Los Angeles** considered buying rural land and setting up a retreat like the Tassajara Center. However, the spiritual leader of the group persuaded them to expand at their city location. They began buying nearby houses and, by the early 1980s, occupied an entire city block, with about 155 people in residence (including 30 children).

As of 2007, the 27 residents of the Zen Center of Los Angeles live in two apartment buildings, which they call Normandie Mountain, after Normandie Avenue, the road that leads to it. According to the Zen Center of Los Angeles Web site, "Geographically, Normandie Mountain is a small hill in metropolitan Los Angeles; spiritually, it is a great mountain. Zen training—awakened living—is the heart of Normandie Mountain" (http://www.zcla.org/AboutUs/Governance/structure.php).

Some residents work for the Zen Center, while others have outside jobs and pay a monthly fee for room and board. The communal food is vegetarian, but residents can eat what they like on their own. Residents are encouraged to have a life of voluntary simplicity, but there are no hard and fast rules. There are no restrictions on sexual behavior. The Zen Center of Los Angeles has run a number of community businesses, including a retail store; nonprofit medical clinic; plumbing, landscaping, and carpentry businesses; and a publishing company (Popenoe and Popenoe 1984, 24–28; Fields 1981, 363).

In the early 1980s, the **Zen Mountain Monastery** was established in the Catskill Mountains of New York. It offers Zen workshops and retreats, including a year-long retreat during which residents engage in meditation, studying Buddhist texts and principles, and performing "work practice" at the center. The Zen Mountain Monastery features a four-story main house with communal kitchen and dining facilities, dormitories, and private rooms. Nearby are cabins and houses for residents (Prebish 1999, 97).

The **Zen Center of New York City,** which is associated with the Zen Mountain Monastery, also has a residential component that is considered "monastic training" for lay people. Residents begin and end their days with meditation and participate in retreats whenever possible. Some residents are on the staff of the Zen Center and others leave the temple to go to work or school. The center has an artist-in-residence program in which residents work on their art or creative writing in addition to participating in Zen training. Residents pay a fee to cover their housing and retreats, and must provide their own food.

While Japanese Zen Buddhism was one of the first and most popular forms of Buddhism in the United States, more and more Americans have become attracted to Tibetan Buddhism, which was first introduced to Americans in the late 1950s, after the Chinese army invaded Tibet in 1959. Until then, Tibetan Buddhism had been largely hidden from the rest of the world. After the invasion, Tibetan Buddhists (including many Buddhist monks—about 20 percent of the Tibetan population was made up of monks) were forced into exile and some of them came to the United States.

The most well-known Tibetan Buddhist teacher in the United States was Chogyam Trungpa Rinpoche. In 1970, he formed the first community of what would become a worldwide organization called Vajradhatu. The organization is now called **Shamb-**

hala and has several residential centers, all of which offer meditation, yoga training, and retreats for the general public. The Karme Choling Residential Center is located on 600 acres in Vermont and features seven meditation halls, a Zen archery range, organic garden, and communal dining facilities. The Shambhala Mountain Center is located on 600 acres in northern Colorado and features a great stupa, a 108-foot pyramidal tower structure with an assembly hall on the ground floor and a large statue of the Buddha. Stupas are traditional to Buddhist architecture. According to the Shambhala Mountain Center Web site, "A stupa is intended to stop you in your tracks. It is an architectural representation of the entire Buddhist path" (http://www.shambhalamountain.org/stupa_history.html).

Potential residents of these centers must fill out an employment application form—they are hired as employees—and must be committed to Buddhist practices while living and working at the center.

Trungpa Rinpoche was also the founder, in 1974, of the Naropa Institute, a university in Colorado based on Buddhist principles.

See also: Hippies

References

Fields, Rick. *How the Swans Came to the Lake: A Narrative History of Buddhism in America.* Boulder, CO: Shambhala, 1981.

Morgan, Diane. *The Buddhist Experience in America.* Westport, CT: Greenwood Press, 2004.

Murphy, Sean. *One Bird, One Stone: 108 American Zen Stories.* New York: Renaissance Books, 2002.

Popenoe, Oliver, and Cris Popenoe. *Seeds of Tomorrow: New Age Communities That Work.* San Francisco: Harper and Row, 1984.

Prebish, Charles. *Luminous Passage: The Practice and Study of Buddhism in America.* Berkeley: University of California Press, 1999.

Seager, Richard Hughes. *Buddhism in America.* New York: Columbia University Press, 1999.

WEB SITES

San Francisco Zen Center: www.sfzc.org/ (accessed July 2007).

Shambhala Practice and Retreat Centers: www.shambhala.org/centers/practice-retreat.php (accessed July 2007).

Zen Center of Los Angeles: www.zcla.org/ (accessed July 2007).

Zen Mountain Monastery: www.mro.org/zmm/index.php (accessed July 2007).

Burned-Over District

The "Burned-Over District" refers to western New York during the first part of the 19th century, when numerous religious revivals were taking place. Although religious revivalism was popular across the country at this time, according to Whitney Cross, "this section [of New York] was the storm center, and religious forces were the driving propellants of social movements important for the whole country in that generation" (1950, vii). A number of utopian communities grew out of this atmosphere.

Over 1,300 revivals occurred in New York between 1825 and 1835 (Barkun 1986, 23). One reason for all this religious interest is that a number of religious scholars had concluded, after analyzing the Book of Daniel in the New Testament, that the "millennium" would begin in the mid-1800s. The "millennium" referred to the thousand years of peace and plenty as promised in the New Testament Book of Revelation (20:1–6). Christ was expected to return to Earth either before or after this thousand-year-long period.

Joseph Smith, the founder of the Mormon religion, and his family were caught up with these revivals. Smith developed the Mormon religion because he wanted to find the truth among all the religious paths he encountered.

John Humphrey Noyes, the founder of the Oneida community, found converts and a relatively welcoming community in the Burned-Over District.

Thomas Lake Harris, founder of the Brotherhood of the New Life, was born and raised in the Burned-Over District and started his community there.

Another religious path that resulted in a few utopian communities was the Millerite movement, which occurred at the height of the religious fervor of the Burned-Over District. William Miller was a farmer and Baptist lay minister. According to his interpretation of the Book of Daniel, Miller concluded that Christ would return to Earth in 1843. He began to spread his message to New England churches, where he found willing converts to his views. One of his converts, Joshua Himes, helped promote Miller's ideas across the country by raising money, printing pamphlets and periodicals, and establishing libraries. Miller did not intend to form his own religion. Instead, he thought that the message of Christ's coming would serve to bring together Christians from the different sects. Miller attracted an estimated 50,000 supporters (Vance 1999, 17).

When 1843 passed without any sign of Christ's second coming, Miller revised his prediction to the spring of 1844 and when that passed uneventfully, to October 22, 1844. In preparation for this day, Millerites paid off debts, closed their businesses, and did not bother to harvest their crops. When the day passed without Christ's appearance, the Millerites were deeply disappointed. The Millerite movement fragmented into several factions, one of which became the Seventh-Day Adventist Church (which continues to the present day and is not communal). Many years later, another utopian communal group formed as an offshoot of the Seventh-Day Adventist Church: the Davidian and Branch Davidian movements.

Years after their great disappointment of 1844, Millerites formed a few utopian communities. The most important was Adonai Shomo in Worcester County, Massachusetts, which started with 30 members in 1861 and lasted until 1896. Members believed in Saturday Sabbath, the equality of men and women, and physical immortality.

People in the Burned-Over District were not just enthusiastic about religion—they were also enthusiastic about new ideas such as the socialist communities of the Fourierist movement, land reform, phrenology (reading personality through the shape of the head), and mesmerism (hypnotism).

See also: Brook Farm and Fourierist Phalanxes; Brotherhood of the New Life; Davidian and Branch Davidian Movements; Millennialism; Oneida Community; Orderville and Mormon Communalism

References

"Adonai Shomo," in *Encyclopedia of Cults, Sects and New Religions*, edited by James R. Lewis. Amherst, NY: Prometheus Books, 1998, 28.

Barkun, Michael. *Crucible of the Millennium: The Burned-Over District of New York in the 1840s.* Syracuse, NY: Syracuse University Press, 1986.

Cross, Whitney R. *The Burned-Over District: The Social and Intellectual History of Enthusiastic Religion in Western New York, 1800–1850.* Ithaca, NY: Cornell University Press, 1950.

Vance, Laura L. *Seventh-Day Adventism in Crisis.* Urbana: University of Illinois Press, 1999.

Camphill Movement

At a Glance

Dates of existence in United States: 1959 to present (since 1939 worldwide)

Locations: California, Minnesota, New York, Pennsylvania, and worldwide

Peak membership: 10 communities in North America with a total of about 800 members; an estimated 100 communities worldwide

Religious or other belief: Anthroposophism

History

Camphill communities are some of the most unique communities in the world. Nondisabled adults and families (known as coworkers) live in community with children and adults who have disabilities (known as villagers). The communities run schools for children and young adults who have special needs and provide work opportunities for the adults.

The first Camphill community was formed in Aberdeen, Scotland, in 1939 by an Austrian physician, Karl Koenig, who had fled his home country after the Nazi invasion. Koenig was inspired by Rudolf Steiner's philosophy of "Anthroposophy" (explained below).

Before fleeing to Scotland, Koenig worked as a physician for a therapeutic institute in Switzerland and cofounded a school for people with disabilities in Silesia (a region in eastern-central Europe, now mostly part of Poland). In Vienna, Austria, Koenig led an Anthroposophy study group for medical students, artists, and educators.

When Koenig and others fled to Scotland, they wanted to establish a spiritual community based on the ideals of freedom and equality. They sought a common task for everyone in the community to work on. Because of Koenig's previous experience working among people with intellectual and physical disabilities, they decided to devote their energies to caring for children who have special needs. As these children grew up, Camphill expanded into providing communities for adults with developmental disabilities (Sherwood 2001, 7).

The first Camphill community in the United States was started in 1959 by Carlo Pietzner. Since then, six other communities have formed in the United States. As of 2008, an eighth U.S. community, in Colorado, was in the planning stages.

Beliefs and Practices

Camphill communities are based on Anthroposophy, a spiritual movement developed by the European scientist Rudolf Steiner in the early 1900s. Steiner believed that all humans have the ability to access spiritual wisdom. Through his lectures and publications, he helped people in many different disciplines to apply Anthroposophical principles. In 1924, shortly before he died, he developed a system called "curative education" to address the needs of people with disabilities.

Curative education is the idea that education itself can promote healing. Included in this kind of education are speech and physical therapy, as well as art, music, handcrafts, and a movement art invented by Steiner called "eurhythmy." "In its widest aspects, curative education is not only science, not only practical art, but a *human attitude*," wrote Koenig (quoted in Hansmann 1992, 23). This attitude is one of respect for all community members, regardless of their intellectual and physical abilities. "Camphill coworkers assume, in their education and therapies, that people with disabilities can learn about and relate to human-wide experiences and feelings, and have something important to teach people who do not have disabilities" (Sherwood 2001, 21).

The volunteer communities strive to integrate people with developmental disabilities into the community life and to create natural rhythms for life. Koenig explained: "The rhythms of learning and relaxing, of work and play, of weekday and Sunday, of term time and holidays are essential to this. In many of our pupils the natural rhythms of breathing, sleeping and waking, eating and digesting, remembering and forgetting, are disturbed and can be newly established through the rhythms of life in home and classroom" (quoted in Hansmann 1992, 20).

The Anthroposophist belief in the spirituality of all humans extends also to those with mental disabilities. Camphill communities strive "to recognize and uphold that beyond the limitations of physical or mental disability there is in each individual an intact, inviolable, spiritual integrity" (Pietzner 1986, 11).

Social life and celebrations are an important part of Camphill communities. The Camphill movement frequently quotes this saying by Steiner: "The healthy social life is found when in the mirror of each human soul the whole community finds its reflection and when in the community the strength of each one is living" (quoted in Sherwood 2001, 12). Living in community is thus a critical part of healing. Villagers and coworkers eat meals together and work together. They play music, sing, dance, and put on plays together. An observer remarked that "Camphill is the first place I ever heard classical music along with people with disabilities and played by people with disabilities" (quoted in Sherwood 2001, 11).

Although the communities are founded on the basis of Anthroposophy, members are not required to believe in this philosophy or to practice it. Other religions and spiritual traditions are welcome. For example, at Camphill Minnesota, the grace said before meals might be an Anthroposophical grace, or one from another tradition, depending on the person saying the grace. Sunday worship rotates between a once-a-month Anthroposophical gathering, a once-a-month service of another faith, and twice-monthly van trips to nearby churches (McKanan 2004).

Living in harmony with nature is important to Camphill members. Food is grown using organic and biodynamic methods.

The outside world might see the Camphill movement mostly as a volunteer-based provider of care for those with mental disabilities, but the movement sees itself mainly as "an intentional community" of people who choose to live and work together. "Camphill's perception of its purposes and realities is of an intentional community that shares life with people with special needs. While Camphill places have a primary responsibility to care for the people with special needs, that is not the only reason that Camphill places were created" (Sherwood 2001, 7).

Daily Life

Camphill communities serve people with mental disabilities, including mild to severe mental retardation, autism, and emotional disturbances. Camphill Beaver Run in Pennsylvania runs a school for students aged 5 through 18. Camphill Soltane in Pennsylvania and Triform Camphill in New York offer a five-year program for students aged 18–23. And several communities welcome adults to live and take part in community work as well as they are able to.

Coworkers do not receive any pay for their services. They are considered members of the community and receive room, board, health insurance, and a small monthly stipend. They are not required to turn over their personal wealth to the community.

Every coworker gets time off periodically. For example, at Camphill Soltane in Pennsylvania, coworkers have one free day per week, several free weekends per year, and several longer vacation times per year.

Coworkers and villagers live together in houses, and they work together to keep the community running. For example, Camphill Village in New York has 240 people living on 600 acres of land. A household generally consists of four to six villagers, two coworkers (along with any children they may have), and a few short-term volunteers (often high school or college students).

Adult Camphill villagers are taught and encouraged to perform work that benefits the community. Such work can include making candles, woodworking, and weaving. Villagers also work in the vegetable garden or on the farm, or help out with cooking meals or cleaning the homes. Some work outside the community at local businesses.

At the children's school at Camphill Beaver Run, two houseparents run each house. Each student shares rooms with other compatible students. Students are cared for by coworkers who teach them skills such as dressing, bathing, and communicating with others in their house. Teachers, therapists, and other helpers also live in the houses. Children are given chores according to ability, such as collecting napkins or sweeping the floor.

A typical day for a child with developmental disabilities might begin by waking up at about 7:00 a.m. to music played throughout the house. After dressing, the student gathers with other community members in the dining room. Before breakfast, members sing a song or recite a verse. Coworkers arrange for villagers to help each other during breakfast. For example, an older, more able-bodied student might help a younger or less able-bodied student. After breakfast, members clear the table, wash dishes, and sweep the floor. Students then go to their classrooms by about 9:00 a.m. School is over by 12:30 p.m., lunch is eaten, and some people rest after lunch. Others might do homework, play outside, do chores, or practice music. Later in the afternoon, students might have woodworking or other craft sessions and rehearsals for a play. After dinner, members sing a song or recite a verse. Younger children go to bed, and older children play until bedtime at 9:00 p.m. (Hansmann 1992, 25–27).

The school curriculum is based on the program of study developed by Steiner for the Waldorf schools, emphasizing not just intellectual development but also social, artistic, and practical skills. Children are taught reading, writing, arithmetic, history, geography, mythology, and sciences, as well as music, crafts, and drama (Pietzner 1986, 14).

How They Make Their Living

The main source of income at Camphill villages is the tuition paid for the care and education of children and adults with disabilities. Government grants cover much of the cost. Families are asked to contribute as much as they can. Camphill communities also solicit funds from private foundations and donors.

In addition, villages raise their own crops, vegetables, and animals, and often sell their crafts in community-run stores that are open to the public. Camphill Village Kimberton Hills in Pennsylvania runs a café open to the public.

Leadership and Decision Making

Each Camphill community is run by a board of directors. Potential board members are selected by a nominating committee and then voted in by the other board members. One-third of the board members are generally long-term Camphill coworkers; one-third are "vested" members (such as parents of Camphill students); and one-third are from outside of Camphill. The communities are also run by a governing board composed of long-term coworkers. This governing board works with the board of directors to make decisions and hire the managers of the community (Lyles 2006).

One challenge at Camphill is how to involve those with disabilities in running the communities. Camphill Village Copake (which serves adults with disabilities) asks a group of lawyers to visit once a year, meet individually with each villager, find out how life is going, and ask about any changes the villager desires. At Triform Camphill (which serves young adults), each villager participates in a "birthday meeting" during which he or she talks with family, friends, and coworkers about how the year has been and what he or she would like to do during the coming year (Sherwood 2001, 40).

How New Members Are Recruited or Chosen

Nondisabled members of Camphill communities are called volunteers or coworkers. Young people (high school and college students) are welcome to apply for short-term volunteer positions. People of all ages can also apply to fill longer-term positions.

Community members who have disabilities are chosen as space is available. At the two Camphill communities for young adults, prospective members must visit for two to four weeks. The community tries to make sure that new members are eager to learn, that they can offer something to the community in terms of sociability or other qualities, and that the community can meet their physical, mental, and emotional needs.

Children and Youth

Nondisabled children of coworkers attend school outside of the community, preferably the local Waldorf school, if one is available. (Waldorf schools are also based on Anthroposophist philosophy.) Coworkers are in charge of their own children and are provided extra money for their care.

Relationship with the Outside World

Camphill communities interact with the outside world in several ways. Parents of students and villagers generally do not live in the community but are frequent visitors. In addition, the communities accept short-term volunteers from around the world. The communities also sell craft products to the outside world. Some adult Camphill villagers work in local businesses outside the community. In addition, members take advantage of local amenities such as parks, swimming pools, hiking trails, and public transportation.

Influence on the Outside World

The Camphill movement serves an extremely small percentage of people with learning disabilities, mental retardation, autism, and other developmental disabilities. However, the movement has taken some action to promote better care for the mentally disabled in the outside world. A Camphill student's mother, Elizabeth Boggs, worked for 40 years to educate lawmakers about the needs of persons with these disabilities. She helped pass legislation benefiting people with special needs, and founded supportive organizations, including the Camphill Association of North America. In 1976, she spearheaded a symposium sponsored by Camphill to discuss ways in which Camphill could help the outside community with the care for people with developmental disabilities, and how the outside community could help Camphill. A second symposium was held in 2001 (Sherwood 2001, 10).

Some people in the outside world urge the Camphill movement to reach out much more. For example, K. Charles Lakin, director of the Rehabilitation Research and Training Center on Community Living at the University of Minnesota, pointed out that "outside the community not many people know what goes on inside Camphill. . . . I think in some ways it is important that we come to understand what Camphill is to the larger world of services to people with disabilities" (quoted in Sherwood 2001, 22).

Future of the Camphill Movement

The Camphill movement seems likely to grow. One future challenge for the Camphill communities is the aging of its members. Because coworkers are members and not employees, they do not leave the community as they age and become too old to work. Camphill members have also never paid into the Social Security system. Currently, Camphill communities support their elderly coworkers out of their operating budgets, but this may become more of a challenge as more and more coworkers age (Sherwood 2001, 13).

See also: Ecovillages; Steiner, Rudolf

References

Hansmann, Henning. *Education for Special Needs: Principles and Practice in Camphill Schools.* Edinburgh, U.K.: Floris Books, 1992.

Lyles, Coleman, President of Camphill Association of North America. E-mail reply to author questions. October 3–4, 2006.

McKanan, Dan. "Doing the Work." *Communities,* Fall 2004, no. 124, 50–54.

Pietzner, Cornelius, ed. *Village Life: The Camphill Communities.* Munich, Germany: Neugebauer Press, 1986.

Sherwood, Kay. *Community-Based Care and Care in Communities: A Dialogue about Responding to the Issues Facing People with Developmental Disabilities.* Report of a symposium sponsored by the Camphill Association of North America, April 3–4, 2001. www.camphillfoundation.org/symposium.pdf (accessed October 2006).

WEB SITES

Anthroposophical Society in America: www.anthroposophy.org/ (accessed October 2006).

Camphill Movement in North America: www.camphill.org/ (accessed October 2006).

Capitalism

Capitalism is a system of economics that emphasizes private ownership of property and business and freedom from government regulation. In other words, society's "capital"—land, businesses, natural resources, and so forth—is owned by a minority of people, who use the capital for their own private benefit. This type of economy is also called a "free market" economy. The U.S. economy is generally capitalist in nature.

The other main type of economy, the socialist economy, relies on government ownership and control of business and property, or cooperative control of business or property (meaning workers or customers might own a business).

Capitalism is associated with the movement toward individualism, according to William Ebenstein and Edwin Fogelman, whereas socialism is associated with the movement toward cooperation and communal living (1980, 147).

Throughout history, most communal utopias rejected the idea of capitalism and private ownership within the community, opting to use a socialist system. Instead of property being owned by individuals, it was owned by the entire community. However, these same communities used and benefited from the capitalist system when selling their communally made goods to the outside world. In fact, communities that were not able to find a way to earn money in the outside free market system often did not survive for long.

Capitalist theory was first promoted in a book published in 1776, *The Wealth of Nations,* by British economist Adam Smith. Before this time, from the 1400s to the 1700s, governments had imposed tariffs (taxes) on imported goods and had given subsidies (financial help) to farms and industries within the country. Countries thought this was the best way to increase their wealth. In the mid-1700s, Smith and others argued that countries could make more money by allowing free trade without tariffs or subsidies.

Smith argued that individuals and businesses should be allowed to act free of government interference. Individuals would choose to buy goods based on preference and price. Businesses would compete with each other to produce those goods that the consumers wanted at the best price. Furthermore, workers would choose their work based on pay and preference, and businesses would compete to attract the best workers. This, Smith said, would produce an economy of "perfect competition" that would encourage efficiency and low prices and in which everyone's needs would automatically be met.

In response to Smith's ideas, the British government and other countries ended their tariffs and subsidies. However, with the coming of the Industrial Revolution in the late 1800s, people began to recognize the shortcomings of capitalism. Often, large businesses had so much power that they were able to get away with paying very little to workers. During the Industrial Revolution, many people—including small children—worked very long hours for low pay in the new factories. Other problems with capitalism include the fact that, left to themselves, businesses sometimes polluted the environment in their quest for efficiency and low prices.

As a result, even in capitalist economies, the government generally does regulate such things as the minimum wage, child labor, and air and water pollution. In addition, even in capitalist countries, governments sometimes own and run certain businesses. In the United States, the government runs the postal service, for example.

Sometimes, the goods and services offered by utopian communities were able to compete very well in a capitalist market. For instance, during the Great Depression, the restaurants and hotels operated by the Peace Mission Movement were able to charge lower rates and offer better food and services than other establishments, because the Peace Mission community members worked without pay. The Harmony Society, one of the wealthiest utopian communities in the United States, discovered oil on its land and grew rich from selling this oil on the free market. The Zoar Society operated canal boats along the Ohio and Erie Canal.

At other times, the free market economy caused utopian communities to lose money when demand for their goods or services fell. During the Industrial Revolution, many goods that were previously made by hand could be made more quickly with the use of machines. Communities such as the Shakers, which had relied on selling their handmade goods, suffered financially because there was less demand for handmade items.

Some communities have had to make hard choices between holding onto their values and competing in the free market. The Amish, for example, do not allow electricity, computers, or many modern conveniences. They have chosen to keep their farms and businesses small and often sell and trade mostly within their own community. Catholic Worker communities have kept more or less separate from the free market system by relying primarily on donations to support their work.

See also: Industrial Revolution; Socialism

References

Ebenstein, William, and Edwin Fogelman. *Today's Isms: Communism, Fascism, Capitalism, Socialism.* Englewood Cliffs, NJ: Prentice-Hall, 1980.

Lekachman, Robert, and Borin Van Loon. *Capitalism for Beginners.* New York: Pantheon Books, 1981.

Catholic Worker Movement

At a Glance

Dates of existence in United States: 1933 to present
Locations: 37 U.S. states and worldwide
Peak membership: 185 communities with varying numbers of members;
 the movement does not keep statistics
Religious or other belief: Catholicism, socialism, anarchism

History

The Catholic Worker Movement is one of the few religious communal movements that also incorporates the socialist belief of helping the poor and needy. While many religious communal utopias cut themselves off from the outside world, the Catholic Worker communities exist for the purpose of serving the needy in the outside world.

Catholic Worker communities are cooperative households that provide food, shelter, clothing, and assistance to those in need. Although each household tends to be small, the movement as a whole is widespread: as of 2008, there were over 185 Catholic Worker households in the United States and throughout the world (www.catholicworker.org).

The movement was founded by journalist Dorothy Day. She rejected religion during her college years because she felt religious people were often hypocritical in their complacency with life. "I did not want just the few, the missionary-minded people like the Salvation Army to be kind to the poor. . . . I wanted everyone to be kind. I wanted every home to be open to the lame, the halt and the blind," she wrote of her feelings as a young adult (Day 1952, 39).

Day was disturbed by the poverty and hardship she saw around her and was drawn to socialist ideas. She joined the Socialist Party as a university student and later worked at socialist newspapers. She was also interested in anarchism.

She learned firsthand of the suffering of the downtrodden when she was jailed twice: once for picketing outside the White House with a group of women suffragists, and another time for being in a house run by a socialist group, the Industrial Workers of the World. In jail, she met prostitutes and sympathized with their plight. She also trained as a nurse for a year, and although she felt drawn to the work of serving the ill, she was more attracted to writing.

As a young adult, Day became familiar with Catholicism through a number of Catholic friends. She entered into a common-law marriage with a man who was an atheist, yet at this time she began praying more and more. She was torn between her socialist views—Socialist Party leader Karl Marx had written that "religion is the opiate of the masses"—and the happiness she felt while praying. At age 30, she gave birth to a baby girl, and her joy was such that she felt "the final object of this love and gratitude was God. No human creature could receive or contain so vast a flood of love and joy as I often felt after the birth of my child" (Day 1952, 139).

She had the child baptized in the Catholic Church and became a Catholic herself, although she knew this would mean the end of her relationship with the child's father.

In 1932, when she was 35, Day met Peter Maurin, a Catholic who often preached on street corners. She was living in New York City at the time. Maurin was interested in combining Catholicism with social change. Together they started a newspaper, the *Catholic Worker*. The first issue was launched on May 1, 1933. The newspaper covered unemployment, strikes, labor unions, racism, anti-Semitism, and other current social issues.

The *Catholic Worker* sold on the street for a penny a copy. By the end of the year, the paper had reached a circulation of 100,000 copies; it grew to its largest circulation—190,000—in 1938. Catholic parishes all over the country and the world bought hundreds of copies for distribution, and volunteers sold it on the streets.

Maurin also promoted the idea of "houses of hospitality" that would provide help for those in need. Soon after the first newspaper was published, Maurin began bringing homeless people to Day's apartment for food. Eventually, Day and the volunteer editorial staff began offering beds to the needy as well. By 1936, the group had grown to 150 people housed in a set of apartments. By 1938, the Catholic Worker soup kitchen fed 1,200 people morning and evening.

As the newspaper reported on its House of Hospitality in New York City, readers asked how they could start one of their own. The editors sent out lists of readers in different locations so they could connect with each other. Within three years, there were 32 Houses of Hospitality around the country.

After the United States entered World War II in 1941, many people refused to buy the *Catholic Worker* because they disagreed with Day's pacifist objections to the war. Even other pacifists felt that the United States was justified in entering this war in order to save the Jews. But Day felt that war is never justified and that the country could have done more good by allowing more Jews refuge before the war began (Zwick and Zwick 2005, 260).

Until her death in 1980, Day served as editor of the *Catholic Worker* and as a spiritual leader of the movement. However, she did not see herself as being in charge of the movement.

As of 2008, the price of the *Catholic Worker* remained a penny a copy, and it had a circulation of about 80,000, according to the Catholic Worker Web site (http://www.catholicworker.org/).

Beliefs and Practices

A 2002 article in the *Catholic Worker* stated that "the aim of the Catholic Worker Movement is to live in accordance with the justice and charity of Jesus Christ" ("Aims and Means" 2002). To this end, the movement emphasizes taking personal responsibility for social conditions; supporting a decentralized society based on land trusts, family farms, worker cooperatives, and so forth; advocating nonviolence; serving the poor and needy; performing manual labor; and promoting voluntary poverty.

One of the original ideals behind the Catholic Worker Movement was the idea that the poor are "ambassadors of God," as Peter Maurin put it (Piehl 1982, 103). The poor and needy, by allowing others to serve them, are in fact aiding the spiritual development of their helpers. For this reason, Catholic Worker houses attempt to treat all of their "guests"—as they call the needy who approach them for help—with dignity and respect. Theoretically, no one in need should be turned away.

Day made a distinction between voluntary poverty and involuntary poverty: "The freely chosen poverty is, for Dorothy, a response to the Gospel message that calls for a non-attachment to material goods as well as a shared spiritual life. Forced destitution, on the other hand, represents the evils of our present society that does not care for others, and reduces people to economic, social and spiritual obscurity" (Ellis 2000, 52).

Day's interest in anarchism—the idea that government is unnecessary—also helped shape the belief that there should be no leadership and no set rules in the movement.

Although each home is different, Catholic Worker homes generally include time for organized prayer.

Daily Life

Catholic Worker homes began during the Great Depression. Houses were often very crowded and lacking in basics, such as working toilets and showers. Donated food was sometimes rotten. A member of a house in Chicago recalls a severe winter in 1937 and 1938: "The old men slept on [cots]; the young ones found places on the floor, under beds and tables, and even on the wide display counter at the storefront window. . . . After the place was chock full . . . it was heartbreaking to tell another hundred standing outside, shivering and pleading, that there was no more room. . . . Inside, the house was heavy with the stench of unwashed bodies and filthy clothes" (quoted in Piehl 1982, 151).

Catholic Worker houses have tended to be shabby and drab, with used furniture and minimal housekeeping. A worker during the 1970s describes his living conditions in St. Joseph's House in Manhattan, where Dorothy Day lived: "The fifth floor is gloomy with little light, brown-gray walls, sagging beds, and lockers for clothes instead of dressers. The bathroom is dirty and the fear of bedbugs and lice is ever present" (quoted in Ellis 2000, 36).

As the wealth of the country has increased, so have donations to the Catholic Worker homes. Typically, 21st-century living conditions are considerably better. For example, a community in Wisconsin, Anathoth Community Farm, features a two-acre organic garden, with homes powered by the sun and wood.

The main emphasis is on providing food and other help to the needy. There are no rules about how much members must work or what work they must do. The Catholic Worker Movement feels that rules are associated with bureaucracy and inflexibility. "With rules things might run a little more smoothly *on the surface*," explained an article in the *Catholic Worker* in 1935. "But in the Catholic Worker community more people do get housed and fed because there is no red tape and so-called efficiency" (quoted in Piehl 1982, 101).

However, after years of struggle, many Catholic Worker houses did institute rules against liquor, drugs, gambling, and violence. They also served meals only at regularly scheduled times, and locked their doors at night.

A highlight of life at a Catholic Worker house was a visit from Dorothy Day, who traveled by bus around the country. She was often able to solve problems and revive morale.

How They Make Their Living

The movement depends mostly on donations to cover rent, food, and the cost of publishing its newspaper. Some Catholic Worker houses run small businesses. In other Catholic Worker houses, the members hold part-time jobs to bring in income.

The Catholic Worker homes believe in voluntary poverty, which is defined as meeting the basic needs of food, clothing, and shelter, without any luxuries. If a Catholic Worker house has extra income, it gives it away.

Leadership and Decision Making

Day and Maurin liked to say that the Catholic Worker Movement was an "organism," and not an "organization," as a way to describe how the movement grew in response to need instead of being planned out. There are no leaders in a Catholic Worker house. "Each Catholic Worker House of Hospitality constituted itself as a free anarchist commune held together only by shared commitment, religion, friendship, experience, and the spiritual leadership of Day and Maurin" (Piehl 1982, 97–98).

The Catholic Worker Web site explains further: "It is unlikely that any religious community was ever less structured than the Catholic Worker. Each community is autonomous. There is no board of directors, no sponsor, no system of governance, no endowment, no pay checks, no pension plans. Since Dorothy Day's death [in 1980], there has been no central leader" (www.catholicworker.org/).

When a House of Hospitality started, Dorothy Day would name a leader for the house, but only if the members requested this.

How New Members Are Recruited or Chosen

In keeping with the idea of the movement as an organism that grows spontaneously, there is no set process for becoming a member of a Catholic Worker house or for founding such a house. "Each individual who came to a House of Hospitality was understood to be acting on his own full responsibility, and to be engaged in discovering for himself the full implications of the Christian Gospel" (Piehl 1982, 97).

Often, people who first come to a Catholic Worker house for food or shelter will end up staying and becoming a working member of the house and serving others in need.

The Catholic Worker Movement Web site explains that anyone can start a House of Hospitality. You do not even need to be Catholic to live at or start a Catholic Worker house. A house in Atlanta, the Open Door Community, is Protestant. Haley House in Boston describes its members as being from "rich and diverse spiritual traditions" (www.catholicworker.org/).

Day did recommend that, before starting a House of Hospitality, prospective members should meet to study and reflect on Catholic social thought.

Children and Youth

At first, families with children were discouraged from living in a Catholic Worker home. Nowadays, more families do live in Catholic Worker homes. Each family is in charge of its own children.

Relationship with the Outside World

In addition to serving the poor, members of a Catholic Worker house are often active in labor unions, human rights issues, cooperatives, and the development of a nonviolent culture.

Influence on the Outside World

While the Catholic Worker Movement supports social change such as labor unions and pacifism, members consider themselves a small part of a larger American movement supporting these issues.

However, the Catholic Worker Movement has been an important influence on the Catholic Church itself. It showed Catholics that they could be socially active within the context of their religion.

The movement also introduced the idea of pacifism into American Catholicism. Two members of a Houston Catholic Worker house remark that "when the United States Catholic Bishops affirmed pacifism and conscientious objection as an expression of Catholic faith in their 1983 pastoral . . . they credited Dorothy Day for her witness, acknowledging the legitimate use of nonviolent means for the defense of one's country" (quoted in Zwick 2005, 302).

The Future of the Catholic Worker Movement

In the past, the Catholic Worker Movement was dominated by single people. Although she was a mother, Day discouraged couples and children from living in Catholic Worker homes. She sent her daughter to boarding school or to stay with friends or relatives.

More and more families with children are now getting involved. A founder of a Catholic Worker home in California comments: "The typical Catholic Worker in the past was single, worked in a soup kitchen, and resisted the war. . . . But now there are Catholic Workers in suburbs and small towns. There are many more families than there were. The Catholic Worker tradition has not been hospitable to families. The struggle of how to be a Catholic Worker and a family is being engaged vigorously on a number of fronts" (Patterson 2003).

Parents are often torn between their commitment to living in a Catholic Worker home, which can include potentially dangerous transients, and their commitment to provide a safe environment for their children. In addition, they can be torn between spending money on extras for their children or giving that money to the needy. On the positive side, parents also feel that living at a Catholic Worker home can be an enriching experience for their children.

See also: Anarchism; Great Depression; Socialism

References

"Aims and Means of the Catholic Worker." *Catholic Worker*, May 2002, www.catholicworker.org/imsandmeanstext.cfm?Number=5 (accessed April 9, 2008).

Day, Dorothy. *The Long Loneliness: An Autobiography*. San Francisco: Harper and Row, 1952.

Ellis, Marc. *A Year at the Catholic Worker*. Waco, TX: Baylor University Press, 2000 (first published 1978).

Miller, William D. *Dorothy Day: A Biography*. San Francisco: Harper and Row, 1982.

Patterson, Margot. "Finding Family at the Catholic Worker." *National Catholic Reporter*, March 7, 2003, ncronline.org/NCR_Online/archives/030703/030703a.htm (accessed April 9, 2008).

Piehl, Mel. *Breaking Bread: The Catholic Worker and the Origin of Catholic Radicalism in America*. Philadelphia, PA: Temple University Press, 1982.

Zwick, Mark, and Louise Zwick. *The Catholic Worker Movement: Intellectual and Spiritual Origins*. Mahwah, NJ: Paulist Press, 2005.

WEB SITES

Anathoth Community Farm: anathothcommunityfarm.org/ (accessed September 2006).

Catholic Worker Movement: www.catholicworker.org/ (accessed September 2006).

Haley House: www.haleyhouse.org/about.htm (accessed September 2006).

Open Door Community: www.opendoorcommunity.org/ (accessed September 2006).

Children and Child Rearing

Utopian communities have a variety of ways of raising children. However, in general, children are often seen as the responsibility of the entire community, not just of their parents.

Historically, in some communities, children lived in a separate building from their parents and were cared for by unrelated adults. This was to allow parents the freedom to work within the community, to socialize the children in community values, and to create in the children a loyalty to the community rather than a loyalty to the biological family. Communal child rearing was practiced in the following communities: Brotherhood of the New Life, Icarian movement, the International Society for Krishna Consciousness (for a time), Moravians, New Harmony, Oneida, Point Loma, Shakers, Twin Oaks (for a time), and Zoar Society (for a time).

In other communities, children lived with their parents but participated in the community through communal child care and schools. This has been the case in the following communities: Amana, Amish, Bishop Hill, Bohemia Manor, Bruderhof, Davidian and Branch Davidian Movements, Ferrer Colony, Harmony, Home Colony, House of David Movement, Hutterites, Jesus People USA, Kaweah, Keil Communities, Koreshan Unity, Llano del Rio and New Llano, Love Family (for a time), Orderville, and Ruskin.

In some communities, children lived with their parents and attended a school of the parents' choice. However, the children might participate in communal activities by eating and socializing together. The following communities follow this pattern: Ananda, Camphill, Cohousing, Fairhope, The Family/Children of God, The Farm, Koinonia, Love Family, Peace Mission Movement, and Renaissance Community.

According to Rosabeth Moss Kanter, communal child rearing can benefit children in that they have many adult role models, many child peers, and the security of the entire community. These children tend to become independent and self-sufficient at a young age. One drawback is that children raised communally may miss a deep, intimate relationship with their own parents (1973, 351–352).

The most extreme example of communal child rearing is probably the Oneida community, where the children did not just live separately from their parents; they were discouraged from seeing their biological parents and from forming emotional bonds with them. Oneida's leader, John Humphrey Noyes, believed that everyone in the community should have an equal love for all other community members and should not form special emotional bonds with a few people. Therefore, children were only permitted to visit their parents for a few hours once a week. If a child or a mother seemed especially attached (for example, if a child cried upon leaving the mother), this privilege could be revoked.

Children and their parents sometimes suffered under this system. Pierrepont Noyes, a son of John Humphrey Noyes, who was raised in Oneida, recalls happy memories of the Children's House but also remembers that "I often wept bitterly when the time came to return to the Children's House" after a weekly visit with his mother. Once, for a punishment, he was forbidden to visit his mother, and he threw a tantrum. His separation from his mother was extended by another week (1973, 370–371).

Twin Oaks, a modern socialist community, also experimented with a communal child care system, in which the children lived in their own building separately from their parents (although parents and children were free to visit with each other at any time). As at Oneida, this system proved difficult for children at times. Eventually the system was abandoned because parents wanted more interaction with and control over their children. Lee Ann Kinkade, the granddaughter of a founder of Twin Oaks, was raised communally with almost no contact with her biological parents for her first five years. "By the time I was five," she said, "all of my original caretakers had left. When someone leaves the community and you're a child, it's like they died. . . . There is a lot of pain associated with that for me" (quoted in Kuhlmann 2005, 105–106).

At the Zoar Society, children between three and fourteen lived separately from and rarely saw their parents. The food and living conditions in the nursery were so poor that one of the leaders of the community refused to send his daughter there, and the system was abandoned.

The International Society for Krishna Consciousness set up a series of boarding schools for children ages five and up. Once at a boarding school, the children rarely saw their parents, who might live hundreds of miles away. Unfortunately, children were physically and mentally abused in these boarding schools, which were closed after a time for lack of funds.

In addition to nontraditional ways of raising children, the end of childhood and the concept of "adulthood" might also be viewed differently within a utopian community than in the outside world. Young people often begin participating in the work of the community as teenagers, but other adult privileges and responsibilities might be delayed until a later age. For example, among the Hutterites and the Amish, young people end their schooling and begin full-time work within the community at the age of 14 or 15. However, they are not allowed to marry until they undergo baptism, generally several years later. Within the Amana community, teens of 14 began working in community, and marriage was not allowed until the ages of 20 to 24.

In the Oneida community, the situation was somewhat reversed. The young people could continue with their education through college. There was no monogamous marriage—instead, all members were considered married to all other members of the opposite gender. Young people thus began participating in the social (sexual) life of the community at puberty—sometimes as young teenagers.

See also: Education; Family; Women, Status of

References

Kanter, Rosabeth Moss, ed. *Communes: Creating and Managing the Collective Life.* New York: Harper and Row, 1973.

Kuhlmann, Hilke. *Living Walden Two: B.F. Skinner's Behaviorist Utopia and Experimental Communities.* Urbana: University of Illinois Press, 2005.

Noyes, Pierrepont. "Growing Up in Oneida," in *Communes: Creating and Managing the Collective Life,* edited by Rosabeth Moss Kanter. New York: Harper and Row, 1973.

Civil Rights Movement

In the United States, the term *civil rights movement* refers to the largely nonviolent campaign for equal rights for African Americans that took place during the 1950s and 1960s and culminated in the passage of the Civil Rights Act of 1964 and the Voting Rights Act of 1965.

African Americans had been fighting for racial equality ever since slavery was outlawed in 1863. The National Association for the Advancement of Colored People (NAACP) began in 1909 to fight for the rights of all people of color. In the 1940s and 1950s, the NAACP brought legal cases against racial discrimination in education and housing. African Americans won a major legal victory in 1954, when the U.S. Supreme Court ruled in *Brown v. Board of Education of Topeka* that segregated educational facilities were "inherently unequal" and thus unconstitutional. While some predominantly white schools integrated, others closed in order to avoid integration.

In late 1955, activists in Montgomery, Alabama, began a one-year boycott of the bus system because African American bus riders were required to sit at the back of the bus. Starting in 1960, black students began sit-ins at lunch counters, restaurants, department stores, libraries, and public beaches that did not admit blacks. Civil rights supporters staged a massive "March on Washington," in 1963, during which Dr. Martin Luther King Jr. gave his famous "I Have a Dream" speech. The following year, President Lyndon Johnson pushed for, and won, passage of the Civil Rights Act, which prohibited discrimination in employment or public accommodations on the basis of race or sex.

However, this law did not guarantee America's black citizens the right to vote. Blacks were often barred from voting due to threats of violence or the requirement to pay a "poll tax" before voting. Dr. King led a massive voting rights drive in Selma, Alabama. In 1965, Congress passed the Voting Rights Act, which prohibited the poll tax and provided for federal supervision of voter registration.

Even before the modern civil rights movement, some utopian communities worked for racial equality by prohibiting slavery or by welcoming black members. For example, one of the first utopian communities on American land, Valley of the Swans, prohibited members from owning slaves. The Shakers also welcomed African American members. Antislavery communities aimed to create self-sufficient communities for blacks. In the first part of the 20th century, the Peace Mission Movement attracted black and white members who worked and lived together in equality.

One major community was especially involved with the civil rights movement: Koinonia Farm/Koinonia Partners. Its location in Georgia, and its goal of fostering equality, friendship, and sharing among blacks and whites, allowed it to serve as host to white and black activists who came to Georgia to work for civil rights.

See also: Antislavery Communities; Civil War; Koinonia Farm/Koinonia Partners; Peace Mission Movement; Shakers; Valley of the Swans

Reference

Levy, Peter. *The Civil Rights Movement.* Westport, CT: Greenwood Press, 1998.

Civil War

The American Civil War was fought from 1861 to 1865 over a variety of issues, including slavery. The Civil War affected a number of utopian communities. It signaled the end of most of the antislavery communities (although it marked the beginning of the Port Royal antislavery community). It helped support the Icarian community, because soldiers bought food and supplies from the community. And it pitted the antislavery beliefs of some communities against their pacifist beliefs. For example, while the Zoar community was pacifist and did not believe in war, a dozen Zoar men chose to fight against slavery.

As of 1860, 15 southern states permitted slavery and 19 Northern states did not. The Northern states did not support slavery, but the southern states considered it an economic necessity for profitability. Most slave owners felt that they would not be able to make enough money if they did not have slave labor to work their plantations.

When Abraham Lincoln was elected president in 1860, the southerners were afraid he would declare slavery to be illegal in the entire country. Southern states began to secede from the rest of the country. They declared themselves a separate country, called the Confederate States of America. The U.S. government under Lincoln said that the Southern states were not allowed to withdraw from the rest of the country. The American Civil War officially began in 1861, when the Southern states took over a military fort in South Carolina and the Northern states attempted to take it back.

In 1863, President Lincoln issued the Emancipation Proclamation, which declared that all slaves in the Confederate states were free. However, the war continued until the Southern states surrendered in 1865. Before the surrender, Lincoln was shot and killed by a southern sympathizer. Slavery ended when the United States ratified the Thirteenth Amendment to the Constitution in December 1865.

See also: Antislavery Communities; Icarian Movement; Zoar Society

Reference

Angle, Paul. *Pictorial History of the Civil War Years*. Garden City, NY: Doubleday, 1967.

Web site
The American Civil War: http://www.civilwar.com/index.php (accessed June 2008).

Cohousing

History

Cohousing is a worldwide movement that aims to bring together the best of communal living and private ownership. It involves communities of privately owned houses and jointly owned common areas where cohousers share common meals, leisure space, and workshop space.

The concept of cohousing was introduced to the United States by American architects Kathryn McCamant and Charles Durrett in their 1988 book, *Cohousing: A Contemporary Approach to Housing Ourselves.*

As young single people, the two architects had studied at the University of Copenhagen in Denmark, where they learned about the Danish concept of *bofoelleskaber* ("living communities" in English), in which private homes are grouped together around a jointly owned common house where some community meals are eaten. The common house often contains children's playrooms, workshops, guest rooms, and a laundry area. Other commonly owned facilities include gardens and outdoor recreation and play spaces.

Bofoelleskaber housing was first conceived in Denmark in 1964 by architect Jan Gudmand-Hoyer. He and his wife were thinking of starting a family, and they did not like any of the available housing options. Neither a single-family home nor an apartment complex offered the mix of privacy and community they sought, so they gathered a group of friends to discuss alternatives. They envisioned a housing complex that would combine the cooperation and social interaction of a country village with a location near the city. They were inspired in part by a book written in 1516— *Utopia* by Thomas More, which describes a fictional island composed of income-sharing cities in which groups of 30 families share common meals.

The group bought land near Copenhagen and planned a development that would look fairly conservative today, with large houses, private backyards enclosed by walls, and an inconspicuous common house. However, when neighbors found out about the plan, they protested, assuming that the group was communist and fearing that the additional children would make the neighborhood too noisy. The group was forced to sell its land, and many of the original families gave up.

Based on this experience, Gudmand-Hoyer wrote an article, "The Missing Link between Utopia and the Dated One-Family Home," which was published in a national newspaper. The article generated over a hundred phone calls and letters from people who wanted to live in a community such as Gudmand-Hoyer described.

Meanwhile, the youth movement had begun in Europe and the United States, and people were more willing to question the status quo. In 1968, Gudmand-Hoyer gathered another group of interested people to try again. Two communities were finished near Copenhagen, one in 1972 and one in 1973; by 1982, there were 22 completed bofoelleskaber communities in Denmark.

Back in the United States in the early 1980s, McCamant and Durrett were a young married couple looking for their ideal place to live. They remembered the bofoelleskaber housing they had encountered in Denmark as students, but they could not get any information on them in English. The couple decided to go Denmark again in order to study and write about the communities. They coined the word *cohousing* to describe this type of community in English.

McCamant and Durrett's book created great interest in the United States. Muir Commons in Davis, California, completed in 1991, was the first cohousing development to be built in the nation. It features 26 homes in three sizes, from 808 to 1,381 square feet. In addition to a large kitchen and dining area, other common facilities include a sitting room with a fireplace, an automotive and wood shop, and a hot tub.

As of 2007, not only were there nearly 90 completed American cohousing communities, but there are also eight architectural and/or development companies listed on the Cohousing Association of the United States Web site that help start, design, and build cohousing developments.

Internationally, there are an estimated 300 cohousing developments, including those in the United States and others in Europe, Australia, and Japan (Bowen, 2006).

Beliefs and Practices

Cohousing was developed to meet the needs of people who want more interaction and cooperation with their neighbors, but do not want to share finances or a common ideology, as is common in other utopian communities.

Cohousing is defined by six main characteristics: a planning process that includes participation by future residents; a neighborhood design that fosters community interaction; common facilities designed for daily use; management of the community by the residents themselves; a nonhierarchical decision-making structure; and no shared community economy.

The impetus for a cohousing development often comes from the residents themselves, who get together, decide where to buy land, and help design their community. Sometimes a housing developer will initiate the process, but even in this case, the future residents must be involved in the planning or it is not considered a true cohousing community.

Cohousing neighborhoods are designed to encourage casual interactions among residents. For example, the private homes are generally clustered together with front doors facing a common pathway or courtyard, and the residents share common parking areas on the edge of the community.

Common facilities are one of the more notable aspects of cohousing. Generally, cohousing communities include a prominent, centrally located common house featuring a large kitchen and dining area, laundry facilities, a children's playroom, and perhaps workshops, an exercise room, a library, a crafts room, and guest rooms. Cohousing communities also often share outdoor recreation spaces, such as swimming pools, tennis courts, gardens, playgrounds, and undeveloped open space.

Cohousing communities are managed by the residents themselves, who also perform necessary maintenance tasks.

In addition, many cohousing developments have incorporated environmentally sensitive design into their development. Communities might include drought-resistant landscaping or wetlands. Housing design might incorporate energy efficiency and solar power. Blueberry Hill, completed in 2001 in Vienna, Virginia, uses geothermal heating and cooling systems.

A few cohousing communities take protection of the environment so seriously that they call themselves "ecovillages." The ecovillage in Ithaca, New York, built in 2004, was one of the first. It not only includes two cohousing developments (with a third in the works), but also organic vegetable and berry farms and a sheep pasture. The community plans to keep 80 percent of its land as green space.

Although the vast majority of cohousing communities do not share any kind of spiritual belief system, a group in California is trying to form a Buddhist cohousing community.

While economic equality is often a goal in utopian communities, cohousing developments struggle with this ideal. Most cohousing homes are just as expensive as, if not more expensive than, other newly built homes in their area, making cohousing difficult for low-income families to afford. Some cohousing developments address this problem by including subsidized houses. Ten percent of the houses in Jamaica Plain Cohousing in Boston, for example, are subsidized by the local government, and the community itself subsidizes additional housing. In order to further reduce wealth differences, Jamaica Plain Cohousing asks that, when people make improvements to their personal homes, they also make a voluntary, anonymous donation to the community (Bowen 2006).

Although cohousing developments incorporate private ownership and privacy, cohousers consider themselves to be part of the "intentional community" movement—their communities are listed on the Fellowship for Intentional Community Web site (www.ic.org), a directory of currently active utopian communities throughout the world.

Cohousers look to other utopian communities for ideas and inspiration. For example, in 1995, Chuck Durrett, one of the founders of the cohousing movement in the United States, worked with the Bruderhof community in New York and came away so impressed with their no-gossip policy that he brought the idea to his own group, Doyle Street Cohousing in California, which instituted a similar policy. Under this system, cohousers agree to settle any disputes in the community by speaking directly to the person with whom they are having trouble. After two such heart-to-heart talks, Durrett noted: "My relationship with those two people changed completely. . . . Our new approach to gossip was a watershed in our community" (Durrett 2006). He later approached the Nevada City, California, cohousing group with the same no-gossip proposal, with similar transformational results.

Daily Life

Cohousing developments in the United States range in size from 7 to 67 households, with most containing between 20 and 40 households.

Cohousing residents own their own homes, as well as a portion of the common areas. In some communities, residents can rent their residences instead of buying them. Each home is self-contained, featuring a full kitchen, living areas, bedrooms, and bathrooms. Cohousing homes are often on the small side compared to other newly built homes in the area, because residents prefer to put more money into common areas and less into their own individual homes.

Members choose how much, if any, interaction they would like to have with their fellow cohousers. Common meals are served one to five times per week. These meals are optional, and those who choose to participate pay a small fee for the meal. Food choices are up to each individual, although most communities frequently serve vegetarian meals or include a vegetarian option.

Residents are expected to contribute some labor toward the maintenance of the community, including cooking community meals and cleaning the common house. Some communities require a set number of hours per week, whereas others are more casual about the communal work requirements.

While almost all cohousing is completely residential, at least one community owns retail space as well: Frog Song in Cotati, California. The city required Frog Song to include retail space as part of its development, and the community decided to maintain ownership of this space, which it rents out to local businesses.

How They Make Their Living

People who live in cohousing developments are responsible for their own finances. They pay dues to the cohousing association to support the common areas.

Leadership and Decision Making

Residents manage their own communities and set up committees to get the work done. For example, Winslow Cohousing in Bainbridge Island, Washington, which was completed in 1992, has created several "clusters" to manage the tasks of the community, including administration, grounds, common facilities, and maintenance. Members also elect a board of trustees every year. Each resident is a member of one of the clusters or of the board of trustees.

Most cohousing communities make their decisions by consensus—by discussing an issue, coming up with a variety of possible solutions, and discussing these until they find one that everyone can live with. They may also have a provision allowing for voting if a decision cannot be reached by consensus.

How New Members Are Recruited or Chosen

Theoretically, anyone who can afford it can buy a house in a cohousing development. In most communities, members are permitted to sell their houses to anyone, although they might be asked to sign a voluntary agreement not to sell to someone who is not interested in participating in the community. Most cohousing developments ask potential members to attend an orientation session and several community meetings before deciding to join.

Children and Youth

Children live with and are cared for by their parents. Children generally attend nearby schools.

At least one cohousing community has started a community school: Heartwood Cohousing in Durango, Colorado. The school started in 2002 and as of 2007 had two classes of mixed ages.

Relationship with the Outside World

Although the outside world in Denmark was initially hostile to the first bofoellesk-aber project, the Danes were soon won over. In the United States, cohousing has attracted very little negative attention.

Influence on the Outside World

Cohousing is the first major communal movement in the United States since the hippie-inspired communities of the 1960s and 1970s. Cohousing could very well change the patterns of development and living in the United States from suburbs of single-family homes surrounded by lawns, to cooperative, densely built communities surrounded by natural areas and recreational facilities. "Cohousing revitalizes the idea of neighborhood in communities where people are feeling isolated," says Dolores Hayden, a professor at Yale University and author of books on residential architecture and sprawl. "We're in an environment where households have gotten smaller and houses larger over the past 50 years. We're a society of more young singles living alone and older people living alone" (quoted in Bowen 2006).

Cohousing could be the "missing link," as Jan Gudmand-Hoyer put it, between communal living and privacy.

The Future of Cohousing

Cohousing is poised to grow. While there were almost 90 completed cohousing developments in 2007, there were also about 100 groups in the formative or building stages.

Cohousing is also growing in a new direction: elder housing. As of the fall of 2006, two elder cohousing communities had been built in the United States and about 25 more were in the planning or building stages (Abraham and Delagrange 2006, 62).

In addition to the other characteristics of cohousing, elder cohousing is designed to meet the needs of an aging population: it might be located near medical facilities, or have an on-site medical provider. Health care treatment rooms might be included in the common house. In addition, the communities aim to foster a setting that is conducive to inner spiritual work as well as social activism and civic participation. Some senior cohousing developments have been built next to multigenerational cohousing, so residents of the two communities can freely interact.

According to Neshama Abraham, who cofounded the Elder Cohousing Network, "baby boomers who began turning 60 in 2006 do not want to retire or grow older in the same kind of aging institutions in which they placed their own parents. . . . Instead, people are drawn to the idea of an old-fashioned, egalitarian neighborhood where neighbors help one another through the minor challenges of everyday life, and support one another through the major ones" (Abraham and Delagrange 2006, 63).

See also: Bruderhof; Ecovillages; Fellowship for Intentional Community; Literary Utopias; More, Thomas

References

Abraham, Neshama, and Katie Delagrange. "Elder Cohousing: An Idea Whose Time Has Come?" *Communities*, fall 2006, no. 132, 60–69.

Bowen, Ted Smalley. "The Closeness of Strangers." *Financial Times* (London), November 11, 2006.

"Completed Cohousing Neighborhoods in the United States," press release, April 2007, www.abrahampaiss.com/resources/2007ListCompletedCommunities.pdf (accessed April 2007.

Durrett, Chuck. "An Open Letter about Gossip." December 2006, http://www.cohousing.org/cm/article/gossip (accessed April 7, 2008).

McCamant, Kathryn, and Charles Durrett. *Cohousing: A Contemporary Approach to Housing Ourselves*. Berkeley, CA: Habitat Press/Ten Speed Press, 1988.

More, Thomas. *Utopia*. Translated by Paul Turner. Middlesex, England: Penguin Books, 1965.

Thompson, Sandy. "A Homeschool with Heart." *Communities*, winter 2004, no. 125, 23–25.

Web sites

Blueberry Hill Cohousing: www.blueberryhill.org/ (accessed May 2007).

Cohousing Association of the United States: www.cohousing.org/ (accessed May 2007).

Ecovillage at Ithaca, NY: www.ecovillage.ithaca.ny.us/ (accessed May 2007).

Elder Cohousing Network: www.eldercohousing.org/ (accessed May 2007).

Frog Song Cohousing: www.cotaticohousing.org/ (accessed May 2007).

Heartwood Cohousing: www.heartwoodcohousing.com/ (accessed May 2007).

Jamaica Plain Cohousing: www.jpcohousing.org/ (accessed May 2007).

Muir Commons: www.muircommons.org/ (accessed May 2007).

Winslow Cohousing: www.winslowcohousing.org/ (accessed May 2007).

Cooperatives

A cooperative is a business or an institution that is owned and run jointly by all of its workers or members. Some common cooperatives today include food cooperatives (which are managed and owned by their consumer members); credit unions (which are owned by and which provide banking services to members of a specific class, such as university employees); producer cooperatives (collections of farmers or other manufacturers who get together to sell their products for a better price); worker cooperatives (in which the business is owned and operated by employees); and housing cooperatives (in which the residents are owners and managers of the buildings in which they live).

A cooperative business is different from a traditional business in that the profits of a cooperative business are used to expand or help the business or are distributed to the workers or consumer members. In a traditional business, the profits are kept by the owners. In addition, cooperative businesses allow workers or consumer members to help run the business by electing and serving on the board of directors.

The National Cooperative Business Association's Web site states the principles followed by cooperatives worldwide, including a membership open to anyone who wishes to join; a leadership elected by members; economic control by members; education and training for members about how cooperatives work; and working together with other cooperatives.

The first cooperative-type business in the United States, an insurance company, was started by Benjamin Franklin in Philadelphia in 1752. Even earlier in the 1700s, cooperative-type businesses were founded in England and France, and by 1830, there were 300 cooperative societies in the United Kingdom.

The origin of the modern cooperative movement, incorporating the principles detailed above, was the Rochdale Pioneers in Rochdale, England. This group of 44 weavers decided to do something about the fact that they could not afford basic food. In 1844, they pooled their resources and started a store that at first sold only flour, oatmeal, sugar, and butter. They made every customer a member with a vote and a share in profits. The success of the Rochdale Pioneers, and the principles they followed, led to an increasing number of cooperatives in Europe.

Utopian communities and cooperative businesses are related in that both are based on a system of collective ownership and decision making. Almost all utopian communities made use of cooperative businesses that were owned and run by the entire community. Even in cases where private ownership was allowed within a community, some businesses might be run cooperatively. For example, the New Deal communities incorporated cooperatively run farms and industry, in addition to privately owned farms and homes.

Customers at the entrance of the Tri-County Farmers Co-op Market in Du Bois, Pennsylvania. (Library of Congress)

Some of the early socialists were advocates of both cooperatives and communal societies as alternatives to the widespread poverty caused by the unregulated private businesses that sprang up during the Industrial Revolution. One of the first secular community-builders, Robert Owen, worked in London to help reorganize industry into cooperatives. Although this attempt was not successful, his ideas influenced the cooperative movement in Great Britain. Another early socialist and community-builder, Charles Fourier, also advocated for cooperative businesses. Followers of Fourier founded the American cooperative movement. Members of the Jewish Agricultural Communities also started a number of cooperatives, such as the Cooperative Poultrymen's Association in New Jersey, the Cooperative Fire Insurance Companies in New York, and the Intermountain Farmers Association in Utah.

See also: Brook Farm and Fourierist Phalanxes; Industrial Revolution; Jewish Agricultural Communities; New Deal Communities; Owen, Robert; Socialism

Reference

Williams, Richard C. *The Cooperative Movement: Globalization from Below.* Burlington, VT: Ashgate, 2007.

WEB SITES

International Co-operative Alliance: www.ica.coop/ (accessed April 9, 2008).
National Cooperative Business Association: www.ncba.coop/ (accessed April 9, 2008).

Cults

A cult is a system of religious or spiritual belief. The word is often used to refer to a group that follows beliefs that are unlike those of the mainstream culture. In this sense, almost any religious or spiritual utopian community in the United States could be defined as a cult.

The word *cult* has taken on a negative connotation, implying a deviant, dangerous religious group that coerces people into joining. Therefore, religious scholars prefer to use the term *new religious movement* when discussing this topic.

Because new religious movements generally challenge some aspects of the dominant society, they are often initially misunderstood and feared by the general public, even if later on they become accepted and even revered. For example, what is today one of the most famous and respected utopian communities, the Shakers, was once reviled as a dangerous cult. A former member accused the Shakers of practicing witchcraft and leading people to hell (Gallagher 2004, 1).

Although most new religious movements are peaceful and keep to themselves, some new religious movements do engage in violence. For example, in 1978 over 900 members of a religious group, the People's Temple, committed suicide together in Guyana, South America. In the 1980s, leaders of Rajneeshpuram pleaded guilty to attempted murder. Reports of these events reignited the public's fear of new religious movements.

Even though new religious movements—and their opponents—have been part of American history since the Pilgrims began arriving, the modern anticult movement started in response to the fact that more and more young adults were attracted to unusual religions beginning in the late 1960s. At this time, some parents and relatives of members of these movements began to fear that their loved ones were being harmed by these groups. These concerned relatives began forming "anticult" groups to "rescue" their loved ones from the grip of these new religious movements.

The anticult movement is based on the idea that no one in their right mind would join an unusual religious group. Therefore, the cults must be coercing or brainwashing people into joining. However, social scientists have shown that people have considerable free will when it comes to joining new religious movements, and that those who do convert do so for a variety of reasons (Gallagher 2004, 225–230).

The Family/Children of God was one of the first utopian communities to be targeted by the modern anticult movement: in 1972, an organization was formed called Parents' Committee to Free Our Sons and Daughters from the Children of God.

In addition, some people developed businesses to "rescue" and "deprogram" members of new religious movements. These deprogrammers would kidnap adult members of new religious movements, detain them, and subject them to verbal or even physical abuse in an effort to get them to renounce their beliefs.

Deprogramming (or "exit counseling," as it is also known) has since been discredited. In 1996, one of the largest anticult groups, the Cult Awareness Network (CAN), declared bankruptcy largely due to a civil suit brought by Jason Scott, who was abducted from a United Pentecostal congregation, detained for a week, and physically abused. CAN was found to provide misleading information about new religious movements as well as referrals to deprogrammers, who charged thousands of dollars per case and then paid CAN a portion of their fee (Shupe et al. 2002, 21–25).

Members of a new religious movement sometimes garner benefits from practices that would be unacceptable to the outside world. Robert Balch interviewed former members of the utopian community known as the Love Family and found that "although many of the defectors I interviewed wondered in retrospect if they had been brainwashed, they still had fond memories of the Love Family. Ironically, some of their best memories were of situations that anticult writers cited to show how oppressive Family life was. At one time, for example, 16 people lived in eight tiny cubicles in a small, windowless room in the basement of Love's house, where they shared virtually everything but toothbrushes. When I asked an ex-member what it was like, he replied, 'Wonderful! It was like summer camp. It was very cramped, but we had a lot of fun. Those people are still my best friends.' Many defectors nostalgically recalled the blissful feeling of merging into the group's collective consciousness while singing, chanting, or meditating together" (1998, 74–75).

According to Larry Shinn, who wrote a book about cults and the Hare Krishnas, "one will not find any two lists of characteristics that agree exactly on what constitutes a cult. . . . One difficulty with such sets of criteria is that when applied equitably they also describe many mainline and accepted religious and political institutions" (1987, 17).

See also: The Family/Children of God; International Society for Krishna
Consciousness (Hare Krishna Movement); Love Family; Rajneeshpuram

References

Balch, Robert. "The Love Family: Its Formative Years," in *Sects, Cults and Spiritual Communities: A Sociological Analysis*, edited by William Zellner and Marc Petrowsky. Westport, CT: Praeger, 1998, 63–94.

Gallagher, Eugene V. *The New Religious Movements Experience in America*. Westport, CT: Greenwood Press, 2004.

Shinn, Larry. *The Dark Lord: Cult Images and the Hare Krishnas in America*. Philadelphia, PA: Westminster Press, 1987.

Shupe, Anson, Susan E. Darnell, and Kendrick Moxon. "The Cult Awareness Network and the Anticult Movement: Implications for NRMs in America," in *New Religious Movements and Religious Liberty in America,* edited by Derek H. Davis and Barry Hankins. Waco, TX: J. M. Dawson Institute of Church-State Studies and Baylor University Press, 2002, 21–44.

Davidian and Branch Davidian Movements

At a Glance

Dates of existence in United States: 1935 to present
Location: Texas
Peak membership: 130
Religious or other belief: Christianity, Adventism

History

The Branch Davidians are best known for the 1993 confrontation between the U.S. government and their community in Waco, Texas, which resulted in a fire that killed over 70 Branch Davidians. Few people realize that the group began during the Great Depression and that it was an offshoot of the Seventh-Day Adventist Church.

The Davidian movement was started in 1929 by Victor Houteff, a Bulgarian immigrant who converted to Seventh-Day Adventism, a Christian sect that started in the mid-1800s. Houteff claimed he received a vision of new teachings that he called the Shepherd's Rod. He hoped to reform the Seventh-Day Adventist Church with his new teachings. The Seventh-Day Adventist Church rejected Houteff's message, so Houteff began teaching in the home of a supporter and attracted a following.

In 1935, Houteff bought land near Waco, Texas. Twelve followers moved onto the land in May, and within a few months 37 members were living on the land. By 1940, the community had 64 members, 10 buildings, water supply and sewage systems, and electricity. The site was named Mount Carmel (Pitts 1995, 21–26).

Until 1942, Houteff called his group the Shepherd's Rod. When World War II started, Houteff changed the name of the group to the Davidian Seventh-Day Adventists, to make it clear to government officials that they considered themselves part of an established pacifist religion. They were excused from active military service (Pitts 1995, 29).

Houteff died in 1955 without appointing a successor. His wife, Florence, declared herself the leader. While Victor Houteff had never predicted the date of Christ's second coming, Florence declared that the process would begin on April 22, 1959. She asked Davidians who did not live at Mount Carmel to move to the community and wait for God's signal to move to Israel. About 900 supporters arrived. Many of them sold their homes and businesses in order to make the trip. The community built 11 barracks-style buildings to house these supporters, and 75 tents were pitched (Pitts 1995, 30; Crowe, 2004, 17, 19). When the Davidians did not receive any sign of Christ's imminent return to Earth, most of the supporters began to leave.

In 1962, Florence Houteff and her executive council resigned and dissolved the Davidian Seventh-Day Adventists. They believed that their movement's literature was mistaken regarding its interpretation of parts of the Bible, and rather than lead a movement that was perhaps false, they chose to dissolve the organization (Pitts 1995, 31; Crowe 2004, 27–28).

One Davidian, Ben Roden, had been challenging Florence's leadership since 1955. He called his movement the Branch Davidians, claiming he received this name through a divine message. He saw himself as leading the third and final stage in the Adventist movement before the second coming of Christ. When Florence Houteff and her followers left Mount Carmel in 1962, Roden sought to buy the land. Although other Davidians challenged Roden, he finally managed to buy Mount Carmel in 1973 (Pitts 1995, 32–33; Crowe 2004, 44–52).

Roden died in 1978. He left instructions that his sons were to carry on the leadership of the community. However, Roden's wife, Lois, challenged the leadership of their oldest son, George. In 1981, a young man named Vernon Howell visited Mount Carmel. Lois was so impressed with Howell's sincerity and his knowledge of scripture that she promoted Howell as a new leader of Mount Carmel; by 1984, most Branch Davidians at Mount Carmel were followers of Howell (Pitts 1995, 37; Crowe 2004, 61–66).

While Lois was ill in 1985, and while Howell was away, George Roden managed to take over Mount Carmel. However, since most residents were followers of Howell, they simply moved away from Mount Carmel to eastern Texas, where Howell was living. Lois Roden died in 1986. The next year, in an attempt to gain control of Mount Carmel, Howell filed a legal document declaring himself the trustee of Mount Carmel. He and Roden ended up facing off in a gunfight at the property. During the subsequent trial, Roden was jailed because he would not stop sending letters asking God to inflict herpes and AIDS upon the judges. While Roden was in prison, Howell and his followers paid back taxes on Mount Carmel and moved onto the land again. The jury could not reach a verdict as to whether Howell and his followers were guilty of attempted murder, and the judge declared a mistrial. In 1990, Howell legally changed his name to David Koresh (Crowe 2004, 82–96; Bromley and Silver 1995, 57).

Starting in 1992, former Branch Davidian members began contacting authorities with complaints of child abuse and illegal weapons at Mount Carmel. A UPS driver reported to the local sheriff's department that Mount Carmel was receiving shipments of firearms and explosives. The sheriff's department asked the U.S. Bureau of Alcohol, Tobacco and Firearms (ATF) to investigate (Wright 1995, 83–89; Kerstetter 2004).

After months of undercover surveillance, the ATF decided that Koresh and his followers were manufacturing illegal weapons; that children were being physically and sexually abused; and that members were under the sway of Koresh and his teachings. Instead of arresting Koresh when he left the community to jog or go into Waco, the ATF chose to force an armed entry into the compound in February 1993. The Branch Davidians, also armed (they had been warned of the ATF's plans), became involved in a gun battle with the ATF that resulted in five Branch Davidians' deaths and four ATF agents' deaths. Some women and children left the compound, and government officials separated the children from their mothers. The other Branch Davidians chose to stay.

For 51 days, the federal government tried to force the Branch Davidians to leave by cutting off their electricity, blaring loud noise into the compound, and shining bright lights day and night. Koresh refused to exit, claiming that he would only leave when instructed to do so by God. A survivor of the siege, David Thibodeau, states that one reason the Branch Davidians did not leave the buildings was that they feared the armed officials outside would shoot them.

Finally, then-U.S. Attorney General Janet Reno, who had been told that children were being abused in the compound, gave permission to spray tear gas into the buildings. At some point, a fire started that killed almost everyone inside, including Koresh and 21 children. Although the government accused the Branch Davidians of starting the fire, and the Branch Davidians accused the government, it is also possible that the fire could have started accidentally: the tear gas was flammable, and the Branch Davidians had been using kerosene lamps because their electricity had been cut off (Boyer 1995; Kerstetter 2004; Rosenbloom 1995; Thibodeau 1999, v–xviii; 157–175, 291).

The U.S. government spent over $100 million dollars and involved over 700 federal officials in the Branch Davidian incident (Wright 1995, 76).

In 1994, several Branch Davidian survivors were found guilty of weapons possession and conspiracy to commit murder during the February ATF attack. They were sentenced to prison (Thibodeau 1999, 316).

In 2000, the Branch Davidians brought a wrongful-death lawsuit against the U.S. government. The judge ruled that the fire was set by the Branch Davidians and that the government was not responsible for the deaths (Hancock 2000).

As of 2007, a small group of Davidians occupied the land of Mount Carmel. They call themselves "the Branch" and do not follow the teachings of David Koresh. They live in mobile homes and plan to build an amphitheater, petting zoo, and wellness center (Jennings 2007).

Beliefs and Practices

The Davidian and Branch Davidian movements consider themselves Seventh-Day Adventists. They believe in the second coming of Christ and in Saturday as the Sabbath. They are vegetarians and for most of their history did not consume alcohol or tobacco. Until the leadership of Koresh, the Davidians were pacifists, like the Seventh-Day Adventists, and refused to bear arms (Pitts 1995, 22).

Victor Houteff did not intend to start a new religion but hoped to reform the Seventh-Day Adventist Church. He believed the Seventh-Day Adventists had grown too worldly, and that Christ would not return until the church was reformed. According to Houteff, his role was to reveal the secrets of the seven seals (as described in the New Testament Book of Revelation) and gather the 144,000 faithful to await Christ's second coming (Bromley and Silver 1995, 46).

During Houteff's time, the community held regular religious services on Friday evenings and Saturday afternoons. Religious study classes were held every evening. Houteff preached against the corruption of the outside world. The women wore modest calf-length dresses with long sleeves and no makeup. Members of the community were not allowed to engage in competitive games (Pitts 1995, 28–29).

Ben Roden believed that Christians should follow the precepts of the Ten Commandments and observe the Sabbath and Jewish festival days, such as Passover (Pitts 1995, 35).

David Koresh claimed that he was a messiah who could lead sinners to salvation. Like Houteff and Roden, he believed he was gathering the 144,000 faithful to await Christ's second coming. During Koresh's time, the community met twice a day for a brief religious ceremony, including a communion service of bread and wine. Koresh often led lengthy Scripture study groups after dinner. One former member described the atmosphere: "We lived, ate and breathed the Bible." While the community continued to be vegetarian, alcohol was permitted (Bromley and Silver 1995, 58, 61; Thibodeau 1999, 30).

Koresh's most striking departure from previous Davidian tradition was in family relationships. In 1989, Koresh had a revelation that he called New Light. He taught that all the men in the community, married and single, must be celibate, and that only he, David Koresh, could have sexual relations with all the women (including teenagers). The purpose of this was to produce children who would rule the future earthly kingdom in Israel that God would set up (Bromley and Silver 1995, 58–60; Thibodeau, 1999, 53–54).

Daily Life

Thibodeau, a Branch Davidian member who survived the 1993 fire, describes his first impressions of Mount Carmel in 1990: There was a dirt track along a series of shabby buildings, including the study house, cottages, and barns. At the top of the hill was a concrete storage room, next to which a new building was being constructed, which would include a communal cafeteria. Only some of the houses had running water.

The community was open and friendly, Thibodeau recalls, and members were from many different ethnic backgrounds and countries. Most had a background in Seventh-Day Adventism. Single people shared housing. Koresh and his family lived in their own house. Meals were prepared and eaten communally. "More than anything, the easy ambiance at Mount Carmel was reminiscent of hippie communes as my mom had described them to me," says Thibodeau (1999, 30).

He notes that while community members shared freely with each other, members could keep their own bank accounts and personal property. The women cooked, sewed, and took care of the children. The men constructed new buildings on the property, worked in the auto shop or landscaping business, or had jobs outside the community (Thibodeau 1999, 28–31).

How They Made Their Living

While the Davidians and Branch Davidians aimed for self-sufficiency, they also took jobs outside the community to bring in extra money. Houteff believed that physical labor was an important part of successful community life. He required everyone to work and paid them wages. During Houteff's time, the Davidians had their own internal money system. Members were required to donate 10 percent of their income for religious work. Houteff introduced a "second tithe"—a donation of 10 percent of the remaining 90 percent, for social needs such as health insurance, schooling, and elder care (Pitts 1995, 26–27).

In Koresh's time, the community earned money through an automobile repair shop as well as the Mag Bag, a business selling guns and hunting products at gun shows. In addition, wealthy members donated significant sums of money (Bromley and Silver 1995, 55).

Leadership and Decision Making

The spiritual leaders of the community were also its administrative leaders. When Houteff headed the community, he was the main leader, and he appointed four officers and a council. Many officers were family members: his wife, Florence, was secretary, and his mother-in-law was treasurer (Pitts 1995 26).

How New Members Were Recruited or Chosen

Generally, the Davidians and Branch Davidians looked to the Seventh-Day Adventist (SDA) Church for new members. They visited SDA churches and passed out Davidian literature. In 1952 and 1953, Houteff sent followers all over the world to contact Seventh-Day Adventist families. Likewise, Roden and Koresh generally tried to gain followers from other Adventist and Davidian groups scattered around the country and the world. For example, in 1988, Koresh led followers to evangelize at SDA churches in Hawaii, England, and Australia (Pitts 1995, 29; Bromley and Silver 1995, 56).

Children and Youth

Under Houteff, the Davidians formed the Mount Carmel Academy to educate their children. In addition to academic subjects, the students studied the Bible, the writings of Ellen White (the founder of Seventh-Day Adventism), and the writings of Houteff. The students also acquired practical skills by working within the community. The school closed in 1948 due to lack of funds and the students went to public schools (Pitts 1995, 27–28; Crowe 2004, 8).

Under Koresh's leadership, the children lived with their mothers and went to school in the cafeteria. They studied academic subjects as well as the Bible. The children enjoyed swimming in the community pool and riding the go-carts and mini motorbikes bought by Koresh for them (Thibodeau 1999, 117–118).

Koresh has been accused of abusing the children in the community. The abuse of children was one of the main reasons given by U.S. Attorney General Janet Reno for the government's use of tear gas that may have caused the deadly fire at the compound in Waco. Former Branch Davidians accused Koresh of paddling babies and young children until he drew blood (Ellison and Bartkowski 1995, 111–112, 120–121).

According to Thibodeau, Koresh did have sexual relations with preteen and teenaged girls with their consent and that of their parents. Koresh is also known to have spanked disobedient children with a paddle. But Thibodeau claims that he did not see any other evidence of child abuse in the community. A 1992 Child Protective Services investigation of the community did not produce any evidence of abuse. Children who left the compound before the fire were found to be in good health (Thibodeau 1999, 118–119; Ellison and Bartkowski 1995, 123, 133).

Relationship with the Outside World

The leadership of the Seventh-Day Adventist Church was always hostile to the Davidian movement. The local community, however, seemed to have few problems with it. For the most part, the rest of the outside world did not hear of the group until 1993.

Influence on the Outside World

The Davidian and Branch Davidian movements aimed to reform the Seventh-Day Adventist Church in an effort to prepare its members for Christ's second coming. However, the leaders of the SDA Church have never been interested in the Davidians, and only a small percentage of Seventh-Day Adventists follow the Davidian movement.

In April 1995, two years after the Branch Davidian fire, a man who was not a Davidian, Timothy McVeigh, bombed a federal building in Oklahoma City, Oklahoma, killing 168 people. McVeigh stated that his action was a justifiable retaliation for the crimes the government committed in their treatment of the Branch Davidians (Kerstetter 2004).

The Branch Davidian tragedy is a reminder to us all that mistrust and fear of alternative religions can lead to violence and mass deaths. The raid and standoff at Mount Carmel suggest, according to one scholar, that "religious freedom extends only as far as the mainstream deems fit. Practices beyond those bounds were 'crazy,' amounting to 'perversion,' and would be dealt with accordingly" (Kerstetter 2004).

See also: Burned-Over District; Cults; Millennialism; Persecution

References

Boyer, Peter J. "The Children of Waco." *The New Yorker*, May 15, 1995, www.pbs.org/wgbh/pages/frontline/waco/childrenofwaco1.html (accessed March 2007).

Bromley, David, and Edward Silver. "The Davidian Tradition: From Patronal Clan to Prophetic Movement," in *Armageddon in Waco: Critical Perspectives on the Branch Davidian Conflict,* edited by Stuart Wright. Chicago: University of Chicago Press, 1995, 43–72.

Crowe, Rebekah Ann. "Because God Said I Was! A History of the Power Struggles within the Davidian and Branch Davidian Sects of the Seventh-Day Adventist Church." Master's Thesis, Baylor University, 2004.

Ellison, Christopher, and John Bartkowski. "'Babies Were Being Beaten'—Exploring Child Abuse Allegations at Ranch Apocalypse," in *Armageddon in Waco: Critical Perspectives on the Branch Davidian Conflict,* edited by Stuart Wright. Chicago: University of Chicago Press, 1995, 111–149.

Hancock, Lee. "Judge Rules Waco Fire Was Solely Fault of Branch Davidians." *Dallas Morning News,* September 21, 2000.

Jennings, Diane. "Reorganized Davidians Envision 'Place of Healing.'" *Dallas Morning News*, March 8, 2007.

Kerstetter, Todd. "'That's Just the American Way': The Branch Davidian Tragedy and Western Religious History." *Western Historical Quarterly*, winter 2004, vol. 35, no. 4, 453–472.

Pitts, William L. "Davidians and Branch Davidians, 1929–1987," in *Armageddon in Waco: Critical Perspectives on the Branch Davidian Conflict,* edited by Stuart Wright. Chicago: University of Chicago Press, 1995, 20–42.

Rosenbloom, Joe. "Waco: More than Simple Blunders?" *Wall Street Journal*, October 17, 1995, www.pbs.org/wgbh/pages/frontline/waco/blunders.html (accessed March 2007).

Thibodeau, David. *A Place Called Waco: A Survivor's Story.* New York: Public Affairs, 1999.

Wright, Stuart. "Construction and Escalation of a Cult Threat," in *Armageddon in Waco: Critical Perspectives on the Branch Davidian Conflict,* edited by Stuart Wright. Chicago: University of Chicago Press, 1995, 75–94.

Ecovillages

Ecovillages are communities that strive to protect the natural environment around them and to minimize their own impact on the environment. According to the Global Ecovillage Network Web site, "Ecovillages are urban or rural communities of people, who strive to integrate a supportive social environment with a low-impact way of life. To achieve this, they integrate various aspects of ecological design, permaculture, ecological building, green production, alternative energy, community building practices, and much more" (http://gen.ecovillage.org/).

Several American utopian communities can be considered ecovillages. Among them are The Farm, Ecovillage in Ithaca (a cohousing community), Twin Oaks, and the Camphill communities.

Although some American communities have been incorporating ecological principals since the 1960s and 1970s, the concept of an ecovillage was developed during the 1990s. In 1991, a group of leaders from communities that were incorporating environmental principles met in Denmark to discuss how to spread the theory of an ecovillage. From this initial meeting, the Global Ecovillage Network was founded in 1995. Its goals are to help start more ecovillages and to spread information about ecovillages throughout the world.

In addition to the communities mentioned above, which are profiled elsewhere in this book, other American ecovillages are being created, including Earthaven in North Carolina, which was founded in 1995. As of 2007, it had 60 members and aimed to grow to 150 people. The community has built homes using ecological techniques, an alternative (off-the-grid) power system, and a wetlands. Members run ecological businesses, including classes in herbal medicine and solar power installation.

See also: Camphill Movement; Cohousing; The Farm; Fellowship for Intentional Community; Twin Oaks Community

Reference

Bang, Jan Martin. *Ecovillages: A Practical Guide to Sustainable Communities*. Gabriola Island, British Columbia, Canada: New Society Publishers, 2005.

WEB SITES
Earthaven: www.earthaven.org/ (accessed May 2007).
Global Ecovillage Network: http://gen.ecovillage.org/ (accessed May 2007).

Education

The education of children is an important part of most utopian communities. Since they are creating a new way of living—one different from that of the outside world—the communities also generally want to educate their children in a new way—one that will socialize and adapt the child to the new, better life that the community is living.

From a historical perspective, Yaacov Oved emphasizes that, in communal schools, the socialization aspect was often more important than intellectual learning: "More than places of learning, their schools served as a socializing agent. It was imperative to instill the values of their special way of life in the young generation" (1988, 393).

Perhaps this is why the American communal movement has not had much influence on the outside world of education. According to Donald Pitzer: "American communitarians have been more educationally imitative than innovative. . . . No American communal society has created a methodology later used by private or public school systems or espoused by noted professional educators. No educational 'schools of thought' have emerged from a communal source. No nationally-recognized educational theorists have risen from their ranks" (1987, 276).

Nevertheless, American communal schools have been innovative in some ways. The New Harmony School in Indiana was one of the first public schools in the United States. The school at the antislavery community of Elgin was started for the children of former slaves but soon began accepting white neighborhood children as well—making it the first racially integrated school in North America. Many communities kept large libraries, which were often, in the pioneer days of the United States, some of the leading libraries in the country. In one case, a community (Fairhope) donated its library to become the town's public library. The Camphill schools have developed unique ways of educating children and adults with developmental disabilities. Communal schools often introduced inventive educational concepts to Americans, such as the methods of the Swiss educator Johann Pestalozzi, Spanish educator Francisco Ferrer, and Italian educator Maria Montessori.

Some communities saw educational experimentation as central to their existence. For example, the anarchist Ferrer Colony revolved around an innovative "Modern School" that it ran from 1911 to 1956 to educate children in an atmosphere of intellectual and social freedom. Based on a coeducational school started by Francisco Ferrer in Spain, the Modern School de-emphasized abstract academic learning, and instead emphasized crafts, manual arts, dance, music, and playing outdoors. The students could attend school any time they liked—there were no formal class periods—and could choose to work in one of the four classrooms dedicated to arts and crafts. There were no punishments and no grades. The Modern School aimed to educate

School building at The Farm in Summertown, Tennessee. (Douglas Stevenson Village Media)

children to learn how to live free of formal authority and free of what the anarchists saw as the selfishness of the capitalist system.

In addition to the school at the Ferrer Colony, the anarchist movement started and ran a number of other Modern Schools, most of which were short-lived, but which may have influenced educators in the 1960s to experiment with new methods of education.

Point Loma, a Theosophical community, was also formed around a school for children. The "Raja Yoga" school ran during the first 40 years of the 20th century and was designed to foster in children a balance of mental, physical, and spiritual traits. Most of the students at the school were boarders and many came from other countries. The students, who were encouraged to work largely in silence, spent two and a half hours per day on academic work and also worked on the community's farm and in the workshops. Girls and boys received the same education until they became teenagers, when they were separated. The students were known locally for the high quality of their theater performances. The leader of the Point Loma community, Katherine Tingley, envisioned a series of such schools around the world, but this ideal never materialized.

Another communal movement with education at its center is the growing and thriving Camphill movement, founded in 1939 in Scotland, and in 1959 in the United States. Camphill communities center on the education of children and adults with disabilities, using a system called "curative education"—the idea that education itself can promote healing. Included in this kind of education are speech and physical therapy, as well as art, music, handcrafts, and a movement art called "eurhythmy." While the Camphill movement's methods are innovative and unique, the communities have not put much emphasis on spreading their ideas to the outside world.

Other communities also experimented with education, even if education was not the primary reason for the community's existence. One of the earliest experiments in innovative education was carried out at Robert Owen's community of New Harmony from 1825 to 1827. Owen recruited teachers who believed in the educational system promoted by the Swiss educator Johann Pestalozzi—that children should learn through doing, and not through rote memorization. Corporal punishment was banned in the New Harmony school, which taught academic subjects as well as manual trades, and was the first public school in Indiana. While the New Harmony community folded after two years, the school continued for about 20 more.

In addition to this school, Owen's family was influential in educational reform in the United States. For example, Owen's son, Robert Dale Owen, promoted the idea of free public education as a member of the Indiana legislature and the U.S. House of Representatives.

The school at Brook Farm, which was open to the public and ran from 1841 to 1847, also aimed to be innovative in that it accepted both boys and girls and did not restrict attendance only to the upper class.

The School of Organic Education was set up in the Fairhope community in 1907 and is still running today. Like the Modern Schools, the School of Organic Education has no grades, no rewards, and no punishments. Academic subjects are taught, but crafts, music, drama, and folk dancing are considered equally important. The founder of the School of Organic Education, Marietta Johnson, believed that her school would help children grow up in freedom and challenge injustice as adults. Johnson also started nine other similar schools around the country. In her time, Johnson was considered one of the country's most influential advocates for progressive education.

The Ruskin socialist colony (1894–1901) ran a school that drew on the philosophies of Johann Pestalozzi and Friedrich Froebel, teaching children the value of manual labor, as well as the academic subjects. Girls were to be provided the same education as boys. The school gave no grades and did not emphasize memorization or competition.

The socialist colony of Llano del Rio set up a preschool from 1914 to 1917 based on the principles of Maria Montessori, a noted Italian educator. In the Montessori system, the teacher creates an optimal learning environment by setting up appropriate games, puzzles, and household utensils, and then allows children the freedom to choose their tasks. This preschool was one of the first Montessori schools in California.

Some of the New Deal communities experimented with education, as well. The Arthurdale community in West Virginia set up a school designed to foster democracy and cooperation by allowing the students to investigate the subjects that most interested them. In high school, even the girls had access to shop classes and gym classes, which was unusual at that time.

The Ananda Colonies, which first started in 1968, run "Living Wisdom" schools for community children as well as outside children. The goal of the Living Wisdom schools is to help students become more balanced, mature, and harmonious in mind, body, and spirit. The curriculum involves the usual academic subjects, along with art, theater, music, computers, and physical education. Hands-on learning and service projects are emphasized, as is participation in spiritual ceremonies.

Traditionally, many of the more conservative Christian communities have put much less emphasis on innovation in education and more emphasis on keeping the children separate from the outside world and socializing them in the community's values. The schools generally taught only the academic basics, as well as community values and songs. Many of these conservative communities ran their school only for younger children. Young people above the age of 12 or 14 were expected to work within the community. This was the case at the Amana Colonies, the Harmony Society, the Zoar Society, the Keil communities, and the House of David movement; among the Amish and in the Hutterite communities.

Many of these communities do not see the value of higher academic education. For example, the Amish equate more education with more sinfulness: they see that the outside world is highly educated but also highly corrupt. Benjamin Purnell, the leader of the House of David movement (which began in 1903), compared education to dung and stated that dung was more useful because of its value as a fertilizer.

However, some of these conservative communities have allowed higher education when it would benefit the community. Amana men were sometimes sent to college to become doctors, teachers, or other professionals needed within the community. The Hutterites have started to allow young people to take high school classes and sometimes even to attend college-level teacher-training programs.

Other Christian communities have been more open to academic education, routinely encouraging young people to attend high school and even college. The school at the Oneida community (1848 to 1881) taught reading, writing, spelling, and arithmetic. After age 12, the students learned a wider variety of subjects, including astronomy, geography, math, sciences, and foreign languages. A number of students were sent to college. The Bruderhof communities, which began in the United States in 1954, also allow community children to attend college. In addition to the basics of reading, writing, and arithmetic, the Bruderhof schools emphasize drama, music, arts and crafts, Spanish, and exploring natural surroundings. There is no homework until fifth grade.

The International Society for Krishna Consciousness (Hare Krishnas), a non-Christian religious community that began in 1965, de-emphasized academic learning in its boarding schools. The schools stressed religious learning: the children were taught stories of the Hindu deity Krishna and they learned Sanskrit (the language of Hindu scriptures), in addition to academic basics. The children were not allowed toys because those were associated with "sense gratification." After the age of 12, girls were taught to cook and sew, while boys continued their education in Krishna texts.

A few communities virtually ignored children, giving almost no thought to how they should be educated. Rajneeshpuram (1981–1987) would fall into this category—the children were often left to fend for themselves. Also in this category, and existing about two centuries before, is the Ephrata Cloister (1732–1786). There was apparently no philosophy about child rearing or education at the Ephrata Cloister, and the children were said to be neglected and undisciplined.

References

Oved, Yaacov. *Two Hundred Years of American Communes*. New Brunswick, NJ: Transaction Books, 1988.

Pitzer, Donald. "Patterns of Education in American Communal Societies," in *Communal Life: An International Perspective,* edited by Yosef Gorni, Yaacov Oved, and Idit Paz. New Brunswick, NJ: Transaction Books, 1987.

Ephrata Cloister

At a Glance

Dates of existence in United States: 1732 to 1786 (partially communal until 1813)
Location: Pennsylvania
Peak membership: 300
Religious or other belief: Christianity, Pietism

History

The Ephrata Cloister was one of the earliest of the American utopian communities and the longest-lived of the colonial communities.

The community was founded by Conrad Beissel, a baker who was born in 1691 in Germany. He did not like the formal Lutheran Church and became attracted to the Pietists, who believed in studying the Bible themselves, without the aid of clergy. While working around the country as a journeyman baker, Beissel began criticizing the baker's guild members for their rowdy banquets. The guild found out that he had cut his ties to the Lutheran Church and had been attending secret Pietist meetings. They had him banished from the guild and the area. He wandered from place to place, earning a living by spinning wool and as a peddler. Beissel had heard about an American spiritual community called the Society of the Woman in the Wilderness. He and a few companions left for America to find this community.

In 1720, upon arriving in Germantown, Pennsylvania (in present-day Philadelphia), the site of the Society of the Woman in the Wilderness community, Beissel found that the community's founder had been dead for 18 years and the community was scattered. Beissel spent a year as an apprentice to Peter Becker in a weaving shop and then traveled west with a companion into the wilderness of Pennsylvania, building a cabin on Mill Creek (near present-day Lancaster County). That same year, he visited another religious community, Bohemia Manor in Maryland, which by that time was in the process of disintegrating.

While living on Mill Creek, Beissel aligned himself for many years with Becker's religious group, the Schwarzenau Brethren. Several followers of Beissel built cabins near his.

However, Beissel began to believe in some ideas that were contrary to Becker's group, such as celibacy, Saturday as the true Sabbath, and following Old Testament dietary laws. In 1728, he broke with Becker's group. Beissel and his followers continued to live in the wilderness. In the winter of 1732, Beissel suddenly resigned as the head of his little congregation, left his cabin, and moved eight miles north to a deserted area that was said to be infested with snakes.

However, in spring, some of his followers arrived and built their own cabins near his. This was the beginning of the Ephrata Cloister. It does not appear that Beissel meant to found his own community, but that is what ended up happening. "The members of the new settlement simply identified it as . . . the Camp of the Solitary. It seemed to have come into being all very naturally, with no grandiose plans or pre-conceptions" (Alderfer 1985, 50).

In 1739, some members formed the secretive Zion Brotherhood within the community, entrance to which required 40 days of penance (see below).

In 1741, Count Nicholas Ludwig von Zinzendorf and his followers, who founded the Moravian movement in the United States, arrived in Pennsylvania. Zinzendorf tried to unite all the religious groups. He personally visited Ephrata, and although he was snubbed by Beissel, Ephrata members did participate in some of Zinzendorf's meetings. However, Ephrata declined to join with Zinzendorf, and he went on to found his own community (Durnbaugh 1997, 27).

In 1743, Beissel bought a printing press for the community, on which it printed not only Ephrata books such as hymnals but also books for the outside community.

At its height, the community had about 80 celibate members and about 200 "Householders" who lived in their own homes nearby.

Beissel became an alcoholic in his old age and was disruptive to the community. He died of tuberculosis in 1768. Peter Miller took his place as leader of the community. At this time, few new members joined, and only 50 elderly "Solitaries" remained. During the American Revolution, Ephrata welcomed and tended to George Washington's wounded troops after the Battle of Brandywine. Unfortunately, typhoid spread throughout the community and about a third of the members died. In 1786, the community began allowing private ownership, although land and buildings were still held in common (Sutton 2003, 12–13).

The last of the Solitaries died in 1813 and the married members formed the German Seventh Day Baptist Church.

Beliefs and Practices

Beissel preached that in order to achieve the highest level of spiritual attainment, his followers should practice celibacy. However, married couples were allowed to join the congregation and live nearby. They were called Householders, and the celibate single people were called Solitaries. He asked Solitaries to give their property to the community but did not require this of the Householders.

Beissel preached that salvation was a gift of God and did not result from good works, although exhausting physical labor did help to banish sin. He saw himself as a prophet like Christ and said that he was the last in line of a series of messiahs. On Friday nights, members had to give written confessions to Beissel. Members prayed and meditated at regular intervals throughout the day (see below). Sometimes Beissel ordered a special celebratory meal, a "love feast," during which members ate bread, apple butter, pickles, and coffee. During this meal the women and men were separated. Within their separate groups, they shook hands with each other, kissed each other on the cheek, and washed each other's feet (Sutton 2003 4–5).

Music was an important part of Ephrata spiritual practice. Beissel, who had learned to play the violin in Germany, developed a unique system of music involving four-, six-, or seven-part harmonies. Most of the parts were sung by the Sisters (the female Solitaries). Instruments were never used: the singing was a cappella. The choir sang in a falsetto voice, with lips partially closed. A listener described the effect thus: "The music had little or no air or melody, but consisted of simple, long notes, combined with the richest harmony." Beissel believed his system came from God and that it was like the sound of angels. He composed hundreds of pieces for his choir, members of which practiced daily and adhered to an even more strict diet than was followed by other members (Sutton 2003, 8–9).

Daily Life

The Solitary members took on new names when they joined the community, and were referred to as Brothers and Sisters. Beissel named himself "Father Friedsam."

The main community (where Beissel and the Solitaries lived) took up about two modern city blocks and consisted of dormitories for the Brothers and Sisters (including common kitchens, dining rooms, and work rooms), small houses for Beissel and a few other members, a bakery, and a printing house. The farms and homes of the Householders surrounded these buildings.

The dormitories were "enormous structures," according to Robert Sutton—"three and four stories, each with tiny, one-window sleeping cells and meeting rooms." All the buildings were constructed according to rules found in Scripture, with walls one foot thick, and no nails or iron used (2003, 4).

The Ephrata members kept to a strict, ascetic routine. They rose at six in the morning and spent an hour meditating and singing hymns. Then they worked until breakfast at nine. After breakfast they worked until eleven and meditated for an hour. Some people ate lunch at noon, but it was considered more devout to skip lunch. After working during the afternoon, members gathered again for a reading from Scripture and meditation, followed by the evening meal. From seven to nine the members read, drew, or meditated. At midnight, they attended a religious meeting during which they apologized to anyone whom they might have offended during the day. They then prayed and marched outside for two hours, singing hymns (Sutton 2003, 5–6).

According to the Ephrata Cloister Web site, each Ephrata member ate about a pound of bread daily. They also ate vegetables, cheese, and on occasion meat. Pork was never allowed. Members drank water or milk. Members were noted for their thin, emaciated appearance. The Solitary members slept on benches with pine blocks for pillows.

At first, the members wore simple clothes similar to those worn by the Quakers. The men grew their beards and all went barefoot when the weather permitted. Later, the Ephrata members adopted a style of dress like that of the first Christians. The men wore a shirt, pants, vest, and a long gown with a hood. The women wore a

The Saron at Ephrata Cloister in Lancaster County, Pennsylvania, was the communal residence of the Sisters of the Ephrata community. (Library of Congress)

skirt instead of pants. During worship services, they wore an additional hooded cloak (Sachse 1971, 296–298).

On the Sabbath, Beissel gave out work assignments to the Solitaries and House-holders. The Sisters worked at spinning, quilting, basket weaving, sewing, canning, and splitting firewood. They also made candles, matches, and other household items, and took care of the community gardens. The Brothers did the heavier community work, including farming, constructing buildings, tending the orchard, cooking, wash-ing clothes, and making shoes (Sutton 2003, 6, 12).

Two special rooms in the Sisters' dormitory were reserved for copying sermons and illustrating Ephrata books. The Ephrata style of art was called *Fraktur*, after the "broken" or "fractured" style of lettering and drawing.

How They Made Their Living

The community was self-sufficient in terms of food, clothing, and other necessities. New members donated their money and property to the community.

Beissel did not intend for the community to become wealthy. He believed in giv-ing away any excess grain or flour. However, when Beissel appointed the Eckerling brothers to be in charge of the community's economy, the brothers soon showed they were more interested in economic success.

Israel Eckerling began to sell lumber in nearby towns, constructed a paper mill and a bookbinding shop, and opened a tannery, a shoe shop, and weaving and pottery workshops. More wheat, flax, and millet were grown. Ephrata products were sold through agents as far away as Wilmington, Delaware. Eckerling also began to take on the spiritual leadership of the community. Beissel and his followers asked Eckerling to repent. He refused and left the community, after which Beissel drastically cut back the industries (Sutton 2003, 11; Alderfer 1985, 90).

Leadership and Decision Making

Beissel was the community's main leader. He appointed other leaders as needed.

How New Members Were Recruited or Chosen

Beissel preached throughout the region to attract new members. At first, anyone who wanted to join was accepted into the community. After 1734, Beissel required new members to serve a year of probation, during which inspectors would note whether they attended the morning and midnight meetings and whether they engaged in loud talking, whistling, or dawdling (Sutton 2003, 6–7).

After 1739, members who wanted to join the secretive Zion Brotherhood, an elite part of the community, had to undergo an ordeal that lasted 40 days. It consisted of living alone on a diet of herb broth, biscuits, and rain water; having blood taken from them; and consuming a secret elixir that caused loss of speech and memory, a high fever, the loss of hair, skin, and teeth, and then the magical renewal of hair, skin, and teeth. This ordeal was supposed to prompt a feeling of spiritual regeneration (Sachse 1971, 358–361).

Children and Youth

Children of the Householders were raised by their parents in their own homes. The community did not have a way to raise children communally.

Robert Sutton notes that "Ephrata children were largely neglected by their parents and were totally undisciplined. . . . They started to dress in gaudy clothes that mocked the plain garb of their elders." Apparently the young people went so far as to organize their own church service, baptize themselves, and hold their own love feasts. Beissel eventually abolished this youth service and burned the offensive clothing (2003, 10).

Relationship with the Outside World

Even in Pennsylvania, which was founded by William Penn on principles of religious freedom, the outside world was often hostile to the Ephrata Cloister because the group kept its Sabbath on Saturday. Government authorities arrested and fined members of the group for working on Sunday. In addition, male settlers were angry at Beissel for attracting their wives and daughters into the community. Beissel and his followers were beaten several times by intruders who entered the community at night (Alderfer 1985, 53).

Despite this harsh treatment, members of the Ephrata Cloister responded with charity. They ran a school for the children of poor German settlers and distributed bread to new settlers in the area.

Reasons for Ending the Community

As Beissel grew older and less able to lead effectively, fewer and fewer members joined. After his death, the new leader, Peter Miller, was not able to attract many new members. As members aged and died, the community dwindled and finally ended.

Influence on the Outside World

The music of Ephrata was some of the first serious music composed in the American colonies. Ephrata manuscripts were lavishly illustrated with calligraphy and intricate drawings. The group also printed books for outsiders on its printing press, including *Martyrs Mirror*, printed for the Mennonites and believed to be the largest single publication of the colonial American period (Durnbaugh 1997, 25–26). Today the site of the Ephrata Cloister is one of the most important historic landmarks in Pennsylvania.

Other Similar Communities

Some members of Ephrata started other communities, of which Snow Hill lasted the longest. In 1798, Peter Miller, the head of Ephrata, asked Peter Lehman to start Snow Hill in Franklin County, Pennsylvania. The community eventually grew to 40 men and women and continued until 1889 (Sutton 2003 13).

Snow Hill was similar to Ephrata in that celibacy was valued, but married couples were allowed to join. Members of Snow Hill did not take on new names. The community was governed by five trustees elected annually by the Cloister members and the lay congregation (those who did not give up their personal property to the society). Like Ephrata members, Snow Hill members were harassed for working on Sundays. For many years, the community paid a fine for this infraction. In 1846, they tried to change the state law but failed.

Members of the community made a living through agriculture; weaving linen and wool fabric; and running workshops for blacksmithing, cabinetry, and the making of barrels, brooms, and bricks. Life at Snow Hill was more comfortable than at Ephrata: the diet was not so meager, the members did not use wood blocks for pillows, and they did not hold midnight meetings, so members were able to get more sleep. Works of charity were as important for Snow Hill members as they were for Ephrata members: Snow Hill sent flour and money to Ireland to alleviate the suffering of the Irish famine of 1845–1847 (Alderfer 1985, 173–183).

See also: Bohemia Manor; Jerusalem/Society of Universal Friends; Moravian Movement; Society of the Woman in the Wilderness

References

Alderfer, E. G. *The Ephrata Commune: An Early American Counterculture.* Pittsburgh, PA: University of Pittsburgh Press, 1985.

Durnbaugh, Donald. "Communitarian Societies in Colonial America," in *America's Communal Utopias*, edited by Donald Pitzer. Chapel Hill: University of North Carolina Press, 1997, 22–27.

Sachse, Julius Friedrich. *The German Sectarians of Pennsylvania, 1708–1742.* Philadelphia: AMS Press, 1971.

Sutton, Robert. *Communal Utopias and the American Experience: Religious Communities, 1732–2000.* Westport, CT: Praeger, 2003.

WEB SITE

Ephrata Cloister: www.ephratacloister.org/ (accessed October 2006).

Fairhope and Single-Tax Communities

At a Glance

Dates of existence in United States: 1894 to present (Fairhope); 1900 to present (three Ardens)

Locations: Alabama (Fairhope); Delaware (three Ardens)

Peak membership: 1,800 leaseholders at Fairhope (not all of whom are members); 1,000 residents of the three Ardens

Religious or other belief: single tax

History

Fairhope is the most significant of the communities designed to showcase the idea of a "single tax"—a tax on land only—which was publicized in the 19th century as a simple remedy to inequalities of wealth. The single-tax idea was developed by Henry George.

Although Fairhope is associated with the single-tax movement, its original founder, Ernest Gaston, first intended to form a cooperative, socialistic community inspired by Edward Bellamy's novel *Looking Backward 2000–1887*. A friend suggested that Gaston might like to make his community a model of a single-tax community. Gaston agreed, and the Fairhope Industrial Association was incorporated in Iowa in 1894.

The community bought land in Baldwin County, Alabama, where the climate was warm and land was cheap. Fairhope started with about 22 people.

By 1896, the community ran its own public school, and by 1898, the residents had started a public library, which received donations from Joseph Fels, a wealthy soap manufacturer and single-tax supporter (Alyea and Alyea 1956, 76–77; www.fairhopelibrary.org/history.htm).

In 1904, the community incorporated in Alabama under a new name: the Fairhope Single Tax Corporation. By 1907, almost 500 people lived on community land. Private businesses included four stores, two bakeries, three hotels, a meat market, a blacksmith shop, a sawmill, a corn grinding and rice hulling mill, and a brickyard (Alyea and Alyea 1956, 84–85).

In 1908, the town of Fairhope was incorporated. The Fairhope Single Tax Corporation became a part of this town. About a quarter of the land in the town of Fairhope was owned by the Fairhope Single Tax Corporation (Alyea and Alyea 1956, 131).

Over the years, Fairhope grew and prospered. As of 1999, 1,800 people leased Fairhope land for renewable terms of 99 years. Of the people who lease the land, only about 10 percent are actually voting members of the Fairhope Single Tax Corporation. In 2003, the Fairhope Single Tax Corporation was granted nonprofit status as a social welfare organization, which means that the government recognizes that it operates not for private profit, but solely to promote the social welfare of its members. As of 2007, the Fairhope Single Tax Corporation owned 4,500 acres in and around Fairhope, Alabama (www.fairhopesingletax.com/).

Beliefs and Practices

The idea behind Henry George's single tax is that land is a finite resource given by nature and that it has value only because of the community's demand for it. Therefore, the community as a whole should share the wealth created by popular demand for land. George urged the government to tax only the increased value of land brought about because of public demand for that land.

Henry George and many of his supporters did not believe that the single-tax theory could be tried on a small scale such as a utopian community. Because it depends on tax collection, only the government can technically form a single-tax community. In addition, pure single taxers were generally opposed to socialist communities because such communities might reduce individual freedom with their emphasis on co-operation. Nevertheless, Fairhope was formed on these two perhaps conflicting principles: the single tax and voluntary cooperation (Alyea and Alyea 1956, 27–29).

The constitution of Fairhope states the following as the community's purpose: "to establish and conduct a model community or colony, free from all forms of private monopoly, and to secure to its members therein equality of opportunity, the full reward of individual efforts, and the benefits of co-operation in matters of general concern" (www.fairhopesingletax.com/).

Fairhope wanted to demonstrate that the single tax could prevent land speculation, create more and better-paying jobs, and redistribute wealth so that there would be no one who was excessively rich or excessively poor. Through its example, Fairhope aimed to influence other communities and governments to adopt the single tax (Alyea and Alyea 1956, 35).

Although Gaston believed in equality for all—and in fact compared private ownership of land to the enslavement of blacks—Fairhope was started for white people only. Gaston was afraid that if he opened up the community to blacks, it would be destroyed by the racism of the outside world in the Deep South. Gaston did talk about starting a separate black single-tax community next to Fairhope but that community never materialized (Gaston 1984, 7–9).

Fairhope's constitution does not allow individuals to own land. The land is owned by the association on behalf of the entire membership.

Although the Fairhope community is called a single-tax community, the community itself does not have the power to tax its members. Fairhope members have to pay the same taxes to the government as anyone else in Alabama. Fairhope then refunds some of those taxes to its members, while at the same time collecting rent from the leased land. In this way, it tries to simulate the idea of the single tax. The rent is used for community projects such as parks and roads (Alyea and Alyea 1956, 6, 112–113; www.fairhopesingletax.com/).

Daily Life

Fairhope members were and are in charge of building their own homes and earning their own money. However, the community did provide employment in building roads, a wharf, and other community amenities. At first, the community paid members with internal money, "scrip" that could be used to pay off debts to the colony (Alyea and Alyea 1956, 70–74).

Residents of the Fairhope colony organized many groups and clubs, including the Progressive League, which met on Sunday afternoons to discuss any subject they chose, including single tax and socialism. Residents also formed the Women's Suffrage Association, a band, a dancing assembly, and the Village Improvement Association (Alyea and Alyea 1956, 82–84).

How They Made Their Living

Members of Fairhope were and are in charge of their own personal finances. As a community, Fairhope has taken in revenue in the form of rent on the land, membership fees, and fees from its wharf. The community has spent this money on such projects as schools, a cemetery, a public library, parks, roads, and land purchases (Alyea and Alyea 1956, 60, 204).

The community has tried several cooperative business ventures. When it first started, it operated a cooperative store, which ended within a year because it was not profitable (Alyea and Alyea 1956, 43–44).

Fairhope built its own wharf, which was economically successful. After building the wharf, members began thinking they would like to have a community boat to bring visitors to Fairhope and increase tourist revenue. Fairhope members worked to build this boat, which was paid for through outside subscriptions and was launched in 1901. The steamer, named *Fairhope*, was not a financial success, and was destroyed by fire in 1905 (Alyea and Alyea 1956, 79–80).

In 1904, the Fairhope community began operating a telephone system with only 12 subscribers. Users had to buy their own phone, but the service itself was free, paid for by the community. Many Fairhope residents who did not have a telephone were upset at this use of community money, when the water system was still inadequate (Alyea and Alyea 1956, 78–79).

Gaston wanted to build a railroad at Fairhope in order to connect it with the outside world and to supplement the wharf they had already built. The community was to provide some of the money for this railroad, with the rest coming from outside investors. By 1916, a mile of track for the People's Railroad had been laid. But the community could do no more—not enough financing was secured, and the wharf, which was not insured, was damaged by a tropical storm, putting additional strain on the community's finances. In 1923, the community decided to abandon its railroad project altogether (Alyea and Alyea 1956, 147–153).

Leadership and Decision Making

Fairhope is ultimately run by its members. An executive council is elected, made up of the leaders of various departments. However, at any time, 10 percent of the members of Fairhope can petition for an issue to be voted on by the entire membership. Except for amending its constitution, Fairhope is ruled by a majority vote. Changes to the constitution require agreement by three-quarters of the members (Alyea and Alyea 1956, 13).

Even from the beginning, nonmembers living at Fairhope outnumbered members. These nonmembers have no voting rights (Alyea and Alyea 1956, 202; www.fairhope singletax.com/).

How New Members Were Recruited or Chosen

Fairhope attracted members from among socialists as well as single taxers. In 1901, a number of socialists from the dying Ruskin community in Georgia joined the Fairhope community (Alyea and Alyea 1956, 93).

The community's progressive school for children, the School of Organic Education, attracted students and families from around the country.

Potential members must be at least 18 years old and must buy at least one share of stock in Fairhope for a membership fee of $100. Applicants must be approved by the executive council and the membership (Alyea and Alyea 1956, 13, 44).

As of 2007, potential members had to enroll in a once-a-week class, which lasts for 11 weeks, on single-tax economics and how the Fairhope land is valued and taxed. Most people who live on Fairhope Single Tax Corporation land are not members, which means that although they pay rent, they cannot vote within the community or serve as an officer (www.fairhopesingletax.com/).

Children and Youth

The community pledged to provide free schooling to its children. The first school was started in 1896. At times when the community did not have enough money to pay the teacher, it sometimes charged students a fee for this school, which was open to non-Fairhope children as well. The state of Alabama also provided some money for the school (Alyea and Alyea 1956, 75–76).

In 1907, a Fairhope member, Marietta Johnson, started a second school within the community, the School of Organic Education. Johnson had worked as a public school teacher in Fairhope and elsewhere; she began to take issue with the idea of "training" children and instead started to see the benefits of "growing" children: "In training we often dominate or force in order to accomplish certain definite external results. In growing we provide the right conditions . . . and the moving power is within! If the child is wholesomely, happily, intelligently employed, he is being educated!" she stated (quoted in Alyea and Alyea 1956, 154).

Johnson's school was free for Fairhope children and charged tuition for outside children. About half of the Fairhope children attended the School of Organic Education. The school accepted students from age four through high school. There were no grades and no rewards or punishments. Johnson did not believe in teaching children to read until they were older than eight. Crafts, music, drama, and folk dancing were considered just as important as academics. Students also were involved in building school buildings, planting gardens, sewing uniforms for the sports teams, and other maintenance activities. High school students learned the usual academic courses—history, literature, languages, mathematics, and science—in addition to the arts and crafts and a class on single-tax economics. Many students from the Organic School went on to attend college (Gaston 1984, 90–100).

Johnson believed that single-tax economics and her Organic School were two sides of the same coin in terms of creating a better world. While single-tax economics was a way to equalize wealth, her progressive education was a way to ensure that children grew up in freedom and would, as adults, challenge injustice. "No great economic reform can be effected by people who have been trained during the growing years to believe that success is in 'passing' at school and in 'making money' in life," she declared (quoted in Gaston 1984, 80).

Joseph Fels, a wealthy single-tax supporter, donated $10,000 to the school. The Fairhope community donated land and buildings until the school had a 10-acre campus. Johnson also conducted fund-raising campaigns across the country. At its height in 1920, the school had 220 students (Gaston 1984, 79, 81–82, 100).

The School of Organic Education was still operating in Fairhope as of 2007, as a private school up to grade eight.

Relationship with the Outside World

Fairhope residents seemed to have had few problems with the outside world. Outsiders often saw Fairhope residents as very intellectual and artistic and generally admired them for these traits (Alyea and Alyea 1956, 83). Outsiders sent their children to Fairhope schools and sometimes joined Fairhope members at their dances (Gaston 1984, 99).

Influence on the Outside World

Although Fairhope aimed to be a model single-tax community that would prove the benefits of the single tax theory, it fell short in that respect. According to C. A. Gaston, who served as Fairhope's secretary from 1936 to 1972 and who wrote a brief history of the community that appears on its Web site, Fairhope was not able to fully demonstrate the benefits of the single-tax theory because its land holdings were too small and of poor quality and because its land was not held in one solid block.

Nevertheless, Fairhope has proven that there is something beneficial about the single-tax theory. Fairhope grew more quickly than other communities in Baldwin County, despite having poor land. Fairhope residents also enjoyed public services earlier than other communities, because they financed these services themselves (Alyea and Alyea 1956, 253–255).

Fairhope has made positive contributions on the local community and the nation. The library started at the Fairhope colony eventually grew to become the public library of the town of Fairhope, Alabama. Marietta Johnson, who started the School of Organic Education in Fairhope, also started at least nine other similar schools in other parts of the country. In her time, she was considered one of the country's most influential advocates of progressive education (Gaston 1984, 84–87).

Other Single-Tax Communities

Besides Fairhope, three other single-tax communities, known as the "three Ardens" in Delaware, have been long-lasting: Arden (founded in 1900), Ardentown (founded in 1922), and Ardencroft (founded in 1950).

Like Fairhope, the Arden communities own their land in common, and residents have 99-year leases. The Ardens are also based on the Arts and Crafts movement founded by William Morris. In fact, Arden first started as a summer arts colony. The name *Arden* comes from the forest in Shakespeare's play *As You Like It*.

In addition to the arts, nature is also very important to members of the three Ardens. Tree-lined paths connect the homes there. About half of the land in Arden is public space, open to anyone. Its community forest is named "Sherwood Forest," from the legend of Robin Hood.

Residents of the Ardens believe in direct democracy. Anyone 18 and above who has lived in the town for more than six months is considered part of the town council and can participate in meetings, which are held four times per year, according to the Ardens' Web site.

As of 2007, the three Ardens had a combined population of about 1,000. The Ardens are listed on the National Register of Historic Places.

See also: Bellamy, Edward; George, Henry; Gronlund, Laurence; Ruskin; Socialism

References

Alyea, Paul, and Blanche Alyea. *Fairhope, 1894–1954: The Story of a Single Tax Colony.* Tuscaloosa: University of Alabama Press, 1956.

Brown, Robin. "Arden: As They Like It." *Delaware Online News Journal*, May 17, 2004, www.delawareonline.com/apps/pbcs.dll/article?AID=/99999999/HOMES05/51228005/1182 (accessed April 2007).

Gaston, Paul. *Women of Fair Hope.* Athens: University of Georgia Press, 1984.

Young, Arthur Nichols. *The Single Tax Movement in the United States.* Princeton, NJ: Princeton University Press, 1916.

WEB SITES

Fairhope Public Library: www.fairhopelibrary.org/history.htm (accessed April 2007).

Fairhope School of Organic Education: www.fairhopeorganicschool.com/ (accessed April 2007).

Fairhope Single Tax Corporation: www.fairhopesingletax.com/ (accessed April 2007).

The Three Ardens: www.theardens.com/ (accessed April 2007).

Family

Utopian communities have a variety of ways to structure families and family relationships within the community. However, in almost all cases, the goal (stated or unstated) is to weaken bonds between married or related people, and to replace these biological family bonds with a bonding of the entire community. Some communities actually refer to themselves as a family or include the word *family* in the name of the group, such as The Family/Children of God; Love Family; and Rainbow Family of Living Light. Others use the word *brother*, as in: Brotherhood of the New Life and Bruderhof (which can be translated as "Brother's Place"). This weakening of biological family bonds helps to make sure that individuals are more loyal to the community than to their spouses or relatives and this in turn helps ensure the survival of the community as a whole.

Sociologist Rosabeth Moss Kanter suggests four basic ways in which utopian communities weaken biological family life within the community: they do not differentiate very much between nuclear families and the rest of the group; the entire community performs functions normally thought of as "family" functions; there is not much difference between domestic work and work for money; and there is a flexible division of labor (1973, 287–288).

Some communities have completely done away with nuclear family bonds. The Shakers, for example, were a celibate community in which men and women lived separately. Groups of unrelated men and women were organized into "families" who lived under one roof (the men on one side of the building, the women on the other).

The Oneida community also completely did away with biological family bonds, but in a very different way: instead of being celibate, every man was considered married to every woman, and they took turns having sexual relations with each other. Members were not supposed to show special affection for any one person. Children were raised separately from their parents and were only permitted to visit their parents once a week, in order to prevent any special attachment between children and biological parents.

Celibacy or unusual sexual practices were prevalent in other communities as well. The Branch Davidian leader, David Koresh, decreed that all the men in the community were to be celibate, and that only he, Koresh, was allowed to have sexual relations with the women, with their consent. The leader of the House of David movement was not as forthcoming about his actions: although he preached celibacy for the rest of the community, even for married couples, he secretly had sexual relations with many of the women. Mormons experimented with polygamy.

Portrait of a Mormon family. Man poses with his six wives, ca. 1885. (Library of Congress)

Some communities do not do away with biological family bonds, but they try to weaken this bond in other ways. The Moravians allowed monogamous marriage, but the married men and women lived in separate houses, just as the single members did. Twin Oaks, a modern secular community, provides separate rooms for each member, whether they are married or partnered, or not. For a time, The Farm experimented with "four-marriages," in which two couples were committed to each other. Married couples in the International Society of Krishna Consciousness (Hare Krishnas) were only to have sexual relations in order to procreate and then only after chanting for six hours. Married members of The Family were allowed to have sexual relations with other members as long as their spouses agreed.

The Amana Colonies allowed couples to marry and to live together, but celibacy was valued more than marriage. When couples got married, and each time they had a child, they were demoted in rank by being made to sit farther toward the front in the church service. Within the Hutterite communities, monogamous marriage is strongly encouraged, as is having children, and biological families live together. However, family bonds are weakened in other ways: the men eat their communal meals separately from the women, and the children have their own dining room. Married Hutterites are asked to vow that, should they leave the community, they will not persuade their spouses to follow. In this way, loyalty to the community is given a higher place than loyalty to one's spouse.

Another way of weakening biological family ties is by taking on new names or by not using last names. The celibate members of the Ephrata Cloister took on new names and referred to each other as Sister and Brother. Members of the Peace Mission Movement were asked to renounce their biological family ties and were given new "spiritual" names. Members of Twin Oaks go by their first names only, and if a new member joins with the same first name as an existing member, that new member must choose a new first name.

Since biological families ties have been weakened, the community often carries out functions traditionally performed within a biological family. Members of utopian communities often eat together in large, communal dining halls. Utopian communities celebrate and worship together. Often, the community's founding day or the founder's birthday are important holidays.

Historically, child rearing was another community function in utopian communities. In a number of communities, children had a separate dwelling where they slept and were cared for. For a time, Hare Krishna children were sent hundreds of miles away from their parents to Hare Krishna boarding schools and were rarely visited by their parents. In other communities, such as the Bruderhof and Hutterites, children live with their parents but are cared for and educated during much of the day in communal nurseries and schools. During The Farm's income-sharing phase, children lived with their parents, but mothers often took turns caring for and even nursing each other's children.

In a utopian community, important life decisions are often made by the community, not by the family unit. The Zoar community decided to be celibate for many years, in order to free the women from childbearing so they could perform community work. When a Hutterite community splits in two, no one knows who will be asked to stay and who will move to the new location. All families pack and get ready to leave before the final decision is made. Marriages within the Moravian community were arranged by the leaders of the community. Among the Amish, members must abide by strict community rules regarding dress, behavior, personal possessions, and livelihood. In many communities, work is assigned by leaders. Various communities have a set schedule for the day, including times for waking up, going to bed, meals, and worship.

Within a traditional nuclear family unit, domestic chores fell to the women and were not considered as important as work done for wages (men's work). Utopian communities tend not to make this distinction between domestic chores and work that brings cash into the community. All members receive the benefits of community life for whatever work they do. For example, members of Twin Oaks must work 42 hours per week, which can include cooking, cleaning, and child care, in addition to hammock making, one of their most important businesses. Members of Ruskin, both women and men, received the same wage per hour no matter what work they performed and mothers of young children were paid a wage for caring for their own children.

While in a traditional nuclear family system jobs are often fixed for life (a concept that began changing late in the 20th century); in many utopian communities, members have always had the opportunity to perform a number of different jobs: Oneida members often switched jobs to avoid boredom. At Twin Oaks, members might be a manager in one area and a worker in another area. The Brotherhood of the New

Life purposely encouraged members to work in areas in which they were not familiar in order to promote spiritual growth.

See also: Children and Child Rearing; Women, Status of

Reference

Kanter, Rosabeth Moss, ed. *Communes: Creating and Managing the Collective Life*. New York: Harper and Row, 1973.

The Family/Children of God

At a Glance

Dates of existence in United States: 1968 to present
Locations: nationwide and worldwide
Peak membership: 10,000
Religious or other belief: evangelical Christianity

History

The Family, one of the more controversial among American utopian communities, was the first group to be targeted by modern anticult activists.

The Family was started by David Berg, who came from a family of evangelical preachers. In 1968, he and his wife and children began preaching to hippie teens at a Christian coffee house in Huntington Beach, California. As such, Berg's group was one of the "Jesus People" groups popular among hippies in the 1960s. People who converted to Berg's views were asked to give up their jobs and education, contribute their savings to the movement, and move into the Berg's home.

Starting in 1969, Berg and his 50 followers began traveling around North America gathering more supporters. At this point, Berg started a relationship with a follower, Karen Zerby, known within The Family as "Maria." She began to lead the movement with him. In 1970, the group settled into two communities, one in Texas and one in Los Angeles.

The movement did not yet have a name, but a member of the media called them the "Children of God," and the name stuck. In August 1971, parents whose adult children had joined with Berg formed a group to "rescue" and "deprogram" members of the Children of God.

Berg and Maria began traveling around the world. In 1972, Berg had a dream about mass destruction in the United States. He asked his followers to leave the United States and set up small colonies around the world. By 1973, the group had 2,400 members in 140 communities in 40 countries. Within two years, this number had grown to over 4,000 members in 725 communities in 70 countries (Van Zandt 1991, 43–44; Chancellor 2000, 5).

Berg reorganized the leadership of the group during the 1970s and gave it the name Family of Love, which eventually became simply The Family. Also in the 1970s, he introduced the controversial practice of "flirty fishing"—women members would engage in romantic encounters and even sexual relationships with men whom they hoped to convert. Flirty fishing was meant to demonstrate God's love to the men.

A group of members from The Family. The Family is an international Christian community focused on sharing the Christian message with others. (Carol Cunningham/The Family International)

The practice was abandoned in 1987, partly because of AIDS and venereal disease, and partly because of public outcry against the practice.

Berg died in 1994. Maria continues to lead the community along with her new husband, Steven Kelly (called "Peter Amsterdam" within The Family). According to the Family Web site, as of 2007 there were about 10,000 members in 1,100 communities in 100 countries.

Beliefs and Practices

The Family is similar to other evangelical Protestant religions in that they believe that (1) the Bible is the word of God, (2) people can be saved and go to heaven through faith in Jesus Christ, and (3) the end of the world is near, and that Jesus will reappear on Earth to save humanity. Its mission is to talk to others about Jesus Christ and persuade them to accept Jesus as their savior.

The Family differs from other evangelical Protestant denominations in that its members do not believe sexuality is sinful. Rather, they see it as beautiful and normal. Berg promoted what he called the Law of Love, which allowed extramarital sexual relations as long as all partners were motivated by love, not selfishness. While marriage is the norm in The Family, adult members are permitted to engage in sexual "sharing" with others to whom they are not married, as long as all spouses agree. They also have a relaxed attitude toward sex among teenagers and toward lesbianism. However, they believe that the Bible prohibits homosexual activity among men. They also believe the Bible prohibits birth control and abortion (Bainbridge 2002, 117–139; Melton "Sexuality," 1994, 73, 76).

The Family believes that Berg, also known as Moses David or Father David, was a prophet who received messages from the spiritual world. Berg's letters to the movement, called "Mo Letters," are seen as important religious documents. The Family believes in living communally, like the early Christian church as described in Acts of the Apostles in the New Testament (Melton "The Family," 1994, 252–261).

The Family does not have churches. It holds informal "Fellowship" evenings, which include singing, Bible reading, and sharing a communion of bread and wine. Family members pray individually and in groups several times a day. Sometimes the prayers are spontaneous and other times they are planned. Members read the Bible and memorize verses and read the letters written by Berg and Maria (Bainbridge 2002, 38, 69–75).

Daily Life

Members live in cooperative group homes all over the world. Each home often includes a dozen or more members, including parents and children. Members can move from one home to another, as long as they can pay their way to the new home and the new home accepts them. Homes in need of new members advertise for them through Family publications and networks (Bainbridge 2002, 25–29).

While some members work at jobs outside the home, most work within the home or engage in Family work such as distributing Family literature and talking with outsiders, and performing volunteer work to help the poor and needy. Work within the group homes includes child care, teaching children, maintaining the home, cooking, and cleaning. Some members help produce The Family's literature tracts, music, or videos (Bainbridge 2002, 38–42).

Although living arrangements vary, in general the married couples are assigned a room together. Children under three sleep with their parents. After that, they move into the sleeping rooms designated for girls or boys. Members wake up between 7:00 and 8:00 a.m. After washing up and quiet reading time, they gather for group prayer or Bible reading. Members then prepare breakfast and clean the house. By 10:00 or 11:00 a.m., everyone is working. By 7:00 p.m., members return home for dinner and some free time. In the evening, members sing and dance. On Sundays, they have more free time (Van Zandt 1991, 57–63).

According to The Family's Web site, each home schedules an hour per day, and one day per week, for parents to spend with their children.

How They Make Their Living

The Family survives on donations of money, food, clothing, and other goods and services from supportive outsiders. When members join, they are expected to give all their money and possessions to The Family. A few members of The Family hold outside jobs that bring in money.

For a time, in some areas of the world (such as Thailand and Australia), women from The Family worked for escort agencies as a way to convert more men and as a way to earn income (Van Zandt 1991, 52).

The Family accepts donations of money from outside supporters. The Family also engages in what its members call "provisioning." They approach grocery stores, restaurants, and other businesses, explain that they are a missionary group, and ask if the business would like to help by providing free food, car repair, medical care, or other services. Some Family homes have arrangements to take leftover food from restaurants or grocery stores at the end of the day.

Housing can be a challenge. Sometimes Family members can find cheap places to stay by offering to rent (without a lease) a home that is unoccupied or by agreeing to fix up a house in exchange for rent (Bainbridge 2002, 31–38).

Leadership and Decision Making

The leadership of The Family has changed over the years. At first, Berg and his extended family were the leaders of the movement. In 1975, he created many more leadership positions and required that these leaders be elected by the members.

At the end of the 1970s, Berg removed almost all leaders between himself and the communal households. Each home was to have an elected leadership, and this leadership was to include citizens of the host nation. Each home was to post Berg's address in a prominent place, and members were asked to write directly to him with any problems (Van Zandt 1991, 45–50).

The organization's headquarters is called World Services, and as of 2007 was led by Maria and her husband, Peter Amsterdam. According to xfamily.org, an online encyclopedia about The Family, World Services has no fixed location but is a collection of undercover homes that handle the finances, publications, and special projects of The Family.

How New Members Are Recruited or Chosen

New members are recruited by personal contact with a member of The Family. The Family has used many techniques to publicize their movement and to attract new members, including handing out tracts of their literature; picketing established churches; opening discos to attract young people; and engaging in romantic or sexual encounters with lonely men.

Children and Youth

Birth control is not allowed in The Family and women often give birth to many children. The children are schooled at home or sometimes sent to local public or private schools.

The Family has been accused of child abuse, including encouraging sexual activity between children and adults. Berg published a book about Maria's son, Davidito, which included photos of Davidito as a toddler engaged in sex play with his female caretakers. The idea was that he should be allowed to explore his sexuality freely. Davidito—who later changed his name to Ricky Rodriguez—left The Family in 2001. In 2005, he killed one of his former nannies and then fatally shot himself. In a video he made before this murder-suicide, he said he had a need for revenge because of his abusive childhood. A reporter for the *New York Times* interviewed several other people who were former members of The Family and found that as children they had also engaged in sexual activity with other children and adults (Goodstein 2005).

Berg's oldest daughter, Deborah Berg Davis, who left The Family in the late 1970s, wrote a book in which she accused her father of attempting to have a sexual relationship with her and of actually having such a relationship with her younger sister.

In 1987, Berg issued guidelines threatening to excommunicate anyone found to have had sexual contact with a minor. In the late 1980s and early 1990s, Berg also made it clear that teens were to wait until they were 16 or 18 to begin engaging in a sexual relationship with other teens (Van Zandt 1991, 170; Melton "Sexuality," 1994, 90–92).

The most comprehensive outside review of The Family's possible connection with child abuse was undertaken by a judge in Great Britain, Lord Justice Alan Ward, in response to a British grandmother who filed for custody of her grandson, who lived in a Family home with his mother. Although in the past Family leadership had denied that children were involved with sexual activity, this case forced them to admit that, in fact, some minors had been subjected to such activity (Chancellor 2000, 30–31).

In 1995, Ward decided that the group had, in the past, been abusive toward some children through cases of sexual abuse and severe corporal punishment. "I am completely satisfied that he [David Berg] was obsessed with sex and that he became a perverted man who recklessly corrupted his flock and did many of them serious damage that he made no attempt to redress and for which he never admitted any personal responsibility," Ward wrote in his opinion. Ward also stated that The Family no longer engaged in these practices and that Family homes were safe environments for children. "I am impressed by the winds of change that have blown and continue to blow through The Family. Although sullied by their participation in the sexual excesses, Maria and Peter Amsterdam have demonstrated convincingly a willingness to change. With Berg's death they have an opportunity subtly yet dramatically to change further. In my judgment, they may be ready to do so" (Ward 1995).

Relationship with the Outside World

The Family refers to the outside world as "the System" and to established churches as "Churchianity." Members believe that the outside world, including established Christian churches, is corrupt.

However, Family members interact extensively with the outside world. They often live in urban areas, spend hours per day talking to outsiders about Jesus Christ, and perform charitable work. Followers often own televisions and are connected to the Internet. However, they keep their identity as members of The Family through their own internal publications and songs that help connect individual Family homes to the larger international network (Bainbridge 2002, 29–31).

Because its members engaged in unusual sexual practices at times in its history, The Family has been the target of persecution. In Mexico, Argentina, Spain, Australia, and France, Family homes have been invaded, Family members jailed, and children removed from their parents because authorities believed the children were being abused. The charges were eventually dropped in these cases (Bainbridge 2002, 1–20; Bromley and Newton 1994, 44).

Family members engage in a variety of volunteer and charitable activities. According to The Family Web site, members have helped with relief work following hurricanes in the United States; floods in France, the United States, Venezuela, and Mozambique; earthquakes in India, the United States, Japan, and Taiwan; and other disasters. They have also reportedly helped in refugee camps in the former Yugoslavia and Kosovo and offered humanitarian aid in Russia.

Influence on the Outside World

The Family spawned the modern anticult movement. It was the first of the 1960s utopian communities to be targeted by deprogrammers.

Ted Patrick, who would later become famous as a deprogrammer, was alarmed when his son came home in a daze after meeting with members of the Children of God. Patrick formed Free Our Children from the Children of God with other concerned parents who were afraid their children had been "brainwashed" into joining the Children of God. Patrick quit his job (he worked for then California governor Ronald Reagan) and began kidnapping some Children of God members and deprogramming them. Deprogramming consisted of locking people in rooms, shouting at them, and not allowing them to leave until they denounced their belief in the Children of God. By the spring of 1979, the anticult movement had grown and Patrick had deprogrammed 1,600 people from a variety of unusual religious movements (Wangerin 1993, 32–33, 150, 154–159).

The anticult movement has since been discredited. In 1996, one of the largest anticult groups, the Cult Awareness Network (CAN), was found to provide misleading information about new religious movements as well as referrals to deprogrammers. These deprogrammers charged families thousands of dollars per case and then paid CAN a portion of their fee (Shupe et al 2002, 21–25).

See also: Bible Communism; Cults; Hippies; Jesus People USA

References

Bainbridge, William Sims. *The Endtime Family: Children of God*. Albany: State University of New York Press, 2002.

Bromley, David G., and Sidney H. Newton. "The Family: History, Organization and Ideology," in *Sex, Slander and Salvation: Investigating The Family/Children of God*. Stanford, CA: Center for Academic Publication, 1994, 41–46.

Chancellor, James D. *Life in the Family: An Oral History of the Children of God*. Syracuse, NY: Syracuse University Press, 2000.

Davis, Deborah (Linda Berg). *The Children of God: The Inside Story*. Grand Rapids, MI: Zondervan Publishing House, 1984.

Goodstein, Laurie. "Murder and Suicide Revising Claims of Child Abuse in Cult." *New York Times*, January 15, 2005, A1.

Melton, J. Gordon. "The Family: Where Does It Fit?" in *Sex, Slander and Salvation: Investigating The Family/Children of God.* Stanford, CA: Center for Academic Publication, 1994, 253–261.

Melton, J. Gordon. "Sexuality and the Maturation of the Family," in *Sex, Slander and Salvation: Investigating The Family/Children of God.* Stanford, CA: Center for Academic Publication, 1994, 71–95.

Shupe, Anson, Susan E. Darnell, and Kendrick Moxon. "The Cult Awareness Network and the Anticult Movement: Implications for NRMs in America," in *New Religious Movements and Religious Liberty in America,* edited by Derek H. Davis and Barry Hankins. Waco, TX: J. M. Dawson Institute of Church-State Studies and Baylor University Press, 2002, 21–44.

Van Zandt, David. *Living in the Children of God.* Princeton, NJ: Princeton University Press, 1991.

Wangerin, Ruth. *The Children of God: A Make-Believe Revolution?* Westport, CT: Bergin and Garvey, 1993.

Ward, Lord Justice Alan. "Complete Judgment of Lord Justice Ward," May 26, 1995, www.xfamily.org/index.php/Judgment_of_Lord_Justice_Ward (accessed February 2007).

WEB SITES

The Family: www.thefamily.org/ (accessed February 2007).

XFamily.org, an online encyclopedia about The Family: www.xfamily.org/ (accessed February 2007).

The Farm

At a Glance

Dates of existence in United States: 1971 to present
Location: Summertown, Tennessee
Peak membership: 1,500
Religious or other belief: eclectic spiritualism

History

The Farm is one of the largest and longest-lasting hippie communities. Although it began as a community in 1971, its roots were established in the early 1960s, when a teacher at San Francisco State University, Stephen Gaskin, became interested in his students' "hippie" lifestyle.

At the age of 27, Gaskin found that marijuana and LSD helped open spiritual doors for him. However, he was concerned about the naiveté of his students. He began holding classes through the Experimental College at the university on subjects of interest to young adults at that time, including world religions, parapsychology, sociology, and psychology. These classes grew so popular that they moved off campus. They were held on Monday nights and were soon referred to simply as the "Monday Night Class." Over a thousand people attended the class each week.

In 1969, the American Academy of Religion invited Gaskin to tour the country and speak. When he told his Monday night class about this opportunity, some of them decided to join him on his tour. As Gaskin toured, more people joined the Caravan, as it came to be called, until at its peak there were 100 vehicles and 300 people. While on this trip, Gaskin decided to give up the use of LSD. After four months, when the group returned to San Francisco, many of the members did not want to re-enter "normal life." They longed to buy land and create a spiritual community of their own, but land was expensive in California.

The group had met some friendly people in Nashville, Tennessee, and Gaskin announced that the Caravan would leave for Tennessee to buy land there. In 1971, they settled in Lewis County, one of the poorest counties in Tennessee, where they began to grow a vegetable garden, including marijuana plants. Gaskin felt that it was acceptable to grow and use marijuana but unacceptable to take money in exchange for it. Gaskin also became a licensed minister: the only requirement in Tennessee was the existence of a congregation and services. At this point, the community had about 300 members.

That same year, the police raided The Farm and arrested Gaskin and three others for growing marijuana. Despite two years of legal appeals, Gaskin ended up serving one year of a three-year prison sentence.

By 1980, The Farm had grown to over 1,400 members. But the community was heavily in debt. Perhaps The Farm was trying to do too much: expand its membership, start a nonprofit organization (Plenty—see below), and keep several businesses afloat.

In 1983, the community experienced a crisis that it calls the Changeover. In order to deal with its financial difficulties, the group decided to change its practice of complete income-sharing. Land is still held in common, but since 1983, each family has been responsible for supporting itself and for paying dues to the community. Because of the Changeover, a majority of members left The Farm.

By 1987, the debt on the land was completely paid off. As of 2006, The Farm had about 200 members.

Beliefs and Practices

Brian Pfaffenberger described The Farm's religion before the 1983 Changeover as "a remarkable syncretism of several religious and philosophical traditions, including Tantric Hinduism, Mahayana Buddhism, Zen, Christianity, and humanistic psychology. These traditions are woven together into a single faith that, in Stephen's [Gaskin] view, expresses the essence of all religions" (1982, 172).

According to The Farm's Web site, the goal of the founders was "To live a 'back to the land' lifestyle while still remaining engaged in social change to make the world a better place. To create a new social experiment based on compassion and a spiritual relationship to your fellow beings on the planet" (http://thefarmcommunity.com/about%5Fthe%5Ffarm/frequently%5Fasked%5Fquestions).

The Farm derived a part of its inspiration from the Book of Acts in the Bible, which describes the communal lifestyle of the early Christians. Farm members were required to sign a vow of poverty, agreeing to give all money to the community (Fike 1998, 9).

When The Farm began, Gaskin was its spiritual leader. He taught that humans are one with other humans, animals, and Earth. He also taught that people can and should get in touch with their "higher self" through such techniques as meditation, consuming marijuana, and making love. Gaskin encouraged members to bridge the gap between generations by visiting their parents and speaking honestly and politely to everyone.

During Sunday morning services, which were held outdoors when the weather permitted, members engaged in an hour of silent meditation and then listened to a talk by Gaskin. Members were encouraged to get involved in the discussion. "Sunday morning services were the focal point of The Farm's spiritual life and, for many individuals, the highlight of the week. They were regarded as a chance to relax and open up, reflect on the cares of the week and then transcend them, to touch base with the rest of the community. Just about everybody attended the services, the adults taking turns staying home and babysitting" (Traugot 1998, 53).

Sex was considered a "holy sacrament," like birth and death, "to be practiced with as few distractions as possible. Thus, sexual union was a time for cleansing oneself of psychic debris, making the subconscious conscious, and dealing with any disagreements the couple may have had during the day. This promoted solid marriages. Hence, making love was at the core of the community" (Traugot 1998, 50).

For many years, The Farm did not believe in abortion or artificial methods of birth control. However, it did feel the need for some way to regulate pregnancy. A member, Margaret Nofziger, researched the subject of natural birth control and in 1976 wrote *A Cooperative Method of Natural Birth Control*. This book became a best seller for The Farm.

The Farm members were vegan (they did not consume any animal products or wear leather), and they did not allow tobacco, alcohol, or hard drugs.

There were some unusual sexual practices on The Farm, most notably "four-marriages," in which four people were committed to each other. "These were not 'swingin' or 'swappin,' but serious attempts at a new, more inclusive kind of family," explains a Farm member. "The four adults considered themselves married in all ways, including raising and providing for all their children, and were sexually faithful to each other. They purposely varied sexual partners to 'split fields,' to get to know both opposite-sex partners as well as possible. They were expected to be very close to their same-sex partner" (quoted in Traugot 1998, 49).

However, most members were fairly traditional in terms of relationships. Gaskin preached that "if you're sleeping together, you're considered engaged, and if you're pregnant, you're considered married." As a licensed minister, Gaskin performed weddings and encouraged couples to get marriage licenses. "The community protected marriage in various ways; couples were given a lot of help and advice in sorting out their relationships, and those who allowed themselves to become romantically involved with someone else's spouse could wind up having to leave the community for 30 days" (Traugot 1998, 46, 48).

Over the years, the beliefs of Farm members have evolved. The Farm's Web site explains their current belief system in this way: "As a church we live in community, and our reverence for life has always been central to our community ways. Within The Farm community people can live together and pursue a spiritual path that includes but is not limited to the following beliefs and agreements." The beliefs and agreements listed include veganism, nonviolence, honesty, and compassion. The church's sacraments include marriage, childbirth, and death. Members believe in nonmaterial planes of consciousness, the highest of which is the spiritual plane (http://thefarmcommunity.com/about_the_farm/our_beliefs.asp).

Since the 1983 Changeover, Sunday morning services are still held, but Gaskin is no longer considered the main spiritual leader of the community.

Daily Life

The Farm is located on three square miles in rural Tennessee. At first, members lived in army surplus tents or built their own buildings, often from salvaged material. Living conditions were crowded and primitive: there was no running water for many

Circle gathering at The Farm in Summertown, Tennessee. The Farm is one of the longest lasting hippie communities in the United States. (Douglas Stevenson/Village Media)

years. As many as 60 people lived in a single building. Some lived in converted buses or vans. There was no electricity. "Each Farm household functioned as a team. People took turns doing the dishes, cleaning, and cooking meals" (Traugot 1998, 49, 51).

Although most Farm members hailed from urban environments, they quickly learned to grow their own food. Peter Jenkins visited The Farm in 1974 and reported on the community's productivity: 85 tons of potatoes, 40 tons of sweet potatoes, 65 tons of soybeans, 1,355 bushels of yellow corn, 166 bushels of cabbage, 25 tons of tomatoes, and 800 bushels of spinach. Farm members worked dawn to dusk to plant, harvest, can, and freeze their food (1979, 209–211).

During its first 12 years of existence, The Farm was completely communal. Everyone received an equal share of food and people requested money for special needs from the "Bank Lady" (Traugot 1998, 52).

In the early years of the 21st century, The Farm members generally live in single-family homes with running water and electricity. Owners often help design and build their homes. Many of the homes incorporate passive solar technology and energy efficiency.

The Farm also includes a grocery store, a medical clinic, a gas station, schools, a pharmacy, a post office, a cemetery, and various businesses.

Despite the fact that The Farm started and grew at the time of the women's liberation movement, Farm members did adhere to some traditional gender roles, at least before the 1983 Changeover. Women were expected to embrace motherhood, to have many children, and to create a beautiful, nurturing home. Men were supposed to support women in this role. However, women were not seen as second-class citizens. Gaskin believed that men and women had different "energies" and that mainstream society tended to ignore the female energy. Gaskin encouraged women to stand up for themselves and refuse to be intimidated by their husbands (Pfaffenberger 1982, 204–208).

After the 1983 Changeover, women's roles broadened. As of 2006, one of The Farm's largest businesses, SE International, which makes radiation-detection equipment, was owned by a woman.

How They Make Their Living

When the community was completely communal, The Farm made a living by providing construction services locally and by selling the publications of its Book Publishing Company. Members also sometimes traveled to other areas to help with the harvest and earn money.

After the Changeover, members became responsible for supporting themselves and for contributing to the running of the community. As of 2006, about a third of The Farm members worked outside the community. The rest worked for The Farm businesses, such as the Book Publishing Company, The Farm Catalog, the Soy Dairy, and so forth. Others worked for community services such as The Farm school, medical clinic, community government, or radio station. Some worked for Farm-sponsored nonprofit organizations (see below).

Leadership and Decision Making

At first, Gaskin appointed the heads of the various work crews. During Gaskin's year in prison (1974), The Farm members became more adept at running things without his leadership. When he returned, the work crew leaders came to be called the Board of Directors. Since the Changeover in 1983, the community has had an elected board. Its members hold town meetings during which the community votes on important issues.

How New Members Are Recruited or Chosen

Gaskin regularly went on speaking tours to talk about The Farm. In addition, The Farm's publishing company sold tapes of the Monday Night Classes.

Prospective members had to agree to The Farm's rules: no alcohol, tobacco, weapons, or violence; hard work; and no ownership of property. They also had to agree to be Gaskin's spiritual students. They were required to live for one year on The Farm before being accepted as permanent members.

Since 1983, when the complete income-sharing aspect of the community ended, prospective members must visit the community several times and be formally accepted by the membership committee. New members are asked to contribute a one-time membership fee.

Children and Youth

Children were and are extremely important to The Farm. Even during the Caravan phase, babies were born into the community, and because Gaskin's followers did not have much money and did not believe in accepting welfare, they decided to give birth outside of the hospital as much as possible. Gaskin's wife, Ina May Gaskin, and a few other Farm women taught themselves to be midwives by attending births, reading medical manuals, and getting informal training from a local Tennessee doctor who was comfortable with the concept of home births (Gaskin 2002, 14–21).

Within four years, half of The Farm's population was children. "Farm family life was different . . . from that of most Americans. The Farm was like a large extended family. Sometimes mothers would nurse each other's babies, blurring the line a little between the nuclear family and the 'clan' or 'tribe.' Children were cared for in groups known as 'kid herds,' different adults taking turns watching them" (Traugot 1998, 49).

The Farm started its own one-room school in 1971, which today is a K–12 school that serves community children as well as those from the outside. The school teaches a curriculum that includes math, science, technology, languages, and other subjects, with the aim of utilizing these skills to promote peace, equality, and sustainability.

Relationship with the Outside World

The outside world was very curious about The Farm. In the 1970s, the community attracted 10,000 visitors per year and film crews from the major television networks visited The Farm.

In the early 1970s, after Gaskin and others were arrested for growing marijuana, they appealed the case all the way to the U.S. Supreme Court. They argued that, just as Native Americans are allowed to use peyote in religious ceremonies, so The Farm should be allowed to grow and use marijuana for spiritual purposes. The Supreme Court refused to hear the case, and Gaskin served a year in prison (Traugot 1998, 57–58).

In the mid-1970s, The Farm started a medical clinic to serve its own community and the surrounding area (the nearest hospital was 30 miles away). The Farm's midwives made a public offer to provide prenatal care and delivery to mothers who were not sure they wanted to keep their babies. The Farm also offered to take care of the babies until the mothers wanted them back. This program ran until 1984, by which time 269 women had come to The Farm to have their babies. Twelve of these mothers left their babies with foster families on The Farm, and about half of these children were later reclaimed by the mothers or other relatives (Gaskin 2002, 123).

In keeping with their goal to have a positive effect on the outside world, The Farm members have started a number of nonprofit organizations. The first was Plenty, which began by giving extra Farm food to local hungry people. The organization also helped with disaster relief in the United States and abroad and worked in Guatemala to improve health care and sanitation. In addition, the group runs Kids to the Country, which brings inner-city children from Nashville to The Farm.

Other Farm nonprofits include PeaceRoots Alliance, to connect farmers in the struggle for peace; Ecovillage Training Center, which offers workshops in environmentally sustainable living; and the Swan Conservation Trust, which works to protect wildlife habitat and water quality in Tennessee.

Influence on the Outside World

The Farm's Book Publishing Company put out cookbooks that helped to educate the public about vegan cookery. Its book on natural birth control became a best seller, garnering bulk orders from the Catholic Church and Planned Parenthood.

Ina May Gaskin has made a name for herself as one of the most well-known midwives in the country. She developed the "Gaskin maneuver," a hands-and-knees birthing position to deliver a baby whose shoulder is stuck after the head has emerged. This is the first obstetrical procedure to be named after a midwife.

See also: Bible Communism; Ecovillages; Hippies

References

Fike, Rupert, ed. *Voices from The Farm*. Summertown, TN: Book Publishing Company, 1998.

Gaskin, Ina May. *Spiritual Midwifery*. Summertown, TN: Book Publishing Company, 2002.

Hutchens, Turner. "State's Most Famous Hippy and Founder of The Farm Turns 70 Today." *Daily Herald* (Columbia, TN), February 16, 2005.

Jenkins, Peter. *A Walk across America*. New York: Fawcett Crest, 1979, 203–217.

Pfaffenberger, Brian. "A World of Husbands and Mothers: Sex Roles and Their Ideological Context in the Formation of The Farm," in *Sex Roles in Contemporary American Communes*, edited by Jon Wagner. Bloomington: Indiana University Press, 1982, 172–210.

Sutton, Robert. *Communal Utopias and the American Experience: Secular Communities, 1824–2000*. Westport, CT: Praeger, 2003.

Traugot, Michael. "The Farm," in *Sects, Cults and Spiritual Communities: A Sociological Analysis*, edited by William Zellner and Marc Petrowsky. Westport, CT: Praeger, 1998, 41–62.

WEB SITES

Ecovillage Training Center: www.thefarm.org/etc/ (accessed October 2006).

The Farm Community: www.thefarmcommunity.com/ (accessed May 2008).

The Farm Organizations: www.thefarm.org/ (accessed October 2006).

Ina May Gaskin: www.inamay.com/ (accessed October 2006).

PeaceRoots Alliance: www.peaceroots.org/Default.aspx (accessed October 2006).

Plenty International: www.plenty.org/ (accessed October 2006).

Swan Conservation Trust: www.swantrust.org/ (accessed October 2006).

Fellowship for Intentional Community

The Fellowship for Intentional Community (FIC) is an organization that helps people connect with existing utopian communities in the United States and around the world, and helps communities connect with and learn from each other. Its Web site (www.ic.org) lists hundreds of utopian communities in existence or in the formative stages. The organization also publishes a magazine, *Communities*, and a print directory of communities, which first came out in 1990.

The FIC takes its name from a term that refers to a group of people who purposely come together to create a community. *Intentional communities* include "ecovillages, cohousing, residential land trusts, communes, student co-ops, urban housing cooperatives, and other projects where people strive together with a common vision," according to the FIC Web site.

The first edition of the FIC's *Communities Directory* listed about 300 communities; the 1995 edition listed 540 communities; and the 2007 edition has 900 communities. The FIC estimates that there might be several thousand intentional communities around the world, based on the fact that not all communities want to be publicly listed. Many of these communities are very small or in the formative stages.

The FIC Web site states: "Intentional communities have for many centuries been places where idealists have come together to create a better world. Although there are thousands of intentional communities in existence today, and many others in the formative stages, most people are unaware of them or the roots from which they spring". (www.ic.org). To remedy this situation, the Fellowship seeks to publicize such community efforts.

A final goal of the Fellowship is "to increase global awareness that intentional communities are pioneers in sustainable living, personal and community transformation, and peaceful social evolution" (www.ic.org).

See also: Cohousing; Ecovillages

WEB SITE
Fellowship for Intentional Community: www.ic.org/ (accessed August 2007).

Ferrer Colony (Stelton)

```
At a Glance

Dates of existence in United States: 1915 to 1956
Location: New Jersey
Peak membership: 200
Religious or other belief: anarchism
```

History

The Ferrer Colony was one of the largest and most successful of the anarchist communities in the United States. The community was built around a school for children, called the Modern School, which grew out of the Francisco Ferrer Association in New York City.

Francisco Ferrer was a Spanish anarchist and educator. He founded and ran the first Modern School in Barcelona, Spain, from 1901 to 1906. This school was free of the control of the church and the government and open to both boys and girls. Students did not learn by memorization, as was common at that time; instead, they learned by doing. The children and their parents participated in running the school. No rewards or punishments, and no grades, were used at the school.

In 1909, Ferrer was accused of leading a rebellion against the Spanish government, and he was put to death. His execution was covered in U.S. newspapers, and American anarchists vowed to start similar Modern Schools along Ferrer's example. In 1910, the Francisco Ferrer Association was established in New York City. Among its founders was Emma Goldman, one of the most famous anarchists in the United States. The group published books about Modern Schools and formed branches around the country. Modern Schools were started in Philadelphia, Chicago, Salt Lake City, Seattle, New York City, Detroit, San Francisco, and Los Angeles. Most of them lasted only a few years.

The New York City Modern School operated from 1911 to 1915. The school experienced ongoing financial trouble and its location in New York City attracted police spies who distrusted the anarchists. The Ferrer Association decided to move the school to Stelton, New Jersey, 30 miles south of New York City.

This was the beginning of the Ferrer Colony. In New York, there was no attempt to live communally, but in rural New Jersey, the anarchists decided to own some land in common. Each member owned his or her own lot of one or two acres, with nine acres communally owned for the school. The colony had tough times at first:

little money with which to build or insulate their buildings and difficulty finding school principals who would stay.

Eventually, the colony was able to secure loans to complete its buildings. In 1920, Elizabeth and Alexis Ferm became coprincipals of the school, providing structure and stability. By 1921, the school had about 120 students. The Ferms were opposed to abstract academic learning and instead emphasized crafts, manual arts, dance, music, and playing in the outdoors. While parents agreed that these things were important, they began to worry that academics were being neglected. In addition, some parents wanted the children to learn about political theories such as anarchism or communism, but the Ferms disagreed. Elizabeth Ferm once stated: "The savior of the world will not be the class conscious worker but the creative artist" (quoted in Avrich 1980, 280). Because of these disagreements, the Ferms left the school in 1925. Their departure marked the beginning of the decline of the school and colony.

Jim and Nellie Dick, who had been involved with the school in New York City and in the early years of Stelton, returned to Stelton in 1928 from the Mohegan colony (see below) and became coprincipals of the Stelton school. They restored the school from the chaos into which it had fallen after the departure of the Ferms. The Dicks were also dismayed by continued interference from parents, and they left in 1933.

The Ferms returned at this point to be coprincipals again. However, even their energy and hard work could not stop the decline of the school and colony. Because of the Great Depression, many parents were not able to pay even the modest tuition of the Stelton school and had to withdraw their students. In the mid-1930s, the school was so short of money that the colony sold the student boarding house, called the Living House, and boarded the students with colony members. By 1938, only 30 students attended the school (Avrich 1980, 319).

In 1940, the U.S. government bought land next to the colony and established Camp Kilmer, which became the largest processing center for troops headed overseas to fight in World War II. Soldiers frequently walked into the colony, homes were broken into, and colonists feared for their safety. Colonists began to move away. Elizabeth Ferm died in 1944; her husband, Alexis, continued as principal until 1948, when he retired. By that time, only 15 young children were enrolled in the school. Enrollment continued to decline until the school was closed in 1953. The Modern School Movement ended in 1961 (Avrich 1980, 320–326).

Beliefs and Practices

The founders of the Modern School Movement believed, in Goldman's words, that the usual public school of that time was "a veritable barrack, where the human mind is drilled and manipulated into submission to various social and moral spooks, and thus fitted to continue our system of exploitation and oppression" (quoted in Avrich 1980, 38).

The Modern Schools hoped to create a free, anarchist culture through education. "A central assumption of the colonists," says Paul Avrich, "was that the anarchist ideal of a free society without formal authority or economic oppression would be realized through the education of a generation of children uncorrupted by the commercialism and selfishness of the capitalist system and undisturbed by the political repression and indoctrination in religion or government as taught in traditional schools." The schools would operate without exams, rankings, and coercive discipline. The students would not sit in rows in front of the raised desk of the teacher (1980, 75–76; 228).

Teachers discouraged academic learning, believing instead that students should learn by doing. Each of the four classrooms in Stelton was dedicated to a different craft or manual-training activity. If students wanted to get involved in academic work, they could use the library (Veysey 1973, 141).

The school was "open" all day long, all year long. "Play and work, education and life were inextricably intertwined. School was not something that started at 9 and ended at 3. It began when the children got up and finished when they went to bed," explains Avrich (1980, 230).

Daily Life

The landscape surrounding the Ferrer Colony was unappealing: flat land that was dry and dusty in the summer, poor soil, and few trees. A brook flowed through the land, attracting mosquitoes (Veysey 1973, 116).

At first, the settlers lived in tents and shacks. One of the children, interviewed as an adult in 1972, remembered that "the nearest telephone was a mile away. There was no electricity and no central heating. We had outhouses for many years and unreliable running water. Dirt roads became impassable in the spring" (quoted in Avrich 1980, 220).

By 1920, a new school building was constructed, including four classrooms and an auditorium, and within two years over 80 houses had been built. Running water and heat were available, and about 120 children attended the Stelton school (Veysey 1973, 122).

However, even when the buildings were finished, visitors were often unimpressed with the looks of the colony. Roads were not paved, and litter was a problem. One visitor in 1921 said that the community was "a very dreary place—all but the school house." In the 1930s, another visitor described seeing "tin-cans, no trees, no shrubs, no paint or shades, a sweat shop left with 20 sewing machines in the center of the colony, no sign on the road, no road worth calling a road" (quoted in Veysey 1973, 127).

The children's lives were unstructured. They attended a morning meeting every day, during which they sang songs and played games. After that each child was allowed to choose how to spend the day. They had access to an art room, a weaving room, a woodshop, and a print shop. If they wanted to learn to read, they asked the reading teacher for help. Some students spent much of their time outdoors, playing games or swimming in the brook (Oral History, Stelton Transcript, 2001).

Every Saturday night the colony held communal dinners that had been prepared by some of the women. The colony held lectures on Saturday evenings on politics, history, or the arts, as well as music recitals and discussions. On Sunday evenings, the members enjoyed singing and folk dancing. Evening classes for adults were available, and plays were produced in the auditorium (Veysey 1973, 124–125).

The anarchists at the colony were interested in experimenting with diet, and sometimes the food was unusual. Most colonists and students ate a vegetarian diet. Students recall times of eating mostly nuts and raisins. One student remembers throwing oranges, tomatoes, and bananas against the wall in order to make them soft, because that was the dietary fad at the time (Avrich 1980, 238).

How They Made Their Living

Some colonists commuted to New York City for work. Others raised poultry and grew vegetables or received money by boarding schoolchildren whose parents did not live in the community.

Tuition and board fees at the Modern School were kept very low in order to allow working-class people to send their children there. Only about a quarter of the school's income came from tuition; therefore, the school did not contribute to the community's income. In fact, the students often performed in New York City, raising money to continue its operation. After 1919, trade unions began contributing to the school (Veysey 1973, 128–130).

Leadership and Decision Making

The only acknowledged leaders of the colony were the principals of the school. The colonists asked certain people to become principals.

However, as Laurence Veysey points out, no community can be as successful as the Ferrer Colony without some leadership. "Much of the credit for the survival of the colony must be given to the striking blend of egalitarianism and shrewd leadership that marked the handling of affairs, even though anarchists do not like to talk about leadership. To begin with, efforts were made to erase customary lines of status. At certain times nearly everyone participated in manual labor. . . . [F]or a while all the teachers took their terms as janitors. . . . The abolition of status differences between teachers and children was also an ideal at Stelton." The colonists had open meetings to discuss important issues, and those who had contributed much to the community, such as Harry Kelly, seemed to have made a great effort not to impose their opinions, but to make sure all colonists had input (1973, 161–162).

How New Members Were Recruited or Chosen

The Modern School Movement published a magazine, called *The Modern School*, to publicize its ideas and innovations. The Ferrer Colony held public "weekends" twice a year for outsiders to visit (Veysey 1973, 121).

Children and Youth

The community revolved around the children at the school. Some of the children lived with their parents in the colony and others were boarding students whose parents lived elsewhere.

The children were seen as capable of being able to choose their own tasks and create their own performances or products. "We did everything ourselves," recalled a former student. "We were gardeners, we were typesetters, we were cooks—we did everything with our own two hands. Instead of merely reading *A Midsummer Night's Dream*, we put on the play, and put it on outdoors" (quoted in Avrich 1980, 231).

The printing teacher helped the children to create their own literary and art journal called *Voice of the Children*. A former student, interviewed in 2001, remembered this publication: "We started the *Voice of the Children,* which was a magazine done by the children completely. We did learn to type-set and to print. A older kid would take dictation from one of the younger kids for stories and then we made prints for pictures on linoleum" (Oral History, Stelton Transcript, 2001).

Although the school did not stress academics, students could and did go on to college or to demanding careers. One student studied architecture and assisted Frank Lloyd Wright; another student became a dancer with the Martha Graham troupe; and a third became a child psychologist (Avrich 1980, 230, 286).

Former students often had fond memories of the school. One student gave the school credit for teaching "the one thing that I really needed to know in order to survive and excel in life, and that was how to learn. They taught me that I could learn anything, and I didn't need a formal, constrained program of education. That I could search and inquire and learn almost anything" (Oral History, Stelton Transcript, 2001).

Relationship with the Outside World

Until Camp Kilmer was built next door, the school and colony were isolated from the outside world by their rural location. While urban anarchists were harassed, the Ferrer Colony was largely left alone (Veysey 1973, 130–133).

Reasons for Ending the Community

The school and community ended because of financial troubles and because of the intrusion of the soldiers from Camp Kilmer on adjacent land. In addition, the anarchist movement was weakening.

A former student had this to say about the ending of the community: "Some people say it was the Camp Kilmer that caused the school to decline. I think perhaps another reason was that socialism became a lot more interesting to a lot of people than anarchism. The children had grown up. Some of the people of the community stayed there, but they didn't have any children. So there really wasn't any room for other children, and the school didn't make a big deal about trying to keep it going. There wasn't really another Alexis and Elizabeth Ferm. It was mostly, people didn't really feel that it needed to go on. There was no thrust. It was . . . the anarchists were there and they wanted their kids to go to the school, and they had grown up. And there were no more anarchists" (Oral History, Stelton Transcript, 2001).

Influence on the Outside World

The Modern School Movement hoped to start schools all over the country, but most of their schools were short-lived. Some students and teachers from the Ferrer Colony went on to teach at other schools and write about education.

In the 1960s, many educators began to experiment with and write about methods similar to those used at the Modern Schools, such as learning by doing and an informal relationship between teachers and students. Some of these educators may have been influenced by the Modern School model (Avrich 1980, 350–351).

Another Modern School Community

Harry Kelly, a founder of the Ferrer Colony, went on to start another colony, Mohegan, in New York in 1923. The physical surroundings of Mohegan were more beautiful than at Stelton: Mohegan was in a hilly, wooded area on a lake. As in Stelton, the Mohegan colonists owned their own land and homes. Many commuted to work in New York City. The school was also similar to that at Stelton: it began with a morning meeting, and the students could choose how to spend their day.

During the 1930s, the school and community suffered financially due to the Great Depression. Some people at the school were open to government support, while others wanted to be free of the government altogether. The school closed in 1941. The colony survived another 15 to 20 years but was wracked by disagreements. People who were identified as communists moved in and tried to take control of the community's leadership. By the late 1950s, community members had grown older, children had moved away, and as new people moved in, the community became a middle-class residential neighborhood (Avrich 1980, 289–311).

See also: Anarchism; Home Colony

References

Avrich, Paul. *The Modern School Movement: Anarchism and Education in the United States.* Princeton, NJ: Princeton University Press, 1980.

Oral History, Stelton Transcript, March 2001, www.talkinghistory.org/stelton/stelton_transcript.doc (accessed October 2006).

Veysey, Laurence. *The Communal Experience: Anarchist and Mystical Counter-Cultures in America.* New York: Harper and Row, 1973.

WEB SITES

History of the Stelton Modern School: www.talkinghistory.org/stelton/stelton.html (accessed October 2006).

Modern School Collection at Rutgers University: www.libraries.rutgers.edu/rul/libs/scua/modern_school/modern.shtml (accessed August 2007).

George, Henry

Henry George (1839–1897) was a newspaper editor who created the "single-tax theory," which was designed to be a simple solution to the problems of poverty and unequal distribution of wealth. He was puzzled as to why poverty persisted and even grew at the same time that wealth grew.

The idea behind the single tax is that land is a finite resource given by nature, and it has value only because of the community's demand for it. Therefore, the community as a whole should share the wealth created by popular demand for land. George urged the government to tax only the increased value of land brought about because of public demand for that land. He felt that all other taxes should be abolished, and people should be able to keep all the revenue they gain as a result of their own labor or their own capital investments. George and his followers argued that this single land tax would be enough to pay all the government's expenses.

During his time, George was very well known—in fact, his name was a household word, according to his biographer Edward Rose. George's book on economics, *Progress and Poverty*, published in 1879, became a best seller (Rose 1968, 1).

George was first struck with his single-tax idea in 1869 or 1870, when, while riding a horse outside of Oakland, California, he asked a passing man about the value of the land he was on. "Like a flash it came upon me that there was the reason of advancing poverty with advancing wealth. With the growth of population, land grows in value, and the men who work it must pay more for the privilege" (quoted in Rose 1968, 41).

Although George did not consider himself a socialist, many socialists supported him. He understood that socialism also aimed to lift people out of poverty, but he was opposed to the political ideology because he felt individual freedom was of the utmost importance. Also, while the socialists aimed to create an ideal society, George did not believe such a society could be created but had to grow based on "the free and natural development of all the parts" (Rose 1968, 75).

George's ideas gained followers who made up the single-tax movement. In 1888, the single-tax movement began circulating a petition to ask Congress to appoint a special committee to study the idea of applying the single tax as a way of raising government revenue. In 1909, a soap manufacturer, Joseph Fels, pledged $25,000 per year for five years in order to promote the single tax in the United States. The movement aimed to influence politicians and governments to try out the single-tax theory (Young, 1916, 133, 163).

Hyattsville, Maryland, experimented with the single tax for several months in 1892 and 1893. It ended the experiment when the Maryland Court of Appeals declared that the single tax violated the state's constitution (Young 1916, 145–146).

Henry George helped launch
an entire generation of
economic and social reform
in the United States with his
best-selling book, Progress
and Poverty *(1880).*
(National Archives)

Several utopian communities tried out the single-tax theory in a modified form. George was not an advocate for communal living—he did not believe the single-tax theory could be put to the test on such a small scale (Young 1916, 256). Nevertheless, some of his supporters went ahead and formed the Fairhope colony, and a few others, based on his single-tax ideas.

See also: Fairhope and Single-Tax Communities; Gronlund, Laurence; Socialism

References

Rose, Edward. *Henry George*. New York: Twayne Publishers, 1968.
Young, Arthur Nichols. *The Single Tax Movement in the United States*. Princeton, NJ: Princeton University Press, 1916.

Great Depression

The Great Depression of the 1930s was a time of poverty and hardship in the United States and around the world. The depression caused hardship for some utopian communities, such as Point Loma and the Llano community, both of which experienced financial troubles during this time.

However, a number of utopian communities formed or grew as a result of the poverty of the Great Depression, including the Catholic Worker Movement, the New Deal communities, and the Peace Mission Movement. These communities hoped to create a new way of living that would offer food, shelter, and jobs for people in need.

The Great Depression was caused by a number of events. After World War I, farmers in the United States were not able to sell their products for a good price. As a result, many farmers were not able to pay the mortgage on their land, and they lost their farms. Because the farmers defaulted on their loans, many banks in agricultural areas were forced to close. In 1929, the stock market crashed—the prices of stocks fell drastically as people frantically sold their stocks, often at a huge loss. Businesses were unable to repay their bank loans, causing more banks to fail. By 1933, about 25 percent of people in the United States were jobless. With no income, many people found themselves living in squalid, rat-infested shelters; some children were not able to attend school because the buildings had closed due to lack of funds; families lost their homes because they could not pay the mortgage; and many people did not even have enough to eat.

The suffering of the Great Depression was eased when the U.S. government created a number of programs, called the "New Deal," to help the needy and create jobs. The New Deal communities were part of this program. The depression ended with the U.S. involvement in World War II in 1941, when the government poured money into the war effort and created so many jobs that the unemployment rate fell to just 1 percent.

See also: Catholic Worker Movement; Llano del Rio and New Llano; New Deal Communities; Peace Mission Movement; Point Loma and Theosophical Communities

Reference

Meltzer, Milton. *Brother, Can You Spare a Dime? The Great Depression 1929–1933*. New York: Facts on File, 1991.

Gronlund, Laurence

Laurence Gronlund (1846–1899) was a Danish-born American socialist. In his day, he was considered one of the most influential socialists in the United States. His book *Cooperative Commonwealth*, published in 1884, was the first attempt to explain Marxism and socialism to the American public.

Gronlund believed that the United States and Great Britain were ideal places to establish a socialist state, yet there was no word in English that explained Karl Marx's version of socialism. By writing about socialism for the American public, Gronlund hoped to convince a significant number of people to lead a peaceful socialist revolution in the United States.

Gronlund's ideas seemed to have influenced Edward Bellamy, whose novel *Looking Backward 2000–1887* popularized socialism in the United States. Those same ideas influenced the formation of socialist utopian communities, including Kaweah Cooperative Commonwealth and Ruskin. Gronlund also wrote pamphlets criticizing the single-tax theories of Henry George, who had spurned the formation of a number of utopian communities. Although many socialists supported George, Gronlund argued that George's reforms were too narrow to really redistribute wealth and alleviate poverty.

See also: Fairhope and Single-Tax Communities; George, Henry; Kaweah Cooperative Commonwealth; Ruskin

Reference

Maher, P. E. "Laurence Gronlund: Contributions to American Socialism." *The Western Political Quarterly*, December 1962, vol. 15, no. 4, 618–624.

Harmony Society

At a Glance

Dates of existence in United States: 1805 to 1905
Locations: Pennsylvania and Indiana
Peak membership: 800
Religious or other belief: Christianity, Separatism

History

The Harmony Society was one of the most financially successful of the American utopian communities. In fact, Karl J. Arndt calls it the "socioeconomic showplace of America in the first half of the nineteenth century" (1971, 367).

Like many other communities, the Harmony Society began when a group of people fled their homeland (in this case, Germany) because of religious persecution.

The group's religion, which came to be known as "Separatist," was founded around 1785 by George Rapp, a farmer's son and a weaver by trade, who became disillusioned with the established Lutheran Church of his time. Rapp was influenced by Pietist leaders, who questioned the rituals and dogma of the Lutheran Church. Rapp felt that the church, the clergy, and the rituals were not necessary for personal salvation, and he began to preach Separatist ideas: that people should not pay church taxes, send their children to church schools, or support the church in any way. By 1802, he had gained over 10,000 active followers. Rapp and his followers were investigated and imprisoned on occasion, because their religion threatened the established church and government power structure.

In 1803, Rapp and a few followers fled to the United States to find land on which to settle. They bought land in Pennsylvania, about 30 miles north of Pittsburgh. In 1805, about 500 followers signed a document committing themselves to live communally and to give all property and possessions to the community. The community named its town "Harmony."

At first, the community was very poor, and its members might have starved during their first winter if it were not for donations from local citizens and credit from the local storekeeper. Over the next 10 years, the community planted, built, and grew, and was able to meet its own needs.

In 1807 and 1808, the group became caught up in religious fervor. Rapp predicted that the second coming of Christ was near, and the Harmony members began to search themselves for sins. The community decided to give up tobacco and to adopt celibacy, even within married life.

Self-proclaimed prophet George Rapp immigrated to the United States from Germany in 1803 with several hundred families of his religious followers. The group eventually settled in Indiana, where Rapp directed a utopian colony called New Harmony, the predecessor of Robert Owen's New Harmony community. Though essentially a religious leader, Rapp proved to be a skilled businessman, establishing the colony as a self-sustaining community and business center. (Pennsylvania Historical and Museum Commission)

Rapp had never intended to live permanently in Pennsylvania—he wanted more land. Consequently, he bought 30,000 acres of land in Indiana along the Wabash River. The first community members to move there, in 1814, were struck with malaria and about 120 died. The swamps, which attracted malaria-carrying mosquitoes, were drained and the community went forward with its construction.

In Indiana, the Harmonists built two-story frame houses and brick buildings, including a tavern, mills, and four large community houses for single members. They built a large church with a roof supported by 28 columns made from local trees. On top of this roof was a balcony where the community's brass band performed. This Indiana town was also called "Harmony" or, alternatively, "New Harmony." The town grew quite prosperous.

In 1824, Rapp decided to move the community again. One reason was that the group needed less land than he had anticipated, since there were fewer followers joining from Europe. Also, Indiana was far from the eastern markets where the Harmony Society sold many of their goods. Rapp sold New Harmony to another community builder, Robert Owen, and bought land about 10 miles north of Pittsburgh.

The community under Rapp called its new town "Economy." Here it established an award-winning silk industry and a museum of natural history. In Economy, some people started to have misgivings about Rapp's leadership abilities. Rapp was not consistent in insisting on celibacy, for example. Before 1826, those who were not celibate were tolerated. After that time, they were asked to leave the community, although Rapp allowed some to return. Members were especially angry over Rapp's favoritism toward a young woman named Hildegard Mutschler, who had been born into the community in 1806. When she ran away to get married in 1829, Rapp welcomed her back with her husband and she bore several children.

In 1831, a charismatic visitor from Germany who called himself Count de Leon stayed with the community. Count de Leon claimed to have found the "Philosopher's Stone," which was supposed to be able to make gold out of other metals. About a third of the members looked to him for leadership. This minority declared that they were the true "Harmonists" and that they no longer viewed Rapp as the community's leader. About 175 dissenters left the community with Count de Leon and established their own community nearby. The new community lasted only one year, after which Count de Leon left for Louisiana and died of cholera. A number of the dissenting members later joined William Keil in his Bethel community in Missouri.

Rapp's town of Economy continued. After Rapp's death in 1847, the remaining 288 members named nine elders as their leaders. The society grew wealthy after discovering oil on its land and forming the Economy Oil Company, but the group continued to insist upon celibacy and did not welcome many new members. As members grew older and older, the society had to hire outside labor and close factories. By 1868, the Harmony Society had only 140 members.

In 1890, people began joining Harmony in order to acquire its wealth. One of these was John Duss, who managed to be appointed a trustee and began using society money for his personal expenses. He spent much of the Harmony fortune on publicity and national tours for an orchestra that he founded and directed. In 1903, he spent $100,000 to create a replica of Venice in Madison Square Garden for performances by the New York Metropolitan Opera.

The community was not attracting new members, and Duss paid some members to leave the community and forced others out. By 1905, the Harmony Society had only a few members and was dissolved.

Beliefs and Practices

In the United States, the Harmonists adopted communal living, as the first Christians did. They adopted celibacy in 1807, even for married couples, although families still lived together. However, families who continued to have children were often tolerated.

The Harmonists believed the second coming of Christ was near, although they never predicted a date for this event. Rapp and his followers used the Bible and had no other written religious books of their own.

The Harmonists valued education and culture. By the 1820s, they had a 360-volume library—which was unusual in a state such as Indiana, where the majority of settlers were illiterate and education was difficult to obtain. The Harmonists engaged in literary competitions, religious discussions, and concerts.

They attended two church services on Sundays, during which men and women sat separately. In addition to the usual Christian holidays, the Harmonists had three holidays of their own: the anniversary of the society's founding (February 15); Harvest Home (in early autumn); and the Love Feast and Lord's Supper (in late October). Music was very important to the Harmonists. They composed many of their own hymns.

Daily Life

The Harmonists are known for the beautiful towns they created. Their first town in Pennsylvania had six main streets. Each family had its own home (built of either logs or bricks), as well as some land, milk cows, and poultry. The society furnished all other needs. Harmony in Indiana featured 180 buildings. The town included public ovens where families could do their baking, and public wells for water. Four large dormitories each housed 60 to 80 unmarried people. The Harmonists also owned a greenhouse on wheels that could be used to cover their citrus trees.

Economy, their second town in Pennsylvania, was also well kept and beautiful. Charles Nordhoff, who visited Economy in 1874, describes "neat frame or brick houses surrounding a square. . . . The broad streets have neat foot-pavements of brick; the houses, substantially built but unpretentious, are beautified by a singular arrangement of grape-vines." Nordhoff also describes a large assembly hall, church, and hotel, where vacationers from Pittsburgh used to stay (reprinted 1960, 64).

In all three towns, the group built a "labyrinth" made of shrubs, vines, and trees, with a small temple or grotto in the center. The twisting paths of the labyrinth stimulated meditation.

The Harmonists wore similar, simple clothing, in order to discourage pride and to encourage equality. The women wore high-waisted ankle-length dresses in a variety of colors, along with aprons and caps. The men wore dark-colored pants, vests and coats, and broad-brimmed hats. Decoration was not permitted.

The Harmonists woke up between 5:00 and 6:00 a.m. Soon after, the community milk wagon came along. The Harmonists poured in the milk from their own cows and took out their day's ration. The milk wagon also brought notices for individuals about work assignments for the day. The Harmonists often sang as they worked or listened to the community band.

Members of the group ate five times a day, like other German communities: breakfast, forenoon snack, lunch, afternoon snack, and supper.

How They Made Their Living

The Harmonists earned a reputation for being hard-working and honest. They planted orchards, vineyards, and grain, and kept sheep. They made and sold whiskey, rope, shoes, leather goods, pottery, and wool, linen, and cotton cloth. Each family was allowed to keep its own animals and its own gardens. From 1814 to 1824, they sold their products in 22 states and 10 foreign countries.

In their second Pennsylvania community of Economy, the Harmonists developed a successful silk industry that produced award-winning silk. The society planted over 10,000 mulberry trees (the leaves of which are a favorite food of silkworms) and created silk cloth, handkerchiefs, women's dresses, silk velvet, and ribbons.

In 1857, they discovered oil on their land and formed the Economy Oil Company. The oil company brought the society immense riches, and with their wealth, they helped finance the building of the Pittsburgh and Lake Erie Railroad.

Leadership and Decision Making

George Rapp was the leader of the society for both spiritual and practical purposes. He heard confessions, led prayers, and oversaw the farm and workshops. Rapp was assisted by his adopted son, Frederick Reichert Rapp, who was the society's business manager. Frederick Rapp appointed seven managers to oversee the various community enterprises.

After George Rapp's death in 1847, the community established a council of nine elders to manage the internal affairs of the society and a council of two trustees to manage the external affairs. Vacancies in these councils were filled by appointment by the council of elders.

How New Members Were Recruited or Chosen

New members often came from Germany. The community tried to make sure that new members shared Harmonist beliefs and asked prospective members to live in the community for some months before formally joining. Young people born within the community were given the opportunity at age 21 to join the community or to leave.

When the community was originally founded, a record had been kept of what each member contributed, with the idea that when a member left, he or she was entitled to the return of this property. In 1818, George Rapp convinced the community to burn this book of records. Rapp argued that burning the book would promote greater equality within the society. It also made it more difficult for members to try to claim their share of the communal property if they wanted to leave the community. After the book was burned, new members were required to sign a document agreeing not to claim any wages or other compensation if they decided to leave the community.

Children and Youth

Although the Harmony Society officially adopted celibacy, children were sometimes born into the community when married members did not follow the celibacy rule. In addition, children came into the community when their parents joined.

The Harmony Society schooled its children within the community, where students ages 6 to 14 were taught not only the basics of reading and writing (in both English and German) and arithmetic but also singing, religious studies, French, geography, history, natural history, physics, and chemistry. At age 14, the boys were apprenticed to a trade and the girls were taught housework, sewing, spinning, and weaving.

Relationship with the Outside World

The Harmony goods gained a solid reputation for being of the highest quality. Their community-run store in the middle of the woods of Indiana was the only place for miles where settlers could purchase supplies. Many neighbors were impressed with the neat, orderly town. However, some others did not trust the Harmonists or their unusual religion. In 1820, outsiders rioted in the streets of Harmony.

The Harmonists were in contact with other utopian communal groups. If they needed goods that they did not make themselves, they preferred to buy from other religious communities. For example, the Harmonists bought cloth from the Amana Colonies when they stopped producing their own cloth.

Reasons for Decline of the Community

The society declined because it was not attracting enough new members, and because some of the later members did not share the same beliefs in communal living and religion. Financial mismanagement sucked away the millions of dollars that the Harmony Society had earned.

Influence on the Outside World

The Harmonists were involved in the founding of Indiana as a state. New Harmony was one of the first towns in Indiana. Frederick Rapp, George Rapp's adopted son, was a delegate to the first constitutional convention in the state and helped to select the site of the state capital. Frederick Rapp also made sure that the state constitution made allowances for conscientious objectors—permitting them to pay a fine rather than to serve in the military. Candidates for public office in Indiana were always interested in seeking the votes of the Harmonists.

The Harmonist wealth was used to support a number of other utopian religious communities. The society gave financial help to the Zoar Society in Ohio, the Mormons, the Hutterites, the Amana Colonies, and the Shakers.

Funds from the Harmony Society also financed the construction of the Pittsburgh and Lake Erie Railroad.

The Harmonist towns in Pennsylvania and Indiana have been preserved for their historic significance.

See also: Keil Communities—Bethel and Aurora; Millennialism; New Harmony and Owenite Movement; Owen, Robert; Zoar Society

References

Arndt, Karl J. R. *George Rapp's Harmony Society (1785–1847)*. Philadelphia: University of Pennsylvania Press, 1965.

Arndt, Karl J. R. *George Rapp's Successors and Material Heirs 1847–1916*. Rutherford, NJ: Fairleigh Dickinson University Press, 1971.

Arndt, Karl J. R. "George Rapp's Harmony Society," in *America's Communal Utopias*, edited by Donald Pitzer. Chapel Hill: University of North Carolina Press, 1997, 57–87.

Kring, Hilda Adam. *The Harmonists: A Folk-Cultural Approach*. Metuchen, NJ: The Scarecrow Press and the American Theological Library Association, 1973.

Nordhoff, Charles. *The Communistic Societies of the United States: From Personal Visit and Observation*. New York: Hillary House, 1960 (first published 1875).

Sutton, Robert. *Communal Utopias and the American Experience: Religious Communities, 1732–2000*. Westport, CT: Praeger, 2003.

Wilson, William. *The Angel and the Serpent: The Story of New Harmony.* Bloomington: Indiana University Press, 1964.

WEB SITES

Historic New Harmony: http://www.ulib.iupui.edu/kade/newharmony/home.html (accessed May 2006).

Old Economy Village: www.oldeconomyvillage.org/home.html (accessed May 2006).

Hippies

During the late 1960s and early 1970s, young adults called "hippies" were active in creating an alternative social movement opposed to the Vietnam War, environmental destruction, and other aspects of the dominant, mainstream culture.

A significant number of hippies turned to Jesus and formed the Jesus Movement, which looked to the early Christian church for an example and rejected much of modern society, including established churches. Other hippies turned to alternative, often Eastern, religions.

The word *hippie* comes from "hip," meaning someone who is aware or tuned-in. The hippie movement grew from the "beat" movement of the 1950s, which also emphasized dropping out of the dominant culture, listening to new music (jazz at that time), and smoking marijuana.

Hippies believed in values such as love, sexual freedom, and honesty. They grew their hair long and wore distinctive, colorful clothing, beads, and flowers. They also believed that drugs such as marijuana and LSD, when used recreationally, could help expand the user's consciousness. The drugs favored by hippies were called "dope" and contrasted with drugs that they viewed negatively, such as alcohol, tobacco, and amphetamines. One writer claimed that "dope turns you on, heightens sensory awareness . . . gives you vision and clarity" (Miller 1991, 26).

A new kind of music, rock and roll, was central to the hippie lifestyle. Discussing rock music's impact on the movement, Timothy Miller states that "dope usually involved inward experiences. Liberated sex in most cases involved interpersonal relationships on a one-to-one basis. Rock, however, was communal, and thus provided a medium for cultural sharing" (1991, 74). In fact, many temporary utopian communities grew around outdoor rock festivals. The most famous of these was the Woodstock gathering in New York in August 1969. "The real point [of the music festivals] was the community offstage. There was a sense of cultural identity at the festivals that simply could not be found elsewhere. The individual faded; the crowd became an organism, 'something alive of itself'" (Miller 1991, 82).

Many hippie communes shared such values as a membership open to anyone who wished to join; the use of drugs; innovative clothing, architecture, and music; sexual freedom; and a rural lifestyle (Miller "Roots").

Hippies formed as many as 1,000 utopian communities, most of them very small and short-lived. The longer-lived, more successful of the hippie communities include The Farm, The Family/Children of God, Jesus People USA, Love Family, Rainbow Family of Living Light, and Renaissance Community/Brotherhood of the Spirit. Hippies saw utopian communities as a way to recreate, on a small scale, a new kind of society—one that emphasized sharing and social freedom.

Hippies were also attracted to communes featuring alternative, often Eastern, religions. The Ananda Colonies, Buddhist communities, and the International Society for Krishna Consciousness (Hare Krishnas) were among these communes.

Synanon started before the hippie movement as a drug-rehabilitation community, but during the hippie era, more and more young people were attracted to its personal-growth philosophy.

In addition to the communities mentioned above, which are profiled elsewhere in this book, descriptions of two other important hippie communities follow:

Tolstoy Farm started in 1963, before the word *hippie* was coined; yet, it is often viewed as one of the first hippie communes. The community (located near Davenport, Washington) had no rules except one: no one should be forced to leave. The community was open to drugs, sex, nudity, and almost anything else. Members lived in a farmhouse or in small homes they had built on community land. They grew their own food. At its height, the community had 80 residents, including many children who were educated in the community's cooperative school. As of 2006, Tolstoy Farm had 50 residents and was no longer an income-sharing community: members owned their own homes. Members sold organic produce at the Spokane, Washington, Farmer's Market.

Drop City was established in May 1965 near Trinidad, Colorado, as an artists' community. Two of the founders, Clark Richert and Gene Bernofsky, started creating "drop art" in Lawrenceville, Kansas. The process involved painting rocks, dropping them from a loft window, and watching the reaction of passersby. The name "Drop City" also came from the hippie injunction to "drop out" of normal society and to make a new way of life. In order to have more financial freedom for their art, they bought land in Colorado and built their own geodesic dome houses, which were covered with automobile tops salvaged from junkyards.

In June 1967, Drop City members went to the "Summer of Love" in the Haight-Ashbury district of San Francisco. This event, with free food, freely available drugs, and free medical care, is often seen as the first mass gathering of the hippie movement. The Droppers invited everyone to come to Drop City. Hundreds of people arrived, and in response to the crush of newcomers, the original members left to set up a more secluded community.

Drop City had no requirements for membership: anyone could show up, stay as long as they liked, and do whatever they chose. There was no organized leadership. The members lived on donations and sometimes food stamps while pursuing their art, which included paintings, sculptures, furniture, one of the first underground comic books, film, and literature. The living conditions were poor: according to a visitor, "the kitchen was filthy, and there was no soap because money was short. Hepatitis has recently swept through the commune. . . . The outhouse was filled to overflowing, and there was no lime to sterilize it" (quoted in Gardner 1978, 40). The community had a garden that no one was in charge of watering, and so it did not grow much. It had goats that one member milked, if he was around (Gardner 1978, 44).

In the winter of 1971–1972, Drop City closed its gates to outsiders. Soon after, the founders decided to sell the land. Drop City ended in 1973.

See also: Ananda Colonies; Buddhist Communities; The Family/Children of God;
The Farm; International Society for Krishna Consciousness (Hare Krishna
Movement); Jesus People USA; Love Family; Rainbow Family of Living Light;
Renaissance Community/Brotherhood of the Spirit; Synanon

References

Drane, James. *A New American Reformation: A Study of Youth Culture and Religion.* New York:
Philosophical Library, 1973.
Gardner, Hugh. *The Children of Prosperity: Thirteen Modern American Communes.* New York:
St. Martin's Press, 1978.
Miller, Timothy. *The Hippies and American Values.* Knoxville: University of Tennessee Press,
1991.
Miller, Timothy. "Roots of Communal Revival 1962–1966," www.thefarm.org/lifestyle/root1.
html (accessed October 2006).

Web sites
Fellowship for Intentional Community, Tolstoy Farm entry:
www.directory.ic.org/records/?action=view&page=view&record_id=1190 (accessed
October 2006).
Tolstoy Farm: www.tolstoyfarm.org/ (accessed October 2006).

Home Colony

At a Glance

Dates of existence in United States: 1896 to 1921
Location: Washington State
Peak membership: up to 500
Religious or other belief: anarchism

History

Home Colony was one of the largest and longest lasting of the anarchist communities in the United States.

It was formed by six former members (three couples) of a socialist community called Glennis, which was located near Tacoma, Washington, and lasted about a year. When it became apparent that Glennis was failing, the three husbands set off in a boat to look for a site for a new colony—a colony that would be based on individual freedom and cooperation. In 1896, they bought land along Joe's Bay in Pierce County. In 1898, they incorporated as the Mutual Home Association, which would own the land.

The purpose of the association was to help members to acquire and own their own homes, and to better their social and moral conditions. Individual families could join by paying for the cost of the land, and then they could build their own homes on that land. The association could use the money it earned only to buy more land to make available to new members. If they wished to move, members could sell their homes, but the land would always be owned by the association.

Almost immediately, members of the colony began to publish anarchist newspapers. These newspapers covered subjects such as politics, working-class struggles, religion, and free love. The newspapers were the cause of many of the clashes between the Home Colony and the outside world (see below). Over the years the newspaper stopped and started publication due to harassment or lack of funds and changed its name from *New Era* to *Discontent, Demonstrator*, and *Agitator*.

In 1899, the community had 54 residents, and by 1910, 213 people lived at the colony. A federal government census during World War I put the population at nearly 500, which may be inaccurate because the boundaries of the community were not clearly defined.

A school for the children was started soon after the colony formed. In 1910, members built a new schoolhouse and community center, which they named Liberty Hall.

In 1909, the Home members revised their original Articles of Incorporation to allow the colony to sell land to individuals. Some members disagreed with this, wanting the land to continue to be owned by the colony. Other members acquired land in this way and then sold it. Property owned by the community—such as Liberty Hall, sidewalks, and the cemetery—was in need of repair, but no money was available for upkeep.

In 1917, two different factions of colony members elected different leaders. The battle for control of the colony ended up in the local court. Judge Ernest Card found that the community was no longer serving its original purpose of offering land to others in order to better their social conditions. In 1919, the judge ordered the community to dissolve. The property was sold off, mainly to colony members.

However, even after the Mutual Home Association ended in May 1921, colony members continued to live in the community and enjoy its freedom. Eleen Greco, who was born just a few months after the judge ordered the community to disband, remembers that every house was full of books, and intellectual discussion was common. "People talked all the time, and they talked about important things. Philosophy, socialism and every other kind of ism. No subject was taboo" (quoted in Hatcher 2000). Gradually, as new people moved in, Home became just another small town, albeit one with an interesting past.

Beliefs and Practices

The anarchists at Home Colony believed, first and foremost, in individual freedom. They started the Mutual Home Association to help lower- and middle-class Americans to own their own homes and enjoy personal freedom in their community (Hall 1994, 78).

Members of Home valued the community because it accepted people who might be shunned in the outside society, such as single mothers and couples who were living together without being married.

The Home colonists were very interested in the labor struggles of the time. At one point, about a third of the adults at Home Colony were members of the International Workers of the World, an international union of the era (Hall 1994, 107).

"Free love" was a concept that many at Home promoted. Several women members believed that marriage was a threat to a woman's freedom and control of her body. They believed that women and men should be free to live with whomever they loved and to end a relationship whenever they wished (Hall 1994, 112).

Some members of Home believed in nude bathing, which they did in Joe's Bay. This belief eventually led to a protracted internal disagreement among the colonists (see below).

Daily Life

Colony members arranged for their own housing. Some single members lived together.

Colonists came from a wide variety of ethnic backgrounds, including immigrants from France, Canada, Scandinavia, Italy, Germany, Holland, and Russia. A number of Jewish families also settled at Home (Hall 1994, 62).

The colonists enjoyed evening lectures, dances, and singing classes. The lectures and discussions included topics such as diet, history, and religion. Famous anarchists such as Emma Goldman and Alexander Berkman came to speak at Home Colony.

Women at the colony felt they had more personal freedom than in the outside world. Sadie Magoon wrote in the community newspaper that she felt safe leaving the doors of her home unlocked and walking at midnight along the bay. Lois Waisbrooker and Olivia Shepard published their own journals on women's issues from the community. Other women were able to take on positions of leadership within the group. Alice Kelly could try out her unusual educational theories as the Home schoolteacher. Two women held the position of president of the Mutual Home Association (Hall 1994, 84–90).

How They Made Their Living

Colonists and families were responsible for their own finances. Some members had to leave the colony periodically in order to find work in the nearest city, Tacoma. One woman was a midwife who served Home members and those in the local community. Many ran poultry businesses. Those who performed labor within the community were paid 15 to 20 cents per hour, which was less than what they could make outside of the colony. The community did start a number of cooperative enterprises that allowed members to work in a lumber mill, as fishermen, and in general stores. Members could choose to work in one of these businesses and get paid according to how much they worked (Hall 1994, 87–114).

Leadership and Decision Making

A board of trustees was elected by the members. Gregory Hall described the Home Colony's leadership in this way: "Through a constant dialogue that encouraged moral self-direction, Home was able to exist, for a time, without the need of a sheriff, an authoritarian administrative body, or the over-riding influence of one person" (1994, 119).

How New Members Were Recruited or Chosen

The public learned about Home through its newspapers and through publicity (often negative) in mainstream newspapers.

The Mutual Home Association never had any rules about who could live in the Home Colony. However, because the land was owned collectively before 1909, potential members had an incentive to make sure they wanted to invest their money in an anarchist community. After 1909, any interested person could buy land in the community. As a result, some families moved in who did not agree with the values of other families. One of the most divisive disagreements in the community was over nude swimming. Some engaged in this practice, and others who lived in the colony were reportedly horrified by it (Hall 1994, 123–124).

Children and Youth

While there was no attempt at raising the children communally, the colony did start a school for the children right away. Although the Home Colony school began before the anarchist Modern School Movement, the teachers of the school believed in some of the same concepts: for example, they did not believe in physical punishment of disobedient or uncooperative children.

The Home Colony school was a public school, and the teacher's salary was paid by the state of Washington.

Relationship with the Outside World

Home had a stormy relationship with the outside world. Early in 1901, the printer of the colony's anarchist newspaper was fined for mailing an article that was considered obscene, in violation of a national law, the Comstock Act, which prohibited sending obscenity through the mail. At that time, "obscenity" could mean information about birth control, in addition to information about nudity or sex.

That same year Lois Waisbrooker was arrested and tried for printing an article about free love in her journal, and Mattie Penhallow was arrested and tried for mailing the article (she was the Home Colony postmistress). The jury acquitted Penhallow but found Waisbrooker guilty. Because the judge disagreed with the guilty verdict, he asked for only the minimum penalty—a fine of $100. However, this kind of official harassment eventually led to the closure of the Home Colony post office. Colonists had to walk to nearby Lakebay to get their mail. The colonists continued to print various versions of their newspaper (LeWarne 1995, 183–185).

After U.S. president William McKinley was assassinated in September 1901 by Leon Czolgosz, who claimed to be an anarchist, the anarchists of Home were attacked in local newspapers, although the Home residents denounced the assassination. An editorial in the Tacoma *Daily Ledger* accused Home residents of being "a collection of outlaws" and "a nest of vipers" (LeWarne 1995, 179).

In 1911, Home Colony became involved in a dispute surrounding nude swimming. Some colonists believed in nude swimming. Other colonists did not, and they brought charges against the nude swimmers. Several Home residents were prosecuted and fined or jailed. In response, Jay Fox, the editor of the Home newspaper *Agitator*, wrote an article about this dispute entitled "The Nudes and the Prudes." Fox was then arrested for his article and spent several months in jail.

Reasons for Ending the Community

The members disagreed with each other about leadership and took their case to court, at which point the judge ordered the community to disband.

Influence on the Outside World

The Home Colony tried to influence the outside world through its newspapers and journals, although these writings were just a "tiny fraction of all the writings that circulated among radicals," according to Charles LeWarne (1995, 235). Home was a haven for those who wanted to discuss and practice ideals that were not dealt with in the mainstream society. LeWarne suggests that Home was ahead of its time in addressing issues such as women's sexual liberation, race relations, and nudity. "When the people of Home encouraged and tolerated those who lived and acted as they chose, then the individualists of Home were addressing themselves to issues that society later would be forced to confront" (1995, 226).

See also: Anarchism; Ferrer Colony

References

Hall, Gregory David. "The Theory and Practice of Anarchism at Home Colony, 1896–1912." MA Thesis, Washington State University, 1994.

Hatcher, Candy. "No Place Like Home." *Seattle Post-Intelligencer*, December 18, 2000, seattlepi.nwsource.com/local/ever18.shtml (accessed October 2006).

LeWarne, Charles Pierce. *Utopias on Puget Sound, 1885–1915.* Seattle: University of Washington Press, 1995.

House of David Movement

<table>
<tr><td colspan="2" align="center">At a Glance</td></tr>
</table>

At a Glance

Dates of existence in United States: 1903 to present
Location: Michigan
Peak membership: 900
Religious or other belief: Christianity, millennialism

History

This unusual community preached celibacy and vegetarianism, and ran an amusement park and sports teams in order to earn money.

The House of David movement was founded by Benjamin and Mary Purnell. Benjamin was a traveling preacher who became a minister for the Jezreelite Church. The founder of this church, James Jezreel, claimed to be the sixth of seven messengers foretelling the second coming of Christ. The Jezreelite Church grew out of a prophetic strain of Christianity that started in England in the 18th century. In 1892, Purnell, his wife, and children joined the community of Michael Mills in Detroit. Mills claimed to be the seventh and final messenger of this church. Around that time Mills was charged with adultery and statutory rape, and sentenced to jail. In 1895, Purnell received a vision that he himself was the seventh messenger (Adkin 1990, 8–12).

The Purnells traveled and preached for seven years. In 1902, they settled in Fostoria, Ohio, where they were taken in by families who were sympathetic to their religious views. Purnell wrote and published a religious tract, *The Star of Bethlehem*.

In 1903, the Purnell's daughter died during an explosion at the factory where she worked. In keeping with their belief that the living should have nothing to do with dead bodies, the Purnells refused to arrange for a burial. The townspeople were so upset by this that the Purnells and a few of their followers fled to Benton Harbor, Michigan. They were soon joined by local supporters and a Jezreelite group from California. With financing from their supporters, the Purnells purchased land for their community and began constructing buildings to house their members (Adkin 1990, 14–17).

In 1904, the Purnells traveled to Australia to preach to followers of the fifth messenger, John Wroe. They later returned to Michigan with 85 members from Australia. By 1907, the community had over 300 members (Fogarty 1981, 55–56; Adkin 1990, 17).

In 1908, the community opened an amusement park on its land and called it Eden Springs Park. It featured a mineral spring, a fish pond, miniature railroad, miniature automobiles, a small zoo, a lake, an orchestra, and souvenir and refreshment stands.

They also began fielding a baseball team. By the late 1920s, the House of David had several teams, including one for young women. The home baseball team played in a baseball stadium constructed next to the amusement park. The traveling baseball team played over 200 games a year around the country and in Canada and Europe (Adkin 1990, 25).

The House of David sponsored several bands as well, including a home band and a traveling band.

Although the community was supposed to be celibate, rumors floated around that Benjamin Purnell approached young women for sex. Twenty marriages were arranged between young women and men of the community in 1910. These marriages were supposed to be celibate, according to the community's rule, and were supposedly arranged so that women and men could travel together as missionaries. They were also apparently arranged to shield Purnell from having to answer to federal authorities for the fact that young community women were no longer virgins.

In 1914, two former members accused Purnell of having sexual relations with them. Lena Fortney stated that Purnell claimed to be Jesus and said that he had the right to have sexual intercourse with her. Further, she stated that he had had such relations with all community girls over the age of 12. That same year a dozen more marriages were arranged. These group marriages were enough to prevent any official investigation (Fogarty 1981, 88–102).

In 1916, about 35 men from the House of David were drafted into the U.S. Army to fight in World War I. The community had tried to get the men listed as conscientious objectors, and when this failed, the men joined and served in noncombat roles. They kept their long hair and beards, and were served meatless meals. The men turned over their military pay to the community. In 1917, several more marriages were arranged so the colony could benefit from the dependent allowance paid by the government (Fogarty 1981, 101–102).

In the early 1920s, several former members accused Purnell of living in luxury while community members did not have enough to eat. Further accusations were made of his having sexual relations with young women of the community. The attorney general of Michigan accused the House of David of deceiving members into giving up their property in order to attain immortality and of permitting immoral and criminal activity within the community. Purnell went into hiding in late 1922 and was not found until four years later. Eighteen more marriages were arranged. While many community members supported Purnell, others began to leave.

Mary Purnell began to challenge her husband's authority, and by 1925, members of the House of David were divided in their loyalty between Benjamin and Mary. In a 1926 police raid of the colony Purnell's hiding place was found. He had, in fact, never left the colony but remained hidden from authorities for four years by making use of a secret hiding place within the community.

Purnell was put on trial in 1927. The judge ordered him and his wife to leave the community. Before Purnell could do so, he died of tuberculosis in December 1927.

Mary Purnell moved across the street, took over some community buildings, and started her own community, which she called the City of David. Thomas Dewhirst took over the original House of David community (Fogarty 1981, 107–121).

The House of David continued fielding baseball teams and running its amusement park. In 1937, the House of David had 300 members and its baseball teams played until the late 1930s. By 1963, the population of the House of David had fallen to 118.

Mary's City of David built a hotel and ran two vegetarian restaurants. Its baseball team played until 1953, the same year that Mary died. During the 1940s and 1950s, the City of David had a basketball team that toured with the Harlem Globetrotters. As both the House of David and the City of David grew smaller, they sold off their property. In his 1981 book, Robert Fogarty described the communities, which had about 50 members combined, as "retirement homes for the believers" (127). As of 2007, Mary's City of David continued as a tourist attraction and hosted vegetarian luncheons and baseball games.

Beliefs and Practices

The Purnells preached a form of "millennialism." In Christianity, this refers to a 1,000-year time period mentioned in the New Testament Book of Revelation. The text of Revelation encourages people to withstand persecution, because the end of the world is near; it promises that God will rescue them and imprison Satan for a thousand years.

The main purpose of the House of David was to gather together the 144,000 members of the tribes of Israel, as mentioned in the Book of Revelation. Purnell preached that people should join his "ingathering" of the 12 scattered tribes of Israel and live a pure life. The community believed in celibacy as a way of keeping the body pure for the coming millennium. Even married couples were supposed to be celibate. The Purnells preached that members must also give up worldly possessions, live communally according to the first Christian church as described in the Book of Acts, abstain from meat and alcoholic beverages, and refrain from cutting their hair or beard. They were not allowed to handle dead bodies. By following these precepts, members would then be prepared for salvation of the body as well as of the soul—Purnell's people would continue to have bodies during the millennium. For a time, Purnell preached that this millennium would begin in 1916 (Adkin 1990, 14, 33–34; Fogarty 1981, 53–54, 60).

The main religious texts of the community were the Bible and Purnell's *Star of Bethlehem: The Living Roll of Life*. The main message of Purnell's text was how to achieve "body salvation" as well as soul salvation (Adkin 1990, 31).

The community had five meetings per week during which Benjamin, and sometimes Mary, preached. The meetings included instrumental and vocal music (Adkin 1990, 31).

Daily Life

Members lived in large dormitories that were two or three stories tall. Women shared rooms with women, and men with men. Sometimes married couples roomed together. They were supposed to maintain their celibate relationship even while rooming together.

The members ate vegetarian meals together in a common dining room. Their food consisted of bread, oatmeal, vegetables, and pies. Although the community produced butter, milk, and eggs, these were not often eaten within the community—instead, they were sold in Benton Harbor for income. The Purnells ate in a private dining room and were served better food (Fogarty 1981, 76).

The men and women of the House of David wore their hair long. The community made its own clothes and members sometimes wore clothing or underwear made out of flour sacks. Some members complained that they did not have enough warm clothes. Mary Purnell apparently had nicer clothes than the rest of the community (Fogarty 1981, 76).

A community rulebook specified that the members were to go to bed at 10:00 p.m. and get up at 5:00 a.m. They were not allowed to play cards, wear black, argue, or mix with outsiders. They were not supposed to leave the community grounds without permission (Fogarty 1981, 75–76, 78).

During the long, cold Michigan winters, community members enjoyed putting on theatrical pageants with religious themes (Fogarty 1981, 68–69).

The community office staff assigned work. Some people were rotated to different jobs, and others maintained the same job for years (Adkin 1990, 27–28).

How They Made Their Living

New members were to turn over their personal wealth to the community. The House of David ran a lucrative amusement park, baseball teams, and bands. The community ran a dairy and a vegetarian restaurant. It had a lumberyard, sawmill, and canning plant.

The community aimed for self-sufficiency. It grew its own fruits, vegetables, and grain. It printed its own publications in the community print shop, mixed its own cement, and sewed its own clothes (Fogarty 1981, 79; Adkin 1990, 26–27).

Leadership and Decision Making

Benjamin and Mary Purnell were the leaders of the community. They appointed a board of 12 trustees, who could be removed with the agreement of the other trustees. In 1908, the Purnells appointed four "pillars" above the trustees. The pillars were in charge of managing the funds of the community. Seven women were called "sweepers," and they performed spiritual cleansing by hearing confessions (Fogarty 1981, 70–71).

How New Members Were Recruited or Chosen

The House of David recruited members from the United States, England, and Australia. They were interested in contacting and recruiting followers of the other six messengers of the prophetic church of which Purnell claimed to be the seventh messenger. Purnell chose missionaries from among the membership to travel around the country and the world. These missionaries worked in teams of two to six men and women. The traveling baseball team also spread the word about the House of David (Adkin 1990, 20, 25).

Potential members were asked to read pamphlets and other literature about the beliefs of the community and to subscribe to the community's newspaper, *Shiloh's Messenger of Wisdom*. They were also asked to fill out a questionnaire about their wealth and family relationships (Fogarty 1981, 56–57).

Children and Youth

Although the community was celibate, children joined with their parents. The Purnells looked down on formal education. Benjamin Purnell compared education to dung and stated that dung was more useful because of its value as a fertilizer.

The children went to school on the colony. At its height, the community school had 175 children and two teachers. The children were taught until eighth grade. They studied the rudiments of math and spelling, along with Bible lessons and Purnell's writings (Fogarty 1981, 76–77).

Relationship with the Outside World

The House of David communities interacted extensively with the outside world through their amusement park, restaurants, and sports teams. However, they kept themselves apart from that world through their appearance—the long hair and beards of the men and boys—and by rules that prevented them from socializing with outsiders.

The public enjoyed the amusements provided by the House of David, but outsiders were shocked by Purnell's sexual behavior.

Influence on the Outside World

At their height, the House of David communities were one of the major economic engines of Berrien County, Michigan (Adkin 1990, 30).

See also: Bible Communism; Millennialism

References

Adkin, Clare Jr. *Brother Benjamin: A History of the Israelite House of David*. Berrien Springs, MI: Andrews University Press, 1990.

Fogarty, Robert S. *The Righteous Remnant: The House of David*. Kent, OH: Kent State University Press, 1981.

WEB SITES

House of David Baseball Team Research Project: www.peppergame.com/history.asp (accessed February 2007).

House of David Museum: www.houseofdavidmuseum.org/ (accessed February 2007).

Israelite House of David: www.israelitehouseofdavid.org/ (accessed May 2008).

Mary's City of David: www.maryscityofdavid.org/ (accessed February 2007).

Hutterites

At a Glance

Dates of existence in North America: 1874 to present (since 1528 outside of the United States)

Locations: Minnesota, Montana, North Dakota, South Dakota, Washington (and many communities in Canada)

Peak membership: 45,000 and growing (United States and Canada)

Religious or other belief: Anabaptist Christianity

History

The Hutterites are one of the largest, longest-lived utopian communities in the United States. They began in 1528, when a group of German, Swiss, and Austrian Anabaptists (those who believe in adult baptism) decided to share their money and belongings. Because of persecution, the Anabaptists had fled from Switzerland to Germany and Austria, and then to Moravia (part of the current Czech Republic). A year later, an Anabaptist minister, Jacob Hutter, arrived and saw that the group was about to fall apart. He helped the group organize and recommit to communal living. The Hutterites take their name from this early leader.

By 1600, the Hutterites had grown to 25,000 members in eight communities. They continued to live in Moravia at this time. However, the group was persecuted for its religious beliefs—many were killed, while others were imprisoned and tortured. As a result, the numbers of Hutterites dwindled to a few hundred. They fled to Russia in 1770, where they lived in peace for about 100 years. When in 1870 the Russian government withdrew its support for the Hutterites, the group decided to flee to North America.

Between 1874 and 1877, about 800 Hutterites arrived in North America. Half of the members decided not to live communally and most of these 400 eventually became Mennonites (another Anabaptist religion). The remaining 400 Hutterites settled in South Dakota in three different colonies, each with its own leader. Each colony was named after its leader: Schmiedeleut, Dariusleut, and Lehrerleut. To this day, each Hutterian colony identifies itself with one of these three *leuts* or groups.

Since then, the Hutterites have prospered and formed new communities, so that as of 2008 there were 460 colonies, with about 45,000 people, in the United States and Canada (http://www.hutterites.org/geographicaldistribution.htm; http://www.hutterites.org/HutteriteHistory/am-worldwar2.htm).

175

Beliefs and Practices

The Hutterites are Anabaptists, like the Amish and the Bruderhof. They believe that people should not become baptized until they are adults and have the capacity to understand and freely choose their faith. Members who leave the community, whether before or after baptism, are generally welcomed back for visits, and are allowed to rejoin the community if they show repentance and declare their intention of living a faithful life.

The Hutterites believe that living communally is the way to reach God. Like other Christians, they believe that Adam and Eve fell from grace and, as a result, humans have a tendency to sin and an attraction for earthly pleasures. However, unlike other Christians, they believe that in order to return to God, one should live communally, share income and property, and remain separate from the rest of the world. Hutterites believe that the individual "self" must be broken, and that every person should work and live for the sake of the entire community.

Although Hutterites believe in monogamous families, they also believe that the community comes before the family. For example, when a Hutterian man gets married, he takes a vow that, if he were to decide to leave the community, he will not ask his wife and children to leave with him.

Their belief in keeping separate from the outside world means that they do not vote or serve on juries. However, they do pay taxes.

Hutterites are pacifists: they do not believe in war and, during World War I, they fled to Canada to avoid having their young men conscripted into the army. Although they buy from and sell to outsiders, Hutterites tend not to socialize with them.

Humans are not equal in the eyes of the Hutterites. They believe in a hierarchy: God rules over the soul, older humans rule the younger, men rule over women, and adults rule over children.

Hutterites are against any kind of birth control, even natural birth control or abstaining from sexual relations. As a result, for much of Hutterian history, their women gave birth to about 10 children each, on average. Because they live communally, the individual parents do not have the burden of cooking and caring for all of their children.

The Hutterites' belief in simple living leads them to reject anything that does not have a practical purpose or that is too individualistic or "worldly." They do not allow radios or television, automobiles, musical instruments, cosmetics, fancy clothes, smoking, dancing, or card playing, for example. Some colonies also prohibit sports.

Hutterites welcome modern innovations that are helpful to their businesses. They use computers, telephones, sewing machines, modern milking machines, electricity, trucks, and so forth. In addition, modern medical care is used when needed.

Hutterites pray before and after meals, attend a short service every evening, and attend longer services on Sundays. They have no separate church building—they believe that God's order should be respected in all buildings and throughout all parts of their lives. They hold worship services in the schoolhouse or the dining hall.

Daily Life

The Hutterites speak their own unique language, which is close to a German dialect spoken in Austria. They also speak English with outsiders.

Each Hutterian colony consists of about 75 to 150 people. Colonies are generally arranged so that the kitchen and dining building are in the center, with the living quarters surrounding it.

While each family lives in its own separate apartment, the apartments have no kitchens, since everyone eats in the central dining hall. Families do not eat together: the women eat separately from the men, and the children have their own dining room. Most apartments have no bathrooms either—the Hutterites use outhouses and common shower houses.

Hutterian buildings are generally plain and free of decoration. Floors are linoleum, walls are painted and not wallpapered. Even flowerbeds are absent from some colonies.

Hutterites wake up early, and breakfast is served around 6:30 to 7:30 a.m. (depending on the colony). The women and girls clean the dining rooms (there is one for adults and one for the schoolchildren). Then the adults go to their work assignments, and the children go to school. A snack is often served during the midmorning. Lunch is served around noon, with a rest period after. Work resumes at about 1:30 p.m. At 5:00 p.m., mothers carry food home for their children under five. Schoolchildren eat supper at 6:00 p.m., after which everyone over six attends a half-hour church service. The adults eat at 7:00 p.m. For the remainder of the evening, members are free to visit one another or engage in a craft or hobby. Singing, chatting, and reading are acceptable leisure-time activities.

Hutterites eat meat at almost every meal, in addition to vegetables, fruit, bread, milk, cheese, and eggs. They drink wine and beer on occasion and enjoy desserts frequently.

Women and men work separately. The women do the gardening, food preparation, sewing, cleaning, and child care. Men do the work for money-making enterprises: farming or manufacturing.

Women wear long dresses in a plaid or flowered fabric and a black head-scarf often polka-dotted with white. Although jewelry is prohibited, eyeglasses are permitted, and women enjoy wearing fancy frames (Wilson 2000, 28). Men wear dark pants with suspenders and shirts of various colors. Men must grow beards after they are married.

Hutterites begin to "retire" at around age 45 or 50, when their workload is generally reduced. However, older people frequently continue to work as they are able to.

How They Make Their Living

Hutterites aim for self-sufficiency: they construct their own buildings, make their own furniture and clothes, manufacture some of their own farm and kitchen equipment, and raise or grow most of their own food.

Children say a prayer before breakfast at the Forest River Colony in North Dakota. The Hutterites, or the Plain People of the Prairie, live a communal life and share the responsibilities of their farms. (Corbis)

In addition, they sell agricultural and livestock products, including grains and peas, hogs, milk, and poultry, to the outside world. Some Hutterian colonies have started getting into small-scale manufacturing of farm and household items such as barn ventilation systems, boilers, windows, doors, sinks, and tubs.

Leadership and Decision Making

Hutterian leaders are chosen through voting. However, the Hutterites believe that men are superior to women. Therefore, women do not vote or hold leadership positions within the community (except for the position of head cook).

Hutterian colonies are run by a minister and an advisory board consisting of the farm manager, the colony manager, the German schoolteacher, and two or three other men. All leaders are elected for life by the adult male members of the colony, and they can be removed if they are not performing their jobs well.

Below these elders are the managers of the various farm divisions, such as cattle, swine, sheep, chickens, ducks, and the mechanical and technical division. Under them is the labor force of all men 15 years and older.

The men also elect the Head Cook, who is a woman. The men often consult with their wives before casting their votes. Women also hold the positions of garden woman, the kindergarten teacher, and the school woman, who supervises the children's breakfast. These are nonelected positions.

A Hutterian colony generally holds decision-making meetings after church on Saturday evening or Sunday. Women do not participate in these meetings. Decisions are made based on a simple majority of voters. Everyone in a colony is well informed about important issues, which are discussed thoroughly before being voted on.

The Hutterites see their decision-making process not simply as a way to run the colony, but as "a means by which the will of God speaks through the assembly of Christians on earth," according to John Bennett. "The 'lot' (vote) is an expression of the spiritual majority who, on that occasion, serve as God's agents" (1973, 199).

How New Colonies Form

The Hutterites do not seek out new members, although genuinely interested outsiders are welcome to join. However, most Hutterites are born into the community; very few outsiders join. Because of their high birthrate, and because the vast majority of people born into a Hutterian family choose to remain Hutterite, their communities grow and spread rapidly.

When a Hutterian colony reaches about 150 people, the colony "branches," or splits in two. Branching is done in order to allow for more leadership positions for adult men. Because leadership positions are held for life, if a colony gets too large, the younger men will not have the opportunity to lead.

The entire colony gives input into where the new colony will be located and land is usually bought within 30 miles of the home colony. Often, the members of a colony don't know who will move and who will stay until the morning of the move. Everyone packs and gets ready to go. The people are divided into two lists, aiming for a balance of ages, genders, and family size, and one list is drawn at random. Those people get into trucks and travel to their new home, while the others unpack.

Children and Youth

Mothers take about six weeks off after the birth of a child, and gradually begin to work until, by the time the baby is three months old, the mother is doing her usual share of work. Before age two, babies are held and played with when the adults are free. However, when the adults are worshipping or eating meals, the babies are often left alone in their cribs. Once they can climb out of their cribs, they are placed in the care of a grandparent or an older child.

At about age two, Hutterian children begin to spend most of their day in the kindergarten building, where they eat, learn, and take naps. Many Hutterite kindergartens have almost no toys. Instead, while indoors, the children are expected to sit still and to learn Hutterian songs and prayers. They also play outdoors. The purpose of the Hutterite kindergarten is to teach the children to obey. Children who disobey are scolded or hit with a willow switch or leather strap.

At about age six, the children begin going to school. The Hutterites have two different schools: the English school, in which they learn English and other subjects taught in American public schools; and the German school, in which they learn the German language and recite passages from the Bible. The English school is generally taught by an outside teacher, hired by the local school district, who often lives in a separate house within the community, while the German school is taught by a Hutterian colony member.

Hutterian youth are considered adults at age 15. They begin to eat in the adult dining hall and begin to work in the different departments around the colony. However, they continue to attend Sunday School and, until they choose to be baptized (usually between 19 and 26), they are allowed somewhat more freedom than baptized adults. At this age, young people often explore the outside world. Some might try playing a harmonica, hiding a radio in their room, smoking, wearing jewelry, reading romance novels, or painting their toenails. Some of the young men live in the outside world for weeks, months, or even years. The young women almost never live in the outside world.

The vast majority of Hutterites who leave choose to come back and live in a Hutterite community. Although they enjoy the variety of outside life, they feel most comfortable within a Hutterite colony (Wilson 2000, 129).

After age 15, Hutterite youth begin to date. They are encouraged to date only people from their own leut but generally must date outside their immediate colony, since they are likely to be closely related to everyone within the colony. The young people frequently visit other colonies in order to help out with work, or to attend weddings, and thus get a chance to meet potential marriage partners. "Dating" consists of walking, talking, or singing together.

Marriage partners must be approved by the young people's parents and by the colony. Before marriage, young people must voluntarily request to be baptized and received as a full member of the Hutterian faith. After marriage, the young woman goes to live in the young man's colony.

Relationship with the Outside World

Before fleeing to North America, Hutterites were subject to persecution in Europe. In North America, Hutterites generally have had good relationships with their neighbors and the outside world. They are known to be honest, hard-working people.

However, there are two issues that have caused conflict with the outside world. Hutterites are pacifists—they do not believe in war—but during World War I, Hutterian young men were drafted into military service. The young men refused to sign admission papers, put on a military uniform, or follow orders. They were tried and sentenced to imprisonment. Many of them were subjected to ridicule and torture. Two Hutterian men died from this mistreatment. During this time, newspapers condemned Hutterite colonies because they refused to buy war bonds. Americans were often suspicious of these German-speaking people, suspecting that that they might be supporters of Germany. As a result, all the Hutterites in the United States fled to Canada (Hostetler 1974, 126–131).

After the war, during the years of the Great Depression, the United States was eager to attract the Hutterites back because they were good farmers and many Hutterian colonies were re-established in the United States. By the time of World War II, the United States had developed a system of alternative service for people who objected to war.

The other conflict involves the purchase of land. As Hutterian colonies have grown and expanded rapidly, they have purchased more and more land. As a result of this need for land, some Canadian provincial governments have become alarmed. In some cases, laws have been threatened or passed to restrict Hutterites from purchasing land. Most of this conflict has taken place in Canada.

Influence on the Outside World

The Hutterites keep to themselves and do not attempt to influence the outside world. However, they have provided inspiration for other religious groups, such as the Bruderhof, a similar communal religious group founded in 1920 in Germany. For two brief periods, the Bruderhof and the Hutterites were united. However, now the Bruderhof are a separate community.

In addition, Christian communal groups in Japan and the Philippines have contacted and visited the Hutterites. Hutterian writings have been translated into Japanese, and a number of Hutterian colonies sent money to these communal Asian groups.

The Future of the Hutterites

The Hutterian way of life changes very slowly, but it does change. In recent years, Hutterites have expanded their businesses into areas other than agriculture because of the difficulty of acquiring large tracts of land. Some Hutterian colonies are also becoming more open to comforts such as indoor plumbing and carpeting.

In addition, Hutterites are becoming more interested in education. Because members use the latest technology in their businesses, they feel the need for better English skills to read farm journals and more math to operate computer software. Some colonies have allowed young people to take high school classes. In addition, two colleges (one in the United States and one in Canada) have begun teacher-training programs specifically for Hutterites who want to teach at the English schools in their communities.

Since about 1960, Hutterian women have begun giving birth to fewer children. Nowadays, Hutterite families might consist of six or fewer children, compared to the 10 or more children common in the past. Experts have suggested that, because of the use of efficient modern technology, Hutterites nowadays do not need so many young people to work on their farms. In addition, because land is more difficult to acquire, larger colonies are harder to support financially. In at least one colony, women are familiar with birth control and report using a number of different methods, such as the birth control pill, IUD, and sterilization. While birth control is still against Hutterian rules, women get around this restriction by asking their doctors to prescribe birth control for health reasons (Curtis-White 2002).

For now, the Hutterites remain one of the most successful examples of a utopian community.

See also: Amish; Bruderhof

References

Bennett, John. "The Managed Democracy of the Hutterites," in *Communes: Creating and Managing the Collective Life*, edited by Rosabeth Moss Kanter. New York: Harper and Row, 1973.

Conkin, Paul. *Two Paths to Utopia: The Hutterites and the Llano Colony*. Lincoln: University of Nebraska Press, 1964.

Curtis-White, Katherine. "Declining Fertility among North American Hutterites: The Use of Birth Control within a Dariusleut Colony." *Social Biology* 49 (2002): 58–73.

Flint, David. *The Hutterites: A Study in Prejudice*. Toronto: Oxford University Press, 1975.

Holzach, Michael. *The Forgotten People: A Year among the Hutterites*. Translated by Stephan Lhotzky. Sioux Falls, SD: Ex Machina Publishing Company, 1993.

Hostetler, John. *Hutterite Society*. Baltimore, MD: Johns Hopkins University Press, 1974.

Hostetler, John, and Gertrude Enders Huntington. *Hutterites in North America*. New York: Holt, Rinehart, and Winston, 1967.

Huntington, Gertrude E. "Living in the Ark: Four Centuries of Hutterite Faith and Community," in *America's Communal Utopias*, edited by Donald Pitzer. Chapel Hill: University of North Carolina Press, 1997, 319–351.

Kephart, William. *Extraordinary Groups: The Sociology of Unconventional Life-Styles*. New York: St. Martin's Press, 1976.

Oved, Yaacov. *Two Hundred Years of American Communes*. New Brunswick, NJ: Transaction Books, 1988.

Peter, Karl. *The Dynamics of Hutterite Society*. Edmonton, Alberta, Canada: University of Alberta Press, 1987.

Peters, Victor. *All Things Common: The Hutterian Way of Life*. Minneapolis: University of Minnesota Press, 1965.

Whitworth, John McKelvie. *God's Blueprints: A Sociological Study of Three Utopian Sects*. London: Routledge and Kegan Paul, 1975.

Wilson, Laura. *Hutterites of Montana*. New Haven, CT: Yale University Press, 2000.

Zehr, Mary Ann. "A World Apart." *Education Week* 19 (2000): 34.

WEB SITES
Hutterite History: http://www.hutteritehistory.org/ (accessed May 2008)

Hutterites: www.hutterites.org/ (accessed May 2006).

Icarian Movement

At a Glance

Dates of existence in United States: 1848 to 1898
Locations: California, Illinois, Iowa, Missouri
Peak membership: 500
Religious or other belief: secularism, socialism

History

The Icarian movement was one of the largest and most successful of the socialist utopian experiments in the United States.

The movement was founded by Etienne Cabet, a French lawyer and political activist. He was opposed to the French monarchy, called for democracy and other reforms, and was exiled from France as a result of his outspoken views. While living in London, he read Sir Thomas More's *Utopia* and met Robert Owen, who had inspired the formation of a number of utopian communities. Cabet wrote his own novel of a utopian community, entitled *Voyage en Icarie (Travels in Icaria),* which describes an ideal communal society with no private property and no money, in which everyone would work and share equally in the products of industry. There would be no wealthy class. The book became a best seller in France.

When Cabet returned to France, he spread his utopian ideas through his own newspaper, *Le Populaire*. He thought about creating a utopian society in France, but for one thing, Marxist socialists, who tended to disdain utopian communities in favor of violent revolution, were gaining influence in France—and Cabet did not believe in violence. In addition, Cabet continued to criticize the government and was not welcome in France. As a result, he decided to form his community in the United States. He told his followers that his community would be founded by 10,000–20,000 people and that a million more would later join.

Cabet acquired land in Texas with the help of Robert Owen (who had started his own utopian community in Indiana some years before). Having never seen the land himself, Cabet nevertheless told his supporters that it was fertile and that the climate resembled that of Italy. He selected 69 men—the "advance guard"—to sail (without Cabet) for the United States in February 1848. These men agreed to pay 600 francs for the privilege of starting the community, and they all signed a contract agreeing that Cabet would be the director of the community.

However, upon landing in New Orleans, the settlers found out that Cabet did not own a contiguous portion of land but instead owned alternate sections, which made it very difficult to start a community. Cabet apparently knew that the land was not contiguous when he agreed to acquire it. Yet he went ahead anyway and did not tell his followers of this difficulty. Furthermore, the land could be reached only via a 300-mile overland journey (there were no roads—only footpaths). The settlers were told that in order to claim the land, they had to build a log house on each of the sections by July.

Although this seemed an impossible task, they set out to claim their land. Twelve of them were killed during the summer by malaria, fatigue, or lightning. In December, Cabet sailed with about 450 followers to rescue his community. When they arrived, almost half of them decided to leave the community to either return to France or to live elsewhere in the United States. Cabet refunded their fees and contributions.

In 1849, Cabet's group found a new site for their community. They bought a number of houses, buildings, and some land in the former Mormon town of Nauvoo, Illinois. Things went well for a few years—they constructed a central dining hall/meeting hall, workshops, and other buildings, started their school, and welcomed new members.

However, back in France, some of the members who had left Icaria were suing Cabet for fraud in connection with the land in Texas. Cabet was called back to France in July 1851. He was found innocent and remained in France for about a year, getting involved with French politics again. When he returned to Icaria in 1852, the community was in disarray: members were bickering and some were protesting by refusing to work. Cabet instituted new rules against smoking, drinking, hunting, fishing, or complaining about the food. People were to remain silent while working. He also asked the community to elect him president for four years (instead of annually, as they had been doing) and asked for the right to appoint inspectors to make sure people were following the rules.

Some members were unhappy with Cabet's rules and demands. Between 1852 and 1856, many community members accused Cabet of being a tyrant and of deceiving the community regarding finances. Cabet continued to push for more power for himself, and the adult male members continued to vote for directors who were opposed to Cabet's rule. In 1856, Cabet was expelled from the community. He and 180 followers traveled to St. Louis in October of that year, where Cabet died of a stroke almost as soon as they arrived (he was 68 years old).

His followers bought three buildings and 39 acres near St. Louis. Although this group was burdened with a number of sick adults and small children, still they persevered, finding jobs in the city and sending their children to public school. However, the community was situated in an unhealthy area, with a sewage-laden river running through the middle, causing disease. By 1864, many young men had left, the community could not pay its mortgage, and the land reverted to the bank.

Meanwhile, the Icarians who had remained in Nauvoo were also experiencing financial troubles. In 1860, they moved to 3,100 acres of farm and timberland near Corning, Iowa. During the Civil War (1861 to 1865), there was a high demand for farm products, and the Icarians were able to make a good living. By 1870, they had paid off their debts and built a relatively prosperous community. However, even this prosperity was apparently not impressive compared to other utopian communities of the time. Charles Nordhoff, who visited a number of communities in the late 1800s, describes the Icarians at Corning as "the least prosperous of all the communities I have visited; and I could not help feeling pity, if not for the men, yet for the women and children of the settlement, who have lived through all the penury and hardship of these many years" (Nordhoff reprinted 1960, 339).

In 1876, a new group of young members arrived in Iowa from France. They demanded voting rights for women and an end to the private gardens kept by some members. In 1878, the community divided into two over this conflict and the older group relocated a mile away.

The new group experienced financial troubles. For one thing, many of them did not like to farm and farming was how they made money. Between 1881 and 1883, some families from this group relocated to the Sonoma Valley in California, near Cloverdale. They called their community "Icaria Speranza," which meant Icaria of Hope. They planted vineyards, peaches, and wheat. However, they were not earning enough to be self-sufficient. They intended to pay their debts from the sale of their Iowa property, but the land did not sell for as much as they had hoped. In 1886, a court ordered the property of Icaria Speranza sold in order to pay the community's debts and the community was dissolved.

The Icarians in Corning (the ones who had moved a mile away) struggled to survive. Many of the young men left the community and they had to hire outside helpers to farm their land. They managed to maintain their community until 1898, when membership dwindled to just a handful. At that point, the members asked the court to dissolve the community.

Beliefs and Practices

The five different Icarian communities all referred to Cabet's novel, *Voyage en Icarie*, as their authority on how to run the community. Their motto was, "All for each and each for all." They wanted to create an ideal society that valued both individualism and community. They believed that each person must work but that a person's work should be freely chosen. Cabet and other socialists felt that living in community would curb the selfish, greedy aspects of human nature.

The issue of private property was a sticky one for the Icarians. In Corning, some members kept private gardens or vineyards, but newer members opposed this practice, saying that everything should be held in common. However, when these newer members moved to California to start Icaria Speranza, they decided to allow a small amount of private property.

Cabet and his followers believed in equality for men and women. However, women and men engaged in different work. Although in many Icarian communities the women did not have full voting privileges, they did speak in the weekly general assembly, when issues of community governance were discussed.

Education was also important to the Icarians. Girls and boys were given the same education. In Nauvoo, they collected a library of over 4,000 volumes—the largest collection in Illinois at that time.

The Icarians valued leisure, entertainment, and culture. In fact, in *Voyage en Icarie*, all the factories close at one o'clock in the afternoon to allow people to socialize and enjoy themselves. While the real Icarians did not have quite so much leisure time, visitors were often amazed at the high quality of the community's music and theater productions. The Icarians organized festive outings, complete with music, dancing, and food, in order to collect walnuts, harvest corn, or enjoy scenery.

There was no official religion in the Icarian communities, but the members met on Sundays to discuss Christian morality or Cabet's writings. Cabet emphasized civic and moral conduct, such as abiding by the Golden Rule: doing unto others as you would have them do unto you.

Marriage was valued, and while divorce was allowed, the divorced members were encouraged to marry again.

Daily Life

Each Icarian family (married couple and young children) was allotted an equal amount of space: two rooms in an apartment (in Nauvoo) or in small private dwellings (log cabins in Iowa, and later frame houses). Each family had the same kind of furniture. People ate in family groups in the dining hall.

In Corning, the community had a large central building that contained a kitchen, dining hall, sewing room, tailor shop, and library. Other buildings housed a pharmacy, a bakery, a laundry, craft shops, barns, and a slaughterhouse.

Although formed in the United States, the community was very much French and members generally spoke French with each other. Its community newspapers were published in French.

In Nauvoo, the Icarians rose at 6:00 a.m., began work, had breakfast at 8:00 a.m., resumed work an hour later, and worked until 6:00 p.m. with a break at 1:00 p.m. for lunch. Members of the community ate a variety of food, including meat, eggs, beans, dairy, vegetables, fruits, and dessert. They drank beer, wine, coffee, and tea.

The men worked either in farming or in one of the workshops, such as the sawmill, the blacksmith's shop, or the tailor's shop. The men also washed the dishes (because this was considered a heavy job requiring strength). The women cooked, did laundry, and took care of the weaving and sewing. The women's work was rotated weekly.

After dinner, the Icarians enjoyed staging Shakespearean plays and performing concerts with their 34-piece orchestra.

How They Made Their Living

The Icarians made their own clothing, shoes, and straw hats, and grew their own food. At first they were able to use royalties from sales of Cabet's novel, *Voyage en Icarie*. When he died, this money was no longer forthcoming.

Members of the communities made their living from various small industries and agriculture, such as a sawmill and a steam-powered flour mill, and by selling cattle and wool from their sheep. They also made wine and sold farm produce.

Leadership and Decision Making

Cabet at first proposed that he should be the only leader for the first 10 years of the community's existence. However, in their first settlement of Nauvoo, he instituted a democratic system in order to win approval of the community charter from the Illinois legislature. Under this system, leaders of the community—including a president and four people in charge of different departments (finances and food, lodging and clothing, education and health, industry and agriculture)—were elected annually by the adult male members. In 1852, when Cabet returned from France and found the community in disarray, he again attempted to take more control, believing that a firm, authoritarian style of leadership was necessary at first. But many members did not want him to exercise so much authority.

For much of the community's history, only adult men voted. However, starting in 1878, some Icarian communities extended the vote to adult women members.

How New Members Were Recruited or Chosen

While he was alive, Cabet spread the word about his community through his French newspaper. Socialists in other European countries were also attracted to the movement. In the 1870s, the Corning Icarian community advertised for new members, distributing pamphlets describing their way of life.

At first, prospective member had to be familiar with Cabet's writing, live in the community for at least four months, pledge $80 to the community, give up all property to the community, and be voted in by three-fourths of the adult male members.

In Icaria Speranza, the membership requirements were tightened. Prospective members had to speak and read fluent French, had to live in the community for one year, and had to be approved by nine-tenths of the adult voting population (male and female).

Children and Youth

Education was very important to the Icarians. Cabet felt that a good education could lay the proper foundation for a happy, productive society. His ideal education, as he spelled out in *Voyages en Icarie*, encompassed physical, intellectual, moral, industrial, and civic education. At Nauvoo, the school building was "the most magnificent structure," according to Lilian Snyder, with two large rooms on the ground floor, two dormitories above, and a fenced yard with garden (1987, 330).

Mothers were taught to promote the physical development of infants and young children, who remained with their parents until the age of three or four. Mothers of young children were released from household duties and could spend all their time with the children. Exercise and dancing were encouraged. From ages three to five, the children played with each other under the supervision of two mothers. At five, the children entered kindergarten.

At the age of four or five, children began living separately from their parents, although they ate meals with their families and visited them on Sundays. From five to twelve, the children learned the usual academics, as well as literature, languages, visual arts, natural sciences, math, and music.

While ideally, Icarian children were to be educated within the community, in Missouri and for a time in Iowa, the children went to public schools.

Relationship with the Outside World

While the Icarians tried to keep themselves separate from mainstream American society (by speaking French, for example), they often interacted extensively with the outside world. For example, in their town of Nauvoo, the Icarians were a minority of only 25 percent. Townspeople in Nauvoo enjoyed the Icarian band concerts so much that the Icarians had to institute a system of ticket taking in order to prevent too large of an audience at any single performance. In Missouri, the Icarians had to accept outside jobs in order to keep the city afloat.

This extensive contact with the public often meant that the community lost members to the outside world.

Reasons for Decline of the Community

The Icarian communities were beset by financial and leadership problems, as well as disease. Because of their insistence on speaking the French language, they were not able to attract many American members and often communities dwindled and dissolved due to lack of able-bodied, hard-working members. Each time they experienced a setback, they started anew, until finally there were no more young members—and there was no more fresh energy—to continue the community.

Influence on the Outside World

Cabet and the Icarians hoped to set up a huge community with as many as a million people. They hoped to create a utopian socialist society that would be the envy of the rest of the world. Instead, they never found a good way to support the communities financially and they were hindered by leadership problems. The Icarians shrank to a handful of members and dissolved completely in 1898.

Their valiant efforts teach us much about how to form and run a communal society. Future communities can learn from the mistakes and setbacks, as well as the successes, of the Icarian movement.

See also: Literary Utopias; More, Thomas; Owen, Robert; Socialism

References

Cabet, Etienne. *Travels in Icaria.* Translated by Leslie J. Roberts, with an introduction by Robert Sutton. Syracuse, NY: Syracuse University Press, 2003.

Holloway, Mark. *Heavens on Earth: Utopian Communities in America, 1680 to 1880.* New York: Library Publishers, 1951.

Nordhoff, Charles. *The Communistic Societies of the United States: From Personal Visit and Observation.* New York: Hillary House, 1960 (first published 1875).

Oved, Yaacov. *Two Hundred Years of American Communes.* New Brunswick, NJ: Transaction Books, 1988.

Snyder, Lilian. "Socialization and Education of the Children in the Icarian Colony in Nauvoo, Illinois, 1849–1860," in *Communal Life: An International Perspective,* edited by Yosef Gorni, Yaacov Oved, and Idit Paz. New Brunswick, NJ: Transaction Books, 1987.

Sutton, Robert P. *Les Icariens: The Utopian Dream in Europe and America*. Urbana: University of Illinois Press, 1994.

Sutton, Robert P. "An American Elysium: The Icarian Communities," in *America's Communal Utopias*, edited by Donald Pitzer. Chapel Hill: University of North Carolina Press, 1997, 279–296.

WEB SITES

French Icarian Colony Foundation: www.icaria.net/ (accessed June 2006).

National Icarian Heritage Society: www.nihs.info/ (accessed June 2006).

Industrial Revolution

Until the late 18th century, most people in Europe and North America made a living by farming or by manufacturing products in their own homes or in small shops.

In the late 1700s, new machines, powered by coal, were invented and installed in factories. Workers were forced to move from their homes in rural areas to cities where the factories were located. The Industrial Revolution allowed the owners of the factories to earn enormous wealth. However, the workers were often forced to toil for up to 14 hours a day for very low wages. The poverty caused by the Industrial Revolution prompted some people to look for another way to organize society, giving rise to the economic theory of socialism and ideas about cooperative, communal ways of living.

The Industrial Revolution began in Great Britain with the development of power-driven machinery. Great Britain had large deposits of iron and coal, which were needed to build and fuel the machines.

For example, spinning and weaving machines were invented that allowed cloth to be made in factories. Before cloth factories were built, spinners and weavers worked at home, where they had the freedom to set their own hours. They could vary their work by doing domestic or farming chores in between the blocks of time they spent making cloth.

With the advent of factories, the workers were forced to move to an unfamiliar urban area and to perform a monotonous job, often without breaks. Children—some younger than 10—worked a full day in the dirty, unsafe factories but were paid much less than adults. Some children were permanently injured or killed by the machines. While children had always helped out in home industries, child labor became a big problem in the factories because of the poor working conditions and very low wages.

The industrialization of production spread during the 19th century to other European countries and North America. Workers in all these newly industrialized countries suffered from low wages and unsafe working conditions. Typically, they lived in crowded, unsanitary conditions, which often led to disease epidemics. Many people in the upper classes of society believed that the working class must be kept poor, or else they would not work hard.

At that time in many countries, workers could not vote. For example, in Great Britain before 1867, only wealthy and middle-class men could vote. Some workers protested their working conditions by forming trade unions (which were generally illegal at that time), by going on strike, or by rioting and destroying machinery.

The poverty created by the Industrial Revolution led to the development of socialist ideas and to the formation of a number of utopian communities that aimed to replace individualism and greed with community and cooperation. The Fourierist phalanxes, the Icarian communities, New Harmony, and the Llano colony were some of the utopian communities formed in reaction to the Industrial Revolution.

See also: Capitalism; Socialism

Reference

Stalcup, Brenda, ed. *The Industrial Revolution*. San Diego, CA: Greenhaven Press, 2002.

International Society
for Krishna Consciousness
(Hare Krishna Movement)

At a Glance

Dates of existence in United States: 1965 to present (although
communal living largely ended by the late 1980s)
Locations: nationwide and worldwide
Peak membership: 5,000 (those who lived communally)
Religious or other belief: Hinduism, Krishna Consciousness

History

The International Society for Krishna Consciousness (ISKCON—also called the Hare
Krishna movement) is the largest and one of the more controversial of the Hindu-
based utopian movements in the United States.

It was started by an Indian businessman named Abhay Charan De, who was raised
in a tradition of Krishna worship. (Krishna is considered to be the incarnation of Lord
Vishnu, one of the three main gods of Hinduism.) As a young married man, De was
initiated as a disciple of the guru Bhaktisiddhanta, who suggested that De ought to
preach about Krishna in English to the rest of the world. In 1959, De became a *sannyas* (someone who renounces the world) and took on the name Bhaktivedanta
Swami Prabhupada.

In 1965, at the age of 69, Prabhupada traveled to New York City to fulfill his guru's
request that he preach about Krishna to the English-speaking world. Prabhupada
found that young Americans were very receptive to his message. On the advice of
one of his first disciples, Prabhupada moved to the Haight-Ashbury district of San
Francisco, which was at the center of a hippie community. Although the official name
of the movement was the International Society for Krishna Consciousness, it was also
known as the Hare Krishna movement because of the chant that was central to the
lives of devotees (see below). Because many of the young followers were transient
and did not have a permanent place to live, the ISKCON temple started communal
living arrangements (Rochford 1985, 159).

Over the next 12 years, Prabhupada's efforts took root. Thousands of young Americans became devotees of his Hare Krishna movement. Prabhupada sent disciples to
other American cities, and even to other countries, to establish temples and communities. Devotees could live communally in the temples if they wished.

The movement also began setting up rural "farm communities." The first of these,
New Vrindaban in West Virginia, was founded in 1968. Prabhupada wanted New
Vrindaban to be a self-sufficient community dedicated to Krishna, like Vrindaban in

Indian guru A. C. Bhaktivedanta Swami Prabhupada (1896–1977), who brought Hare Krishna to the West, sits on an improvised dais and talks to his followers in the V.I.P. lounge at Heathrow Airport, London, September 12, 1969. (Express Newspapers/Getty Images)

India (Krishna's birthplace). He envisioned a sort of Krishna theme park, "a spiritual Disneyland capable of attracting large numbers of visitors," according to Burke Rochford (Rochford and Bailey 2006, 8). New Vrindaban grew to 600 residents by the mid-1980s. Members built the Palace of Gold, a temple dedicated to Prabhupada, featuring stained glass, Austrian crystal chandeliers, walls and floors decorated with marble and onyx inlays, and intricately carved teakwood doors.

Unfortunately, New Vrindaban's guru, Kirtananda, was linked to several crimes, including trademark violations, mail fraud, and conspiracy to commit murder. After several trials, he was jailed for eight years and, after his release in 2004, the Executive Committee of ISKCON prohibited him from visiting any ISKCON temple or community. During the 1990s, while Kirtananda was going through his legal troubles, most residents left the New Vrindaban farm community. New Vrindaban now functions as a tourist attraction and Hindu pilgrimage place, not as a self-sufficient community (Rochford and Bailey 2006, 11–12).

Prabhupada died in 1977. By 1983, there were 50 Hare Krishna communities in the United States and almost 150 throughout the rest of the world (Rochford 1985, 277).

Although the movement was begun by single young adults, over the years, more and more Hare Krishnas married and had children; by the early 1990s, the movement was dominated by married couples with children. During the 1980s, ISKCON was no longer able to support as many members communally and more and more of them began working outside the communities. Also, the movement's system of boarding schools collapsed amid considerable controversy, so parents were again responsible for their children. Although some members still live communally within the temples, ISKCON has gradually taken on the role of a community church, with most devotees living outside the temples (Rochford 1997).

As of 2007, there were 46 ISKCON centers in the United States (www.iskcon.com).

Beliefs and Practices

The Hare Krishna philosophy is part of an ancient Hindu tradition of Krishna worship.

The Hare Krishna goal is "to develop a loving relationship with the Supreme Godhead" (www.iskcon.com). While the Hare Krishnas call this supreme being "Krishna," they recognize that this being has "unlimited names," including Buddha, Jehovah, and Allah. The Hare Krishnas believe that the self is spiritual and not material, and that chanting the Hare Krishna mantra ("Hare Krishna, Hare Krishna, Krishna Krishna, Hare Hare, Hare Rama, Hare Rama, Rama Rama, Hare Hare") is the best way to purify oneself. Hare Krishna devotees abstain from drugs and alcohol, gambling, illicit sex, and eating meat, fish, and eggs (www.iskcon.com).

Devotees are given 108-bead necklaces on which to chant their mantra. They are asked to work up to 16 "rounds" of the mantra (chanting the mantra on each of the beads 16 times). This takes about two hours per day.

The seven purposes of the movement, according to its Web site, include the following three key points: spreading spiritual knowledge to society in order to achieve peace and unity; spreading the knowledge of Krishna as revealed in Hindu scriptures; and teaching and encouraging the Hare Krishna chant (www.iskcon.com).

While Prabhupada preached that men and women were equal spiritually, he also taught that women must be subservient socially. The highest aim for a man was to be celibate, according to Prabhupada, but for a woman the highest aim was to be married, under the protection of her husband, and the mother of children. For those who wished to marry, matches were arranged by temple presidents and other ISKCON leaders (Rochford 1997).

Daily Life

At the movement's height, about 5,000 devotees lived communally in one of the Hare Krishna temples or rural communities.

The daily schedule at most of these communities involved waking up very early (about 3:30 a.m.); showering; worshipping and chanting in the temple; reading scriptures and listening to a lecture; and eating breakfast at about 8:30 a.m. From 9:00 a.m. to late afternoon (about 4:00 p.m.) devotees were engaged in work activities, including fund-raising, with a break for lunch and rest. After worshipping, they ate dinner, attended an evening class at the temple, and went to sleep at about 8:30 p.m. (Shinn 1987, 106).

Men and women lived separately and they wore traditional Indian garments (saris for women, and dhotis for men). The men shaved their heads.

In each community, the housing arrangements were different. A former devotee in Los Angeles describes living in a clean, spare apartment with several other women. Sleeping bags were rolled up every day, and since the women ate while sitting on the floor in traditional Indian style, the bare linoleum floor was washed several times a day. There was no furniture, which was considered to be unnecessary (Muster 1997, 32–33).

Men and women often worked together and lived in the same building, but because celibacy was valued, they often went to extremes to avoid interacting with each other. A woman who lived in a Boston commune describes turning her face to the wall to avoid looking at a man walking by (Rochford 1997).

A former member recalls, "Women generally got the worst accommodations, waited at the end of the food line, and prayed at the back of the temple" (Muster 2004, 315).

How They Make Their Living

The main purpose of ISKCON is to spread the message of Krishna consciousness through chanting, singing, and handing out books about Krishna. This activity is called *sankirtan*. Prabhupada believed that handing out printed material was the best way to convert others to Krishna consciousness, so great emphasis was put on printing and distributing books. The movement is supported by donations from devotees and from outsiders.

Gradually, sankirtan came to mean any kind of activity that brought in money to be used for printing and distributing more books. Hare Krishnas began selling cookies, oil paintings, and other items. Often the Hare Krishnas wore street clothes and wigs (to disguise their shaved heads) when selling these items and did not identify themselves as Hare Krishnas. Sometimes, deception was involved: certain devotees implied that the cheap oil painting reproductions, mass-produced in Hong Kong and Korea, were originals by local artists (Muster 1997, 91).

Perhaps the most serious allegation against the Hare Krishnas involved their knowingly accepting money from drug dealers. In the 1970s, the Laguna Beach Hare Krishna temple president, Rishabdev, accepted large donations from ISKCON supporters who happened to run a drug-smuggling ring. Rishabdev was also said to have helped other devotees become drug smugglers. According to the *Orange County Register*, this drug-smuggling ring was one of the largest in the history of Southern California; however, many Hare Krishna members did not realize that drugs were a major source of revenue for the movement (Muster 1997, 61–65).

Today, the movement is supported almost entirely through donations and it is struggling financially (Kress 2005).

Leadership and Decision Making

While Prabhupada was alive, he was the spiritual and administrative head of the movement. In 1970, he established the 14-member Governing Body Commission (GBC) to help him manage the movement. Before his death in 1977, he appointed 11 close disciples as gurus for ISKCON. The gurus were responsible for initiating new disciples into the movement, and they were to share the responsibility of leading ISKCON with the GBC.

After Prabhupada's death, these two groups—the Governing Body and the guru leadership—were in conflict for many years over who was to really lead the movement (Rochford 1985, 222–223).

As many of the gurus began to vie for power, and as some were expelled for inappropriate and even criminal activities, ISKCON members began to lose faith in the guru system. A reform movement during the 1980s resulted in the GBC appointing 50 gurus. Each guru has less power and prestige than the former 11 gurus, and Prabhupada is again seen as the ultimate master of all gurus and disciples (Deadwyler 2004, 167–168).

How New Members Are Recruited or Chosen

At first, Hare Krishna devotees were almost invariably young (under 30) and unmarried. They encountered the Hare Krishna movement by seeing devotees chanting in public or by being introduced to the philosophy by a friend (Rochford 1985, 78, 150–153).

By the beginning of the 21st century, Hare Krishna temples were attracting a sizeable number of families from India who were seeking Hindu temples, rituals, and philosophy in the United States (Kress 2005).

Children and Youth

The Hare Krishnas value celibacy, although they allow marriage. Married couples are to have sexual intercourse only for the purpose of procreation and then only after chanting for six hours.

For many years, children were generally sent to *gurukulas* (Hare Krishna boarding schools) at the age of five. There were about a dozen gurukulas in North America. They were designed to train the children in living a spiritual life. The schools concentrated on teaching stories of Krishna, Sanskrit (the ancient language of India), and English, as well as some mathematics, history, and sciences. The children were not allowed toys because they were associated with "sense gratification." Students were kept apart from the outside world. After the age of 12, girls were taught to cook and sew, while boys continued their education in Krishna texts. Hare Krishna girls were often married as teenagers (Muster 1997, 73, 75; Shinn 1987, 115–117).

Unfortunately, some of the children were abused in the gurukulas. While Prabhupada made statements against hitting children, he does not seem to have done anything substantial to end the mistreatment. Finally, after years of rumors of abuse, ISKCON asked a sociologist, Burke Rochford, to investigate. His damning report was published in the *ISKCON Communications Journal*, and the information was picked up by the major media.

Rochford found that abuse was far more prevalent in some gurukulas than in others. A high school in Vrindavan, India, where adolescent boys were sent, was one of the worst: the majority of boys were beaten and subjected to sexual abuse. In the United States, some children were beaten and humiliated for infractions such as wetting their beds. The Dallas gurukula, the first one opened in the United States, apparently had a practice of daily beatings for children as young as five. Some children were sexually abused, as well. Many of the students felt lonely and abandoned by their parents. Note, however, that these conditions were not universal; in some gurukulas with a stable, caring staff, abuse was not a problem (Rochford and Heinlein 1998).

Rochford blames the situation on the fact that the Hare Krishna movement did not value children or the gurukulas, which were underfunded. Teachers were not trained and were often sent to work in the gurukulas because they were not good fund-raisers. Parents rarely visited their children. ISKCON closed the gurukulas in the mid-1980s because they could not afford to maintain them, and children began living with their parents and attending local schools (Rochford and Heinlein 1998; Rochford 1997).

In 1999, about 100 young people who had attended the gurukula system sued ISKCON for $400,000. Many temples filed for bankruptcy, and ISKCON negotiated a settlement. They asked abused gurukula alumni to file claims, which about 400 did, in addition to the 100 who had filed the lawsuit (Kress 2005).

According to the ISKCON Web site, the Hare Krishna movement is now concentrating on training its teachers. Its Bhaktivedanta College in Belgium is a seminary offering a bachelor's degree in theology to prepare students to become preachers, teachers, and other religious leaders (www.iskcon.com).

Relationship with the Outside World

The Hare Krishnas have had a rocky relationship with the outside world. The Hare Krishna sankirtan (selling books, chanting, and asking for donations) often took place in public areas such as airports, zoos, and state fairs, which annoyed the public. In 1978, O'Hare International Airport in Chicago banned the Hare Krishnas. In 1981, the U.S. Supreme Court ruled that ISKCON did not have the right to hand out literature and ask for donations at state fairs. In response, the Hare Krishnas cut back on their public distribution of literature (Rochford 1985, 186–187).

While some parents of devotees were glad that their children were off drugs and involved in a spiritual practice, other parents were distrustful of the Hare Krishnas. Former devotees or their parents have, in some cases, sued the Hare Krishnas. In one important case, Robin George and her mother sued ISKCON for kidnapping and brainwashing George in 1974, when she was 15 years old. The suit was initially filed in 1977, and in 1984 the jury awarded George $32 million, one of the largest awards in California's history. The case made its way through appellate courts to the California Supreme Court and ultimately to the U.S. Supreme Court, during which time the courts overturned the decision that George had been brainwashed. The award was reduced to $4 million. In 1992, the Georges and ISKCON settled out of court for an undisclosed amount of money (Shinn 1994).

On a more positive note, ISKCON started public feeding programs in India and Africa in 1974. This grew into Food for Life, which distributes free vegetarian meals to those in need around the world.

New Vrindaban's Palace of Gold is one of the most popular tourist attractions in West Virginia, with up to 500,000 visitors per year (Rochford and Bailey 2006, 9).

Influence on the Outside World

According to A. L. Basham, an expert on Indian civilization, the Hare Krishna movement marks the first time that an Asian religion has been openly practiced by large numbers of Westerners in the West. Unlike other Eastern spiritual imports, Hare Krishna is not just a philosophy or an interesting idea. Devotees often changed their names, way of dress, and way of living. "As such, I don't think anything like it has occurred in the European context since the days of the Roman Empire when Christianity, Judaism, Mithraism and other religions made numerous converts in the West. . . . We have, in fact, people of purely western blood coming from families of the Christian or Jewish tradition who are doing, in the streets of western cities, all the things and more that religious Hindus do in the streets of Calcutta. . . . This being the case, I feel that . . . it is a very important historical phenomenon" (quoted in Gelberg 1983, 164).

The Future of ISKCON

Current and future challenges in ISKCON include acquiring stable funding; determining the role of women within the movement; and attracting and training enough priests and leaders to keep the movement going (Kress 2005).

See also: Cults; Hippies

References

Deadwyler, William. "Cleaning House and Cleaning Hearts: Reform and Renewal in ISKCON," in *The Hare Krishna Movement: The Postcharismatic Fate of a Religious Transplant*, edited by Edwin F. Bryant and Maria L. Ekstrand. New York: Columbia University Press, 2004, 149–169.

Gelberg, Steve, ed. *Hare Krishna, Hare Krishna: Five Distinguished Scholars on the Krishna Movement in the West*. New York: Grove Press, 1983.

Kress, Michael. "Hare Krishna Comes of Age: The Movement Has Matured into a Mainstream Religion after Years of Tumult and Scandal, but Escaping the Past Is Never Easy." *USA Today (Magazine)*, July 1, 2005, www.findarticles.com/p/articles/mi_m1272/is_2722_134/ai_n14814238 (accessed February 2007).

Muster, Nori J. *Betrayal of the Spirit: My Life behind the Headlines of the Hare Krishna Movement*. Urbana: University of Illinois Press, 1997.

Muster, Nori J. "Life as a Woman on Watseka Avenue," in *The Hare Krishna Movement: The Postcharismatic Fate of a Religious Transplant*, edited by Edwin F. Bryant and Maria L. Ekstrand. New York: Columbia University Press, 2004, 312–320.

Rochford, E. Burke Jr. *Hare Krishna in America*. New Brunswick, NJ: Rutgers University Press, 1985.

Rochford, E. Burke Jr. "Family Formation, Culture and Change in the Hare Krishna Movement." *ISKCON Communications Journal*, vol. 5, no. 2, December 1997, www.iskcon.com/icj/5_2/5_2rochford.html (accessed February 2007).

Rochford, E. Burke Jr., and Jennifer Heinlein. "Child Abuse in the Hare Krishna Movement: 1971–1986." *ISKCON Communications Journal*, vol. 6, no. 1, June 1998, www.iskcon.com/icj/6_1/6_1rochford.html (accessed February 2007).

Rochford, E. Burke Jr., and Kendra Bailey. "Almost Heaven: Leadership, Decline and the Transformation of New Vrindaban." *Nova Religio: The Journal of Alternative and Emergent Religions,* vol. 9, no. 3, February 2006.

Shinn, Larry. *The Dark Lord: Cult Images and the Hare Krishnas in America.* Philadelphia: The Westminster Press, 1987.

Shinn, Larry. "The Maturation of the Hare Krsnas in America." *ISKCON Communications Journal,* vol. 2, no. 1, January 1994, www.iskcon.com/icj/2_1/shinn.html (accessed February 2007).

WEB SITES

Bhaktivedanta College: www.bhaktivedantacollege.com/ (accessed February 2007).

Food for Life Global: www.ffl.org/ (accessed February 2007).

International Society for Krishna Consciousness: www.iskcon.com/ (accessed February 2007).

New Vrindaban: www.newvrindaban.com/ (accessed February 2007).

Jerusalem/Society of Universal Friends

At a Glance

Dates of existence in United States: 1788 to 1819
Location: New York
Peak membership: 260
Religious or other belief: Christianity, Society of Universal Friends

---

Jerusalem was a utopian communal society associated with the Society of Universal Friends, the first religious movement started by a native-born American woman—Jemima Wilkinson.

Wilkinson was born in 1752 in Rhode Island. Her father was a Quaker and as a child she began attending Quaker meetings. Her mother, after giving birth to 12 children, died when Wilkinson was in her early teens. As a young adult, Wilkinson joined a group of "New Lights," a zealous, emotional Christian movement that emphasized conversion experiences. As a result, she was expelled from the Quaker society in 1776.

That same year, Wilkinson developed a serious fever that resulted in delirium, making her believe that she had died and that her body was taken over by "the Spirit of Life from God," as she later wrote. She also received the message that this spirit, in her body, "had descended to earth, to warn a lost and guilty, perishing dying World, to flee from the wrath that is to come; and to give an Invitation to the lost Sheep of the house of Israel to come home" (quoted in Wisbey 1964, 13).

About a week after this vision, Wilkinson had recovered from her illness. She began calling herself the "Universal Friend" and no longer used the name "Jemima Wilkinson." She preached her first sermon under a tree in the churchyard of a Baptist meetinghouse. She also started holding religious meetings in her home and the homes of her friends, and in public places in nearby towns.

From 1776 to 1785, the Universal Friend traveled in New England and Pennsylvania, speaking and attracting followers. The beliefs of the Society of Universal Friends were similar to those of other Christians, with an additional emphasis on interpretation of dreams and, for a time, faith healing. Wilkinson preached about the approach of the millennium (the thousand years preceding or following the second coming of Christ), the punishments of Hell, and the importance of repentance. Herbert Wisbey suggests that her powerful presence was at least as important as her message: "The emotional impact of her personality, strengthened by the aura of mysticism that surrounded her, opened new insight and gave new meanings to the familiar biblical texts and stories that she recited" (1964, 29).

Wilkinson is remembered as an attractive woman with loose black ringlets of hair that fell to her shoulders. She wore clothes typical of male preachers: a brimmed hat and flowing black robes with a man's white kerchief at her neck. Indoors, she took off her hat, as was the custom for men at that time, whereas women were not seen in public without a cap. Her presence was said to be confident and sincere.

In about 1785 or 1786, Wilkinson began to think of buying land and forming a community away from the corrupt outside world. She was, perhaps, growing tired of the opposition and harassment she sometimes faced while preaching. She may have been influenced by the successful Shaker community in Niskayuna, New York, or by the Ephrata Cloister in Pennsylvania. In fact, the beliefs of the Universal Friend and the Ephrata Cloister were very similar: both believed celibacy was more virtuous than married life but both accepted marriage. Wilkinson's group adopted the Saturday Sabbath, as did the Ephrata Cloister.

Her followers were actively working on purchasing land for a community in western New York, in the Finger Lakes region. At that time, this area was occupied by the Iroquois, and the fertile, wooded land was coveted by many white people. The community first acquired land in 1788 near Seneca Lake, where followers worked hard to clear land, plant wheat, and build log houses, a gristmill (flour mill), and a sawmill. The Universal Friend arrived to live on the property in 1790. There were about 260 followers on the land at that time.

The community did not own property in common, although wealthier members were asked to donate land and labor for the Universal Friend and poorer followers. They had a community house used for religious meetings and a school.

However, the community was not able to acquire a valid title to the land, due to political and legal wrangling. Some followers had bought a township about a dozen miles to the west, near Keuka Lake, and Wilkinson moved there in 1794. This town consisted of 23,000 acres and was named Jerusalem. Wilkinson refused to own any property in her own name, so "her" land and house at the new site were held in the name of a faithful follower.

Wilkinson and about 16 followers lived in a log house with a middle section used for religious meetings. The Universal Friend also offered lodging to any needy guests. Near the house were log barns and a workshop for spinning, weaving, and sewing. Wilkinson was active in helping the new community get started: she sawed wood, worked in the garden, and oversaw the work on the farm. The Jerusalem community cleared land, planted wheat and rye, erected a sawmill, kept sheep and cattle, and made maple sugar. Wilkinson also ministered to the sick and helped to settle disputes.

Religious meetings were held on Saturday mornings, during which the Universal Friend gave a sermon of an hour and a half. Following Quaker tradition, other members could speak after the sermon if the Spirit moved them. Also similar to Quaker tradition, no singing was allowed in the meeting. On Saturday evenings, the community held a silent meeting of prayer and meditation.

A visitor describes the community's food as being "frugal" but of better quality than any he had eaten since leaving Philadelphia. He enjoyed meat, pudding, and salad. Members ate together, although the Universal Friend dined alone in her room (Wisbey 1964, 131).

Few new converts joined the community after the move to Jerusalem, and as members moved away or died, the community began dwindling. Some observers speculate that the land chosen was too choice—the community was never able to escape from the outside world, since the outside world was determined to have a piece of this good land for itself. Also, as Wilkinson aged, her presence may not have been as commanding as it was before.

The community was also saddled with legal troubles: some followers tried to claim ownership of the land held in trust for the Universal Friend. This legal wrangling went on until long after Wilkinson's death in 1819.

The community effectively ended when she died. Members were never able to find another spiritual leader. However, Wilkinson's followers continued to live on the land until 1863, when the last follower died.

See also: Ephrata Cloister; Millennialism; Shakers

Reference

Wisbey, Herbert A. *Pioneer Prophetess: Jemima Wilkinson, the Publick Universal Friend*. Ithaca, NY: Cornell University Press, 1964.

Jesus People USA

History

Jesus People USA (JPUSA) grew out of the "Jesus Movement" that was part of the hippie era in the United States. In the late 1960s, some hippies turned away from drugs and toward Christianity. They started coffee shops and formed communes to welcome others who wished to get off drugs and turn to Jesus. This Jesus Movement looked to the early Christian church for an example of how to live and rejected much of modern society, including established churches. Members of the Jesus Movement rejected drugs, but they spoke about their belief in Jesus as a mind-altering experience. James Drane noted that "Jesus People are 'high' on Jesus. They have an intense emotional experience of Jesus" (1973, 120).

The Jesus Movement spread throughout the country and up to 300,000 people may have been part of the movement (Drane 1973, 112). Those involved in the movement were called "Jesus People," "Jesus Freaks," or "Street Christians."

The group that eventually became Jesus People USA was an offshoot of Jesus People Milwaukee. In 1972, some members of the Milwaukee group started traveling by bus to spread their views on Jesus through "witnessing" (talking with strangers about their faith in Jesus Christ), playing concerts, and handing out copies of their newspaper, *Cornerstone*. They called themselves the "Jesus People USA Travelling Team." During a stay in Gainesville, Florida, many outsiders confused them with another Christian communal group, the Children of God, which also had a community in Gainesville. Jesus People USA found it difficult to attract new members in Gainesville.

During Christmastime of 1972, members of Jesus People USA traveled back north to visit relatives and were invited to play concerts in many churches. In mid-1973, the Faith Tabernacle Church in Chicago offered to let them stay in its basement for two weeks. They began witnessing in Chicago, and more and more people joined them. The group ended up staying in the basement of Faith Tabernacle Church for two years and growing to 120 people.

During the early 1970s, Jesus People USA weathered several controversies. A married elder of the group, John Herrin, was accused of making sexual advances toward a young woman in the group. The group urged him to attend counseling, which did not help. He eventually left the group. Another controversy was the "spanking" era, described below (Shupe 1998, 35).

Meanwhile, JPUSA was looking for a way to move out of the basement of the Faith Tabernacle Church. In 1975, the members bought a six-apartment building in a middle-class Chicago neighborhood. Using loft beds and triple bunk beds in all the rooms, they managed to squeeze their entire membership into this building. In 1977, they bought another building to house their growing membership.

That same year the group was approached by a new African American group, New Life, which was a Christian community of 15 married couples. New Life was struggling and Jesus People USA helped by exchanging members with them and typesetting their magazine. In 1978, the two groups decided to merge.

In 1979, Jesus People USA decided to settle in a poor neighborhood of Chicago in order to be closer to many of the needy people it served. The group bought a run-down hotel in Chicago's Uptown neighborhood. People from the neighborhood began joining Jesus People USA for dinner and these "guests" grew to up to 300 per night in the early 1980s. At this time, Jesus People USA started noticing more and more homeless people. It began putting up people who were being evicted from their homes or who were escaping abusive situations. Over the years, the group bought more buildings to house its members and those it was serving.

In 1984, the group held their its Cornerstone Christian music festival.

Jesus People USA wanted to be a part of a larger Christian movement. In 1989, the group joined the multi-ethnic Evangelical Covenant Church, which has congregations throughout the United States and Canada. Jesus People USA is one of the only congregations of this church that lives communally.

Also in 1989, Jesus People USA formed Cornerstone Community Outreach. With help from the city of Chicago, the group bought a building and renovated it into a homeless shelter for women and children that includes a daycare center. Cornerstone Community Outreach also runs after-school programs, a senior housing center, and temporary housing centers. In addition, Jesus People USA provides weekly dinners and food bags for those in need; parenting and life-skills classes; job training; counseling; affordable housing assistance; and other services.

Beliefs and Practices

The Jesus People USA Web site has a "statement of faith" that describes the collective beliefs of the community, including the belief that the Bible is the "Word of God"; that Jesus Christ was both divine and human; that God created humans in his image; that Adam and Eve's sin resulted in a separation of humanity from God, and only through Christ's death on the cross can humans be reconnected to God and receive forgiveness and eternal life; that believers in Christ can live a "godly life" even within the "fallen world" because of the Holy Spirit residing in them; and that Jesus Christ will "personally and visibly" return to Earth to judge humans, although no human can predict when this will happen (http://www.jpusa.org/faith.html).

Jesus People USA believes in living communally, like the first-century Christians as described in the New Testament Book of Acts. According to their Covenant, printed on the group's Web site, "We believe that Christ has shown us that ordinary people, by pooling their resources, can accomplish extraordinary things" (http://www.jpusa.org/covenant.html).

At first, the group concentrated more on educating themselves and others about the Bible and Jesus Christ—it held regular classes for this purpose. The members were also involved with street witnessing and playing Christian rock concerts. Its work serving the needy grew gradually. While witnessing, members came across people who were homeless or who needed other material help. A longtime member explained: "We never set out to start a soup kitchen—or a shelter! All of it really just came to us, just happened organically. People just started dropping folks on our doorstep. . . . At that time we were young kids in the 1970s looking for deeper meaning in our lives and looking for ways to be living our faith" (quoted in Fenger 2006).

In 1974, a man named Jack Winters began coming to Jesus People USA from a nearby Christian community to teach classes. Winters preached that the rebellious younger generation needed discipline in order to deal with its rebellion. He instituted a practice of "spanking" members for their sins. Members voluntary asked to be spanked with a thin pine dowel as a way to promote spiritual growth. However, the group eventually decided that this practice was not helpful to its spiritual growth and abandoned it by 1978 (Shupe 1998, 35; Trott "A History").

Jesus People USA believes in voluntary poverty. For example, the community does not provide health insurance for its members but uses public health services. Still, they do enjoy a certain level of comfort. "Members do not go hungry or barefoot like medieval mendicants [religious beggars], nor do they forego health and medical assistance. Rather, in a disciplined way, they have attempted to eliminate social class distinctions within the group" (Shupe 1998, 31; Jesus People USA Covenant).

Within the community, sexual relations outside of marriage are prohibited. Violence or abuse toward spouses or children is considered sinful (Shupe 1998, 33).

Although the group agrees that men and women are equal before Christ and that women can serve as leaders, they do not agree with feminism. They also reject homosexuality and abortion (Trott "A History").

Daily Life

At first, living conditions were crowded: members lived in a church basement or in overcrowded homes. During the time they lived in the basement of the Faith Tabernacle, they woke up at 7:00 a.m. and moved their belongings out of the church's way. At 9:00 a.m. they prayed together. They held two classes at 10:00 and 11:00 a.m., had lunch, and spent the afternoon witnessing, with a break for dinner. After dinner, they did more witnessing and studying. They took Mondays off to relax (Trott "A History").

The group currently lives in a former hotel in downtown Chicago. Single people share rooms with other singles of the same gender, and couples are assigned a room together, which they can decorate however they like. Young children share a room with parents and older children room together near their parents. Meals are cooked and served in a common kitchen, although members are free to take food back to their rooms (Shupe 1998, 32–33; http://www.jpusa.org/covenant.html).

New members are typically assigned housework or maintenance work. After some time, they usually begin to work in one of the community's businesses. The Council of Elders makes work assignments, taking into consideration the members' talents and desires, as well as the community's needs (http://www.jpusa.org/covenant.html).

The group shares all the income from their business, as well as community cars. Drinking and smoking are not allowed. In their free time, they enjoy reading, playing games, picnicking, and playing sports.

How They Make Their Living

At first, the group relied on donations from people they met during street witnessing. In 1975, Jesus People USA started businesses to support itself. The group sold painting and home repair supplies, started a typesetting business and a moving company, and organized a carpentry crew.

As of 2006, the group continued to run home repair businesses. Other community businesses include Belly Acre Designs, which prints corporate or band logos or designs on T-shirts and hats; *Cornerstone* magazine and its companion book publishing arm, Cornerstone Press; and Grrr Records, a recording label for Christian rock musicians.

Leadership and Decision Making

When the group first settled in Chicago, it had one elder, John Herrin, with a council of deacons and deaconesses to help him make decisions. After his departure, the deacons and deaconesses chose two elders to serve together. In 1978, the number of elders was increased to eight. There are no set terms of office. Under the elders are deacons, deaconesses, and group leaders. Men and women can both serve as leaders (Shupe 1998, 32; Trott "A History").

The Jesus People USA Covenant, printed on its Web site, states that "the leaders submit one to another, to other members of the community, and to God's Word, the Bible. No final authority lies with any one individual" (http://www.jpusa.org/covenant.html).

How New Members Are Recruited or Chosen

According to the Covenant printed on the JPUSA Web site, prospective members of Jesus People USA must be at least 18 and "profess a born-again experience with Jesus Christ, as well as a continuing personal relationship with Jesus as Lord of his or her life." The community stresses that members must agree with the Jesus People USA statement of faith. While the community recognizes that other Christians might have differing but valid interpretations of the Bible, "when people live as closely as we do, doctrinal contention over significant points of faith within our membership can cause destructure, discord and strife" (http://www.jpusa.org/covenant.html).

After living at the community for a two- or four-week trial period, prospective members are accepted (or rejected) by the Council of Elders for a one-year provisional membership period. After that, by mutual agreement, the membership becomes permanent.

Members are not obligated to turn over all their assets to the community, but they are asked to store their assets away from the community and not to draw from personal bank accounts while at the community. Members are allowed to retain ownership of certain personal items such as clothing, small appliances, and bicycles.

Children and Youth

Decisions about whether or not to have children, and how many children to have, are left up to the individual couple. The community believes that life begins at conception but sees nothing wrong with preventing conception, so birth control is allowed. Children are not raised communally—they are considered to be the responsibility of their parents.

The community runs a school for its children, the Uptown Christian School, which as of 2006 had about 70 children from preschool to 12th grade. After high school, the young adults are asked to make a choice about whether they want to go to college, work within the community, or enter a nine-month "discipleship program," which involves some work within the community, as well as classes, readings, and discussions on religious and social justice issues. College students are allowed to remain part of the community as long as they abide by community rules and take part in church services, meetings, and chores.

Young people who wish to work outside of Jesus People USA generally leave the community. An exception would be if the outside work corresponds with the purpose and values of JPUSA (such as teaching, social work, or medical work). In that case, the worker could conceivably continue to live at JPUSA if he or she is willing to contribute his or her wages to the community and abide by community rules.

The young adults do not date but instead go out in groups. If two young people are serious about each other, their parents and mentors in the community help them decide whether or not they should pursue a relationship that could lead to marriage. Young adults joining the community are asked to refrain from a serious relationship for one year (Kaiser 2006).

Relationship with the Outside World

In addition to serving the needs of people in their neighborhood, Jesus People USA also runs the Cornerstone Festival, an annual art and music festival drawing about a 100 Christian bands and musicians. About 20,000 people attend the Cornerstone Festival. *Cornerstone* magazine also reaches outsiders.

In 1993, Jesus People USA was publicly criticized by an evangelical Christian sociology professor, Ronald Enroth, who had interviewed a number of former members. Enroth wrote that Jesus People USA implemented harsh discipline bordering on abuse and that leaders lived a better lifestyle than the rank-and-file members.

In an effort to defend the group, Jesus People USA invited Enroth and other sociologists to visit the community. Enroth never did visit, but Anson Shupe did, and wrote about his findings. Shupe suggests that the former members who criticized

Jesus People USA, and Enroth himself, do not understand how a communal group works:

> Most of the accusations of "abuse" that Enroth reported seem, in retrospect, to represent snippets of communal living that can be embellished to appear outrageous, especially to someone unfamiliar with the realities of communal life. Still other complaints come from unhappy memories of times spent in such a group. An example illustrates the point. A leader's child wore newly purchased shoes on one occasion while another member's child wore older shoes. JPUSA provides each family with a periodic modest allowance of discretionary cash to use for whatever purposes it wishes. One couple had chosen to use its allowance for a new pair of shoes, the other had not. Later, accusations of leadership favoritism were made.
>
> Similar examples abound in Enroth's accusations of abuse. Hurt feelings and misperceptions are probably inevitable within groups whose first-generation members are exploring the dimensions of their lifestyle on a daily, experimental basis. Bitterness over larger issues elicits from angry ex-members a retrospective avalanche of minor complaints that become defined as "abuse." The pain associated with departure from a religion sometimes parallels the pain associated with some divorces. . . .
>
> JPUSA does not seem to be an internally dangerous or abusive group. It works well for the majority of its members. There is steady, but minimal, turnover of those for whom it doesn't work (Shupe 1998, 35–38).

Influence on the Outside World

In the 1960s and 1970s, Jesus People USA helped young people who were adrift and looking for meaning in their lives. Although at first it was simply one of many small Jesus-based communes, Jesus People USA has grown and prospered to become one of the largest, longest-lived of the Jesus communities.

Jesus People USA has also helped thousands of needy people through its housing and feeding programs. In 2002, Jesus People USA began raising money for a Romanian Christian organization called Osana, which serves needy people in Romania. According to the Cornerstone Community Outreach Web site, Jesus People USA hopes to further expand its international activities.

See also: Bible Communism; The Family/Children of God; Hippies

References

Drane, James. *A New American Reformation: A Study of Youth Culture and Religion.* New York: Philosophical Library, 1973.

Fenger, Darin. "Communities That Serve Others . . . and LOVE Doing It." *Communities*, summer 2006, 48–52.

Jones, Timothy. "Jesus' People." *Christianity Today*, September 14, 1992, 20–25.

Kaiser, Wendi (a founding member of Jesus People USA). Phone interview with the author, November 30, 2006.

LeBlanc, Doug. "Conflict Divides Countercult Leaders." *Christianity Today*, vol. 38, no. 8, July 17, 1994, 58–59.

Shupe, Anson. "Jesus People USA," in *Sects, Cults and Spiritual Communities: A Sociological Analysis*, edited by William Zellner and Marc Petrowsky. Westport, CT: Praeger, 1998, 27–40.

Trott, Jon. "A History of Jesus People USA." *Cornerstone*, www.jpusa.org/life.html, accessed November 2006.

WEB SITES

Cornerstone Community Outreach: www.ccolife.org/aboutus.cfm (accessed November 2006).

Jesus People USA: www.jpusa.org/ (accessed November 2006).

Jesus People USA Covenant: www.jpusa.org/covenant.html (accessed November 2006).

Religious Movements Home Page at the University of Virginia: http://religiousmovements. lib.virginia.edu/nrms/jpusa.html (accessed November 2006).

Jewish Agricultural Communities

At a Glance

Dates of existence in United States: 1881 to 1941
Locations: nationwide
Peak membership: 100 colonies with varying memberships
Religious or other belief: Judaism, secularism, socialism

History

The Jewish farming communities were an attempt to provide a livelihood for the increasing numbers of Jewish refugees from Eastern Europe arriving in the United States at the end of the 19th century. Jewish aid groups in the United States and Russia hoped that these farming communities would help to relieve overcrowding in urban areas where Jews tended to settle, and also to establish Jews as farmers, when for years Jews had been barred from owning land or farming in Eastern Europe. The Jews formed almost 100 farming communities across the country, almost all of which were short-lived.

A handful of these Jewish farming communities were started even before the wave of Russian-Jewish immigration. The first, Ararat in New York, began in 1820. Its ending date is uncertain. Shalom, also in New York, started in 1837 and ended five years later.

In the late 19th century, Jews began fleeing from Russia because of persecution in that country. A group called Am Olam was founded in Russia to help Jews escape, move to the United States, and establish themselves as farmers.

By teaching them how to farm, Am Olam hoped to change the image of Jews. Because they had been barred from farming in Eastern Europe, Jews generally worked as peddlers and merchants. They were often accused of making money off of other people's hard work. Am Olam hoped that, by becoming farmers in the United States, Jews would be able to avoid this negative stereotype in their adopted country.

Groups of American and Western European Jews also helped the Russian Jews travel to the United States and start communities. These groups included the Alliance Israelite Universelle, a French group; the Mansion House Committee in London; the Jewish Colonization Society founded by a German man, Baron Maurice de Hirsch; and the American-based Hebrew Emigrant Aid Society.

Many of the Jews involved in the farming communities were probably influenced by the socialist writings of Robert Owen and Charles Fourier, who called for cooperative communities as a way to avoid the evils of the Industrial Revolution (Herscher 1981, 26).

The first farming community of Russian Jews was Sicily Island, Louisiana, which started in 1881 and lasted for less than a year. The land proved unsuitable for agriculture: it was a swamp. The colonists were for the most part unfamiliar with farming, and they contracted malaria and yellow fever due to the mosquitoes attracted by the flooding of the Mississippi River.

In 1882, some 20 different Jewish farming colonies were founded, the largest number of any year. Nine more colonies were begun that decade. Some of the more successful communities—located in New Jersey—combined agriculture with industry, so they were not in as bad shape if their crops failed. They were also close to New York City and Philadelphia, where they could sell their crops and products. In addition, maybe because they were closer to Jewish population centers, these communities received more outside funding than some of the others. The other state with a large number of Jewish colonies was North Dakota, a place where it was easy to acquire land and where wheat-growing was profitable (Bartelt 1997, 354, 359–362).

Although most colonies were funded by Jewish organizations, some also received funding from outside sources. Happyville in South Carolina (1905–1908) was financed by the South Carolina Immigration Bureau, because South Carolina wanted to attract immigrant farmers to the state. Clarion in Utah (1911–1916) was funded in part by the Mormon Church. The Mormons wanted to attract more farmers to Utah and they were sympathetic to communal living. They saw Jews as their "biblical brethren" (Bartelt 1997, 365).

By the early 1900s, the Jewish agricultural communities were fading. In their place were organizations and publications to help individual Jewish farmers: the Jewish Agricultural Association, which began in 1900, and *The Jewish Farmer*, a publication that started in 1908 and lasted until 1959 (Bartelt 1997, 366, 369).

Years after the Russian-Jewish farming communities had ended, one more Jewish farming community was started: Sunrise Colony, which began in Michigan in 1933 and moved to Virginia. While this was started by a Russian-born Jewish man and attracted Jewish settlers, its members were American-born Jews, and its belief system was rooted in anarchist ideals (Shor 1987, 175).

Uri Herscher speculates that the Jewish agricultural communities were short-lived because of poor planning. "They were conceived in haste and planned in stress. Indeed, their organizers tended to ignore or discount the complexities and dangers, the depressed state, of post–Civil War American farming." Most of the Jews involved had no experience with farming and often the land they were given was unsuitable for farming (1981, 31, 109–110).

Below are descriptions of some of the longest-lasting and/or more significant of the Jewish agricultural communities.

Alliance, New Jersey (1882–1906): Alliance, located in Salem County, just 35 miles from Philadelphia, was begun by 40 families and grew to 70 families by the end of 1882 (Herscher 1981, 129).

Families at first lived in barracks and later built individual houses consisting of two rooms, one above the other. The community established a school to teach the children English and to prepare them for public school in a nearby town. The members did not work on Saturday (the Jewish Sabbath). However, they built four synagogues, and the community also had a public library and a night school for adults, as well as lectures and concerts.

The families planted trees, grapevines, berries, and vegetables. They also worked for neighboring farmers in order to make extra money. In addition to the individual farms assigned to each family, the community started a cigar factory in 1883 and later added a shirt factory. However, a fire destroyed these buildings. After a benefactor donated a sewing machine to each family, home tailoring also brought in income. In 1897, two Philadelphia businessmen established a canning factory at Alliance.

By 1885, the farmers were able to earn a profit from their farms, and they continued to enjoy this income until 1888. After this time, the income from farming started to fall, as prices for farm products fell all over the country. The farmers were increasingly in debt (Bartelt 1997, 360–361; Herscher 1981, 74–84).

New Odessa, Oregon (1882–1888): Before forming this community, the potential members worked for a while near Hartford, Connecticut, to learn farming techniques. By the spring of 1883, they had moved to Oregon and as many as 50 people lived in the community. They wanted it to be completely communistic, with money and goods held in common. They built a large two-story building, in which they slept on the second floor, and used the first floor as a communal kitchen and dining hall. They began raising wheat, oats, and peas, but it was difficult to transport the crops to buyers. However, they were able to make a good living from selling their timber to the Oregon and Pacific Railroad, being built nearby.

The people of New Odessa believed in living frugally: they ate beans, peas, and coarse bread. They enjoyed evening discussions and a once-a-week recital on a pipe organ. They did not believe in religion and so did not keep the Jewish Sabbath.

Despite their relative prosperity, New Odessa eventually failed perhaps more for ideological reasons than economic reasons. The community broke into two factions led by two different leaders. William Frey, who was not Jewish, wanted New Odessa to follow his "religion of humanity," which involved multiple marriage partners. Paul Kaplan and his followers felt that Frey was too idealistic. Frey and 15 of his followers left in 1885. Eventually, New Odessa's members began to move away due to the lack of women in the area to marry, the isolation of the colony, and a fire that destroyed their community building (Bartelt 1997, 359; Herscher 1981, 39–48).

Palestine/Bad Axe, Michigan (1891–1899): This community began when a group of Jewish peddlers in Bay City, Michigan, came together to buy a large tract of land in Bad Axe from wealthy bankers. Each family bought its own parcel of land. At first, colonists lived in tents and many returned to Bay City when winter came. Some who stayed in Bad Axe were helped by a neighboring farmer who gave them milk and bread. Unlike other Jewish colonies, which were founded by philanthropic organizations, the settlers at Bad Axe did not seem to have any outside source of funding. They built 10 one-room shacks that housed 23 adults and 34 children and called their community Palestine.

A retired Jewish farmer came to their aid. He raised enough funds to provide each family with clothing, food, and a cow. He bought oxen, plows, and other equipment for the community, and trained them in growing oats, peas, and potatoes.

Despite this help, the community did not survive long. Its land was poor, and it was far from markets. By 1899, the colonists still could not pay for their land, and they began moving away. The troubles of the colonists at Palestine led to the formation of the Jewish Agricultural Society, which helped Jewish farmers to succeed (Bartelt 1997, 362–363; Davidson 1943, 234–249).

Woodbine, New Jersey (1892–1941): One of the best known Jewish agricultural communities, Woodbine was located 56 miles from Philadelphia and started with 60 families.

Like Alliance, Woodbine combined farming with industry. The men arrived first and were each given 30 acres. They were to clear 10 acres, leave 20 wooded, and build their own houses. Each man was to plant four and a half acres of fruit trees and berries. Colonists helped each other get their farms ready. By 1893, the settlers at Woodbine had built a hundred miles of roads, cleared 650 acres of farmland, and built houses with plumbing. Woodbine had a machine shop, clothing factories, a knitting mill, a hat factory, and a box factory. The railroad opened a station at Woodbine and the community built a hotel.

The year 1894 was called "The Year of Trouble," because the funders of Woodbine decided to stop subsidizing the colony—they thought the community could be self-sufficient. However, when the colonists protested, the trustees took a second look and decided to continue their support. More industries were set up at Woodbine to replace ones that had failed.

Also in 1894, the Baron de Hirsch Agricultural School was started at Woodbine. It offered free education in agricultural techniques to boys and girls 14 or older. The school continued until 1917.

By 1901, the population of Woodbine had grown to 194 families—1,400 people total. Thirty-four of the families were not Jewish. The community had built a synagogue, a Baptist church, a public bathhouse, and two school buildings. Industries included a machine and tool company, a lock company, clothing factories, and a brick company. The community had a volunteer fire department and a board of health (Bartelt 1997, 363; Herscher 1981, 84–107).

In 1903, Woodbine was incorporated as a borough of Cape May County, New Jersey, and was considered the "first self-governed Jewish community since the fall of Jerusalem," according to the Woodbine Web site. In 1941, the Baron de Hirsch Fund, which had supported the community, allowed individual settlers to purchase land, after which the rest of the land was given to the borough of Woodbine. The town is still in existence today, although most of its people are no longer Jewish (www.boroughofwoodbine.net).

Why did Woodbine succeed, for the most part, when other Jewish agricultural communities failed? According to Uri Herscher, the main reason was the financial support of the Baron de Hirsch Fund. "Woodbine . . . had the benefit of careful planning, expert direction, and large resources. Most important of all, it became evident that only as an agro-industrial community would Woodbine survive and flourish" (1981, 106).

Influence on the Outside World

Although the Jewish farming colonies did not succeed as communities, they did succeed in dispersing Jews across the United States and in introducing Jews to farming. According to the Jewish Agricultural Society, the number of Jews in farming grew

Woodbine, New Jersey, Jewish agricultural community. (American Jewish Historical Society)

from 1,000 in 1900 to 100,000 in 1937. Jewish farmers also started a number of rural cooperatives such as the Cooperative Poultrymen's Association in New Jersey, the Cooperative Fire Insurance Companies in New York, and the Intermountain Farmers Association in Utah (Bartelt 1997, 367–368).

The American experiments in Jewish farming communities were useful to the kibbutz movement in Israel, which has grown into one of the largest communal movements in history. The Jews in Israel learned from the mistakes of the American Jews, although these mistakes pointed mainly to "the steps to be avoided rather than the positive measures to be taken" (Herscher 1981, 118).

See also: Anarchism; Orderville and Mormon Communalism; Socialism

References

Bartelt, Pearl. "American Jewish Agricultural Colonies," in *America's Communal Utopias*, edited by Donald Pitzer. Chapel Hill: University of North Carolina Press, 1997, 352–374.

Davidson, Gabriel. *Our Jewish Farmers and the Story of the Jewish Agricultural Society.* New York: L. B. Fischer, 1943.

Herscher, Uri D. *Jewish Agricultural Utopias in America, 1880–1910.* Detroit, MI: Wayne State University Press, 1981.

Shor, Francis. "An American Kibbutz? Sunrise Colony and the Utopian Problematics in Comparative Perspective." In *Communal Life: An International Perspective*, edited by Yosef Gorni, Yaacov Oved, and Idit Taz. New Brunswick, NJ: Transaction Books, 1987.

Web site

Borough of Woodbine: www.boroughofwoodbine.net/ (accessed February 2007).

Kaweah Cooperative Commonwealth

At a Glance

Dates of existence in United States: 1885 to 1892
Location: California
Peak membership: 300
Religious or other belief: socialism

History

Although short-lived, Kaweah was an ambitious attempt to create a community based on socialist principles. Its demise was brought about when the government took over its land in the formation of Sequoia National Park.

Kaweah was started by a group of socialists in California. One of them was Burnette Haskell, a lawyer and editor of his own small newspaper. In 1882, in search of news, Haskell stumbled upon a meeting of the Trades Assembly, a socialist organization. Haskell, who had never heard of socialism before, was so impressed by what he learned during the meeting that he offered his newspaper, *Truth*, as the official voice of the Trades Assembly. He became a voracious reader of socialist literature and started another socialist organization, the International Workingmen's Association, which helped build the labor movement in California.

Influenced by Laurence Gronlund's 1884 book *Cooperative Commonwealth*, which gives a blueprint for forming a socialist community, Haskell and a few friends decided to start such a community. They organized a land purchase company, requiring members to pay a monthly fee to join.

One of the members of this land purchase company was Charles Keller, who found out that a giant forest of sequoias (a type of redwood tree) had been opened for sale. Keller suggested that the company buy this land. Although this forest had no roads into it, and was cut off from the land around it by deep gorges, Keller thought the community could make a good living from selling timber.

The region was unique for its concentration of giant sequoias, some of which were 30 feet in diameter and 300 feet tall. In addition to the giant sequoias, the forest contained firs, cedars, and pines.

It is unclear whether Keller was proposing to log the giant sequoias, or only the other trees. A U.S. government land agent who visited the community in 1889 stated that "they have no idea at all of denuding the forest and leaving a desert of stumps. They propose to first work up the fallen timber then to thin out the thick growth and foster the remainder, to clear the ground of stumps and cultivate and improve the thus opened spaces" (quoted in O'Connell 1999, 69).

216

Federal law prohibited large corporations from buying this land. Instead, it was supposed to be made available to individuals, who could buy a maximum of 160 acres at $2.50 per acre. Accordingly, 53 members of the land purchase company filed claims for adjacent sections of this land in October 1885 (Tweed 1986, unnumbered; O'Connell 1999, 30).

However, because these individuals applied for land together and because many of them listed the same San Francisco address (a boarding house), the government became suspicious of their motives. Were they a front group for a corporation? When the members of the land purchase company returned in December with their money, they were told that their claims were being investigated and they could not complete the purchase of the land.

Haskell, Keller, and their fellow members were not discouraged. They were confident that the government would soon realize they were not a front group for a corporation. They decided to go ahead and settle on the land they had claimed.

In the spring of 1886, the members established a camp on the north fork of the Kaweah River and pondered the problem of how they could gain access to the land. They decided that building a railroad to take out the timber would be too expensive but that a wagon road would be feasible. Over a hundred members worked until mid-1890 to build this road. When the road finally reached the edge of their forest, they set up a small sawmill powered by a steam engine that had, with difficulty, been hauled up the road. The community started logging some of the smaller trees. The production of the sawmill did not meet Haskell's expectations. He complained that the mill was producing only a tenth of its capacity, because of a number of excuses, including inexperienced loggers, lame oxen, bad foremen, and time off for picnics and meetings (Tweed 1986, unnumbered; O'Connell 1999, 108–113).

Meanwhile, the federal government continued to delay approving the land claims of the Kaweah members. In addition, farmers and conservationists began calling for protection of the giant forest of sequoias. Farmers in the valleys around the Sierra Nevada wanted the forest protected because, by slowing the snowmelt, the forest ensured a good supply of water in late summer. A small group of conservationists was calling for the protection of the forest for its own sake. In 1890, bills to create Sequoia National Park were passed in the U.S. Congress. The park was to include the land claimed by the Kaweah Cooperative Commonwealth. Although private land was protected within the park, because the Kaweah Cooperative's land claims were never approved, they were forced to move.

The Kaweah members next leased private land within the park boundaries. However, the federal government forced them to move again in 1891, claiming that the land was not private. A few weeks later, the government realized their mistake and allowed the colonists to return, but the stress of moving so often had begun the disintegration of the community. In 1892, the community was officially disbanded.

Beliefs and Practices

Kaweah was meant to be a cooperative refuge from the competitive outside world, where a member "shall be given such freedom for growth and development that he . . . shall tower far above the foundation walls. . . . Here shall be Joy, Music, and

Laughter, Art, Science, and Beauty, and all things else for which Poets have sung and Martyrs died, and of which in the outer world we see but the palest phantoms," according to literature put out by the community. Kaweah was not just intended to be a haven for its members, but an example to the outside world (quoted in Hine 1966, 86).

Daily Life

While the road was being built, members lived at "Advance," their name for the camp they set up at the beginning of the road. Members lived in large tents.

A U.S. land agent who visited Kaweah reported that "at colony headquarters . . . I found some 300 men, women and children concentrated in nicely constructed tents, and they appeared to be a wonderfully 'happy family' of enthusiasts. They eat from a public table. . . . Every colonist who labors in any capacity is credited with his or her time on book . . . and no money is circulated in the Colony." The tent homes were apparently furnished with homemade rugs, and tapestries and pictures hung on the canvas walls (O'Connell 1999, 72, 84).

Advance also housed the printing office that produced the community newspaper, the *Kaweah Commonwealth.*

Although women were considered equal to men, women tended to perform work traditional to their gender, such as teaching children, cooking, and cleaning (O'Connell 1999, 83–84).

Kaweah members enjoyed baseball games and swimming in the river. They took overnight trips into the giant sequoia forest. They named the large trees after famous socialists—the largest was called "Karl Marx" and is now known as "General Sherman." They had a band and an orchestra, and enjoyed dancing on occasion. They sometimes held literary and scientific classes for adult members (Hine 1966, 89–90).

How They Made Their Living

New members were required to pay $100 before moving into the community, and this brought in much-needed money. Not all members of the community lived there: about 500 people joined in order to support the effort, but the population of Kaweah at any one time was between 150 and 300 people. Some members gave much more than was required. Other members had to work outside the community in order to make ends meet (Tweed, 1986, unnumbered; O'Connell 1999, 58).

Leadership and Decision Making

When the road work started, the community still had no legal existence, but was a voluntary association of individuals and families. Haskell proposed that the community should be organized as a limited partnership, in which the community could screen those who wanted to buy shares and join as members. This, Haskell thought, would ensure that only like-minded socialists would join the community. Keller wanted the community to be organized as a corporation, in which anyone could buy a share. Keller argued that this was the only way to raise enough money to achieve their goals.

In 1888, Haskell's side won in a vote put to the membership. In response, Keller and 50 other members left the community. Under the new bylaws, each member was entitled to one vote (women were included as members). Members were to work eight hours per day and were to be paid 30 cents per hour. The payment was in the form of "time checks" that could be exchanged for items at the community store or could be used to buy goods and services from other members (O'Connell 1999, 47–54).

Kaweah's organization was adapted from Laurence Gronlund's book, *Cooperative Commonwealth*. There were eight departments, each with a superintendent. The Board of Trustees was above the superintendents and above the trustees was the General Meeting, in which all members could participate. The General Meeting was held on the first Saturday of the month (Hine 1966, 87–88).

How New Members Were Recruited or Chosen

Potential members heard about the community through Haskell's newspaper, *Truth*, through the community's newspaper, the *Kaweah Commonwealth*, and through Nationalist Clubs formed across the country to promote the ideas of socialist writer Edward Bellamy.

According to the community's bylaws, new members were to pay $500 to join. Once the first $100 was paid, the member could live and work within the community and pay off the rest with labor, goods, or money.

Children and Youth

Kaweah ran a school in a tent that, as of 1890, had 52 students. The children called their teachers by their first names. The children were free to attend school or not, as the mood struck them (O'Connell 1999, 127–128).

Relationship with the Outside World

The outside world, including the U.S. government, was suspicious of the Kaweah community. The federal government investigated the community several times and while some agents wrote favorable reports, the government did not approve the community's land claims.

Newspapers in the outside world also wrote negative articles about Kaweah, including accusing it of trying to defraud the public by soliciting donations for the community. In 1892, the government charged the trustees of Kaweah with using the mail to defraud the public. Because of insufficient evidence, Kaweah was found not guilty (Hine 1966, 95–98).

Reasons for Ending the Community

The community's leaders miscalculated when they decided to go ahead and live on land to which they had no legal claim.

Influence on the Outside World

The wagon road built by the Kaweah members was for 36 years the only way to access to the forest of giant sequoias. Colony members never received any money from the government for their work creating this road.

Charles Keller, a founder of the community and the main instigator behind the road and the idea of cutting timber, was interviewed in 1937, when he was 91 years old. He expressed deep satisfaction with the creation of Sequoia National Park. "I am glad, very glad it worked out as it did, and I know now that it was as God intended. When I visited Sequoia last year and saw the wonderful roads, the thousands of people getting away from the cities and that wonderful place accessible to all people, I was very happy. . . . I didn't fail when I founded the colony and my visions have worked out today and are continuing to work out. Now rather than that beautiful place owned and enjoyed by a few, it is as I would have it—enjoyed by all and protected and preserved for them forever" (quoted in Tweed 1986, unnumbered).

See also: Bellamy, Edward; Gronlund, Laurence; Socialism

References

Hine, Robert V. *California's Utopian Colonies*. New Haven, CT: Yale University Press, 1966.

O'Connell, Jay. *Cooperative Dreams: A History of the Kaweah Colony*. Van Nuys, CA: Raven River Press, 1999.

Tweed, William. *Kaweah Remembered*. Three Rivers, CA: Sequoia Natural History Association, 1986.

Keil Communities—Bethel and Aurora

At a Glance

Dates of existence in United States: 1844 to 1881
Locations: Missouri, Oregon
Peak membership: 650 (Bethel); 600 (Aurora)
Religious or other belief: Christianity

History

The Keil communities were started by William Keil, who was born in Germany, learned the trade of a tailor, and immigrated to the United States as a young married man. He quickly set up a tailoring shop in New York City. While there, he studied pharmacology, found that he had a gift for healing people, and moved his family to Pennsylvania, where he opened a drug store and sold medicines. He began to call himself "Dr. Keil."

In Pennsylvania, Keil attended an evangelical Methodist revival meeting, became converted to Methodism, burned the book that contained his secret medical formulas, and became a preacher in 1839. After about a year, he broke with the Methodists and became an independent evangelist. He converted German-speaking people, including several former members of George Rapp's Economy colony (the last phase of the Harmony communities). He and his followers decided to travel west to find land on which to form their community.

In 1844, they settled in Shelby County, Missouri, where they farmed and became nearly self-sufficient. The community grew to about 650 people and was the largest town in the county. In 1850, it established a satellite community about 50 miles away, in Adair County, which was named Nineveh. Keil decided to start a second community in Oregon. Perhaps he wanted to move because of his natural restlessness or perhaps because Missouri was growing too fast for him—in 1852, a railroad station was opened 13 miles south of Bethel, Missouri (Snyder 1993, 43, 49–50).

In 1856, Keil and about 400 people from Bethel moved to an area 29 miles south of present-day Portland. Keil left Andrew Giesy in charge of the Bethel community. The settlers named their Oregon community Aurora, after Keil's daughter.

In 1862, an Aurora colony member took care of a neighbor outside the colony who had smallpox. This member brought the disease back into the community and several members died, including four of Keil's children (Snyder 1993, 69).

Keil had held all community property in his own name. Starting in 1872, he began to transfer the title to much of the community property to individual families.

Perhaps Keil knew that there was no strong leader to succeed him and wished to make provisions for his community after his death. However, the families continued to live as one community.

Keil died in 1877. Without his strong leadership, the members decided to end their community. Bethel disbanded in 1879 and Aurora in 1881. Although some property was still held in Keil's name, his wife and children signed away their rights to it, acknowledging that this property was being held for the community as a whole. The property was divided among the members (Snyder 1993, 87–88, 100).

Beliefs and Practices

William Keil was an uneducated man who had read little except the Bible. He believed in one fundamental Christian truth: "Love one another." Keil felt that this ideal could only be attained through a communal way of life in which members shared goods and services. He was also influenced by the description of the early Christian church, when Christians lived communally (Hendricks 1933, 40).

The Bethel and Aurora communities held church services every two weeks. Women and men entered the church separately and sat on different sides. Keil preached "persevering industry . . . , humility, simplicity, prayer, self-sacrifice, and neighborly love," according to Eugene Snyder (1993, 69). They celebrated Christmas, New Year's Day, and Keil's birthday, at which time "there was music, community singing, and feasting and dancing" (Hendricks 1933, 120–121).

The main rule of the community was that every member must give all goods and money to the community treasury. The purpose of this community treasury was to "do good to the poor, that by our means we might be of benefit not only to the brethren that are with us at present, but also to the poor in the future." However, the community did promise to return the property of departing members (Hendricks 1933, 16).

Daily Life

Families at Bethel and Aurora lived in their own separate houses or apartments. Charles Nordhoff visited Aurora and Bethel in 1873, and he described their homes as very clean but spartan, without carpets or easy chairs. Nordhoff complained that the communities were not beautiful. Of Bethel, he said: "It has one main street, poorly kept, and in parts even without a sidewalk; cattle and pigs were straying about it." Each family tended its own garden patch and kept chickens. Families took the food they needed from the common stores, and no accounts were kept of this (1960, 312, 315, 324).

At Bethel, members built a three-story house for Keil, which included a second floor used for community banquets, dances, and meetings. The third floor was Keil's office and laboratory, where he made herbal treatments for his followers. They also built a large multipurpose building that included a storeroom and a hotel for outsiders. Their church featured interior woodwork of walnut, a floor of red tiles, and a gallery for the band (Snyder 1993, 37–39).

At Aurora, the members again built a three-story house for Keil, along with a hotel. The community church had a 114-foot steeple, rose windows, and two balconies where the community bands could play. The community held picnics, dances, and concerts in a park with a rose garden and a building called the Park House (Snyder 1993, 73–75).

The food at Aurora was said to be quite good. An article in the Portland *Oregonian* praised the community's fried potatoes, pig sausage, smoked ham, bread, cottage cheese, candies, jellies, and cakes (Hendricks 1933, 175). Nordhoff declared Aurora to have "the most extensive orchards in the state, in which are apples, pears of all kinds, plums, prunes . . . and all the commoner large and small fruits" (1960, 311).

While they farmed and raised animals of their own, the colonists at Aurora also enjoyed Earth's natural bounty. A man who was raised in Aurora "tells of the wonderful Oregon salmon, the trout, crawfish, strawberries, blackberries, thimbleberries, and so on, and of the pigeons that used to thicken the air; and the grouse, and the venison. 'Oregon was indeed a great state for epicures,' he declares" (Hendricks 1933, 156–157).

Nordhoff noted that the people at Bethel and Aurora did not have a peculiar way of dressing—they wore plain but customary clothes of that time period. Even during a wedding, the bride and guests did not wear fancy clothes (1960, 312).

Smoking tobacco and drinking wine and whiskey were all allowed in moderation.

How They Made Their Living

The Keil communities aimed for self-sufficiency. They farmed, kept animals, grew fruits and vegetables, and established gristmills, sawmills, and woolen mills. Members made shoes and clothing for each other.

The communities sold excess supplies to the outside world. Bethel was noted for four products in particular: deerskin gloves, plows, wagons, and whiskey (Snyder 1993, 41).

Although members were supposed to contribute all income to the community coffers, families did sometimes sell excess goods to the outside world so as to have some cash for a few luxuries (Nordhoff 1960, 319–320).

Both communities ran hotels and restaurants for outsiders, which brought in cash.

Leadership and Decision Making

Keil was the religious and practical leader of the communities. Eugene Snyder describes him as "a father figure. He saw that everyone was taken care of, in old age and in sickness. He assigned jobs, sometimes approved or discouraged marriages, and generally was a patriarch looking after the Colony members." He appointed trustees to help him (1993, 81).

How New Members Were Recruited or Chosen

Members of the communities were generally German-speaking immigrants. Children born within the community usually stayed. Potential members were sometimes first hired as outside workers and given wages. If they wanted to join the society, they were required to donate all their property and money to the community (Nordhoff 1960, 313).

Children and Youth

Both Bethel and Aurora had schools to educate their children, who were taught only the basics: reading, writing, and arithmetic. Keil did not believe in higher education that did not have a practical use in the community. He told Charles Nordhoff that the community would pay for education in practical knowledge or skills that would benefit society as a whole. "But if a young man wants to study languages, he may do so here, as much as he likes—no one will object; but if he wanted to go to college for that—well, we don't labor here to support persons of such undertakings, which have no bearing on the general welfare of the society" (1960, 317).

Although Keil did not value higher education, the first Oregon student to attend Harvard, Henry Finck, was raised in Aurora. In preparation for college, he was privately tutored by an educated member of the community (Hendricks 1933, 152, 157).

Relationship with the Outside World

The Keil communities voted and took part in local politics. In Bethel, during the Civil War, they tried to be politically neutral although they opposed slavery. In Oregon, they were openly political. Community members became county commissioners, a county treasurer, members of the legislature, a mayor, and a county clerk (Hendricks 1933, 117).

The Aurora members interacted extensively with the outside world: they set up a food booth at the state fair, welcomed travelers to their hotel, and rented their park to outside groups. Their musicians played in towns and cities nearby (Snyder 1993, 4).

Reasons for Decline of the Community

Without the strong leadership of William Keil, the community members decided to disband.

Influence on the Outside World

The members of Bethel and Aurora were among the first white settlers in Missouri and Oregon. Both Bethel and Aurora have been preserved as historic sites.

See also: Bible Communism; Harmony Society

References

Hendricks, Robert J. *Bethel and Aurora: An Experiment in Communism as Practical Christianity*. New York: The Press of the Pioneers, 1933.

Nordhoff, Charles. *The Communistic Societies of the United States: From Personal Visit and Observation*. New York: Hillary House, 1960 (first published 1875).

Snyder, Eugene Edmund. *Aurora, Their Last Utopia*. Portland, OR: Binford and Mort Publishing, 1993.

WEB SITES

Aurora Colony Museum: www.auroracolonymuseum.com/ (accessed April 24, 2008).

Historic Bethel German Colony: www.bethelcolony.missouri.org/ (accessed April 24, 2008).

Koinonia Farm/
Koinonia Partners

At a Glance

Dates of existence in United States: 1942 to present
Location: Georgia
Peak membership: less than 50, plus hundreds of visitors and volunteers who are considered part of the community
Religious or other belief: Christianity, racial equality

History

Although Koinonia has always been a small community, it is important in terms of breaking racial barriers in the southern United States and offering inspiration to others working toward racial equality. It is also the birthplace of Habitat for Humanity, an international organization dedicated to providing housing for low-income people.

The community was founded by Clarence Jordan, a Baptist preacher who wanted to foster racial equality and help poor black southerners become economically self-sufficient. The name *Koinonia* is Greek for "church," "fellowship," or "community." The word is used in the Greek New Testament to refer to the early Christians, who shared their wealth and lived communally. With money provided by a wealthy businessman in Louisville, Kentucky, Jordan bought land in Sumter County, Georgia, in 1942.

During the 1940s, Koinonia members concentrated on improving their own land and creating a "demonstration" farm that would show others how to improve the soil and become economically secure. They began holding classes for black and white farmers, and organized black farmers into a seed cooperative.

The Koinonians also reached out to African American churches, teaching a study course for ministers, holding an interracial Sunday school and a vacation Bible school, and bringing black and white Christians together for study and singing. At this time in the South, blacks and whites did not eat or socialize together and schools were segregated, so Koinonia was breaking significant barriers.

During the first half of the 1950s, Koinonia was growing; the group concentrated on solidifying its community by creating a formal membership process and leadership structure. Koinonia started an interracial summer camp in 1955. By this time the community had about 60 residents—including members, visitors, and workers—about a quarter of whom were African American (K'Meyer 1997, 81).

From 1956 to 1958, members of Koinonia became the target of a hate campaign because of their racial views. As civil rights became a national issue, outsiders began to take more notice of Koinonia's interracial activities. Vandals tore down the farm's sign and shot at the storefront of the farm's roadside market. In 1957, the community store was blown up; guns were fired into homes at Koinonia, but the local police refused to help.

The region's white community also began to boycott Koinonia. It refused to buy eggs from the farm and would not sell fertilizer, seed, and other necessary supplies to the farm's members. Insurance companies cancelled Koinonia's policies. Koinonia began processing pecans and selling them via mail order to replace the egg business. Friends and supporters bought supplies secretly for Koinonia. Volunteers came from across the country to participate in work camps at the community. Supporters sent cash donations and set up an insurance fund for Koinonia.

The violence began to die down, but Koinonia struggled to survive. The community was heavily in debt. By 1959, the violence had scared away almost all members and visitors at Koinonia. Only three families and a few guests were still living on the farm. They again began visiting their African American neighbors and helping those in need. The Koinonians hired blacks at good wages for their pecan-processing plant. New members began to arrive, as well as visitors and volunteers. Up to 1,000 people per year came to help out (K'Meyer 1997, 97, 135).

In 1962, the price of pecans fell and Koinonia was not doing well financially. Koinonia decided to give up the common purse and have each family be in charge of one economic area, such as farm management or mail order. The community still struggled and considered dissolving.

Within a year, Jordan saw hope in the fact that the civil rights movement had reached Georgia. Koinonia became a haven and a place to stay for black and white activists who came to participate in the civil rights movement. In particular, leaders of the Student Nonviolent Coordinating Committee, one of the main organizations of the civil rights movement, visited and ate at Koinonia. Another major organization, the Congress of Racial Equality (also known as CORE), held classes in nonviolent resistance at the farm. Koinonia took care of children whose parents were arrested during this struggle and offered rest and recreation for the activists. The civil rights movement gave Koinonia members a reason to keep going (K'Meyer 1997, 151–154).

Between 1965 and 1968, Koinonia again struggled financially, and the members again considered disbanding. In 1968, a man named Millard Fuller and his family came to work with Koinonia. Fuller was a wealthy white businessman from Alabama who had, after a marital crisis, decided to dedicate himself to Christ and service to blacks. The Fullers decided to join Koinonia and help revitalize the community. The community changed its name to "Koinonia Partners," and the focus shifted to partnerships between families. Each family would be able to start its own enterprises with loans from a common fund. Koinonia also proposed to provide land and help people build their own houses. Families would continue to share socially and spiritually.

Jordan died in October 1969. In the 1970s, volunteers again began arriving at the community, housing construction boomed, and craft industries were started. In the early 1970s, new middle-class members revived the idea of the common purse, and Koinonia again began providing for the necessities of full members. Most African Americans preferred to work at Koinonia for a paycheck and did not participate in the common purse (K'Meyer 1997, 179).

In 1976, Koinonia Partners and Fuller founded Habitat for Humanity in order to build houses all over the world on the partnership model started at Koinonia. During the 1980s, Koinonia members engaged in peace activism by demonstrating at nuclear power plants and participating in vigils (http://www.koinoniapartners.org/History/Timeline.html).

In the 1990s, in response to the fact that African American employees did not feel part of the community, Koinonia again re-evaluated its structure. Workers felt that they were not able to participate in making decisions to the same extent as full members who pooled their money, because only full members could take a turn as community leaders. Koinonia ended up discontinuing the common purse and having everyone earn a salary (K'Meyer 1997, 187–188).

As of 2007, about a quarter of Koinonia's 33 members identify themselves as nonwhite (http://directory.ic.org/records/?action=view&page=view&record_id=647).

Beliefs and Practices

Jordan envisioned a community of people living a Christian life of sharing all resources, similar to the early Christian church as described in the New Testament Book of Acts. He also wanted the community to foster racial equality, because he believed that the teachings of Jesus pointed toward the need for fellowship among the races. He believed that in order to be a true disciple of Christ, one must live in an interracial community (K'Meyer 1997, 30–31).

For many years, members of the community were conflicted between their two main beliefs: living in a Christian community that pooled all its money and fostering racial fellowship. Generally speaking, poor southern blacks were not attracted to a community that required them to share whatever little money they had. Also, blacks were sometimes afraid to associate with Koinonia because of the threat of violence from unsympathetic whites. One black family in the process of achieving full membership was scared away by the violence and threats confronting the community. So it seemed for many years that members of Koinonia would not be able to live by both of their main beliefs.

Although the outside world often saw Koinonia only as a place that promoted racial integration, Koinonia members believed that their Christian community was just as important as their racial goals. They struggled for years with the notion of leaving the southern United States, given the violence and hate they encountered there. Some members believed strongly in staying in the South in order to continue to be a witness for racial fellowship. Others thought that the Christian community ought to move somewhere else where they could live in peace. Starting in the 1950s, Koinonia developed a friendship with the Bruderhof when members of this utopian Christian community visited Koinonia. From them, some Koinonia members came to accept the idea that individuals should surrender to the will of the group, which represents the will of God. Other Koinonia members were not convinced that the will of the group was the same as the will of God. This continued to be a source of conflict within Koinonia. The Bruderhof encouraged the Koinonians to join with them. Although Koinonia remained independent, some Koinonia members moved away to join the Bruderhof.

Koinonia has always been a pacifist community. In 1948, when the United States started a peacetime draft, Jordan signed a petition encouraging young men to refuse to register. For Koinonia, nonviolence was not just a political tactic; it was a way of life, a way of following Jesus' words to love one's enemies. While Koinonia supported the civil rights movement, Jordan also began to wonder if the movement was nonviolent enough. By 1965, Koinonia had broken its ties with the organized civil rights movement because of differences over nonviolence (Lee 1971, 54; K'Meyer 1997, 156–157).

Daily Life

When Jordan and the first members began living on their land, the soil was poor and eroded, and the buildings were in disrepair. They first built a shop/apartment building. The two original families pooled all their money and decided together how to spend it.

In the early years, Koinonians woke up early and started their day together with meditation and prayer. They worked and ate together, and in the evening talked or sang songs on the porch of the main house (K'Meyer 1997, 54–55).

Koinonia made no effort to break up the nuclear family. While members turned their shop into a communal kitchen, families were encouraged to eat the evening meal together by taking the food to their homes. Eventually all the individual family homes or apartments had their own kitchens, so they could eat some meals in privacy (Lee 1971, 72–73).

As of 2007, according to the Koinonia Partners Web site, the community schedule involves prayer at 7:45 a.m., as well as services and pauses for prayer and meditation several times during the workday. The community often eats the noon and evening meals together. On Sundays, members and guests can attend the local church of their choice (http://www.koinoniapartners.org/intern/index.html).

How They Make Their Living

Koinonia's first business was selling eggs in a cooperative business with their neighbors. They combined the eggs from their own hens with those from neighbors and sold all the eggs to local hotels, stores, and restaurants. When the local boycott of the farm destroyed their egg business, Koinonia developed a business processing pecans and selling them via mail order across the country (K'Meyer 1997, 47, 93).

As of 2007, according to the Koinonia Partners Web site, the community sells pecans and pecan products, books by Clarence Jordan, fair trade coffee and tea, and a few crafts. It also has an organic garden that supplies some of its own food (http://www.koinoniapartners.org/business.html).

Leadership and Decision Making

Koinonia has gone through a number of different leadership structures. At first, it had no designated leaders at all. The community made decisions by meeting and discussing issues until it was able to reach consensus. In the early 1950s, Koinonia developed a more formal leadership structure. Each farm enterprise had a supervisor, and the community as a whole had a president, secretary, and treasurer, all of whom were elected for one year (K'Meyer 1997, 53, 68).

In the 1970s and 1980s, when the common purse was revived, full members (those who pooled their money and received necessities from the community) rotated through various leadership positions. In the 1990s, the community was restructured again: it hired an executive director and created paid leadership positions. This new structure allowed African Americans, most of whom preferred to earn a salary, to participate in leadership. In 1994, an African American employee became the executive director of Koinonia Partners (K'Meyer 1997, 188–189).

How New Members Are Recruited or Chosen

Jordan spoke about the community at college campuses, Baptist student meetings, and other sympathetic venues.

At first, anyone who wanted to could come to Koinonia and be considered part of the community. Koinonia included students, ministers, volunteers, and laborers who worked in the fields. They all shared meals and participated in the community as much as they wanted. Some workers shared the common purse and others received wages, as they preferred (K'Meyer 1997, 53).

In 1950, Koinonia developed a more formal membership process. First, the newcomer was considered a novice and after a few months, a provisional member. After about six months, the full members voted as to whether the new person was ready for full membership. As full members, individuals were to give all their belongings and money to the group. In return, they were provided with food, shelter, medical care, and money for clothing and other personal necessities (K'Meyer 1997, 67–68).

Children and Youth

Children were and are raised by their parents.

Relationship with the Outside World

Initially, Georgia's white community tolerated Koinonia's integrationist racial views. Minor conflicts erupted in 1948 and 1950, when Koinonia members invited nonwhite men to attend a local white-only church. Church officials eventually banished Koinonia from the church (K'Meyer 1997, 59–60).

From 1956 to 1958, the community was the target of a massive campaign of hate and violence, including an economic boycott. Not only did the local police not help, but the community was accused of inflicting the violence themselves, in order to gain sympathy and contributions. In addition, the Koinonians were accused of being communists (K'Meyer 1997, 90–91).

Influence on the Outside World

Although it has always been a very small community, Koinonia has been an inspiration to people all over the country who were working toward racial equality. In the mid-1960s, during a low point in the community, it had a mailing list of 10,000 supporters (K'Meyer 1997, 166).

See also: Bible Communism; Bruderhof; Civil Rights Movement

References

Hollyday, Joyce. "The Dream That Has Endured: Clarence Jordan and Koinonia." *Sojourners*, vol. 8, no. 12, December 1979, www.koinoniapartners.org/History/Dream.html (accessed May 2, 2007).

K'Meyer, Tracy Elaine. *Interracialism and Christian Community in the Postwar South: The Story of Koinonia Farm*. Charlottesville: University Press of Virginia, 1997.

Lee, Dallas. *The Cotton Patch Evidence*. New York: Harper and Row, 1971.

WEB SITES

Habitat for Humanity: www.habitat.org/ (accessed May 2007).

Koinonia Partners: www.koinoniapartners.org/ (accessed May 2007).

Koinonia Partners in the Fellowship for Intentional Community Database: directory.ic.org/records/?action=view&page=view&record_id=647 (accessed May 2007).

Koreshan Unity

At a Glance

Dates of existence in United States: 1869 to 1982
Locations: Florida, Illinois, New York
Peak membership: 200
Religious or other belief: Koreshanity

History

The Koreshan Unity was founded on the unusual belief that the planet Earth is a hollow sphere containing the entire universe within it.

The community was started by Cyrus Reed Teed, who was born in 1839 in New York to a family of Baptists. He became a medical doctor and also was interested in alchemy—a way to transform base metals into gold. One midnight in 1869, while he was in his laboratory, he had a vision of a woman surrounded by purple and gold light. She told him that God was male and female, that Earth was hollow and enclosed the universe, and that all humans are reincarnated. She also told him that humans must live communally, as did the early Christians, and that he, Cyrus Reed Teed, was the prophet who would bring this message to the world.

While continuing to practice medicine, Teed started a study group to spread these teachings. However, he felt compelled to proselytize to his patients, but the townspeople had little patience for his bizarre message. Teed moved from one New York town to another in an effort to keep his medical practice afloat. He took the name "Koresh," which is the Hebrew form of "Cyrus."

In 1880, discouraged by his foundering medical practice and his failure to attract large numbers of followers, he moved to Moravia, New York, and took over his family's mop-making business. Within two years, this business also failed. He then moved to Syracuse with a few followers, including his wife, his sister, and a cousin.

In 1886, Teed's wife died and the group moved to New York City. There, he met a woman from Chicago who invited him to her hometown to give a speech at a meeting of the National Association of Mental Science. In his speech, Teed explained how brain forces could be used to restore health. He invited any ill members of the audience to come forward and receive healing. The association was so impressed that the members elected him their president and organized a series of lectures in Chicago.

Teed and his followers moved to Chicago, and by 1888, they had set up their community with about 60 members, mostly women. Within five years, the community had grown to 123 members and had moved to a mansion in Washington Heights

232

(now part of Chicago) called Beth-Ophrah. Teed opened a university, called the College of Life (later the Koreshan University), which offered classes on Koreshanity. He also started two societies dedicated to miracle cures, as well as the Guiding Star Publishing House to print his literature, including a weekly newspaper.

Teed traveled around the country giving speeches. He lectured to other utopian communities such as the Shakers and the Harmonists. Koreshan Unity branches were opened in a number of cities, including San Francisco, Denver, Baltimore, and Boston. However, these branches were not successful financially and followers often moved to Chicago.

Teed was looking for land on which to build his community. In 1894, he bought 300 acres of land in Estero, Florida (near Fort Myers), at a low price from Gustav Damkohler, a German immigrant who was inspired by Teed's writings. Some of Teed's followers moved to Florida to begin building the community. By 1903, the entire community had moved to Florida. By 1906, the community owned 7,000 acres of land.

Between 1896 and 1899, Teed and a follower, Ulysses Grant Morrow, conducted scientific experiments to prove that Earth's surface was concave. Morrow invented a surveying device, which he called the "rectilineator," and using a telescope and this device, Teed and Morrow believed they had proved their theory. They published the results of their experiments in 1899.

The Koreshan community had a rocky relationship with the outside world. The local people of Estero and Fort Myers were not happy that a few hundred Chicagoans had moved in and voted as a bloc. In response, Teed started his own political party, the Liberty Party, and started publishing his own newspaper, *The American Eagle*.

In October 1906, Teed and the community's candidate for county commissioner were attacked by the Fort Myers town marshal. Teed never recovered from his injuries and died in December 1908.

Teed had told his followers that he was immortal, and so the community kept a vigil for three days, praying and waiting for him to come back to life. He did not and the county health officials buried the corpse.

Annie Ordway (also called Victoria Gratia), who was the second in command of the community, took over its leadership. However, she left in 1909 to start another Koreshan community in Seffner, Florida (which did not survive long). In 1910, another group of Koreshans moved to Fort Myers, lived communally, and supported themselves for 20 years by operating a commercial laundry.

The Estero community dwindled. By 1940, only 35 people lived there. A few leaders tried to revive the community. A refugee from Nazi Germany, Hedwig Michel, joined the group, and Lawrence Bubbett, the son of early Koreshan converts, agreed to return to Estero to help lead the colony. Under their leadership, the Koreshans opened a restaurant, managed a gas station, and restored buildings and gardens. Despite all this renewed activity, the community decided that the only way to preserve the Estero property was to donate it to the state of Florida.

In 1961, the governor of Florida accepted the 300-acre property and created the Koreshan State Historic Site.

Michel died in 1982, and with her the community ended. She is considered to be the "last Koreshan," the last person to be officially accepted into the Unity and to live on Koreshan land.

Beliefs and Practices

Teed believed that Earth's surface was 100 miles thick and that the entire universe was contained within it. The sun was in the center and was half light and half dark. Outside of this sphere there was nothing.

This unusual belief did not originate with Teed. A number of earlier scientists, such as Scottish physicist Sir John Leslie and English astronomer Edmund Halley, had also theorized that Earth might be hollow. However, Teed was unique in combining science, religion, and communal living. Teed taught that the belief in a concave, hollow Earth was the same as belief in God and Christ. "To know of the earth's concavity and its relation to universal form, is to know God; while to believe in the earth's convexity is to deny him and all his works. All that is opposed to Koreshanity is Antichrist," he declared in the introduction to one of his books (quoted in Landing 1997, 376, 379, 387).

The community valued celibacy and the celibate members had the highest status. However, married couples were allowed to join, as were people who believed in Teed's teachings and sent financial support but did not live in the community.

Teed preached that God was both male and female and argued for women's suffrage, equal wages for women and men, and a uniform standard of morality for both genders (Kitch 1989, 145).

Daily Life

When the community bought the land in Florida, Teed imagined building a star-shaped city. In reality, the community constructed 35 buildings along the banks of the Estero River. A visiting Shaker described the community this way: "The buildings are mostly set in a park along the right bank of the Estero River for about a mile. This park contains sunken gardens filled with flowers, banana trees loaded with fruit, paw-paw trees in fruit, [and] palm trees of many varieties" (quoted in Landing 1997, 388).

The arts were important to the community. Its kitchen and dining building housed an organ that was used during evening singing sessions. In 1904, it built the Planetary Court, a two-story house with seven bedrooms and one meeting room. The next year, it built an art hall with a stage and rooms for classes, lectures, and concerts. Its orchestra, which played for outside and community audiences, performed popular and classical works. It produced plays on the Bamboo Landing next to the river.

Koreshan Unity members enjoyed "fire fishing" at night during the fall. They attached wire baskets to the bows of their boats and lit pine knots in the baskets. The fish, seeing the light, would jump out of the water, and some would land in the boats (Rea 1994, 38).

Its bakery was capable of producing 600 loaves of bread per day. Men and women ate at separate tables. When the community was first being established, members had to rely on fish and alligator meat for food. They enjoyed swimming in the Estero River and picnicking on the beach (Sutton 2003, 142).

How They Made Their Living

The Florida settlers farmed, planted fruit trees, and built a sawmill. The community also kept bees and had a machine shop, concrete works, and a blacksmith and plumbing shop. Its power plant produced electricity not only for its community but also for the surrounding area. Its printing press accepted orders from outside the community. Members also made money through a bakery, a store, and a boat building business (Rea 1994, 31–33, 49, 52).

Leadership and Decision Making

Teed was the leader of the group. He chose a woman, Anne Ordway (whom he named Victoria Gratia) to rule with him. He created the Planetary Chamber of six women, the Stellar Chamber of four men, and the Signet Chamber of six men and six women, to lead the community. Although Teed assigned both women and men to leadership positions, he was in fact the main leader of the community. Sara Rea Weber explained that Teed "controlled day-to-day affairs as well as long range planning. Unity members followed Dr. Teed's counsel or left the settlement" (1994, 50).

How New Members Were Recruited or Chosen

Teed's speeches and writings inspired new members to join.

Children and Youth

The community's school in Florida taught reading, writing, history, geography, music, and manual arts (Rea 1994, 51).

Relationship with the Outside World

The outside world was often skeptical of or opposed to the Koreshan Unity. In New York, Teed's patients and neighbors were hostile to his spiritual views. In Florida, the local people did not welcome the 200 or so Chicagoans who voted together. A newspaper editor in Fort Myers accused Teed of violating the community's celibacy rule. Rumors circulated that the community was the site of free love and drunkenness.

Influence on the Outside World

Teed had visions of helping the entire country with his scientific inventions. In 1891, he told a Pittsburgh newspaper that he planned to build a railroad between the Atlantic and Pacific coasts, along with a pneumatic passenger transport system that could carry someone across the country in 12 hours. He also announced that he was in the process of patenting a device that would allow him to set type for all the newspapers in the country from his office in Chicago (Carmer 1949, 271).

Although Teed's grandiose dreams went unfulfilled, he managed to convince hundreds of people of the validity of his beliefs, and to create a prosperous community that lasted more than a century.

References

Carmer, Carl. *Dark Trees to the Wind: A Cycle of York State Years*. New York: William Sloane Associates, 1949.

Kitch, Sally. *Chaste Liberation: Celibacy and Female Cultural Status*. Urbana: University of Illinois Press, 1989.

Landing, James E. "Cyrus Reed Teed and the Koreshan Unity," in *America's Communal Utopias*, edited by Donald Pitzer. Chapel Hill: University of North Carolina Press, 1997, 375–395.

Rea, Sara Weber. *The Koreshan Story*. Estero, FL: Guiding Star Publishing House, 1994.

Sutton, Robert. *Communal Utopias and the American Experience: Religious Communities, 1732–2000*. Westport, CT: Praeger, 2003.

WEB SITE

Koreshan State Historic Site: www.floridastateparks.org/koreshan/ (accessed November 2006).

Leadership
and Decision Making

One of the most important aspects of a utopian community is its leadership structure—how decisions are made. A decision-making structure that members have trouble working with often means the end of a community.

One major challenge with leadership systems in a utopian community is that often the members are embarking on what they see as a completely new way of life, so they must create all systems from scratch. According to Hugh Gardner, "starting a commune is like building a new nation from the ground up. There are leaders to choose [or disallow], rules to make [or not make], work to organize [or leave to karma], goals to agree on [or dispute], and situations to hassle out [or avoid]. Communards are Pilgrims, starting from scratch just as surely [or unsurely] as their ancestors did. In a setting such as this, with so many things to be decided and so little practical experience to draw on, it is inconceivable that the affairs of a commune can be conducted without conflict. But conflict is not supposed to exist, for if communes were not a much better way to live there would be little incentive to make the drastic personal changes required to establish them. This is a paradox that has haunted utopian history" (1973, 150).

Despite these seemingly insurmountable difficulties, throughout history, utopian communities have successfully used a wide variety of leadership and decision-making structures, from authoritarian leadership by a charismatic leader, to democracy, consensus decision making, and anarchy. Communities have also changed and adapted their leadership structures over time to better meet their needs.

Charismatic Leaders

Many of the communities profiled in this book were originally founded by what could be called "charismatic leaders." Max Weber, a founder of the study of sociology, was one of the first to describe charismatic leadership and to contrast it with leadership based on rational grounds (established laws and rules) and traditional grounds (such as the idea that the oldest son of a king will become king after him). Charismatic leadership is different from both of these—it rests on "devotion to the specific and exceptional sanctity, heroism or exemplary characteristic of an individual person" (1968, 46). In other words, the charismatic leader is one who has proved to followers that he or she is extraordinary or exceptional in some way, and thus worthy of being followed. Charismatic leaders are considered to be "endowed with supernatural, superhuman, or at least specifically exceptional powers or qualities" (Weber 1968, 48).

The founder of the Bishop Hill community, Eric Jansson, experienced a miracle at the age of 22—he was cured of his rheumatism. He also received a vision that he had been deceived by the Lutheran Church. Based on this miracle and vision, Jansson began preaching while selling wheat flour door-to-door, and he attracted a following. Thomas Lake Harris, who founded the Brotherhood of the New Life, attracted followers by preaching he would be the one to announce Christ's second appearance on Earth. Benjamin Purnell, founder of the House of David movement, received a vision that he was the seventh messenger of a particular branch of Christianity. Cyrus Reed Teed, the founder of the Koreshan Unity, received a vision that Earth was hollow and enclosed the entire universe within it, and that he, Teed, was the prophet to bring this message to the world. Bhagwan Shree Rajneesh claimed to be the reincarnation of a spiritual master from the 12th century. Father Divine, leader of the Peace Mission Movement, was believed to have miraculously caused the death of a judge who had sentenced him to a year in jail. Michael Metelica, founder of the Renaissance Community, experienced psychic visions from a young age.

Charismatic leaders are sometimes unquestioningly obeyed by the members— after all, they joined the group because they wanted to follow that particular leader. This leader may appoint other members to manage certain aspects of the community, but there is generally no formal way for the rank-and-file members to have a say in terms of leadership or decision making. If members are unhappy with the way things are being run, often their only recourse is to leave the community.

John Humphrey Noyes, the founder of the Oneida community, appointed managers as he saw fit and invited everyone's input during daily community meetings, but everyone recognized Noyes as the ultimate authority in the community. Teed, founder of the Koreshan Unity, set up a complicated leadership structure involving three "chambers" of members—men and women—to lead the community. However, it was apparently understood that Teed was the main leader of the community and anyone who disagreed with him had to leave.

One down side of charismatic leadership is that, unless these communities can find a way to transition to a new leader, they often wither away after the original founder dies or leaves. This was the case with the Oneida community, which broke up after Noyes left. The Koreshan Unity withered away after the death of its leader. Members of the Brotherhood of the New Life scattered after their founder left the community. Rajneeshpuram and the other communities set up by Rajneesh collapsed when he and his top manager were arrested and deported from the country. The Peace Mission Movement dwindled after the death of its leader, Father Divine. The Renaissance Community ended soon after members asked the founder, Michael Metelica, to leave.

The Shakers, on the other hand, survived for generations after the death of their original charismatic leader, Ann Lee. After Mother Ann died, the Shakers accepted James Whittaker as their leader. When he died, the Shakers chose a new leader by praying and waiting for a sign from God. In this way, Joseph Meacham was selected and he chose Lucy Wright to lead with him. The top leaders appointed others to be in charge of various departments, such as farm work and food production.

The International Society for Krishna Consciousness has survived the death of its charismatic leader, Swami Prabhupada—but unlike the Shakers, the group experienced years of leadership conflict. Before his death, Prabhupada appointed two different leadership bodies, and the two bodies were in conflict until one of them finally won out.

John Humphrey Noyes was the founder and, for 30 years, the head of the Oneida community, the most successful of the utopian socialist communities established in 19th-century America. (Oneida Ltd.)

Democratic Leadership

Socialist communities, because they value equality, often choose some form of democracy as a way to make decisions, giving each member a vote. However, conflicts can arise over questions such as, Who is considered an official member of the community and thus entitled to a vote? And who should participate in community meetings? The Llano del Rio community, one of the first socialist communities in the United States, struggled with these questions. Its board of directors was elected every year by all full members age 18 and over. However, the community invited all colony members to attend meetings and often the meetings became chaotic with everyone trying to participate. The Icarian socialist communities believed in equality for all but for many years barred women from voting within the community. This rule created conflict within the community.

Twin Oaks is another socialist community that relies on democracy—one person, one vote—in order to make decisions. But because Twin Oaks wants to make sure that everyone's opinion is heard and valued, even those in the minority, the group has a number of ways for people to give input and discuss an issue before a vote is taken. In addition, on important issues such as the election of their three "planners" (the managers of the community), at least 80 percent of members must agree.

Some religious communities also rely on democracy to make decisions. The Hutterites are a Christian community founded many centuries ago. They probably had a charismatic leader at the beginning, but since coming to the United States they have ruled themselves democratically. Only the men vote, and almost all community leaders are male. They believe that this system of voting is a way to allow God to make his will known to the community.

Orderville, a Mormon community, elected its nine-member Board of Management to supervise its property and make work assignments. This Board of Management appointed leaders for the various work departments.

Consensus Decision Making

Consensus decision making involves discussing an issue, coming up with a number of possible solutions, and considering these solutions until the community finds one that everyone can live with. The advantage of consensus decision making is that, by and large, everyone's needs are met and there is no dissatisfied minority. The down side is that it can be quite time consuming. Very few large communities are able to use consensus decision making. The process is most useful when a group is small. Only a handful of communities or movements in this book use forms of consensus decision making; among them are the Bruderhof, cohousing groups, and the Rainbow Family of Living Light.

The Bruderhof is a Christian community founded in the early 1900s. They believe that, for every problem, a decision exists that will be satisfactory to every member of the community. Their goal is to find this correct decision, which to them is God's will. In order to discern this decision, they discuss an issue thoroughly. Their leader, who is called the Servant of the Word, then tries to articulate the group's decision. Women and men participate in these meetings.

While the cohousing movement is quite large and encompasses thousands of people, each cohousing community is small—between seven and 67 households. Within each community, people generally make decisions by consensus, although they may also have a policy that allows voting if a decision cannot be reached via a consensus process.

The Rainbow Family of Living Light is a very large community—as many as 20,000 people. It uses consensus decision making, but since the community is temporary, existing for only several weeks out of each year, the decisions made do not affect the daily lives of members when they are not at the Rainbow Gathering. Each Rainbow Gathering makes decisions using "councils," or open meetings, and everyone who might be affected by a decision must be invited to attend. Everyone present at a meeting must be able to live with a decision before that decision becomes final. Even one person who disagrees can block consensus. The Main Council makes decisions about the Rainbow Gathering as a whole, such as where to hold the next year's gathering.

Anarchy

Several communities profiled in this book are anarchist, and have no designated leaders and no formal way of making a decision. Successful anarchist communities obviously did find some way to make decisions, but often the method is shrouded in obscurity because the community refused to admit that it had leaders or a decision-making structure.

The Ferrer Colony did not acknowledge any leaders except for the principals of their school. The community tried to get rid of status and class distinctions: at times, everyone had to participate in manual labor or take a turn as a janitor. The community held open meetings to discuss issues.

The Home Colony, another anarchist community, did elect a board of directors. However, it tried to encourage dialogue on all important issues, in an effort to avoid domination by one person or one group of people.

The homes that are part of the Catholic Worker Movement have no formal leadership structure or decision-making process. In fact, the movement as a whole has no leadership structure either and there are very few rules about how to set up a House of Hospitality—organizers do not even need to be Catholic. Despite this lack of formal structure, the movement is growing and thriving.

The Rainbow Family of Living Light is an anarchist community with no designated leaders. It makes decisions using a consensus process. In effect, those who participate most in the open meetings tend to become the leaders of the community—their viewpoints often prevail, since they are the ones who take the time and effort to show up for meetings.

Other Forms of Decision Making

Some decision-making systems used in utopian communities fall outside the four categories discussed above. The Moravians, for example, made many decisions using "the lot," in which they placed various possible decisions in a box and drew one at random. This method, they believed, allowed them to involve God in their decision making.

The Rugby colony was governed by the people who owned the land: they were neither elected nor were charismatic leaders. It was like a "company town," in a way, because the landowners hoped to make a profit from the community.

Multiple Forms of Leadership and Decision Making

Some communities included multiple forms of leadership and decision making. The Amana Colonies combined charismatic leadership with democracy. They referred to themselves as the "Community of True Inspiration" to indicate that God spoke directly to them through their leaders, whom they called "instruments." In addition to these charismatic, inspired religious leaders, the Amana Colonies were also led by a Great Council, members of which were elected each year by men over 21 and single women over 30.

The Zoar community also combined an elected Board of Directors with a spiritual leader.

Change and Adaptation in Leadership

Some communities have modified their leadership structure over the years. When the Koinonia community began, it was very small and members were able to make decisions by using consensus decision making—discussing and coming to an agreement on issues. It had no designated leaders at that time. Later, it began electing officers, such as a president, secretary, and treasurer. Still later, full members took turns filling various leadership positions. Currently, the community hires its leaders and pays them a salary.

The Farm originally started out with a charismatic leader named Stephen Gaskin. He appointed the managers of the work crews. When he was jailed for growing marijuana, the community members got used to running things without him and the leadership structure gradually evolved into an elected Board of Directors.

See also: Anarchism

References

Gardner, Hugh. "Crises and Politics in Rural Communes," in *Communes: Creating and Managing the Collective Life,* edited by Rosabeth Moss Kanter. New York: Harper and Row, 1973.

Weber, Max. *On Charisma and Institution Building*. Chicago: University of Chicago Press, 1968.

Literary Utopias

Since ancient times, people have written stories describing ideal ways of living and idyllic societies. Thomas More wrote about an imaginary ideal society in his book *Utopia* in 1516, and since then, literature about such ways of life has been termed *utopian* literature. However, even before More's book, writers addressed the topic of the model society. Plato's *Republic,* written in ancient Greece, describes an ideal city. The Old Testament's Book of Genesis describes a Garden of Eden, and the New Testament's Book of Revelation describes an ideal world without death or pain.

Utopian communities are always created as a reaction against the current mainstream society. Therefore, those who start a utopian community must be able to imagine something different and better. Fiction and literature can help inspire people to imagine a different world and can even provide a blueprint for such a world.

One major literary source of a "better life" and of utopian communities is the Bible, especially the Book of Acts, which describes the early Christian church and how followers lived communally, without private property. A number of Christian communities have been directly influenced by the Book of Acts, including Bishop Hill, Bohemia Manor, The Family/Children of God, The Farm, Harmony Society, the House of David Movement, Jesus People USA, the Shakers, and the Zoar Society.

The New Testament's Book of Revelation has inspired several communities to form for the purpose of preparing for the second coming of Christ and the millennium (1,000 years of peace and plenty). These communities include the Branch Davidians, the House of David Movement, and the Society of the Woman in the Wilderness.

Secular literary utopias have influenced the formation of actual utopian communities as well. Edward Bellamy's novel *Looking Backward 2000–1887* spurred the formation of Nationalist Clubs all over the United States and inspired the formation of the utopian communities Point Loma, Llano del Rio, and Ruskin. The founder of the Icarian movement, Etienne Cabet, wrote a novel about an ideal society called *Voyages en Icarie (Travels in Icaria),* which helped him to attract followers and members and served as a guide for the actual formation of the community. Charles Fourier wrote a detailed description of an ideal society, which led to the formation of the Fourierist phalanxes in the United States. B. F. Skinner's novel *Walden Two* inspired and guided the Twin Oaks community.

In addition to the communities profiled elsewhere in this book, another notable American community, Altruria, was inspired by a novel: *A Traveler from Altruria*, written by William Dean Howells and published in installments in 1892 and 1893. The novel tells of a traveler from a utopian land called Altruria who arrives at a New England hotel and describes to Americans his ideal society. This society had solved the problems plaguing the United States at that time, including poverty, class divisions, and overly long working hours. Altrurians had dispensed with making products that were ugly and of poor quality; they worked only at making products that were long lasting, useful, and beautiful. Therefore, their work hours were much shorter. The people of Altruria practiced economic equality, and everyone took a turn at farming or producing necessary goods. Money was not used. Artists were held in high esteem, and the aim of Altruria was to allow for as much personal freedom as possible, without infringing on the freedom of others.

Altrurians believed themselves to be the true followers of Christ. Because everyone's basic needs were fulfilled and because they saw Altruria as one big family, the Altrurians were able to be compassionate and care for others in need, whether or not they were biologically related.

From this novel, the actual community took its name. Altruria was founded by Edward Payne, a Unitarian minister, and about 25 of his followers. In October 1894, they moved to land they had bought near Santa Rosa, California. Their aim, as they described in their community newspaper, was to create "an ordered and balanced adjustment of interests, in which each individual shall have place and part and privilege, but shall at the same time hold sacred the part, the place, the privilege, of every other" (quoted in Hine 1966, 101). Their constitution called for elected leaders and equality of goods within the community. Individual ownership of goods and property was also allowed. Families often lived in separate houses but some families shared housing.

The community members were allowed to work whenever they liked, at whatever job they chose. Thus, during the nine months of the community's existence, members were involved in a variety of pursuits, including weaving, woodworking, making bamboo screens, blacksmithing, and making wooden chairs and easels. The community also aimed for self-sufficiency, keeping gardens, orchards, poultry, cattle, and bees.

Its most ambitious project was to build a hotel on its creek to attract tourists. This hotel was never completed. The community disbanded in June 1895 because of financial problems. The members divided into three different groups, two of which moved away from Altruria and one of which stayed on the land. All three groups continued to try to live cooperatively for another year, after which they ended communal living.

See also: Bellamy, Edward; Bible Communism; Millennialism; More, Thomas; Skinner, B. F.

References

Hine, Robert. *California's Utopian Colonies.* New Haven, CT: Yale University Press, 1966.

Howells, William Dean. *A Traveler from Altruria.* New York: Harper and Brothers, 1908.

New York Public Library. *Utopia: The Search for the Ideal Society in the Western World.* New York: The New York Public Library, 2001.

Snodgrass, Mary Ellen. *Encyclopedia of Utopian Literature.* Santa Barbara, CA: ABC-CLIO, 1995.

Llano del Rio and New Llano

At a Glance

Dates of existence in United States: 1914 to 1937
Locations: California and Louisiana
Peak membership: 1,100
Religious or other belief: secularism, socialism

History

The Llano colony was one of the largest and most successful of the socialist utopian communities started in the United States.

Llano del Rio was started by Job Harriman in 1914. He was from Indiana, where he studied theology first and then became a lawyer. Harriman moved to California in 1886 and joined the Socialist Party. In 1899, he ran for vice president of the United States on the same ticket as Eugene V. Debs. In 1911, Harriman ran for mayor of Los Angeles. He was supported by labor unions and was thought to have a good chance to win.

Around the same time, however, Harriman became embroiled in a scandal. In 1910, he had agreed to be the defense lawyer for two socialists who were accused of setting off a bomb in the Los Angeles Times building. Harriman and other socialists believed the men were innocent, but in 1911 the men confessed their guilt—just four days before the mayoral election.

Harriman lost the election and grew disillusioned with politics as a way to change society. He decided instead to form a model socialist community based on equality of ownership, wages, and opportunity. He wanted his community to visibly demonstrate how socialism could work. Harriman once stated in an interview: "I assumed that if a cooperative colony could be established . . . that would afford each individual an equal and social advantage, that they would . . . react harmoniously to this environment and the extreme selfishness and greed as it appears in the capitalist . . . would be done away. . . . I thought that if this could be done we could use this community as an example by which other communities could be built" (quoted in Oved 1988, 286).

To achieve this goal, Harriman and his supporters bought 9,000 acres about 45 miles north of Los Angeles in 1913 and began selling shares of stock at $1 per share. Those who wished to live on the colony were required to buy—or at least pledge to buy—2,000 shares.

The colony officially opened on May 1, 1914, with five people and a handful of animals. By January of the next year, over 150 people lived in the colony, and by the summer of 1917, over a thousand people called Llano del Rio home.

Portrait of Job Harriman, founder of the utopian Llano colony. Harriman was a California lawyer with political aspirations. He ran for mayor of Los Angeles and for vice president of the United States with Eugene V. Debs in 1899. (Library of Congress)

Yet the colony was not an economic success: there was not enough water to irrigate the land for farming. Harriman began looking around for another site, and bought land in Louisiana in 1917. Some of the California Llano colony members moved to New Llano, and along with some Texas families who joined, the New Llano colony had about 300 members in January 1918. By the spring of 1918, the California land was sold and the California colony was closed.

In New Llano, things did not go well either: many of the colonists left because of lack of money and food. In 1920, George Pickett was elected vice president of the colony and effectively ran it, since Harriman, the president, was mostly absent—he had tuberculosis and was trying to regain his health. Pickett succeeded in raising a large amount of money for the colony from socialists who wanted to see the experiment succeed. The colony was then able to build a brick kiln, a sawmill, and a dairy. New Llano was back on its feet, and restarted its school and social activities.

Harriman died in California in 1925, but the community continued under the leadership of Pickett. By 1930, colony membership had grown to 500. This was the time of the Great Depression and many people joined not because they believed in socialist ideas, but because they hoped to find relief from poverty and unemployment.

In the 1930s, New Llano's enterprises began making less money. Pickett tried to raise money through outside donations, but because of the grave economic situation throughout the country, there was not much money to be had. He tried to salvage the colony by attempting, unsuccessfully, to drill for oil on the group's land, and he simultaneously sought to expand the community by buying land in Texas, southern Louisiana, and New Mexico. These two ventures wasted an enormous amount of money.

Around this time, a group of members became unhappy with Pickett's leadership. Poverty increased and the standard of living deteriorated: members often did not have shoes to wear and their clothing was ragged. Roofs leaked and porches sagged. The food consisted mostly of sweet potatoes, rice, and occasional meat. Members were often ill because of their meager diet. Opposition to Pickett grew stronger. A new board of directors was elected in 1935, but Pickett refused to give up his leadership. The new leadership tried to expel him from the colony. This battle dragged on for about a year and sometimes involved violence, with members brandishing or shooting pistols and forcibly occupying buildings. Ultimately, the conflict hindered the community from reviving its businesses.

Also in the mid-1930s, a group of ex-members sued the community, demanding a return of their share of money, as their contract had stated. The court decided that the ex-members should be paid. In the midst of this chaos, Pickett was reelected leader of the community in 1937, but the community was dying. Most able-bodied workers had left, the land was leased to neighbors, the industries closed down one by one, and New Llano ended in 1937.

Beliefs and Practices

The socialists who founded the colony wanted it to be a demonstration of cooperation, sharing, and unselfishness. Their Declaration of Principles stated such values as "the rights of the community shall be paramount over those of any individual; things used productively must be owned collectively; talent and intelligence are benefits that should rightly be used in the service of others; only by identifying his interests and pleasures with those of others can man find real happiness" (Conkin 1964, 120).

Yet Harriman, Llano's main founder, saw that many colonists could speak about these values but could not put them into practice. Colonists could be selfish, arrogant, greedy, lazy, and critical. In an interview toward the end of his life, Harriman reflected, "It became apparent to me that people would never abandon their means of livelihood, good or bad, capitalistic or otherwise, until other methods were developed that would promise advantages at least as good as those by which they were living" (quoted in Oved 1988, 286).

There was very little attempt to teach Llano colony members about the ideals of the community. Under Pickett's leadership, the community did hold weekly "psychology meetings," during which he would give an inspirational talk about the ideals of cooperation and communal life. Members were encouraged to discuss their own faults at these meetings, which were not mandatory: some members attended often and others never attended.

Daily Life

The colony's ideal version of living conditions was very different from its actual living conditions. Harriman and others drew up plans involving a community center surrounded by six dormitories to house 10,000 members.

At the beginning in California, many members lived in tents. Gradually, two-room adobe houses were built, clustered around a central building where meetings and dances were held. The colony built its own post office, dairy building, laundry building, and swimming pool. Later, a dining hall, a hotel, warehouses, and industrial buildings were added. At the time the socialists moved to Louisiana, the site of the New Llano colony already had a hotel, some small houses, and other buildings, to which were added additional industrial buildings and houses. The homes had electricity (generated on colony property) and some had running water.

The colonists often lacked food. At one point the only vegetable they had was carrots, and at another point, they ate beans three times a day. Although the food was prepared communally, families often chose to take the food home to eat. Single people ate together in the dining hall.

In the early days of the colony, members were given a wage of $4 per day, which they could spend in the colony's cooperative store, where goods were offered at cost. Later, in Louisiana, the wage was discontinued. Every adult member was to work 48 hours per week in exchange for food, housing, and other basics of life, such as education and health services. Members were allowed to keep any money they gained from outside the colony.

Although the colony was often poor and the work was difficult, the people of Llano kept up a vibrant social and intellectual life. Adult education classes were held in the evenings. Every Sunday afternoon members attended a forum on politics or philosophy. The community had a library that grew to contain 5,000 volumes. A drama group and a mandolin orchestra gave performances. Colonists enjoyed tennis, baseball, basketball, and other sports. Dances were held on Saturday nights. The dance floor at New Llano was said to be the best in the region.

The colony celebrated its birthday every May 1 with a picnic, speeches, and entertainment, in addition to celebrating other holidays and members' birthdays. Every evening would find colonists gathered informally to discuss almost any subject under the sun: Marxism, Einstein, mysticism, to name a few. Colonists were allowed to spend their leisure time any way they liked.

How They Made Their Living

The Llano colony members had many more ideas for industries than those that they actually put into operation. At one time or another in California, they had a shoe shop, a blacksmith shop, a sawmill, a cabinet shop, a print shop, a flour mill, a bakery, and a fish hatchery, among other enterprises. The business ideas that did not work or that never got off the ground included: manufacturing a low-priced airplane for the consumer market, gold prospecting, and turnip farming. The colony often relied on donations from sympathetic socialists.

In Louisiana, the colony grew vegetables and raised some animals. It also had a print shop, a carpentry shop, a dairy, and a cannery, among other industries. The most successful venture in Louisiana was an ice plant that provided ice for the nearby town of Leesville.

The Llano colony was often in precarious financial circumstances. This was partly because the colony made some poor decisions and kept poor financial records and partly because a large proportion of its members were either retired, not healthy enough to work a full day, or dissatisfied and refused to work.

Leadership and Decision Making

The Llano colony struggled over power and leadership. The board of directors was elected every year by all full members 18 years old and over. (Full members were those who had paid their full share of stock.) The board then appointed managers for the colony. At first everyone in the colony was invited to the meetings of these leaders and often the meetings degenerated into chaos, with everyone trying to talk at once. The community created many different rules and ways of governing, only to change things a short time later.

After 1920, George Pickett was elected many times as vice president or president of the community. He assumed much more control of the community than previous leaders had: there were no more general meetings with everyone talking at once. Although some people felt his style of leadership was not democratic enough, other people felt that he was doing a good job and ought to be left alone to do it.

How New Members Were Recruited or Chosen

The colony publicized its venture through socialist publications that it owned. People who wanted to become members of the colony were required to buy 2,000 shares of stock but could pay for most of the shares out of the wages they received for working the land. Some members never ended up paying their shares. Most people who joined the community were socialists but others were not. Although members were asked whether they agreed with the colony's Declaration of Principles, there does not seem to have been any effective method of screening people who did not understand or believe in the ideals of the colony.

Children and Youth

Children lived with their families and were not raised communally. The Llano colony was very interested in the education of its children. It established a nursery for the youngest children (above age two), a preschool based on the methods of Maria Montessori, and a school through eighth grade for the older children. This Montessori preschool was one of the first such schools in California.

A section of the community was set aside for a "children's farm": the children raised some vegetables and cared for their own horses, goats, rabbits, and chickens. The children also helped out on the main colony. Their schooling integrated practical work experience with the normal school subjects: half a day for schoolwork and half a day for practical work.

Relationship with the Outside World

The members of the Llano colony saw themselves as a model that the entire world could and should follow. They were very interested in socialist experiments going on around them, such as the Russian Revolution and the New Deal communities. They visited other communities and were, in turn, visited by members of other communities. In 1933, Pickett worked with a Texas senator to propose national legislation to expand the colony into a nationwide movement as a way to solve unemployment. However, Pickett's bill did not pass.

The nearby townspeople had little trouble with the Llano colony. Townspeople sometimes attended dances and other celebrations at the community. However, the fact that the colony was not religious (members could practice whatever religion they wished) was shocking to some of the conservative people of rural Louisiana.

The colony had an uneasy relationship with the Socialist Party, which saw the Llano community as detracting from the party's political goals. In addition, expelled members spread negative propaganda about the colony and sometimes sued the colony or caused it to be investigated by authorities.

Reasons for Ending the Community

The Llano community was begun with high ideals. Unfortunately, there was little attempt to teach new members these ideals. The community members had trouble agreeing on basics, such as a way to select leaders and make decisions. In addition, the community suffered from poor land and poverty.

Influence on the Outside World

Although the community did not succeed in forming a nationwide movement, the Llano colony remains—in its successes and its failures—an instructive example of communal living.

See also: Socialism

References

Conkin, Paul. *Two Paths to Utopia: The Hutterites and the Llano Colony.* Lincoln: University of Nebraska Press, 1964.

Hine, Robert V. "California's Socialist Utopias," in *America's Communal Utopias*, edited by Donald Pitzer. Chapel Hill: University of North Carolina Press, 1997, 419–431.

Oved, Yaacov. *Two Hundred Years of American Communes.* New Brunswick, NJ: Transaction Books, 1988.

Pitzer, Donald. "Patterns of Education in American Communal Societies," in *Communal Life: An International Perspective,* edited by Yosef Gorni, Yaacov Oved, and Idit Paz. New Brunswick, NJ: Transaction Books, 1987.

Web site

The Center for Land Use Interpretation, New Llano entry: http://ludb.clui.org/ex/i/LA3144/ (accessed May 2006).

Love Family

At a Glance

Dates of existence in United States: 1969 to present
Location: Washington State
Peak membership: 300
Religious or other belief: Christianity

History

The Love Family is one of the more controversial utopian communities in the United States. This community was started by Paul Erdmann, who in the mid-1960s apparently had a vision after taking the hallucinogenic drug LSD (lysergic acid diethylamide). The belief system of the Love Family grew out of this vision.

In 1968, Erdmann moved to Seattle, where he started living communally with three other people who considered him their spiritual leader. He took on the name "Love Israel."

By 1980, the community had 300 members and owned 17 houses in the Queen Anne Hill area of Seattle, two ranches in Washington State, a rural home on Lake Roosevelt in the eastern part of the state, and a cannery.

In 1983, about 85 percent of the members left the community. Members accused Love Israel of misusing community money to buy cocaine and luxuries for himself. A few former members sued Love to recover money they had donated to the community. Love agreed to a settlement in which he gave almost all the Seattle property to one former member.

After 1983, Love Israel maintained a smaller community with about 40 loyal members living on a ranch in Arlington, Washington, north of Seattle. In 2004, the group sold this ranch to pay off debts and moved to rural Stevens County in the northeastern part of the state.

Beliefs and Practices

The Love Family believes in three principles: "We are One, Now is the Time, Love is the Answer" (www.loveisraelfamily.com/).

Members of the Love Family believe they are Israelites, or God's "chosen people." For many years they wore Old Testament–style robes and took on Old Testament names. The community considers itself to be Christian. Its members read the Bible and believe in Jesus Christ.

Loyal members are given "virtue" names by Love Israel, such as Understanding, Fun, and Logic. Members are assumed to have eternal souls and before 1983 were not allowed to give out their legal names, birthdates, or Social Security numbers.

One important aspect of community life was the idea that members should be of one mind. "Deviance in the Family was equated with 'being separate,' not just physically but socially and, most important, mentally" (Balch 1998, 73). Members were generally not allowed to go anywhere alone. There was almost no privacy. At the community's ranch outside of Seattle, the outhouses did not have doors, and the opening faced the walking trail. At night in Seattle, members on the "night watch" would walk from house to house, waking each member and asking about their dreams. The community kept out radios, televisions, clocks, books, and newspapers in order to shield its members from the outside world. The outside world was considered Satanic and a threat to the Love Family. An observer noted that even the behavior of Love Family members was similar: "Members spoke softly, went through their routines quietly and efficiently, and always seemed cheerful about what they were doing" (quoted in Balch 1998, 74).

Love Israel encouraged members to have spiritual experiences through meditation, chanting, or taking drugs. The most common drug was marijuana, which was smoked almost every day. LSD was generally used only if provided by guests. In the early 1970s, the community also sniffed the industrial solvent toluene: members would dip a napkin in toluene, put it in a plastic bag, put the bags over their heads, and inhale. These drugs were called "sacraments." The Love Family felt that drugs had the potential to bring a person "into a closer relationship to his brother and to God" (Balch 1998, 71–72).

After the deaths of two members from toluene inhalation, the Love Family discontinued the use of this chemical, but issued a statement defending the practice: "Our belief in Jesus Christ has freed us from the fears that, in the mind of the world, surround the use of these chemicals. We have seen that we have eternal life, that the God in us can never die. . . . God is stronger than any chemical. . . . We do maintain the right of any man to seek God through the use of any means as long as he does not infringe on the rights of his neighbors" (quoted in Allen 1982, 70–72).

Before 1971, all members except Love Israel and a few women were required to be celibate. Gradually, more and more members were allowed to partner up if the partnership was approved by Love Israel. Elders were encouraged to find a partner and start a family but were also encouraged to have sex with other women. Love Israel had two wives, Honesty and Bliss.

One member commented that, within the community, it was impossible to commit adultery because "we're all married to each other." However, the community favored monogamous relationships because "that way if a child is born we'll know who the parents are" (quoted in Allen 1982, 84).

During the early 1970s, the community used physical punishment to discipline adults who broke the rules. Members might be subjected to beatings with a wooden rod, or being asked to kneel with their forehead on the ground.

Although the community believed that "we are all one," this proclamation did not include social equality. The community was structured as a hierarchy, with Love Israel at the top. To emphasize rank differences, members bowed to those of higher status: children bowed to adults, women to men, rank-and-file members to elders, and everyone bowed to Love Israel (Balch 1998, 79).

One of the most important holidays for the Love Family is Passover, the Jewish celebration of Moses leading the Jews out of Egypt, where they had been slaves. A visitor described the preparations for the holiday in 1980. Classes were held to explain the significance of Passover, the barn was decorated to hold 300 people for dinner, a meal with wine was served, and afterwards members and guests sang and danced (Allen 1982, 153–158).

Daily Life

In Seattle, 10 to 15 people shared each house. The Love Family attempted to create a communal living arrangement out of its single-family homes in Seattle by taking down fences between the houses. There were no mirrors in the houses because "members were expected to see themselves in their friends" (Balch 1998, 74).

Comedian Steve Allen visited his son at the Seattle commune in 1972. He saw "a group of old but beautifully restored, cleaned and painted homes in the hilly, attractive Queen Anne section of the city. . . . I could see at once that the members of the Love Family freely interacted with neighbors, neighborhood merchants and visitors" (Allen 1982, 73).

On their ranch north of Seattle, members lived in yurts (circular tents). A visitor describes the Love Family's ranch in 1980: "The ranch . . . was in a secluded, wooded valley in the foothills of the Cascade mountains. It conveyed an impression of order, tranquility, and harmony with nature. A muscular, long-haired man was plowing a field with two Belgian horses, and several women were singing a song about New Jerusalem while working in the garden. On the far side of a meadow, children were laughing as they splashed in a lake" (quoted in Balch 1998, 64).

Because Love Israel was seen as the "king" of the community, he lived in a nicer house, ate better food, wore nicer clothes, and had access to more sexual partners than other members. Likewise, higher-ranking members enjoyed more privileges than lower-ranking members (Balch 1998, 76–80).

How They Make Their Living

In Seattle, members ran a health food store, a woodworking shop, and an art gallery. In Arlington, Washington, the group ran a gourmet restaurant. At times, members worked in the outside world to bring in money.

New members were required to turn over all possessions and money to Love Israel, and one member in particular, named Richness by Love Israel, contributed over a million dollars to the community.

Leadership and Decision Making

The Love Family is a hierarchy, with Love Israel at the top. At the community's height, Love Israel appointed a Council of Elders to be in charge of the various households. Most of the elders were men, and the women elders were generally partners of high-ranking men (Balch 1998, 77–78).

How New Members Are Recruited or Chosen

A former member said that the Love Family did not do much street preaching. She joined because she was "looking for a Christian house. I asked around the University up in Seattle and someone told me about the Love Family, and I just walked in" (quoted in Allen 1982, 103).

Some new members came from another communal group, the Source in Hawaii, after its leader was killed in a hang-gliding accident (Balch 1998, 81).

Children and Youth

Birth control was not allowed at the Love Family. At first, children were sometimes mistreated by being locked in a closet for crying or by being spanked with a wooden rod. Later, Love Israel banned corporal punishment for children (Balch 1998, 81).

At its height, the community had its own school that was accredited by the state of Washington. Because the community did not use birthdates, the children were grouped by ability rather than age. Later, children were sent to public school, where they were free to participate in all activities. One of Love Israel's sons, Clean, was a high school football star. Love Family children could go to college if they desired (Brooks 2004).

The Love Family children have a reputation of being well-behaved and polite. Steve Allen, whose grandchildren were born and raised for many years in the Love Family, commented that the children were "sweet, free little spirits, though in no way wild or uncontrolled. They laugh readily, have a remarkably well-developed sense of humor for children so young, and are well-behaved" (1982, 205).

Relationship with the Outside World

For many years, the Love Family believed the outside world to be Satanic and tried to keep it out as much as possible. However, parents of members were allowed to visit (a special outhouse with a door was built at the ranch just for visitors), and members sometimes worked in the outside world to bring in money. In addition, Love Israel cultivated relationships with politicians and religious leaders in Seattle (Balch 1998, 75–76).

Although they tried to separate themselves from the outside world, the Love Family did have a practice of sending clothing, food, and money to two orphanages in India. It also had an "abundance table" outside one of its stores in Seattle, where members would put out free food to be picked up by anyone who wished (Allen 1982, 235, 237).

The Love Family has had a rocky relationship with the outside world. In 1971, two members died of suffocation as a result of the community practice of putting plastic bags containing the solvent toluene over their faces and inhaling. After this incident, the Love Family became known to the outside world and was often accused of being a cult (Balch 1998, 71).

At the instigation of their parents, several adult members were kidnapped from the community and subjected to "deprogramming" in order to get them to renounce their beliefs in the group. One woman, Kathy Crampton, was kidnapped repeatedly, although she tried to get help from the local police. She was locked in a motel room or a private home for almost a week, and verbally attacked for her belief in Love Israel. Her parents allowed CBS News to film the deprogramming in the hopes that it would protect other young people from similar "cults." Crampton eventually escaped and returned to the community. In another case, a former member was tranquilized and subjected to electroshock treatment as part of his deprogramming (Allen 1982, 87–97; Balch 1998, 73–74).

The Seattle community eventually came to accept the Love Family. The Seattle Police Department agreed to issue drivers licenses without birthdates to Love Family members. Neighbors in Seattle appreciated the fact that the Love Family renovated old houses and created beautiful gardens (Brooks 2004).

Influence on the Outside World

The Love Family seems to have had very little influence on the outside world. Even within the hippie counterculture, the Love Family was viewed with skepticism because of its hierarchical power structure. The group often participated in the Rainbow Family of Living Light Gathering, a nomadic utopian community. When the Love Family attended a Rainbow Gathering in 1984—shortly after its misused funds crisis, which caused most members to leave—an observer reported that "many Rainbow people were glad the Family had broken up because in their eyes, Love had always been a dictator" (quoted in Balch 1998, 91).

Future of the Love Family

Although the community has moved away from the Seattle area, Love Israel says he would like to create a cultural center for his community in Seattle (Brooks 2004).

See also: Cults; Hippies; Rainbow Family of Living Light

References

Allen, Steve. *Beloved Son: A Story of the Jesus Cults*. Indianapolis, IN: Bobbs-Merrill, 1982.
Balch, Robert. "The Love Family: Its Formative Years," in *Sects, Cults and Spiritual Communities: A Sociological Analysis*, edited by William Zellner and Marc Petrowsky. Westport, CT: Praeger, 1998, 63–94.
Brooks, Diane. "Controversial, Colorful Israel Family Moves to More Open Spaces." *The Seattle Times,* April 19, 2004, http://community.seattletimes.nwsource.com/archive/?date=20040419&slug=loveisrael19m (accessed April 22, 2008).

WEB SITE
Love Family: www.loveisraelfamily.com/ (accessed October 2006).

Millennialism

Millennialism is the belief in the second coming of Christ, to be preceded or followed by a period of a thousand years (a millennium) of peace, as described in the New Testament Book of Revelation. The "Second Advent" refers to the second coming of Christ and so millennialism is also called "Adventism."

While all Christians believe in the second coming of Christ, they do not all agree on when this will happen. Has Christ already appeared for a second time? Is the advent near at hand? Or will it occur in the far distant future? They also do not agree on whether Christ will come before the 1,000 years of peace, or after. Also, will the second coming of Christ be a quiet event or a cataclysmic event? Will it be gradual or sudden? Can the date be predicted by humans?

A number of utopian communities have been founded on the belief in this second coming of Christ. For example, the Society of the Woman in the Wilderness traveled to North America from Europe in order to await the millennium in the wilderness. The Shakers believed that Christ returned to Earth a second time in the body of Ann Lee, their founder. The leader of Jerusalem preached that followers must repent because the millennium was near. The founder of the Oneida community, John Humphrey Noyes, preached that Christ had returned to Earth in 70 CE. The Davidian and Branch Davidian movements predicted 1959 as the date for the second coming of Christ. The House of David movement existed in order to purify its members in preparation for Christ's second coming.

See also: Burned-Over District; Davidian and Branch Davidian Movements; Harmony Society; House of David Movement; Jerusalem/Society of Universal Friends; Oneida Community; Shakers; Society of the Woman in the Wilderness

Reference

Sandeen, Ernest. "Millennialism," in *The Rise of Adventism*, edited by Edwin Gaustad. New York: Harper and Row, 1974.

Moravian Movement

At a Glance

Dates of existence in United States: 1741 to present (communal life was gradually ended between 1762 and the mid-1800s)

Locations: Indiana, New Jersey, North Carolina, Pennsylvania, South Carolina, Wisconsin

Peak membership during communal era: 1,300 (Bethlehem, Pennsylvania); 350 (Wachovia region of North Carolina)

Religious or other belief: Moravian Christianity

History

The Moravian movement founded a number of American communities in the 18th and 19th centuries, the largest of which were Bethlehem, Pennsylvania, and Salem, North Carolina. Some of its communities were fully communal, while others were only partially communal. Today, the Moravian movement is not a communal movement at all; it is simply a church.

The Moravians in the United States are part of a larger movement that had its roots in 15th-century Bohemia and Moravia (part of the present-day Czech Republic), when a man named Jan Hus and his followers began to protest the abuses they saw among the Catholic clergy. Some of Hus's followers and their descendants eventually took on the name of "Unitas Fratrum" (unity of the brethren). They left the sinful influences of the city to live in the countryside and farm. They believed the essential things of life were faith, love, and hope, and saw church rituals as useful but not essential (Smaby 1988, 4).

The Unitas Fratrum grew larger and members were persecuted by the Catholic Church: those who worshipped publicly were tortured, their books were burned, and their children were taken away to be educated in Catholic schools. By the mid-1600s, as a result of this persecution, the Unitas Fratrum had almost died out in Bohemia and Moravia. A small number of followers worshipped privately.

In the early 1700s, Count Zinzendorf of Saxony (in present-day Germany) offered refuge to the Unitas Fratrum on his land. The Moravians appointed him a bishop of their church. Under Zinzendorf's leadership, the Moravians decided that their mission was to teach non-Christians about Jesus Christ. By 1737, they had mission settlements all over the world—in Africa, South America, Greenland, and Russia (Smaby 1988, 9).

A group of Moravians first came to the New World in 1737, when Zinzendorf bought land for them in Georgia. Within a few years, this community had ended because of disease and other difficulties. Some Moravians from Georgia moved to Nazareth, Pennsylvania, where they helped build a school for evangelist George Whitefield, who hoped to educate blacks. Within a few months, however, the Moravians had a religious disagreement with Whitefield.

The Moravians in Pennsylvania were instructed to buy land for a permanent American settlement. In 1741, they bought 500 acres near Nazareth and started building the town of Bethlehem. Zinzendorf arrived later that year. He attended meetings in Pennsylvania, trying (in vain) to unify all Christians under one umbrella. In this quest, he visited with another Pennsylvania utopian community, the Ephrata Cloister (Smaby 1988, 9; Hamilton, 1971, 106–107; Durnbaugh 1997, 27).

In 1753, Zinzendorf bought 100,000 acres of land in North Carolina. This tract was named "Wachovia" and is now part of Winston-Salem, North Carolina. Ten single men from Bethlehem traveled there to start the community of Bethabara. A second settlement, Bethania, was started in 1759. Salem was begun in 1765 and was designed to be the central town of the region. By 1772, about 350 people lived in the three communities (Hamilton 1971, 171; Thorp 1989, 11, 35, 49).

Meanwhile, Bethlehem was growing. By 1759, its population reached 600. The next year, Count Zinzendorf died. By 1761, Bethlehem consisted of 1,300 people, 50 buildings, and 50 industries on 2,500 acres, including fields, orchards, and gardens. Members also built other communities nearby, which contained another 50 buildings and 5,000 acres of land. In addition, they sent missionaries to Native American settlements and to the West Indian slaves (Smaby 1988, 27, 86; Gollin 1967, 198).

In 1760, Bethlehem began transitioning away from a completely communal economy. The Moravian leadership in Germany wanted Bethlehem to cut back on its missionary activities and to contribute more money to decreasing the movement's debts. By 1771, the community's families were living together, raising their own children, and being responsible for supporting themselves. The farms, inns, store, and other businesses continued to be communal. Land was owned by the community and leased to members (Smaby 1988, 33–36). Within a year, Bethabara in North Carolina was also transitioning away from a completely communal economy and outsiders were gradually allowed to settle in Wachovia.

After Bethlehem's finances collapsed in 1842 as a result of an economic depression and floods, the group decided to allow Moravians and non-Moravians to buy land in Bethlehem. It also set out to establish a secular government. Bethlehem was on its way to becoming just another American town (Smaby 1988, 44–46). Moravians were even allowed to marry outsiders, and by the time of the Civil War (1861) the Moravian town of Salem was surprisingly similar to the rest of rural America (Hamilton 1971, 242; Thorp 1989, 203–205).

Beliefs and Practices

The Moravians believe that the Bible is the source of all religious truth and that Jesus Christ (and not the pope, as Roman Catholics believe) is the head of the church. Under Zinzendorf's leadership, the Moravians took on the idea that feeling is more important than understanding, in terms of religious experience. Humans cannot hope

Moravians ascend the Delaware River in the 1700s. Originally from Bohemia and Moravia, a number of Moravian Brethren left Germany during the 18th century to do missionary work in America and Great Britain. (Library of Congress)

to understand God with their brains. However, through the love of Christ, humans can hope to become close to God (Gollin 1967, 9–11).

The Moravians believe that everyone is born with a sinful nature. They also believe that anyone who gave themselves to Jesus Christ would receive forgiveness and eternal life. The goal of Moravian life is to encourage members to recognize their sinful nature and to develop a childlike trust in Jesus. According to the Moravians, the community could help individuals attain this conversion experience. The Moravians had found, while living on Zinzendorf's land in Herrnhut, Germany, that members of a similar age and life situation encouraged each other's spiritual growth and conversion. So in Bethlehem, they organized their living arrangements into "choirs" in order to allow people of similar ages and life experiences to live together (Smaby 1988, 10, 151).

Moravians have always been encouraged to marry. Marriage was considered a holy sacrament and was important in helping the group to achieve its religious goals. Moravians sent out husband-and-wife teams as missionaries, so the husband could minister to the men, and the wife to the women. For many years, Moravian members were not allowed to marry outside of their faith (Gollin 1967, 110–111).

Hard work, diligence, punctuality, frugality, and simplicity were considered important values to the Moravians (Gollin 1967, 143).

Easter was the most important holiday for the Moravians, because they emphasized Christ's sacrifice in order to save human souls from death. They also celebrated historic Moravian events, such as the martyrdom of Jan Hus and the founding of the Unitas Fratrum (Smaby 1988, 18–19).

Singing and music were important to the Moravians. They composed some of their own music and sang in a variety of styles, sometimes in unison and sometimes in harmony. They used musical instruments, including an organ, brass instruments, and stringed instruments. Visitors were often impressed with the quality of Moravian music, comparing it to the music of the royal courts in Europe. The Moravians sang to wake each other up and to accompany their daily routines (Smaby 1988, 21–22).

The Moravian Church had a history of pacifism. However, the Moravians in America were divided on this issue. By 1818, the Moravians had abandoned pacifism, (Smaby, 1988, 39).

Daily Life

Moravian communities were divided between those who lived together in a settlement that was closed to outsiders and those from a geographical area who simply gathered to worship together. Among the closed Moravian settlements, some were economically communal, and in others, families were responsible for their own finances (Smaby 1988, 25).

Bethlehem was the oldest and largest of the American Moravian communities and for many years practiced a communal economy, which allowed them to support a large number of missionaries and to care for the missionaries' children. Bethabara in North Carolina was also communal for a time. Members were to devote all their time and labor to the community and in return they received shelter, food, clothing, and education for the children (Gollin 1967, 139–140; Thorp 1989, 40–41).

Members in Bethlehem and Bethabara were organized into choirs of the same gender and marital status and similar age. Members of a choir lived together and often worked and prayed together. Married people had their own choir. Mothers and fathers usually lived in separate buildings. Babies lived with their mothers but had frequent contact with their fathers (Smaby 1988, 10, 147).

After 1762, when Bethlehem started transitioning away from a completely communal economy, married people and their children lived in their own houses or apartments. Single people continued to live in choirs (Smaby 1988, 107).

The Moravian elders generally arranged the marriages with the help of the "lot." Members were encouraged but not compelled to marry the spouses chosen in this way (Gollin 1967, 111–112).

Hymns were sung at 5:00 a.m. to awaken the Moravians. Breakfast was at 6:00 a.m., and work started an hour later. Members sang hymns before and after their noon meal and returned to work by 12:30 p.m. They ate supper at 6:00 p.m., followed by a devotional walk around the community. At 7:00 p.m. the community gathered for worship, after which the individual choirs had a short service. At 9:00 p.m. the entire community met again for a service, and at 10:00 p.m. they went to bed. Throughout the night, the night watchman sung hymns on the hour. On Sundays, they did not work but attended a number of services (Smaby 1988, 14–17).

Bethlehem members ate meat about twice a week. Staple foods were soup, wheat pudding, and vegetables. Butter and eggs were not as common. They drank a coffee made of barley, as well as herbal tea. They drank beer rarely (Gollin 1967, 163).

How They Made Their Living

Bethlehem and the Wachovia settlements aimed for economic self-sufficiency. Bethlehem and Wachovia farmed wheat, corn, and flax; kept animals; built their own buildings; and made their own clothing, including shoes. They traded some of their products with outsiders to buy such things as sugar, glass, and iron (Gollin 1967, 156–158, 162; Thorp 1989, 112–113).

Leadership and Decision Making

Moravian communities all over the world were under a central leadership, which was supposed to include representatives of all the Moravian settlements. However, the German Moravians in Herrnhut were largely in control of the communities. While he was alive, Zinzendorf was the leader of the Moravian movement.

There was often tension between Bethlehem's desire to govern itself and the desire of the leadership in Germany to exert their control over the movement's main American branch. The Herrnhut council appointed leaders for Bethlehem, but Bethlehem did not always communicate in detail with Herrnhut. Finally, in 1845, Bethlehem cut all political ties to the German Moravians, although it still considered itself part of the same religious group (Gollin 1967, 42–49).

The Moravians used a unique system of decision making called "the lot," which was essentially the process of drawing, at random, one of a number of possible answers from a box. After formulating the question that needed an answer, generally the Moravians put three possible answers in the box: yes, no, and a blank piece of paper (which signified that the decision should not be made at that time). The Moravians believed that this system allowed them to involve God in the decision making by determining what God wanted them to do. In general, the Moravians believed in using the lot only if the community could not come to a decision on its own.

In Bethlehem, the lot was used most often to arrange marriages and to decide who should go on missionary work. It was not often used for economic decisions (Gollin 1967, 50–58).

How New Members Were Recruited or Chosen

The Moravians were conflicted about whether they were supposed to gain members from other Christian denominations or only from outside of Christianity. Count Zinzendorf wanted to unify all Christians and did not believe in the concept of separate Christian denominations. He therefore decided that the Moravians would not look for members from within other Christian denominations but would rather find converts among those who were not Christian, such as Native Americans (Smaby 1988, 27–28).

Although they did not seek to convert other Christians to their particular beliefs, if other Christians wished to join the Moravian movement, they were considered for membership. The first step was for a potential member to request permission to live in the community. Once this was granted, the person had to be accepted into the membership. Next, the person was allowed to observe communion celebrations, and then he or she received First Communion, which was a significant event in that person's life. In some cases, the community in Bethlehem decided whether or not to admit someone, and whether or not to advance him or her to the next stage, by using the system of lot described earlier (Smaby 1988, 22–23; Gollin 1967, 51–52).

Only a few of the Native Americans they converted lived in Bethlehem with the white members and adapted to life in the choirs; most lived in their own settlements nearby. The Moravians did not expect the Native Americans to abandon their own way of life and so felt it was better for the two cultures not to mix (Smaby 1988, 99–100).

Children and Youth

During Bethlehem's fully communal phase, babies lived with their parents until about 18 months of age, when they were weaned and sent to live in the communal nursery. The children in the nursery were raised by single sisters. They had little contact with their parents from this time on (Smaby 1988, 145, 148–149).

After the age of four, boys and girls lived separately in the Little Girls' Choir and Little Boys' Choir. They were cared for by single members of their own gender, and attended religious services just for children. At age 12, they moved into the Older Girls' and Older Boys' Choirs. At the age of 19, they graduated into the single people's choirs (Smaby 1988, 10, 145, 148, 150–151).

Between the ages of 15 and 19, the young person generally experienced a religious awakening and conversion and was accepted as a member of the "Gemeine," or Moravian community (Smaby 1988, 151).

Relationship with the Outside World

The Moravians were admired for their well-built towns, skillful work, modern farming methods, and the quality of their products (Durnbaugh 1997, 28).

Although they tried to keep themselves separate from the outside world, the Moravians traded with outsiders as needed. The Bethlehem and Bethabara communities built inns to house and feed travelers, so these people could be served and yet kept separate from the community. They charged a small fee for this service. Outsiders also patronized the Moravians' shops and doctor. In addition, the Moravians sometimes hired outsiders if they were short of labor (Thorp 1989, 117–119; Smaby 1988, 99).

During the American Revolution (1775–1783), Bethlehem was the site of a hospital for the colonial army and also supplied the army with food and other needs (Hamilton 1971, 252–253).

Reasons for Ending the Communal Aspect

Communal living was not an integral part of the Moravian religion. At times, communal living seemed a practical way of organizing life, such as when building a new community in the wilderness, or when supporting large groups of missionaries. But when communal living no longer served their purposes, the Moravians had little difficulty with abandoning it.

Influence on the Outside World

The Moravians started the towns of Bethlehem, Pennsylvania, and Winston-Salem, North Carolina.

See also: Ephrata Cloister

References

Durnbaugh, Donald. "Communitarian Societies in Colonial America," in *America's Communal Utopias*, edited by Donald Pitzer. Chapel Hill: University of North Carolina Press, 1997, 27–30.

Gollin, Gillian Lindt. *Moravians in Two Worlds: A Study of Changing Communities*. New York: Columbia University Press, 1967.

Hamilton, J. Taylor. *A History of the Church Known as the Moravian Church*. New York: AMS Press, 1971 (reprint of 1900 edition).

Sessler, Jacob John. *Communal Pietism among Early American Moravians*. New York: AMS Press, 1971 (reprint of 1933 edition).

Smaby, Beverly Prior. *The Transformation of Moravian Bethlehem: From Communal Mission to Family Economy*. Philadelphia: University of Pennsylvania Press, 1988.

Thorp, Daniel B. *The Moravian Community in Colonial North Carolina*. Knoxville: University of Tennessee Press, 1989.

WEB SITES

Historic Bethabara Park, NC: www.bethabarapark.org/maphome.htm (accessed April 2007).

Historic Bethlehem, PA: www.historicbethlehem.org (accessed April 2007).

Historic Salem, NC: www.oldsalem.org (accessed April 2007).

Moravian Church in North America: www.moravian.org/ (accessed April 2007).

Moravian Historical Society: www.moravianhistoricalsociety.org/ (accessed April 2007).

Sun Inn, Bethlehem, PA: www.suninnbethlehem.org/ (accessed April 2007).

More, Thomas

Thomas More (1478–1535) was an English scholar and statesman who in 1516 wrote a book called *Utopia,* which is a fictional account of an ideal society in which people live cooperatively, without private property.

More coined the word *utopia* from two Greek words—*ou* and *topis*—meaning "no place." Based on More's description of his ideal society, the word has come to mean a place or society of harmony and happiness.

More was educated at Oxford University and worked in both the legal and political arena. He was a councilor and ambassador for King Henry VIII. As he worked with his own government and those of other countries, he came to disagree with the way some issues were handled. In *Utopia*, he has his main character, Raphael Hythlodaeus, complain about the fact that thieves in England are condemned to death, when poverty often drives people to steal food or other necessities. More also uses *Utopia* to criticize the corruption and greed of European rulers.

More wrote *Utopia* in Latin because in the early 16th century Latin was a more universal language than English. Book One features a criticism of current European politics and society, and Book Two describes an idyllic society located on an island somewhere in the New World (North and South America, which had just been discovered by Europeans). The people of Utopia have no private property and they disdain gold so much that they use it to make chamber pots and manacles for prisoners. They take turns farming, share their food equitably, and elect their own rulers. They wear simple linen clothing. Their work day is just six hours long and in their free time they enjoy attending public lectures, playing music, and talking. Groups of 30 families eat together at common dining houses. Each household takes a turn at planning the menus and cooking the meals. The common dining houses also feature nurseries where women can breast-feed their babies and put them to bed during dinner. Criminals are punished by being forced to work as slaves for the community; however, they can be released from slavery for good behavior.

More even takes on issues that are controversial in modern times, such as euthanasia and women priests. In Utopia, terminally ill people who suffer from unrelievable, excruciating pain are encouraged to kill themselves through starvation or drugs. Priests in Utopia are elected by the entire community. Women and married men are allowed to be priests, although the only women eligible for priesthood are elderly widows.

To modern readers, some aspects of Utopia might not seem acceptable: residents were not allowed to travel outside of their home city without official permission; everyone wore the same kind of colorless clothing; husbands had the authority to punish their wives; and adultery was punished by slavery. Still, Utopia suggests comparatively humane solutions to the problems facing society in More's day, such as poverty, greed, and corruption.

English philosopher Thomas More is credited with coining the term utopia *to describe an ideal community. His 1516 book* Utopia *is a fictional account of an island society where the inhabitants live communally.* (Library of Congress)

Although *Utopia* can be seen as a serious attempt to promote reform in European society, More used humor in his book. The traveler who tells the story of Utopia is called Raphael Hythlodaeus—the last name can be translated as "nonsense." The major river in Utopia is called "Anydrus," or "no water." And the exact location of the island of Utopia is not known because just as Raphael was giving the location, someone coughed and no one heard what he said. Paul Turner, in his introduction to his translation of *Utopia*, suggests that More may have used these comical names and incidents because he enjoyed jokes, or to remind readers that the book was fiction, or to avoid getting into trouble at a time when kings could and did imprison and kill those who disagreed with them.

Despite this caution, More was in fact ordered to be executed by King Henry VIII—although his crime was not writing *Utopia*. More was beheaded because he refused to agree that Henry VIII was ranked higher than the pope and should be allowed to annul his marriage to Catherine of Aragon in order to marry Anne Boleyn.

More's *Utopia* was a best seller in his time and has retained its popularity since then. More was canonized as a Catholic saint in 1935. *Utopia* has been said to have influenced socialism and communism and was an important influence in the formation of cohousing communities.

See also: Cohousing; Literary Utopias

Reference

More, Thomas. *Utopia*. Translated by Paul Turner. Middlesex, England: Penguin Books, 1965.

New Deal Communities

At a Glance

Dates of existence in United States: 1933 to 1954
Location: nationwide
Peak membership: 10,000 families (approximately 50,000 individuals—
   one survey found that the average family size was 5.2 people)
Religious or other belief: secularism

History

The "New Deal" is the name given to all the U.S. government programs during the 1930s designed to help Americans who were poor and unemployed in the aftermath of the Great Depression. Some New Deal programs created cooperative settlements for those in need. This was the first time the federal government had tried to promote communal living. The New Deal communities also represent one of the most ambitious attempts at community building in the history of the United States.

As part of the New Deal, President Franklin Delano Roosevelt and the U.S. Congress passed a number of laws—including laws aimed at banks, investors, farmers, businesses, and workers—to help ease the suffering of Americans caused by the worst economic downtown the country had ever seen. A few of the programs attempted to help poor people by settling them in cooperative communities where they could work together and help each other, while at the same time maintaining their own individual family homes and land.

The New Deal community programs can be divided into two classes: subsistence homestead communities for farmers, miners, and other unemployed workers, and "greenbelt" suburbs that were designed to provide an alternative to inner-city slums.

A total of 99 different New Deal communities were funded, providing housing and employment for about 10,000 families.

The government hoped that these communities would not only alleviate poverty but would also lead to a more cooperative society. Other countries during the Great Depression had turned away from democracy and toward dictatorial governments. "The whole history of the New Deal communities could be related to the ideal of cooperation, which was to replace competition and extreme individualism," says historian Paul Conkin (1959). "The architects of the New Deal communities were attempting to develop cooperation as the new institution best suited for the modern environment. No more concerted effort was ever made in the United States to develop cooperatives of all kinds. Voluntary, democratic cooperation was to be the alternative to the economic insecurity and chaos of an individualistic, capitalistic past and to the involuntary, totalitarian collectivism of both fascism and communism" (Conkin 1959, 202).

The federal government's subsistence homesteads program ran from 1933 to 1935. In addition, another agency, the Federal Emergency Relief Administration, gave money to states to set up their own subsistence homestead programs. The work of both these agencies was taken over in 1935 by the newly created Resettlement Administration. This new agency went on to develop the greenbelt suburbs program.

While the New Deal helped many people to survive the Great Depression, prosperity returned to the United States only with the U.S. entry into World War II in 1941. At this time, the New Deal community program came under attack by Congress and other critics as being a waste of money and as being antithetical to the American values of individualism and free enterprise. The government began selling the communities starting in 1944. The subsistence farmstead units were sold at market value to low-income families, and the greenbelt homes were also sold to low-income settlers when possible. Despite the sales, the U.S. government lost a huge amount of money on the venture. The sales continued through the 1940s and early 1950s.

Subsistence Homestead Communities

A "subsistence homestead" meant a home and land on which the family could grow or raise most of the food they would require. Subsistence homesteads were envisioned as communities with between 25 and 100 families settled on one to five acres of land, which would include an orchard, a vegetable garden, poultry, a pig, and sometimes a cow. The settlers were supposed to eventually own their land, and would share some land and amenities with the other settlers in their community. The communities were appealing to the suffering public: by June 1934, almost 14,000 people had applied for 2,176 proposed homesteads.

At the urging of First Lady Eleanor Roosevelt, the subsistence houses were not merely shacks but durable homes with at least four rooms, plumbing, and electricity. In some communities, the settlers themselves helped to build their own houses. In others, outside labor was used.

In addition to homes and land, education was seen as extremely important to foster an economically successful community. The subsistence homesteaders benefited from the presence of experts to teach them better techniques for farming, canning, and food processing and from study groups to teach adults how to operate a cooperative business.

While the poor and unemployed were eager for subsistence homesteads, the program was not welcomed by everyone. Established farmers were afraid that the government-supported subsistence farmers would cut into their market. Businesses were afraid that any government-sponsored industry in the communities would threaten their livelihood. Some members of Congress were opposed to the cooperative, communal aspect of these communities, labeling them communistic.

The subsistence homestead communities succeeded in lifting people out of poverty and in providing them with decent housing, education, and other necessities. However, most of the communities were not able to make enough income to pay the government back and to become self-sufficient communities, as had been envisioned. Because of this failure, they were criticized as being a waste of money.

Many of the communities involved part-time subsistence farming and part-time employment in industry. Arthurdale was one of the first and most publicized of the communities.

Arthurdale: Several projects were planned to benefit unemployed miners in West Virginia, including Arthurdale, near the town of Reedsville. The project began when First Lady Eleanor Roosevelt visited this poverty-stricken area of West Virginia, where she found the residents living in shacks overrun by rats and having access to only dirty gutter water.

The U.S. government bought 1,200 acres of land to start the community in 1933. Eventually, 165 homes were built, along with several school buildings, an administration building, a gas station, a forge, a cooperative store, a furniture factory, a flour mill, a barbershop, a weaving room, a health clinic, and other community buildings.

The low-income settlers were selected based on their education, physical fitness, agricultural experience, and attitudes. The residents were responsible for paying rent on their homes and working their own farms. They also found employment constructing buildings on the community and working at the school and community businesses. Social activities included plays put on by the schoolchildren, competitive sports, and dancing.

One of the most innovative aspects of Arthurdale was its school, which was designed to foster democracy and cooperation by allowing the students to investigate the subjects that most interested them. Sometimes students would study the same theme in different subject areas. Much of the learning involved hands-on activities in addition to textbook work. In high school, vocational training was emphasized. Even the girls had access to shop classes and gym classes, which was unusual at that time. After the first few years, the school began to drop its innovative curriculum because the residents decided they wanted a more traditional education for their children.

The residents of Arthurdale enjoyed comfortable homes, education, health care, and an active community life. A visitor described the village: "Little white homes, chattering visitors, mountain scenery of the Allegheny plateau" (quoted in Conkin 1959, 249).

However, Arthurdale never managed to make enough money to justify the federal government's investment in it. The government was unable to find a suitable industry that could provide cash income to supplement the subsistence farms and community businesses and that would allow the settlers to pay an adequate amount of rent.

The U.S. Post Office offered to place a factory at Arthurdale in order to produce hardware and furniture for use in post offices, but Congress blocked this because it was feared that this factory would compete with existing private furniture businesses. Later, General Electric built a vacuum cleaner factory at Arthurdale, but the factory was not a financial success and was closed after a year. Next, a clothing manufacturer took over the vacuum cleaner building for the purposes of collar assembly, but this soon closed because of labor troubles in its home factory. A tractor assembly factory was also unsuccessful: it was never able to find enough buyers for its products. The most successful factory was one that made radio cabinets, which employed 100 people in 1942, although it too closed down because it could not find materials due to scarcities brought on by World War II.

However, with the U.S. involvement in World War II, prosperity returned. The coal mines reopened nearby and the Hoover Aircraft Corporation leased several Arthurdale factories and buildings for manufacturing defense-related materials. Between 1942 and 1946, the homes and buildings of Arthurdale were sold to private owners.

Today, Arthurdale is preserved as a historic site.

Other Subsistence Homestead Projects

Jersey Homesteads: Another famous community was Jersey Homesteads near Hightstown, New Jersey, started in 1936. It was planned for unemployed Jewish garment workers from New York City. The community was to include a cooperative garment factory, a cooperative farm, and a community store. The completed town included 200 concrete-block homes with five to seven rooms, modern bathrooms, and electric refrigerators, each on one acre of land. The residents shared a modern, air-conditioned garment factory, town hall, nursery school, library, elementary school, various stores, and a health clinic.

Like Arthurdale, Jersey Homesteads never managed to produce an income sufficient to pay back the government. The garment factory suffered during its first year because many of the houses had not yet been built, so the factory did not have enough workers to fulfill all of its orders. Even in its second year, when all housing had been completed, the factory was a financial failure, perhaps because of bad management. The cooperative farms were somewhat more successful but still did not bring in regular profits. Many of the settlers did not want to be farmers. The grocery and meat stores were a bit more prosperous. Many houses remained unoccupied: only 120 families at the most lived at Jersey Homesteads.

However, despite the financial troubles, many of the settlers were happy with the social life of the community. They organized a drama club, sewing circle, and baseball club, among others. Most did not want to leave the community even when they had to in order to take a job elsewhere.

After World War II, the homesteads were sold to private individuals, and in 1954 the settlers renamed their town "Roosevelt," after President Franklin Delano Roosevelt, who had just died. Today, Jersey Homesteads is a historic district within the town of Roosevelt.

Dyess Colony: In terms of the state-run programs, one of the largest was Dyess Colony, near Wilson, Arkansas, started in 1934. About 500 homes were built on 20 to 40 acres, along with a community center, warehouses, a mule barn, a theater building, a hospital, a school, a seed house, a cotton gin, a store, a credit union, a cafe, a lumber mill, a furniture shop, a cannery, a blacksmith shop, and other businesses and amenities. By 1936, about 3,000 people lived in the community. A scholar describes it as "a small city, with city blocks, paved streets and sidewalks, stores, offices, and residential sections" (Holley 1975, 44–45).

The community's prospects looked hopeful. In 1936, the community's lawyer said, "I predict that within ten years, this will be the most prosperous community in

Arkansas or any other state. . . . There will be no rich people here, but everyone will be well-to-do" (quoted in Holley 1975, 50). However, the colony was not able to become financially self-sufficient. It was sold to private owners beginning in 1943.

Greenbelt Towns: Three greenbelt towns were constructed under the New Deal: Greenbelt, Maryland; Greenhills, Ohio; and Greendale, Wisconsin. These were the largest of the New Deal communities, together containing over 2,000 family units.

"Based on world-wide influence, the greenbelt cities, next to the Tennessee Valley Authority, were probably the most influential creations of the New Deal," says historian Paul Conkin. "They represented . . . the most daring, original and ambitious experiments in public housing in the history of the United States" (1959, 167, 305).

The Greenbelt towns were built to allow low-income people to escape the slums of the city, but still be near enough to the city to find employment. They were designed to provide decent, affordable housing surrounded by parks, woodland, and/or farmland.

Greenbelt, Maryland, near Washington, D.C., was the first town to be completed, in 1937. It grouped houses into five neighborhoods, each containing a central park. The houses were connected with pedestrian walkways—no roads were within the neighborhoods. The town also contained a lake, a school, a restaurant, a movie theater, a swimming pool, a community-controlled retail stores, and a community gardens.

Greenhills, near Cincinnati, was planned more for the automobile and less for pedestrian traffic. Like Greenbelt, it featured parks, stores, and so forth, but the town was bisected by a main highway, along which ran the community center. Families began settling in Greenhills in 1938.

Greendale, near Milwaukee, was also started in 1938 and was surrounded by farms. It was designed to resemble a normal country village, with houses arranged in city blocks.

The towns were envisioned as more than just a collection of housing and amenities. Regarding Greendale, one expert explained: "The vision of the Greendale planners extended far beyond the mere physical plan of the town. It recognized government housing as more than the provision of shelter—it is the creation of communities in which democratic processes of living can best be developed" (quoted in Arnold 1971, 205).

The cooperative stores, credit unions, and health care services within each community were financially successful. In fact, residents were so enthusiastic about cooperatives that, in Greenbelt, the schoolchildren operated their own cooperative store to sell candy, pencils, and other childhood necessities.

The settlers in each city were also enthusiastic about fostering community feeling. They organized a plethora of clubs and social activities. For example, Greenbelt residents had access to a hobby club, garden club, preschool mothers' club, school-age mothers' club, radio club, swimming club, choral group, drama club, and newspaper, among others.

Each town was governed by an elected city council. There was no elected mayor. Instead, the city council appointed a city manager.

The major criticism of the Greenbelt towns was their cost. The towns ended up being quite expensive to build, and the rent had to be subsidized because the low-

Cinder block house in Greendale, Wisconsin, in 1937, which was part of the federal government's Subsistence Homesteads program designed to assist people affected by the Great Depression. (Library of Congress)

income residents could not afford to pay for the full cost of the housing and community services. Other critics felt it was inappropriate for the federal government to compete with private business in building housing. Finally, some people did not like the cooperative aspects of the towns.

Nevertheless, the public was intensely curious about these new towns. A "Guest Day" at Greenbelt attracted 4,000 visitors. Town planners from all over the world were fascinated by the greenbelt towns experiment. People were interested in the idea of decentralized public housing, and in government planning of towns. The towns were radical in that (1) they gave low-income residents living in government-subsidized housing control over their own local government, and (2) they planned for a system of cooperative institutions to serve the residents.

By the late 1940s, the federal government decided it did not want to own the cities any longer. Over the next several years, it sold portions of the greenbelt cities to the residents, to churches, to city park services, and to other private owners. The government suffered financial losses in these transactions. All three towns are still thriving today. Greenbelt is a National Historic Landmark.

Influence on the Outside World

Despite the fact that the New Deal communities were often financial failures, they attempted something very ambitious. They aimed to help people to help themselves by providing them with decent housing, health care, education, and employment. And while the communities may have been too expensive and extravagant, the New Deal communities did succeed in lifting people out of poverty and in fostering a feeling of community and cooperation.

Experts suggest that the successes and challenges of the New Deal community experiment can help us to understand how to create communities that allow people to help themselves and to prosper.

See also: Cooperatives; Great Depression

References

Arnold, Joseph. *The New Deal in the Suburbs: A History of the Greenbelt Town Program, 1935–1954.* Columbus: Ohio State University Press, 1971.

Conkin, Paul. *Tomorrow a New World: The New Deal Community Program.* Ithaca, NY: American Historical Association, Cornell University Press, 1959.

Davis, Kenneth. *FDR, The New Deal Years, 1933–1937: A History.* New York: Random House, 1986.

Holley, Donald. *Uncle Sam's Farmers: The New Deal Communities in the Lower Mississippi Valley.* Urbana: University of Illinois Press, 1975.

Wuenstel, Mary. "Participants in the Arthurdale Community Schools' Experiment in Progressive Education from the Years 1934 to 1938 Recount Their Experiences." *Education,* summer 2002, www.findarticles.com/p/articles/mi_qa3673/is_200207/ai_n9109083 (accessed April 22, 2008).

WEB SITES

Arthurdale Heritage: www.arthurdaleheritage.org/ (accessed June 2006).

Greenbelt CityLink, Greenbelt, MD: www.greenbeltmd.gov/ (accessed June 2006).

Jersey Homesteads History: http://pluto.njcc.com/~ret/Roosevelt/history1.html (accessed June 2006).

New Deal Network: http://newdeal.feri.org/ (accessed June 2006).

Village of Greendale, WI: www.greendale.org/ (accessed June 2006).

Village of Greenhills, OH: www.greenhillsohio.org/ (accessed June 2006).

New Harmony and Owenite Movement

At a Glance

Dates of existence in United States: 1825 to 1827 (New Harmony); 1825 to 1860s (Owenite movement)
Locations: Indiana (New Harmony); Illinois, New York, Ohio, Pennsylvania, Wisconsin (Owenite movement)
Peak membership: 1,000
Religious or other belief: secularism, socialism

History

Although short-lived, New Harmony is important because it was the first nonreligious, socialist community in the United States. In addition, Robert Owen, founder of New Harmony, inspired the formation of a number of other communities, all of which lasted for just a short time.

Robert Owen was a British factory owner who turned to utopian community-building after his efforts at promoting factory reform failed. Owen had created a model factory town in New Lanark, Scotland. While he could see that the machines of the Industrial Revolution were producing vast quantities of consumer goods as well as immense wealth for a few factory owners, he was also concerned about the poverty of the factory workers, as well as their lack of education and what he viewed as immoral behavior on the part of the factory workers. He wanted to create a new way of living that combined material prosperity with education, health, and morality for everyone. His town featured cleaner, nicer housing and shorter working hours than was common in factory towns of the day. In addition, he provided free education from infancy through adulthood.

Since few British factory owners were interested in adopting the reforms Owen promoted, he decided to turn his attention to building communities from scratch. He wanted to create living examples of the ideas he was trying to promote. In 1817, he collected his writings into a book called *A New View of Society*, in which he argued that communal villages would solve the problems of unemployment and poverty. He distributed 40,000 copies of this document to the public and to influential leaders. Over the next several years, he traveled throughout the United Kingdom, spoke about his ideas, and tried to raise money to start a community.

By 1824, Owen had not raised enough money to buy land in the United Kingdom. In August of that year, he found out that the Harmony Society in Indiana had put its land up for sale. Owen left his oldest son, Robert Dale Owen, in charge of the New

Karl Bodmer painting of the utopian community of New Harmony around 1832. (Library of Congress)

Lanark mills and traveled to the United States in October 1824 to look at the land. The purchase was finalized in January 1825. The village he bought contained 30,000 acres of land and 180 buildings, including housing for 700 people.

Over the next three months, Owen journeyed through the United States giving public lectures about his proposed community. The top leaders of the United States welcomed him: Owen spoke in the U.S. Capitol, with President John Quincy Adams and former President James Monroe in attendance along with members of their cabinets, in addition to both chambers of Congress and the Supreme Court. *A New View of Society* was published in the United States, and Owen's speeches were printed in newspapers across the country. Owen published a manifesto inviting anyone who liked his ideas to join his community in New Harmony. In April, Owen returned to New Harmony and drafted a constitution for his society. By May, Owen's community had attracted between 800 and 900 people.

Although he had declared himself leader of the community for the first year, in mid-1825, Owen left the community to be run by a committee of seven men. He did not tell anyone when he would return. Owen ended up being absent for seven months, during which time he traveled and lectured in the eastern United States and in England, where he commissioned a six-foot-square model of his ideal community. He brought this model to the United States and arranged for its display in New York, Philadelphia, and the White House. Despite the fact that his son had written to him of the difficulty of building anything new on the Indiana land, Owen proclaimed publicly that the actual buildings depicted in his model would be constructed soon on this land.

While Owen was away, the Indiana summer was hot, the housing was crowded, free-roaming hogs devoured many of the vegetables in the garden, and community members grew dissatisfied with the amount of store credit they were awarded for their community work. They awaited the return of Owen to put things right. Meanwhile, the community began printing its weekly newspaper, *The New Harmony Gazette*, which helped spread the views of Owen within the community and to the outside world.

Owen returned to New Harmony in January 1826. At the time, the community had a population of about 1,000. A few weeks later, several scientists, educators, and artists recruited by Owen arrived at the community, along with Owen's oldest son, Robert Dale. Owen dubbed this crew the "Boatload of Knowledge." Owen proposed that a new constitution be drafted, creating a community of common property and full equality. A committee of seven men was elected to write the constitution.

However, about two weeks after this constitution was adopted, the department leaders, distressed by the chaos of the community, asked Owen to reassume leadership of the community. He agreed, but many members were upset about the state of the community and left. A few offshoot communities were formed, and Owen provided them with land. Among the remaining members at New Harmony was a high proportion of "drifters, parasites and fanatics" (Bestor 1950, 186). One new member, Paul Brown, spent months publicly complaining about Owen and the community.

Despite these difficulties, Owen chose a portion of land on which to build his ideal community and gave speeches to commemorate the occasion. However, the chaos within the community grew worse. Owen reorganized New Harmony several times and finally, in January 1827, he agreed to lease the land to anyone who wanted to form a community based on his ideas. One man, William Taylor, acquired 1,500 acres in this way and promptly set up a distillery. (Owen had prohibited liquor in New Harmony.)

Owen left the community in June 1827, and this was the end of the community experiment at New Harmony. However, Owen continued to promote the concepts behind his communities. In 1828, he asked the government of Mexico to grant him the entire province of Texas (which was at that time part of Mexico) for the purpose of building Owenite communities. His request was turned down.

Owen's sons continued to live on their family's land in Indiana, and Owen visited them periodically.

Beliefs and Practices

Owen felt that environment shaped a person's character. A clean environment full of educational opportunities, he felt, would produce the happiest, most productive workers. He had experimented with creating such an environment at his factory town of New Lanark. Accordingly, he drew up plans for a series of communities based on New Lanark.

Each community, providing housing and work for 500 to 1,500 residents, would feature buildings in a square formation surrounding a central quadrangle. The houses would have hot and cold running water. In addition, within the village complex, residents would have access to a library, kitchens, dining halls, baths, laundries, stores, schools, a museum, gymnasium, music rooms, and lecture halls. Outside of the village square would be mills, factories, and farmland. These villages would allow everyone's needs to be met. Private property would cease to exist and everyone would live in equality. Owen imagined that as these ideal villages came to dominate the Earth, human character would be so well formed, and happiness so prevalent, as to extend the average life span to 140 years.

Owen believed that the existing town in New Harmony was only a "half-way house" to his ideal community. He drafted a constitution for the society in April 1825 that combined communal ownership with private property and communal work with private enterprise. The constitution stated that members would provide their own furniture and tools. In exchange for their communal work, they would receive credit at the community store. If they did not wish to work within the community, they could pay for their goods with cash.

In 1826, at his urging, a committee drafted a permanent constitution that called for equality of rights for men and women; equality of duties (with consideration given to physical and mental abilities); community property; and freedom of speech and action. The constitution further specified such values as sincerity, kindness, order, and the acquisition of knowledge. Unfortunately, this constitution was never put into practice because of the turmoil that enveloped the community.

Daily Life

Following Owen's plan, the community engaged in dancing on Tuesday nights; a committee business meeting on Wednesday nights; a concert on Thursday nights; and lectures or sermons on Sundays. Although Owen was an atheist, he declared that the people of New Harmony should be free to worship in whatever way they chose, and visiting preachers frequently spoke in the New Harmony church.

Owen designed clothes to be worn by community members. The men wore white, full pantaloons and a boy's jacket without a collar. The women wore undertrousers tied at the ankles and a full skirt that reached to the knees. One woman described the men's costume thus: "A fat person dressed in the elegant costume I have heard very appropriately compared to a feather bed tied in the middle" (quoted in Wilson 1964, 147).

How They Made Their Living

Although the community started out with too many members for the housing it could provide, they did not have enough skilled craftspeople to operate the machinery left behind in the town. For example, the wool and cotton spinning industries did not have enough spinners, and the dye-house was not in use because there was no one knowledgeable enough to manage it. The community did not have potters, saddlers, harness makers, coppersmiths, or any of a number of other occupations that would have been useful.

The only viable community industries seemed to have been the manufacture of soap, candles, glue, hats, and shoes. In addition, carpenters, bricklayers, and stonecutters worked to create extra living quarters. The community also put to work the butchers, bakers, blacksmiths, and tailors in their midst. Owen's wealth was the main income source of the community, making up for the lack of community industry.

Leadership and Decision Making

The New Harmony constitution that Owen drafted in 1825 stated that he would be in control of the community for the first year and would appoint a committee to manage the affairs of the community. After the first year, the members would elect three additional members of the committee. In reality, Owen appointed four members of the committee and, right away, asked the community to elect three more.

The permanent constitution that was adopted in 1826 divided the community into six departments: agriculture, manufacturing, education, domestic economy, general economy, and commerce. Each department would have a manager chosen by the people who worked in that department and confirmed by an assembly of all members. Laws would be made by all members of the community above age 21. However, this system was not used—almost as soon as the department leaders were chosen, they asked Owen to take over, because the community was in such disarray.

How New Members Were Recruited or Chosen

At first, Owen never made it clear how members were to be chosen. Apparently, a significant portion of the first people who arrived in New Harmony did not agree with or understand Owen's views.

The permanent constitution adopted in 1826 specified that prospective members had to be approved by a majority of current members. Members could leave on one week's notice and were entitled to the return of whatever property or money they had originally contributed to the community.

Children and Youth

Owen believed that education was the key to producing happy, healthy, productive human beings. He felt that children should be removed from their families at an early age in order to provide them with an ideal education as soon as possible. In New Lanark, Owen started an infant school for children as young as one or two. In his plans for his communal villages, Owen proposed that children over two would live together in a nursery, separately from their parents.

At New Harmony, the children lived in a separate building and were almost never allowed to see their parents. One woman who spent time in New Harmony as a child recalls, "I saw my father and mother twice in two years" (quoted in Wilson 1964, 145).

Owen recruited William Maclure, a geologist and naturalist, to take charge of the school at New Harmony. In addition, the teachers included Joseph Neef and Madame Marie Fretageot, who had been in charge of schools in Philadelphia before coming to New Harmony. All of these teachers believed in an educational system promoted by the Swiss educator Johann Pestalozzi, whose philosophy was that children should learn through doing. Students learned from objects such as maps, skeletons, and outdoor observation as much as possible. Corporal punishment was banned in the New Harmony school. It was one of the first public schools in the United States and the first public school in Indiana.

At its height, the New Harmony school had 400 students. The school taught sciences, mathematics, reading, geography, French, and Spanish. Maclure believed that the students ought to learn practical skills as well as academics, so the boys learned engraving, printing, taxidermy, carpentry, wheelmaking, blacksmithing, agriculture, and so forth. The girls were taught sewing, cooking, and dressmaking (Pitzer 1987, 282).

Maclure continued this school, renamed the School of Industry, for about 20 years after the communal experiment at New Harmony ended.

Relationship with the Outside World

The American public willingly accepted Owen's experiment in communal living. His audiences included some of the most powerful people in the United States. The more controversial question at that time was Owen's atheism. He spoke openly about his disdain of religion and was often criticized for these views.

Reasons for Decline of the Community

New Harmony hardly got off the ground for many reasons. Owen, the self-declared leader of the community, was absent for much of the first year, and even when he returned, he was not able to create order out of the chaotic community. Owen put much energy into speaking about his ideas, and not enough energy into making those ideas a reality. In addition to this lack of leadership, Owen did not screen those who wanted to live in the community and thus attracted some people who were only interested in living off his wealth instead of contributing to the community.

Influence on the Outside World

Robert Owen was much more influential as a speaker and as a promoter of ideas than as a founder of a community. His views on education, for example, were far ahead of his time. He introduced the educational principles of Johann Pestalozzi to the United States and promoted the education of girls and boys together. He was one of the first and most influential leaders to promote ideas about economic security, equality for women, and religious tolerance.

Owen envisioned that his community plan would be adopted all over the industrialized world. Although this never happened, he did inspire the formation of at least 19 Owenite communities in the United States, and about nine in Great Britain. One of the most successful, in Kendal, Ohio (now part of Massillon, Ohio), began in 1826 and ended in 1828. Although the community members in Kendal were getting along with each other and the industries were producing income, the members decided to end it because they no longer wished to live communally.

None of the Owenite communities managed to build the grandiose village Owen envisioned and most lasted less than two years. They often suffered from the same kinds of problems as New Harmony: bickering about how exactly the community work and property should be allocated and a lack of funds and/or leadership.

Owen also inspired one of the first antislavery communities: Nashoba in Tennessee. Its founder, Fanny Wright, visited New Harmony several times.

Owen's Boatload of Knowledge, which brought prominent scientists and educators to the wilds of Indiana, "contributed to the opening of the Midwest personally and through their influence upon the next generation of scholars," according to Donald Pitzer (1989, 140).

See also: Antislavery Communities; Harmony Society; Owen, Robert; Socialism

References

Bestor, Arthur E. *Backwoods Utopias: The Sectarian and Owenite Phases of Communitarian Socialism in America: 1663–1829.* Philadelphia: University of Pennsylvania Press, 1950.

Branigin, Richard. "Robert Owen's New Harmony: An American Heritage," in *Robert Owen's American Legacy: Proceedings of the Robert Owen Bicentennial Conference,* edited by Donald Pitzer. Indianapolis: Indiana Historical Society, 1972.

Holloway, Mark. *Heavens on Earth: Utopian Communities in America, 1680 to 1880.* New York: Library Publishers, 1951.

Oved, Yaacov. *Two Hundred Years of American Communes.* New Brunswick, NJ: Transaction Books, 1988.

Owen, Robert. *A New View of Society.* Harmondsworth, England: Penguin, 1970.

Pitzer, Donald. "The Original Boatload of Knowledge Down the Ohio River: William Maclure's and Robert Owen's Transfer of Science and Education to the Midwest." *Ohio Journal of Science,* December 1989, vol. 89, issue 5: 128–142.

Pitzer, Donald. "Patterns of Education in American Communal Societies," in *Communal Life: An International Perspective,* edited by Yosef Gorni, Yaacov Oved, and Idit Paz. New Brunswick, NJ: Transaction Books, 1987.

Pitzer, Donald E. "The New Moral World of Robert Owen and New Harmony," in *America's Communal Utopias,* edited by Donald Pitzer. Chapel Hill: University of North Carolina Press, 1997, 88–134.

Wilson, William. *The Angel and the Serpent: The Story of New Harmony.* Bloomington: Indiana University Press, 1964.

Web site

Historic New Harmony: http://www.ulib.iupui.edu/kade/newharmony/home.html (accessed May 2006).

Oneida Community

At a Glance

Dates of existence in United States: 1848 to 1881
Locations: Oneida, New York, with a smaller community in Wallingford, Connecticut
Peak membership: about 300
Religious or other belief: Christianity, Perfectionism

History

The Oneida community was one of the first American communities begun by a native-born American with a membership composed mostly of native-born Americans.

The community was founded by John Humphrey Noyes, a Vermont minister who converted to the idea of "Perfectionism." He believed that the second coming of Christ had already occurred in 70 CE; therefore, he reasoned that humans could, if sincere and faithful enough, live in this world free from sin.

Noyes declared that he was perfect and free of sin. This proclamation prompted Yale University to withdraw his license to preach. Noyes lost his church. For the next few years, he wandered through New England and New York as a missionary, preaching and gathering followers. In 1838, he married Harriet Holton, and six years later he and about two dozen followers, including two of his sisters, a brother, and his mother, began to live communally in his hometown of Putney, Vermont: they shared their homes, worked together on the Noyes family farm, ran a store, and educated their children themselves.

In 1846, Noyes began a practice that was to bring him fame and notoriety: a system he called "complex marriage," in which every man of the community was married to every woman. This system shocked the people of Putney, and Noyes was accused of adultery, jailed, and released on bail. Noyes and his community were afraid the residents of Putney would physically harm them, so Noyes fled to New York, and many community members left Putney as well.

In 1847, about 50 of Noyes's followers re-formed their community in Oneida County, New York, on land donated by a follower. This was during an era of fervent religious revival in western New York—a region now termed the *Burned-Over District*. More people joined the community, many of whom were affluent and able to donate money and property. The complex marriage system was investigated in court in 1850, but by this time the Oneida community had developed a reputation for honesty and fairness in its dealings with the outside world. Many of the community's

The large Mansion House at Oneida was the center of life in the prosperous communal society. (George Wallingford Noyes, ed. *The Religious Experiences of John Humphrey Noyes.* New York: Macmillan Company, 1923.)

neighbors came to its defense, signing a declaration that the Oneida members were people of good behavior, and that since their unusual marriage system was restricted to their own community, it was not harmful to the rest of society.

By 1851, there were 250 people living in the Oneida community. The group struggled to earn a living through farming and manufacturing consumer items such as furniture and brooms. In 1855, it began what would become its most lucrative business: manufacturing steel traps for the fur trade.

Oneida prospered throughout the 1860s. Members built a large brick building, named the Mansion House, where they lived, ate, and socialized. In 1869, they began an experiment called "stirpiculture," in which certain men and women were selected to become parents of a "superior" generation.

By 1877, Noyes was growing old, and he appointed his son, Theodore, to be the community's leader. Theodore was not able to hold the community together during a period of internal division, and the community officially dissolved in 1881 and became a business: Oneida Ltd., which is today the world's largest manufacturer of silverware.

Beliefs and Practices

The Oneidans believed that God spoke to them through John Humphrey Noyes, and he in turn preached that community members should strive toward "Perfection"—becoming unselfish and loving one another equally. Noyes felt that living in community could help his followers achieve Perfection. The community would shield them from the influences of the outside world and give them the opportunity to work for the good of the whole community, rather than just for themselves and their own families.

While working together was important, so was learning together. Noyes believed that intellectual efforts were as important as spiritual concerns. In addition to educating its children, the Oneida community held daily adult education classes.

Another practice to help the members achieve Perfection was the complex marriage system. Noyes believed that the practice of monogamous marriage was contrary to Biblical principles. "When the will of God is done on earth," he wrote to a friend, "there will be no marriage. The marriage supper of the Lamb is a feast at which every dish is free to every guest. Exclusiveness, jealousy, quarreling, have no place there. . . . In a holy community there is no more reason why sexual intercourse should be restrained by law, than why eating and drinking should be, and there is little reason for shame in the one case as in the other" (quoted in Oved 1988, 169).

The complex marriage system allowed any man in the community to ask any woman to have sexual relations with him. This was usually done by means of a go-between (an older woman, generally), who would convey the man's request to the woman. She was free to accept or refuse. However, Noyes did not believe in having two people especially attached to each other. He felt that all men should love all women, and vice versa. If two people were found to be falling in love exclusively with each other, they were ordered to stop seeing each other for a while (Kephart 1976, 80–82).

Further, Noyes felt that a woman's health was harmed by frequent pregnancies and childbearing (his own wife had suffered four stillbirths within the first six years of their marriage). Therefore, he taught the men in the community to withhold their ejaculations as a means of birth control. This system worked: from 1848 to 1869 there were only 31 accidental births among the community, although the adult population was generally over 200 (Carden 1969, 49–51).

A fourth way to help his followers achieve Perfection was the system of "mutual criticism." Members would take turns offering themselves for a mutual criticism session, during which other members would comment upon the faults of the person being criticized and offer suggestions for personal improvement.

While Noyes always insisted that men were superior to women, he nevertheless allowed women considerable freedom within the community. Because they were freed from the burden of pregnancy and caring for children, and because they were encouraged to participate in the same classes and many of the same jobs as men, women's status within the community was much higher than it was in the outside world at that point in history (Carden 1969, 66–67).

As the community became more prosperous, Noyes felt it was time to allow babies to be born within the community. However, he was opposed to random, unplanned pregnancies and births. His interest in science led him to believe that parents should be carefully selected for superior physical, mental, and spiritual qualities. Accordingly, about 100 women and men were chosen to become parents, resulting in the birth of 58 children. This experiment, called stirpiculture (from the Latin word for "root"), was just as shocking to the outside world as complex marriage (Carden 1969, 61–63).

Daily Life

The Oneida community house contained kitchens, a dining hall, an assembly hall with stage, a parlor, and a library with thousands of volumes, including newspapers and magazines. On the upper floors were the sleeping rooms: each adult generally had a private sleeping room (Nordhoff 1960, 277).

Adult community members woke up between 5:00 and 7:30 a.m. and went to the dining hall for breakfast and Bible reading, after which members would go to their work assignments. Men and women often worked together, talking and laughing as they carried out their tasks. Members sometimes switched jobs in order to become proficient in a number of areas and to avoid boredom. If there was a large job to be done, the community would announce a "bee" in which anyone interested was invited to participate. Members might call a bee to pare apples, pick strawberries, or to sew the traveling lunch bags that the community sold for a time (Klaw 1993, 99–104; Nordhoff 1960, 280–281).

In general, Oneidans had two meals per day, with the second one around 3:00 p.m. The Oneidans ate meat about twice a week; they preferred fruits, vegetables, milk, butter, cheese, and cake. They drank coffee or an herbal tea made of strawberry leaves, but used no tobacco or alcoholic beverages. After dinner, members met for adult education classes in French, mathematics, sciences, literature, music, and the arts (Nordhoff 1960, 282).

After the classes came perhaps the most important event of the day: the evening meeting. The Oneidans did not have Sunday worship services, because they believed every day was holy. Instead, they met every evening to discuss religious subjects, as well as the day-to-day running of the community. Noyes would often give a speech about how Perfectionist theology applied to everyday life, after which the community would deal with practical matters: hearing reports from the various committees, or discussing letters from applicants who wished to join the community. After the meeting, members were free to amuse themselves with dancing, singing, games, reading, or writing letters. Card playing was not permitted (Carden 1969, 46–47).

While the male members wore typical clothes of that period, the women at Oneida had a unique costume. Noyes felt that women's fashions of the day took too much time to put on and hindered movement. Accordingly, the women at Oneida cut their hair (so it would be easier to style) and wore calf-length dresses with pants underneath (Kephart 1976, 64–65).

During their free time, the Oneidans enjoyed parties, picnics, swimming, fishing, skating, hiking, sleigh riding, and camping. They put on dramatic and musical performances for each other. They played croquet year-round on the lawn in front of the Mansion House (Klaw 1993, 94–97).

How They Made Their Living

The Oneida community was involved with a number of business enterprises, including farming and manufacturing furniture, silk thread, and other consumer items. However, the most lucrative of their businesses—begun in the 1850s—was manufacturing steel traps for the fur trade. One of its members had developed a better animal trap and orders came in from all over the United States and Canada. In 1877, the community began manufacturing silverware (Carden 1969, 37–42).

Leadership and Decision Making

The Oneida community was not a democracy. Noyes was its leader and those who did not accept his leadership generally did not join the community.

However, Noyes did not run every aspect of the community. He chose certain spiritually advanced "central members" to run the day-to-day business of Oneida. In addition, there were 21 committees and 48 departments in charge of such things as finance, roads and lawns, painting, water and steam power, haircutting, printing of the community newspaper, running the various business enterprises, and caring for the children. At the evening meeting, any member was allowed to speak up about any subject. Women and men both served as central members and as members of committees and departments (Kephart 1976, 61–63).

The community members were extremely loyal to Noyes, and it was only when he grew too old to lead that the community broke up.

How New Members Were Recruited or Chosen

The Oneida community circulated Noyes's writing to the public. In addition, because of its unusual practices, outsiders were curious about the community and many came to visit. The Oneidans received many letters from people who wished to join, but the group was mainly interested in those who were familiar with Perfectionism and Noyes's writings. Part of the acceptance process might involve a session of mutual criticism via letters. Once invited to live in the community, new members passed through a probationary period of a few months to a year before becoming full members (Kephart 1976, 66; Carden 1969, 77–78).

Children and Youth

Babies in Oneida lived with their mothers until weaned. Between the ages of 15 months and 12 years, children lived in their own separate wing of the Mansion House, cared for by their own staff of nannies and teachers. Because all adults were supposed to love all children and vice versa, mothers and fathers were not supposed to develop a particular love for their own offspring. The children were allowed to spend only a few hours per week with their own mothers and fathers. In fact, children who cried for their mothers were sometimes punished by not being allowed to see them even for a weekly visit (Klaw 1993, 142–144).

The children ate meals with the adults in the dining hall, and as soon as they were able, the young people began to work an hour or more per day on the farm or in one of the factories.

The Oneida school taught reading, writing, spelling, and arithmetic. After age 12, the students learned a wider variety of subjects, including astronomy, geography, math, sciences, and languages. A number of students were sent to college.

Once a young person experienced puberty, he or she began participating in the complex marriage system. Many youth were thus sexually active as young teenagers (Klaw 1993, 181).

Relationship with the Outside World

The Oneidans rarely left their community. However, the outside world was very curious about their way of life, and beginning in 1850, Oneida opened its doors to visitors. Thousands of people came to see this unusual community, and tourism became an important way to earn income. In 1866 alone, about 6,000 people came to visit the community (Carden 1969, 81).

The Oneidans also hired outside workers in their businesses. Sometimes the number of outside workers was equal to the number of community members. Because they paid generous wages and provided better working conditions than other workplaces of the day, the Oneida fields and factories were popular places to work (Nordhoff 1960, 263).

Despite their unusual marriage practices, they had only sporadic trouble with the outside world regarding this subject. For example, in 1852, a number of religious newspapers began attacking the Oneida community because of complex marriage, leading the community to abandon the practice for six months. However, criticism of its marriage system eventually helped to bring about the end of the community.

Reasons for Decline of the Community

The Oneida community was held together by Noyes. He was a persuasive and an effective leader. The community fell apart when he grew too old to lead.

From the outside, problems came in the form of a minister, John Mears, who began attacking the community in the mid-1870s for its practice of complex marriage. Within the community, a new group of 12 people had joined, along with their minister, James Towner. Towner and his followers challenged the leadership of Noyes, who resigned in 1877 and appointed his son, Theodore, leader of the community. However, Theodore was not able to hold the community together in the face of Towner's criticism.

In 1879, John Humphrey Noyes left the community for Canada. From there, he asked the community to stop its practice of complex marriage. At that point, many Oneidans married in monogamous unions. Often, mothers married the fathers of their children. The community decided to disband in 1881. Members formed a private company—Oneida Ltd.—out of their many business enterprises. Each former member was given some stock in the company, the opportunity to rent living quarters in the Mansion House, and the opportunity to work in the company for wages.

Influence on the Outside World

While the community itself dissolved long ago, the Oneida name is still known today as the world's largest manufacturer of silverware. The company also makes plates and other dinnerware.

Although the community was popular and even notorious in its day, today few people know the history of the Oneida community. Nevertheless, Oneida was ahead of its time. In an era when sexuality was seen as sinful, Noyes declared that it was not, and he converted hundreds of people to his practice of complex marriage. In an era when birth control was not commonly available and women were burdened with frequent pregnancies and too many children, Noyes instituted a successful method of birth control. He showed, through his successful community, that there were other ways to live a happy, prosperous life.

See also: Burned-Over District; Millennialism

References

Carden, Maren Lockwood. *Oneida: Utopian Community to Modern Corporation.* Baltimore, MD: The Johns Hopkins University Press, 1969.

Foster, Lawrence. *Religion and Sexuality: Three American Communal Experiences of the Nineteenth Century.* New York: Oxford University Press, 1981.

Foster, Lawrence. "Free Love and Community: John Humphrey Noyes and the Oneida Perfectionists," in *America's Communal Utopias,* edited by Donald Pitzer. Chapel Hill: University of North Carolina Press, 1997, 253–278.

Kephart, William. *Extraordinary Groups: The Sociology of Unconventional Life-Styles.* New York: St. Martin's Press, 1976.

Klaw, Spencer. *Without Sin: The Life and Death of the Oneida Community.* New York: Penguin Books, 1993.

Nordhoff, Charles. *The Communistic Societies of the United States; From Personal Visit and Observation.* New York: Hillary House Publishers, 1960 (reprint of 1875 edition).

Oved, Yaacov. *Two Hundred Years of American Communes.* New Brunswick, NJ: Transaction Books, 1988.

Thomas, Robert David. *The Man Who Would Be Perfect: John Humphrey Noyes and the Utopian Impulse.* Philadelphia: University of Pennsylvania Press, 1977.

Web sites

History of Oneida: http://www.oneida.com/index.cfm/fuseaction/content.page/nodeID/c41889b4–6e42–48ac-bf36-c18f0861ff0b/ (accessed April 2006).

Oneida Community: www.oneidacommunity.org/ (accessed April 2006).

Orderville and Mormon Communalism

At a Glance

Dates of existence in United States: 1875 to 1885 (Orderville)
Location: Utah (Orderville)
Peak membership: 700 (Orderville)
Religious or other belief: Church of Jesus Christ of Latter-day Saints (Mormons)

History

From its beginnings, the Mormon religion has valued economic cooperation. At different times and in different places, Mormon communities have set up systems to foster such cooperation. The most ambitious of these experiments lasted for 10 years in Orderville, Utah.

Mormonism was founded by Joseph Smith, who grew up in upstate New York, an area that was in religious ferment in the early 19th century, with Unitarians, Shakers, Methodists, Presbyterians, and others holding revival meetings and attracting converts. The first half of the 1800s in western New York has been termed the *Burned-Over District* because of this religious excitement. Smith's family was divided religiously: several members of his family were Presbyterian, he himself was drawn to the Methodist faith, and his father was a free thinker. Smith was troubled by this religious division and pluralism and wanted to find the one true way. He experienced a series of visions that led him to found the Church of Jesus Christ of Latter-day Saints in 1830.

Smith claimed to have translated, from gold plates given to him by the angel Moroni, the Book of Mormon, which was published in 1830. The Book of Mormon is believed to contain the history of three groups of Middle Eastern peoples who arrived in what is now America around 600 BCE, and were subsequently visited by Jesus Christ after his resurrection. After this visit, these American Christians lived in a communal society where they shared all things in common, similar to the early Christian church as described in the Acts of the Apostles in the New Testament.

Smith and his followers believed that their church was a restoration of the true Christian church. In 1831, Smith described the "Law of Consecration and Stewardship," which was to be a way of redistributing wealth and fostering economic cooperation and equality. Under this system, followers were to "consecrate" their land and belongings to the church. In return, the church would appoint them as "stewards" over whatever land or belongings they needed to make a living and maintain their households. The followers were also to give any surplus farm produce or goods

The angel Moroni delivers the plates of the Book of Mormon to Joseph Smith on September 22, 1827. Smith claimed to have been visited by the angel Moroni who told him of the location of ancient gold plates, from which he transcribed and published the Book of Mormon. Smith founded the Mormon Church in 1830. (Library of Congress)

to the church. The idea was that, as followers gave the church more property and goods than they themselves needed, this excess could be used to support families in need. Smith's followers put this law into action first in Missouri between 1831 and 1833.

However, the Mormons were persecuted by the non-Mormons in the area—their homes were burned, their printing press was destroyed, and they were driven out of the area. The Mormons attempted settlements in Ohio and in other parts of Missouri. They set up cooperative farms and businesses. Again, they were persecuted and expelled from their land. They then moved to Illinois and attempted to set up a model city they called Nauvoo. In this area, they replaced the Law of Consecration and Stewardship with the concept of tithing: followers were to give 10 percent of their wealth to the church, or if they had no property, were to work one-tenth of the time for the church (Arrington 2005, 7). In Nauvoo, the surrounding citizens again persecuted the Mormons, and in 1844, Smith and his brother were assassinated. Brigham Young then took over the leadership of the Mormons. Members were pressured to leave the area and in 1846 they set out for the western United States. (Buildings and land in Nauvoo were later sold to another utopian community—the Icarians.)

The Mormons traveled cooperatively. All income was pooled, and families were organized into groups to make the journey. Some groups were assigned to find work along the way to contribute to the common fund, and other groups were to plow and plant unclaimed land so it could be harvested by groups coming later. In 1847, the Mormons settled in Utah (Arrington 2005, 18–22).

Their Utah settlements were run cooperatively, although individual families owned their own land and homes. The settlers farmed land together, built houses for each other, and shared excess food with those in need. The church also started a number of cooperative industries, although many of these later failed. Members were asked to give to the church 10 percent of their property, labor, and/or the increase of their production (Arrington, Fox, and May 1976, 45–62; Arrington 2005, 130–137).

In the mid-1860s, a group of Mormons living in Brigham City, Utah, created a cooperative community with a cooperative retail store and cooperative industries. Inspired by their example, Brigham Young started a cooperative retail store in Salt Lake City, the Zion's Cooperative Mercantile Institution, and encouraged such stores to be established in all Mormon towns. The Mormon Church also started a cooperative bank, textile factory, and iron works.

In the 1870s, Young and other church leaders revived a version of the Law of Consecration and Stewardship, which they now called the United Order of Enoch. Young encouraged congregations to organize themselves into United Orders. Ideally, members of each United Order were to contribute their economic property and labor to the Order. Members were to live frugally, to use only products of the Order, and to obey their leaders. However, each individual congregation was allowed to decide how far to go toward full communal living. The Order of Enoch was to bring a time "when there shall be no rich and no poor among the Latter-day Saints . . . when every man will love his neighbor as he does himself; when every man and woman will labor for the good of all as much as for self," according to a church apostle (quoted in Arrington, Fox and May 1976, 138; Arrington 2005, 328–329).

Many of these United Orders ended within a year. Some United Orders simply set up or continued one or more cooperative enterprises but did not ask members to give over all their property or labor. A few, however, were fully communal. The most important of these was in Orderville, Utah. In addition, United Order communes were started in Price City, Springdale, and Kingston, Utah; Bunkerville, Nevada; and several places in Arizona. Some of these were as small as 50 people (Arrington 2005, 333).

Orderville was founded in 1875 as a United Order city. The original 150 settlers came from the destitute "Muddy colonies," which were started in the 1860s to grow cotton for a Mormon cotton factory. At first, the communal efforts at Orderville resulted in the settlers being better-off economically than their non-Mormon neighbors. In the late 1870s, when silver deposits were found nearby, the non-Mormons became more prosperous and the young people of Orderville became envious. Orderville began moving away from communalism and toward more private ownership. The community continued to prosper and grow to about 700 people. In 1885, the federal government began enforcing an antipolygamy law. Orderville leaders, including its president, were convicted and sent to jail for practicing polygamy. The Mormon Church recommended that Orderville disband (Arrington 1954).

Brigham Young died in 1877, and the general United Order movement ended that year. By the late 1880s, private enterprise was the norm for Mormon communities. It was not until the 1930s, during the Great Depression, that the Mormons began another significant experiment in cooperation. In 1936, they launched their Church Welfare Plan, under which the church would acquire farms and factories to grow or make products specifically for those in need. Members would provide volunteer labor for these efforts. This Church Welfare Plan continues to operate today (Arrington 2005, 337–338; May 1997, 151–153).

Beliefs and Practices

Mormons are Christians and believe in the Bible and Jesus Christ. They also have their own religious texts such as the Book of Mormon.

Leonard Arrington describes the basic principles of the Mormon Church: (1) Mormons must gather the believers together in villages; (2) property should be distributed and regulated by the church (because of their belief that "the earth is the Lord's"); (3) the Mormons should make Earth productive; (4) they should be frugal and economically interdependent upon each other, but self-sufficient and not dependent on the outside world; (5) they should be unified under a common leadership, and cooperate with each other; and (6) families should be economically equal (2005, 24–28).

Based on a vision received by Joseph Smith, Mormons for many years believed in polygamy (the practice of a man being married to more than one woman at a time). This arrangement, they believed, was similar to the polygamous marriages of Bible patriarchs such as Abraham, Isaac, and Jacob. A Mormon who wished to marry more than one wife had to get the approval of church elders and of his first wife. This practice was declared illegal by the U.S. government in 1882, and even before that, only a minority of Mormon men had more than one wife. In 1890, the Mormon Church officially abandoned polygamy.

Daily Life

Orderville was founded in Kane County in southern Utah. At first the community recognized no private property, although each person was the "steward" over his or her own clothing, beds, and other personal necessities. Families lived in separate apartments that were owned by the community. Each dwelling consisted of one or two rooms. Until 1880, when the dining hall was flooded, the community ate together in a common dining hall.

Bells or bugles woke the members up and signaled the times of meals and work. For the first few years, men ate first, and women and children afterwards. In 1879, the members decided to eat in family units in the dining hall, so two dining shifts were organized. The members ate bread, meat, potatoes, fruits, and milk. Mormons do not smoke or drink alcohol, tea, coffee, or soft drinks. These rules come from one of Joseph Smith's visions (Arrington 1954, 9–11).

How They Made Their Living

Orderville aimed to be economically self-sufficient, and it came very near to achieving this goal. Residents owned farms, orchards, and vegetable gardens; they kept poultry, ran a dairy, and raised sheep. They owned a gristmill to grind flour, and molasses mills to press sugar cane. They made their own brooms, soap, clothing, buckets, leather goods, furniture, and buildings. They sold their excess wool, furniture, and leather goods to other Utah cities. Orderville also had its own midwives, an herb doctor, and blacksmiths, clerks, artists, and musicians.

During the first two years, everyone worked without wages or credits and took whatever food and supplies they needed from the storehouse. In 1877, they started a wage credit system. Men, no matter what work they did, received a standard credit per day. Women received half this amount. From these credits, families were to pay for their housing, food, and other necessities. At the end of each year, surplus credit was to be given back to the Order and surplus debt was wiped out.

In 1883, the community moved further away from communal living. The wage credit system was modified to allow certain jobs to earn more credits than other jobs. Families were allowed to purchase their own lots and homes, and the community businesses were leased to their foremen. Credits and debts were no longer wiped away at the end of each year (Arrington 1954, 11–17, 25–32).

Leadership and Decision Making

Orderville was governed by the nine-member Board of Management, all of whom were men. This Board of Management was elected each year. It supervised the property, bought or sold property for the Order, and made work assignments. However, important issues were discussed by the community as a whole during regular meetings. Under the Board of Management were 33 departments, each headed by a foreman selected by the Board. Women served as "foremen" of departments such as millinery and sewing (Arrington 1954, 18–20).

How New Members Were Recruited or Chosen

Members were asked whether they were willing to abide by the rules of the community, including living frugally, maintaining the peace, and refraining from using tobacco, alcohol, coffee, and tea. Unlike other utopian communes, Orderville gave significant wealth to those who left the community: departing members were paid an equivalent to what they had contributed and debts of these members were often cancelled (Arrington 1954, 22–23).

Children and Youth

The community ran a school during the winter months and sometimes during the evenings all year round. Only the younger children attended school; the older ones worked within the community (Arrington 1954, 14).

Relationship with the Outside World

Orderville, and Mormons in general at that time, tried to have as little as possible to do with the outside world. This was partly because of the persecution the Mormons had suffered at the hands of the outside world.

Why were the Mormons persecuted so severely, when other unusual religions or communities of the same time period—such as the Shakers—were allowed to live largely in peace? Leonard Arrington and Davis Bitton suggest that non-Mormons feared and hated Mormons for religious, racial, economic, and political reasons.

First, many non-Mormons viewed the Mormon religion as full of superstition (because of the religious visions of Joseph Smith). The young Protestant congregations of the Midwest feared that the Mormons would convert their members. In Utah, when the Mormons practiced polygamy more openly, this became another source of opposition from the outside world.

Because Mormons preached to Native Americans and to free blacks, they were seen as threatening the racial order. Mormons believed that Native Americans were descendants of the Americans who were visited by the resurrected Jesus Christ, as described in their Book of Mormon.

Mormons believed in economic self-sufficiency, so that when a large group of Mormons arrived in an area, they did not benefit the local businesses, but instead kept their money to themselves. In addition, outsiders feared that the Mormons would buy up all the land.

Members of the Mormon Church tended to vote as a bloc—they cast all their votes for the same candidates and issues. Outsiders who disagreed with Mormon politics wanted them out of the area.

As a result of these fears, non-Mormons harassed the Mormons, stoned and burned their buildings, destroyed their fields, murdered their leaders, and forced them to flee (Arrington and Bitton 1979, 46–64).

Reasons for Ending the Community

Orderville and the other communal United Order settlements ended largely because their leaders were jailed or prosecuted for polygamy (Arrington 2005, 333).

Influence on the Outside World

The Mormon communal experiments seem to have had the most influence on the larger Mormon community. For example, even as late as the 1940s, over 50 years after the ending of the United Order, researchers at Harvard University found that, for Mormons, the ideal society was a communal one—whereas for non-Mormons, the ideal society was more individualist (May 1997, 151).

Although the communal experiments of the United Orders were short-lived, Arrington points out that by emphasizing self-sufficiency, they "assured a more rapid development of resources, particularly in areas where Utah had a comparative disadvantage. The United Order . . . helped to keep Utah economically independent of the East longer and more completely than would otherwise have been the case" (2005, 338).

See also: Bible Communism; Burned-Over District; Cooperatives; Icarian Movement

References

Arrington, Leonard J. *Orderville, Utah: A Pioneer Mormon Experiment in Economic Organizations.* Logan: Utah State Agricultural College Monograph Series, vol. 2, no. 2, March 1954.

Arrington, Leonard J. *Great Basin Kingdom: An Economic History of the Latter-Day Saints, 1830–1900, New Edition.* Urbana: University of Illinois Press, 2005.

Arrington, Leonard J., and Davis Bitton. *The Mormon Experience: A History of the Latter-Day Saints.* New York: Alfred A. Knopf, 1979.

Arrington, Leonard J., Feramorz Y. Fox, and Dean L. May. *Building the City of God: Community and Cooperation among the Mormons.* Salt Lake City, UT: Deseret Book Company, 1976.

Kephart, William. *Extraordinary Groups: The Sociology of Unconventional Life-Styles.* New York: St. Martin's Press, 1976.

May, Dean L. "One Heart and One Mind: Communal Life and Values among the Mormons," in *America's Communal Utopias,* edited by Donald Pitzer. Chapel Hill: University of North Carolina Press, 1997, 135–158.

Owen, Robert

Robert Owen (1771–1858) was a British factory owner who influenced the formation of utopian communities, cooperatives, and labor unions. Although he did not manage to form a successful utopian community, his views have been influential in Europe and the United States in terms of cooperatives, labor unions, educational reform, and gender equality.

Owen was born in Wales to a working-class family: his father was a saddlemaker and a blacksmith. Young Owen attended school until the age of 10, when he was apprenticed to a clothier. He was treated well and spent about five hours a day reading books in his employer's library. During this time, he decided that he no longer believed in organized religion.

Before the age of 20, Owen had become a manager and partner of a large cotton mill in Manchester, England. He then persuaded the other partners to buy a mill in New Lanark, Scotland.

In New Lanark, Owen found that crime was widespread, sanitation was poor, housing conditions were unacceptable, and the people were uneducated. Owen believed that a person's character was formed in response to outside influences. He criticized society for promoting circumstances that lead to criminal behavior and then punishing that behavior. In 1813, he began writing essays detailing his philosophy, which were published in 1817 as *A New View of Society*. In these essays, Owen repeatedly stresses "that the character of man is, without a single exception, always formed for him; that it may be, and is chiefly, created by his predecessors; that they give him, or may give him, his ideas and habits, which are the powers that govern and direct his conduct. Man, therefore, never did, nor is it possible ever can, form his own character" (Owen 1817, 92).

Owen aimed to create a positive influence in New Lanark. He improved the housing in the town and encouraged his workers to be clean and frugal. Instead of employing children as young as five, as was common in other factories, he started a school for them, where students learned through play, singing, and dancing. He also instituted adult education classes and lectures.

In order to be competitive with other mills, Owen did employ children above 10 years old. And while he was able to reduce the working hours for his employees, the working day was still a long 10.5 hours at New Lanark. Despite his liberal thinking, Owen saw himself as the boss: for example, to curb crime he instituted curfews and random searches. He did not see his employees as equal to himself. In fact, in one of his essays he compares employees to machines and tries to convince other factory owners that they ought to institute his reforms as a way of taking just as good care of their "vital machines" as they do of their inanimate machines. "When you shall acquire a right knowledge of [employees], of their curious mechanism, of their self-adjusting powers; when the proper main spring shall be applied to their varied movements, you will become conscious of their real value, and you will be readily induced to turn your thoughts more frequently from your inanimate to your living machines; you will discover that the latter may be easily trained and directed to procure a large increase of pecuniary gain, while you may also derive from them high and substantial gratification" (Owen 1817, 72–73).

The New Lanark mills were successful both as a business and as a social experiment. Between 1815 and 1825, an estimated 20,000 people visited the mills, including reformers and politicians. In 1815, Owen began to speak publicly about factory reform, trying to convince other factory owners to follow his example. But few were interested.

Owen became interested in community building because he felt that only in a favorable community could people develop good characters. He was particularly captivated by the idea that a group of people could create a community right away, without waiting for a class revolution or action from the government. As John Harrison explains, "In order to build [his new society] it was necessary to withdraw partially from existing society and its corrupting influences" (1972, 31).

Owen had learned about utopian communal groups, such as the Shakers and the Harmony Society, in the United States. He began to publicize his ideas for cooperative villages in which about 1,000 people would live and work together on 1,000 to 1,500 acres. Owen came up with this size because it was similar to the size of the village of New Lanark. Everyone was to live together in one large building, with common kitchen and dining rooms. Each family was to have its own apartment and to care for its children until age three, at which point the children would be raised communally and see their parents at meals and other times.

Many people were in favor of Owen's ideas until he declared publicly, at a London meeting, that he did not believe in religion.

In 1825, Owen bought 30,000 acres of land in Indiana from the Harmony Society and started his New Harmony community. Despite the enormous amount of publicity the community garnered, and support from top American leaders, the community ended in 1827, partly because Owen was absent from the community much of the time—traveling to publicize his views—and partly because Owen allowed anyone who wanted to join the community, whether or not they understood its principles or were willing to work on behalf of the community.

In addition to his attempts at community building, Owen was involved in factory reform. He was one of the first people to speak publicly about the evils of the Industrial Revolution and to propose humane solutions. Starting in 1815, he tried to influence the British parliament to pass laws against employing children under 10, in favor of four years of compulsory schooling before employment and a limit of 10.5 hours per day of work for youth. From 1820 to 1830, supporters formed a variety of organizations and journals to promote Owen's views. In 1833, the British Parliament did finally pass a law that came close to meeting Owen's demands.

After the failure of New Harmony, Owen returned to England and was regarded as the leader of the trade union, or labor union, movement, which had been formed based on his views. He traveled the country, speaking and working to promote labor unions.

In England, Owen was involved with another effort at community building at Queenwood, Hampshire, which existed from 1839 to 1845.

In addition to Robert Owen's personal influence in the United States, he brought several of his children to the United States. His son Robert Dale Owen was elected to the Indiana legislature and the U.S. House of Representatives, where he worked on behalf of women's rights and free public education, and against slavery.

See also: Industrial Revolution; New Harmony and Owenite Movement; Socialism

References

Harrison, John F. C. "Robert Owen's Quest for the New Moral World in America," in *Robert Owen's American Legacy: Proceedings of the Robert Owen Bicentennial Conference*, edited by Donald Pitzer. Indianapolis: Indiana Historical Society, 1972.

"Owen, Robert." *The New Encyclopedia Britannica,* 2005 ed., vol. 9, 23–24.

Owen, Robert. *A New View of Society; or Essays on the Principle of the Formation of Human Character.* Glencoe, IL: The Free Press (facsimile reproduction of the 3rd edition printed in London in 1817).

Pacifism

Pacifism is a rejection of violence and war as a way to solve problems. Many utopian communities include a belief in pacifism.

Pacifists refuse to participate in war and sometimes refuse to engage in violence even for self-defense. In some cases, pacifists believe that one must cultivate a feeling of love or goodwill toward other people and not merely avoid hurting them.

The earliest American pacifists generally based their peaceful beliefs on religion, and often these pacifists were forced to flee Europe in order to maintain their beliefs. The Shakers were an early pacifist community. They first arrived in the American colonies in 1774, shortly before the American Revolution, which started in 1775. In 1780, while the war was still going on, the Shakers began attracting attention by preaching against war. Six Shakers, including Mother Ann (their leader), were arrested for trying to persuade others not to take up arms. The colonial government was afraid they were British sympathizers. In the end, the government realized that the group was simply an unusual religion, yet Mother Ann was kept in prison for five months (Brock 1968, 274).

At first the Shakers paid fines rather than allow their young men to be drafted into the military, although some states allowed them to be exempted from military service without paying any fines. By the time of the Civil War, the Shakers were instructing their young men to refuse both service and fines. Some Shakers were arrested and imprisoned for this (Brock 1968, 430–431, 828–829). Furthermore, the Shakers would not allow any members who had formerly been in the military to accept a military pension from the government, even though this money would have gone into the common fund (Brock 1968, 427–428, 430).

Sometimes a belief in pacifism conflicts with other beliefs. The Zoar Society, a Christian sect, started in 1817 as a pacifist community. However, a dozen Zoar men chose to fight against slavery in the Civil War.

Another early pacifist community was the Amish, who are Anabaptists (they believe that people should be baptized only as adults, when they can understand and accept their religion). The Amish started arriving in the New World in 1727. "For Anabaptists . . . participation in war and violence was wrong, both because it had been forbidden in the New Testament and because spiritual weapons alone were thought to be consistent with Christian discipleship," explains Peter Brock (1968, 5–6).

Other pacifist Anabaptists who formed utopian communities in the United States include the Hutterites (who began immigrating to the United States in 1874) and the Bruderhof (whose first American community started in 1954).

The Anabaptists do not even believe in violence for the purpose of self-defense. When called for military service, they generally elected to pay fines, hire substitutes, or perform a civilian assignment. During World War I, the Hutterite and Amish conscientious objectors were sent to military camp for training, and if they refused to put on a military uniform or participate in drills, they were subjected to punishment such as solitary confinement and physical abuse. Two Hutterite men died from this mistreatment. During this time, newspapers condemned Hutterite colonies because they refused to buy war bonds. Americans were often suspicious of the German-speaking Hutterites, fearing that they might be spies for Germany. As a result, the entire community in the United States fled to Canada.

During World War II, a number of pacifist churches (Mennonites, Quakers, and Brethren) succeeded in passing a law allowing conscientious objectors to bypass military training and to perform service projects with government agencies or nonprofit organizations.

The Amana Colonies, a Christian community that started in the United States in 1843, were also pacifist for many years. Members of these communities generally paid for replacements for any of their young men who were called to war. When the community gave up a fully communal economy in 1932, they also began allowing church members to follow their own conscience when it came to military duty, and many Amana Church members did participate in World War II.

The Point Loma Theosophical community, which began in 1897, worked to end all war in the early 1900s, as World War I began in Europe. The leader of the community, Katherine Tingley, lobbied U.S. president Woodrow Wilson, as well as the nation's governors and mayors, to set aside September 28, 1914, as a "Sacred Peace Day for the Nations." Wilson declined to do so. Tingley organized a "Parliament of Peace" at Point Loma in 1915, and fought for draft exemptions for the men of Point Loma.

The Davidian and Branch Davidian movements, which began in 1935, were pacifist for many years. They are an outgrowth of the Seventh-Day Adventist Church, which is a historically pacifist church. However, the Branch Davidians gave up their pacifist beliefs under leader David Koresh in the 1990s and actually started a business selling guns and gun equipment.

The Peace Mission Movement, which promoted racial equality and positive thinking, was not pacifist despite having the word *peace* in its name. The movement began in 1917 and reached its height during the Great Depression of the 1930s. When World War II started, the Peace Mission Movement leader, Father Divine, spoke out against German leader Adolf Hitler, who was carrying out a policy to exterminate Jews and people of other ethnic minorities. Father Divine told his followers to consult their own conscience regarding military service. A number of members did fight in World War II.

The Catholic Worker Movement, which is a socialist, anarchist movement to help the needy, was criticized for its pacifist stance during World War II. Many people refused to buy the *Catholic Worker* newspaper because they disagreed with founder Dorothy Day's pacifist objections to the war. Even other pacifists felt that the United States was justified in entering this war in order to save the Jews. But Day felt that war is never justified and that the United States could have done more good by providing more Jews with a safe haven in the United States before the war began.

Koinonia, a Christian community founded in 1942 on the premise of racial equality, has a firm belief in pacifism. While members of Koinonia supported the civil rights movement for African Americans, they wondered if the movement was non-violent enough. They believed that nonviolence must be accompanied by love, and not by hate.

Hippie communities were often pacifist, since the hippie movement was founded on a protest of the Vietnam War.

See also: Persecution

References

Brock, Peter. *Pacifism in the United States from the Colonial Era to the First World War.* Princeton, NJ: Princeton University Press, 1968.

Chatfield, Charles. *The American Peace Movement: Ideals and Activism.* New York: Twayne Publishers, 1992.

Meltzer, Milton. *Ain't Gonna Study War No More: The Story of America's Peace Seekers.* New York: Harper and Row, 1985.

Peace Mission Movement

At a Glance

Dates of existence in United States: 1917 to present
Locations: New York, New Jersey, Pennsylvania, Washington State,
    California, and across the United States and internationally
Peak membership: up to 10,000
Religious or other belief: Christianity, "New Thought," racial equality

History

Before the civil rights movement, the Peace Mission Movement was calling for racial integration. At a time when most black churches emphasized the joys of the hereafter but did little to help followers who were unemployed or hungry, the Peace Mission Movement housed, fed, and found jobs for the poor. At its height, this movement attracted tens of thousands of people, both black and white—yet it is largely forgotten today.

The Peace Mission Movement was founded by a man who called himself Father Divine. He generally refused to divulge his birth name or any details about his life before he became "Father Divine." However, he is believed to have been George Baker Jr., born in Rockville, Maryland, in 1879. He left home at the age of 18, worked in Baltimore as a gardener and began to be influenced by "New Thought" ideas (Watts 1992, 5–21).

He took on the name "The Messenger" and traveled to the southern United States to spread the word about positive thought and celibacy. Black women were attracted to his teachings, and some of them left their husbands or began practicing celibacy. Black men—including other ministers—became angry at The Messenger and had him arrested a few times. Finally, in 1917, The Messenger traveled to New York City with a few of his followers. He rented an apartment in Brooklyn and they began living communally. The Messenger acted as an employment agency, finding jobs for his followers as domestics. He pooled their income and bought discounted food and clothing. Because he taught his followers to work hard, and asked them to refrain from smoking, drinking, gambling, profanity, and accepting tips, his followers were in demand as employees.

The Messenger changed his name to Major Jealous Divine, or Father Divine, around 1919. He bought an eight-room house in Sayville, a predominantly white town on Long Island. By this time, he had married one of his followers by the name of Peninniah. It was a chaste, "spiritual" marriage. Peninniah was one of his most devoted and capable followers, and upon their marriage she became Mother Divine. At this point, he had less than a dozen followers.

For many years things went well on Long Island. The white neighbors tolerated Father Divine, a quiet, well-dressed man who provided good household help. However, slowly Father Divine's movement grew. He added onto his house and new followers arrived to live there. Worship services, which were open to the public, sometimes attracted close to 100 people. The Great Depression had started with the stock market crash of 1929, and many desperately poor people flocked to Father Divine for help.

Father Divine's Long Island neighbors had him arrested in 1931 for disturbing the peace. After his release on bail, he began preaching widely throughout New York City, attracting more and more worshippers. In addition, the newspapers covered his conflict with his neighbors, which gave him additional publicity. In 1932, he was sentenced to one year in jail. Three days after this sentence, the judge in his case died of a heart attack. The black newspapers proclaimed it a miracle. Father Divine's lawyer managed to get him released from jail about three weeks later, until his case could be appealed (Weisbrot 1983, 46–53).

His popularity soared, as did the number of his followers—not just in New York, but all over the country and even in other countries. The group was mostly black, but increasingly Father Divine attracted whites as well, many of whom were from the middle and upper classes. He moved his headquarters to Harlem in New York City in order to lecture more easily in the city. He and his disciples began buying small businesses and hotels, which they ran cooperatively.

At first, Father Divine did not try to control the growth of his movement: any follower who wished could set up a Peace Mission. Sometimes affluent followers donated their houses for Peace Missions. Others pooled savings to buy a business and run it cooperatively. Although no records were kept of the size of the group, Robert Weisbrot estimates that Father Divine may have had 10,000 hard-core followers during the 1930s. In addition, tens of thousands more were likely sympathetic to his views. His supporters were predominantly women. A 1930s issue of a Peace Mission newspaper listed 158 Peace Missions, with the largest numbers in New York, California, New Jersey, and Washington State (Weisbrot 1983, 68–69; Hoshor 1936, 207–208).

In addition to running businesses and spreading their religious teachings, Father Divine and his followers attempted to influence politicians to support racial integration. The Peace Missions also continued to make inroads into white culture. In fact, in 1938, Father Divine's followers bought him an estate on the Hudson River across from the Hyde Park mansion of President Franklin Delano Roosevelt!

Toward the end of the 1930s, Father Divine's Peace Mission Movement began having problems with some followers who were gaining power but were not following Father Divine's teachings. One wealthy white man decided that he was Jesus Christ. He began preaching in Peace Missions and convinced a 17-year-old white woman that she was the Virgin Mary and should have a baby by him. Another disciple by the name of Faithful Mary accepted a large cash donation from a follower and refused to return it when Father Divine asked her to. A former follower, Verinda Brown, sued Father Divine to return money she had given him years earlier. The courts ordered him to pay, although she admitted she had given the money freely (Watts 1992, 144–147, 152–155).

As a result of these scandals, Father Divine formed an official church in order to protect himself and to have more control over what was going on in the Peace Mission Movement. After 1941, any follower who wanted to start a Peace Mission had to have approval from one of the three church branches. In 1942, in order to avoid having to pay Verinda Brown, Father Divine left New York City and made Philadelphia his headquarters.

The next year, Mother Divine died. Father Divine decided to marry a 21-year-old white follower, Edna Rose Ritchings, who took on the spiritual name "Sweet Angel." He explained that Mother Divine had been reincarnated in the body of Sweet Angel. At a time when interracial marriage was illegal in many states, Father Divine married Sweet Angel in a civil ceremony in 1946. Again, it was a purely spiritual marriage, and the new Mother Divine was assigned a constant female companion in order to prove to followers that Father Divine was celibate (Watts 1992, 168–169).

During the 1940s, the movement remained strong, but was not attracting many new members. A number of Peace Missions began to close. Father Divine retired from public life in about 1955. After his death in 1965, the number of followers decreased sharply. Today, the movement, led by Mother Divine, is very small.

Beliefs and Practices

New Thought was a philosophy, popular in the late 19th and early 20th century, that taught that God's spirit existed in all people, and that this spirit could be channeled, through positive thinking, to cure physical illnesses and restore health. Positive thinking, coupled with hard work, could also help people be successful financially.

While many New Thought adherents were well-off whites, Father Divine introduced this philosophy to poor blacks. He felt that their social and economic woes were a result of negative thinking, not racial prejudice. Father Divine believed that anyone could be healthy and successful with the right thoughts and the right faith. He did not believe in dwelling on the subject of race. He encouraged black and white followers not to mention race, and to work together, eat at the same dinner tables, and even room together (Watts 1992, 21–24).

Father Divine saw his followers as his children, and encouraged them to renounce their family ties and take on new spiritual names such as Great B. Love, Brilliant Victory, Merriness Truth, and Evangeline Faithful. Father Divine and his followers insisted that they were reborn and refused to talk about their lives before taking on their new names.

In addition to new names, Father Divine encouraged his followers to adopt new, positive language. His followers said "peace" rather than "hello," and frequently punctuated their speech with the phrase, "It is wonderful!"

Father Divine disagreed with the common church practice of soliciting funds from worshippers. He refused to ask for donations or to pass a collection plate. However, if people freely gave him money or gifts, he would accept them on behalf of the community.

Father Divine did not believe in borrowing money. He encouraged his followers to pay all their debts and to be scrupulously honest in their financial dealings. He did not believe in stock investments, banks, or government welfare. Disciples who were guilty of stealing, even if the crime had been committed years ago, were encouraged to send the money back, along with a letter explaining the circumstances (Hoshor 1936, 225–227).

Although the name of the movement included the word *peace*, the movement was not particularly pacifist. During World War II, Father Divine railed against Nazi leader Adolf Hitler and told his followers that they should consult their own conscience regarding whether or not to join the military. A number of his followers did join.

Father Divine preached that anyone with enough faith would enjoy eternal life. When followers—including the first Mother Divine—began to die, he changed his ideas about death by explaining that disciples might choose to come back to life in a younger, healthier body.

The main spiritual service of the Peace Missions was the Holy Communion Banquet. At least once a week, but sometimes more often, a huge banquet would be served, featuring beautifully laid tables. The feasts were extraordinarily lavish, with generally about 50 different types of food served: hot and cold meats, a dozen different kinds of cooked vegetables, fruit and vegetable salads, several different kinds of bread, many condiments, and a variety of hot and cold drinks. Dessert might consist of a variety of cakes or ice cream.

The Holy Communion Banquet was free and open to anyone. Father Divine blessed each dish by inserting a serving spoon or cutting the first serving. Followers were encouraged to eat heartily. At a time when many black people did not have enough to eat, Father Divine aimed to show that faith and positive thinking could produce an abundance of nourishment.

During the meal, followers would stand up and talk about how their belief in Father Divine had restored their health, or had cured them of alcoholism or other social ills. Often, followers would shout, clap and stamp with joy, or sing songs of their own composition praising Father Divine.

The highlight of a Holy Communion Banquet was Father Divine's speech. He told listeners that they could lead prosperous lives now, in this world, without waiting for heaven in the future. He encouraged them with visions of a world in which all men and women would be equal. During the height of his movement, he had as many as 25 personal secretaries to take down his words. His speeches were reprinted in Peace Mission newspapers (Watts 1992, 63–64; Weisbrot 1983, 34–36; Kephart 1972, 107–113).

As the movement grew and more and more Peace Missions formed, Father Divine could not be physically present at all Holy Communion Banquets. However, a place was always laid for him, and a secretary would read one of his previous speeches.

Daily Life

Because each Peace Mission was different, daily life was not consistent across the missions. Most followers worked within a Peace Mission business in exchange for food, clothing, and shelter, but no wages. Other followers remained in the home to perform domestic duties. Within each household, each member had an equal voice in household decisions.

Some followers did not work within Peace Mission businesses. Instead, they paid a small amount to live at the Peace Missions.

Although the Peace Mission followers were celibate, often destitute single mothers joined with their children. The young children were cared for by the followers who remained at home, freeing the mother for other work. School-aged children were sent to local public schools.

Followers were encouraged to hold Holy Communion Banquets at least once a week. Anyone caught smoking, drinking alcohol, cursing, or violating the celibacy rule was asked to leave (Weisbrot 1983, 72–74; Watts 1992, 102).

How They Made Their Living

The community first earned money through Father Divine's domestic service employment agency. Around 1932, the Peace Missions began buying and running restaurants in New York City and Newark, New Jersey. These restaurants offered good food for a low price and became very popular. Soon, Peace Missions bought hotels, food markets, and garages, often in the poorer parts of a city.

Peace Mission businesses succeeded where other businesses failed because they had a built-in low-cost labor pool: honest, hard-working disciples who would work for no wages other than room and board. By offering their goods and services at rock-bottom prices during the Great Depression, Peace Missions were able to outcompete other businesses. Since Father Divine did not believe in borrowing money, businesses were bought out of savings or through donations from followers, and there was no debt to worry about repaying.

In 1935, several disciples pooled their money and began buying farms in rural Ulster County, in upstate New York. Four years later, the Peace Missions owned 2,000 acres. These cooperative farms were able to supply the city-based Peace Mission hotels and restaurants with high-quality, low-cost food (Weisbrot 1983, 122–131).

Leadership and Decision Making

Father Divine was the leader of the movement, and he selected many of the people who worked closest with him as personal secretaries or managers of large enterprises. Since Father Divine preached that anyone with enough faith would achieve eternal life, he made few provisions for who would succeed him after he died. Although the second Mother Divine is a capable leader, she was not able to command the kind of following that Father Divine had enjoyed while in the prime of his life (Kephart 1976, 141).

How New Members Were Recruited or Chosen

There seems to have been no formal way of joining the Peace Mission Movement. Interested people typically attended a lecture by Father Divine or visited a Peace Mission. Persons willing to abide by the rules of the Peace Mission could join.

Relationship with the Outside World

Because they were often located in poor areas, and because they encouraged their members to be honest, hard-working citizens, the Peace Missions had a reputation for reducing crime in their areas. In Los Angeles, for example, a municipal judge estimated that, in an area housing a number of new Peace Missions, about 2,600 fewer people were arrested in one year. In addition, by helping poor people find employment, Peace Missions saved money for governments by reducing the number of people needing welfare. A New York City official maintained that, during the Great Depression, the Peace Mission Movement saved the city over $2 million in welfare payments (Weisbrot 1983, 92–94).

However, outsiders were sometimes suspicious of this unusual religion that preached racial integration. Father Divine was at times accused of seducing young women followers and of overseeing sexual orgies. In 1930, the Suffolk County district attorney's office sent an undercover agent—a young black woman—to infiltrate the movement. She spent about two weeks living in the house and participating in the Holy Communion Banquets. She attempted to seduce Father Divine but reported that he was uninterested in her advances. She reported no sign of any wrongdoing and stated that she was welcomed and that the atmosphere of the household was deeply religious (Watts 1992, 63–68).

Unlike many other religious utopian communities, Father Divine did not believe in living completely separate from the outside world. While the Peace Missions did insulate members from many of the negative influences of the outside world, they also actively engaged the outside world. Father Divine encouraged his followers to vote. In fact, a number of prominent politicians—including the candidates in the 1932 U.S. presidential election—courted Father Divine in order to get his followers' votes.

Father Divine frequently spoke out against racial intolerance and helped raise money for the "Scottsboro Boys," a group of nine young men in Alabama who were believed to have been wrongly convicted of raping two white girls. The Peace Mission Movement supported various political parties and wrote a political "platform," or set of ideas, which included equal job opportunities, school desegregation, and an end to capital punishment. It tried to get one of the major political parties to adopt their platform, but failed. In 1940, the Peace Missions gathered 250,000 signatures on a petition in support of a law to prevent lynching; however, the law did not pass (Weisbrot 1983, 147, 151–161; Watts 1992, 108, 133, 139, 164).

Instead of insulating themselves against the outside world, the Peace Missions hoped that by engaging the outside world, they could change it to be more in line with their own philosophy.

Reasons for Decline of the Community

Experts speculate that the community most likely declined because, as the United States grew more prosperous, there were fewer needy people who required the help provided by the Peace Missions. Perhaps new converts decreased because Father Divine grew too old to effectively attract new members, and there was no other leader within the movement who was as successful as he had been at the movement's height. Since members of the Peace Mission Movement were celibate and no children were born within it, the lack of outside converts meant a fatal decline (Weisbrot 1983, 211–212).

Influence on the Outside World

Although few people today have heard of the Peace Mission Movement, it was extremely well known in its day. Father Divine introduced and promoted the idea of racial integration at a time when many churches, schools, and places of business were segregated. He proved that racial integration could work within his movement, with businesses that catered equally to blacks and whites, and with white and black followers working and living together.

Some Peace Mission businesses were still running as of 2006, such as the Divine Tracy Hotel in Philadelphia. At this budget hotel, women and men were required to stay on different floors. Smoking, alcohol, and cursing were prohibited, and guests are even asked not to wear shorts or miniskirts! (Watts 1992, 176).

See also: Great Depression

References

Hoshor, John. *God in a Rolls Royce: The Rise of Father Divine, Madman, Menace, or Messiah.* Freeport, NY: Books for Libraries Press, 1971 (first published 1936).

Kephart, William. *Extraordinary Groups: The Sociology of Unconventional Life-Styles.* New York: St. Martin's Press, 1976.

Watts, Jill. *God, Harlem, USA: The Father Divine Story.* Berkeley: University of California Press, 1992.

Weisbrot, Robert. *Father Divine and the Struggle for Racial Equality.* Urbana: University of Illinois Press, 1983.

Weisbrot, Robert. "Father Divine and the Peace Mission," in *America's Communal Utopias*, edited by Donald Pitzer. Chapel Hill: University of North Carolina Press, 1997, 432–447.

Web site

Father Divine's International Peace Mission Movement: http://fdipmm.libertynet.org/ (accessed May 2006).

Persecution

Although the United States was set up as a land of religious and personal freedom, and although many persecuted religious groups fled Europe in order to live in peace in the United States, still some religious sects and secular groups have experienced persecution in the United States, both from the government and from hostile outsiders.

The Ephrata Cloister, which lived communally in Pennsylvania from 1732 to 1786, believed in keeping Saturday as their Sabbath. They were arrested and fined for working on Sundays. In addition, male settlers, angry because their wives and daughters were attracted to the community, beat the Ephrata leader several times.

Several Shakers were jailed within the first two years of their arrival in the American colonies, because they were preaching pacifism at the time of the American Revolution. Even after their release from prison, the Shakers were beaten and stoned by suspicious members of the public. Mother Ann (their leader) was stoned and beaten on several occasions, which may have led to her early death at the age of 48 (Kephart 1976, 162–163).

The Amish (who first began immigrating to the United States in 1727 and who now live in many eastern and midwestern states) were persecuted by the government for refusing to send their children to high school. Traditionally, the Amish do not value formal education and have set up their own schools through eighth grade, in order to keep their children separate from the outside world. In Pennsylvania during the first half of the 20th century, some parents were arrested numerous times for not sending their children to public high school. In the 1960s in one Iowa county, school authorities began fining Amish parents for sending their children to a sub-standard school (the Amish schoolteacher was not state certified). Also in the 1960s, a Wisconsin county arrested three Amish fathers for refusing to send their children to public school. In addition, the Amish were persecuted for their pacifist beliefs. During World War I, Amish men were abused and jailed when they refused to wear a military uniform or follow orders.

Like the Amish, the Hutterites (who began arriving in the United States in 1874 and who now live in many western states) were also persecuted for their pacifist beliefs. Two Hutterite men died from mistreatment at the hands of military officers.

The Mormon religious movement, which began in New York in 1830, was the target of repeated persecution by non-Mormons, mainly because the Mormons valued economic cooperation and tended to try to become economically self-sufficient wherever they lived. The outside world resented the fact that Mormons did not trade with them, and so Mormon homes were burned, their printing press was destroyed, and they were driven out of Ohio, Missouri, and Illinois. In Illinois, the Mormon leader Joseph Smith and his brother were assassinated.

Fire engulfs the Branch Davidian compound near Waco, Texas, on April 19, 1993. Eighty-one Davidians, including leader David Koresh, perished as federal agents tried to drive them out of the compound. (AP/Wide World Photos)

The Koreshan Unity, a mystical Christian community that was established in Chicago, and existed from 1869 to 1892, was persecuted for its politics. After the Koreshans relocated to Florida, the local people were not happy that a few hundred Chicagoans had moved in and were voting as a bloc. After Koreshan leader Cyrus Reed Teed started his own political party, he was fatally attacked by the Fort Myers town marshal.

The socialist Kaweah Cooperative Commonwealth, which existed in California from 1885 to 1892, ultimately ended because its land claims were not approved. Government suspicion of the community may have prevented approval of its effort to buy land.

The anarchist Home Colony (which existed from 1896 to 1921 in Washington State) was harassed by the government for its "obscene" mailings (some members mailed newsletters about free love). The community was fined and eventually the Home post office was shut down. One member was jailed for writing an article about nude swimming.

Koinonia Farm, which started in Georgia in 1942, was harassed by the public because of Koinonia's belief in racial equality and fellowship. Its store was vandalized and eventually blown up, and homes were shot at. The local police refused to help. Local merchants would not sell to them or buy their products, and insurance companies cancelled Koinonia's policies.

The hippie communes of the 1960s were persecuted by the public and harassed by the government. According to Benjamin Zablocki, communities across the country were burned and members were shot at or beaten (1980, 54–55). The Renaissance Community/Brotherhood of the Spirit had its very first residence, a treehouse, burned; its members had trouble buying property because of their appearance; and a member of the community was murdered. The Rainbow Family of Living Light, which holds massive Gatherings in national parks, has been harassed by the Forest Service: at one particular Gathering, the Forest Service prevented vehicles from carrying fresh water and latrine covers from entering the Gathering site and arrested the clean-up crew. Synanon, a racially integrated community of former drug addicts, had part of its new facility bulldozed by the Santa Monica (California) Police Department.

The anticult movement, which developed in the 1960s and 1970s, harassed unusual religious sects such as The Family/Children of God and the Love Family by kidnapping and "deprogramming" sect members. Deprogramming involved locking members in a room and subjecting them to verbal and sometimes physical abuse in order to convince them to recant their religious beliefs.

One of the most recent examples of persecution, according to some experts, is the government siege of the Branch Davidian home, Mt. Carmel, in Waco, Texas, in 1993, resulting in a fire that killed over 70 Branch Davidians. Stuart Wright stated: "The holocaust at Mt. Carmel represents a tragic episode in the history of sectarian religion in America. It belies some of our deepest and most sacred convictions about the sanctity of religious freedom and tolerance for individual differences and beliefs. We should find it odd that a nation founded by religious sectarians (Puritans attempting to escape religious persecution at the hands of the state) should itself so easily forget the lessons of history. . . . Sectarian or non-traditional religion . . . is a critical source of cultural innovation, revitalization, and social change" (1995, xvii).

See also: Cults; Pacifism

References

Kephart, William. *Extraordinary Groups: The Sociology of Unconventional Life-Styles*. New York: St. Martin's Press, 1976.

Wright, Stuart, ed. *Armageddon in Waco: Critical Perspectives on the Branch Davidian Conflict*. Chicago: University of Chicago Press, 1995.

Zablocki, Benjamin. *Alienation and Charisma: A Study of Contemporary American Communes*. New York: The Free Press, 1980.

Point Loma and Theosophical Communities

At a Glance

Dates of existence in United States: 1897 to 1942 (Point Loma)
Location: California
Peak membership: 500 (Point Loma)
Religious or other belief: Theosophism

History

Point Loma was the largest and longest lasting of the "Theosophical" communities in the United States.

The Theosophical Society was founded in New York by a Russian woman, Helen Blavatsky, in 1875. In the 1880s and 1890s, many Theosophists were drawn to the ideas of the author Edward Bellamy and his novel, *Looking Backward 2000–1887*, which describes a secular utopian society that has been freed of labor unrest and class distinctions because the government has taken over all industry. Theosophists founded and were involved with a number of Nationalist Clubs to promote Bellamy's ideas; the two groups split, though, when the Nationalists wanted to align themselves with socialist politicians. The Theosophists were wary of political solutions and did not believe in engaging in partisan politics (Melton 1997, 397–400).

However, the idea of forming a utopian society was still present among Theosophists. In 1897, an American philanthropist and social worker named Katherine Tingley became the head of the Theosophical Society in America and spearheaded a campaign to form a community based on Theosophical ideas.

Before becoming a Theosophical leader, Tingley had tried to provide help to the poor and unfortunate by taking in an orphan boy, by forming an organization to visit inmates of prisons and hospitals, and by starting a mission to feed the needy. Tingley felt that the help she provided was unsuccessful: "In spite of all my efforts to help them, to teach them how to begin anew, feeding them, clothing them, finding them positions (and then after a week or two having them back at our mission to feed and clothe again) lo! to my dismay, I found that I was actually encouraging them in pauperism those whom I would most serve" (quoted in Greenwalt 1955, 77).

Tingley hoped that a Theosophical community would strike at the root of the problems of humanity. She aimed to start a school at the community to train children from birth in Theosophical principles and ideas, and in this way to start them off well in life.

She had an inspiration to buy land on Point Loma, California—an arm of land enclosing San Diego Bay—although she had never seen the place. The land was bought in early 1897 through donations from Theosophists.

During the next two years, Tingley continued to build support for her Point Loma community. She also organized a relief expedition to Cuba, whose people were suffering after the Spanish-American War.

By 1899, the first building had been erected and Theosophists from around the world gathered in Point Loma to begin community life. Most lived in tents while more buildings were put up.

The community school began with students from Theosophist families who paid tuition, as well as a number of Cuban children and poor children from Buffalo, New York, who were educated for free.

By 1910, the community grew to 500 members. Three hundred of these were students at the school, and 65 were teachers.

Tingley died in 1929 as a result of an automobile accident in Germany, and her successor, Geoffrey de Purucker, discovered that the community was heavily in debt. He cut back on activities, including the plays, musical entertainment, and water for the orchards and gardens. He sold some land to pay some of the debts. Many members left, and enrollment in the school dropped. The huge glass domes topping the main buildings were damaged by the vibrations from firing practice at the nearby naval base. The school was closed in 1940, and in 1942, de Purucker sold the property.

The community moved to Covina, California (north of Los Angeles). The school never reopened, but the community did run a Theosophical university. About 75 residents lived at the community as of 1945, but as members died or moved away, the community dwindled (Ashcraft 2002, 175–176).

Beliefs and Practices

The Point Loma community was based on a philosophy called Theosophy, or "divine wisdom." It involved the comparative study of religions and spiritual traditions. The goals of the Theosophical Society were to connect with spiritual reality by engaging in the study of ancient and modern religions and sciences and to investigate psychic powers and unexplained natural phenomena.

Theosophists believed in the "Brotherhood of Humanity" without regard to race, gender, ethnicity, or social class. Tingley recruited students from all over the world to attend her school, and at one point, 26 countries were represented by students at the school.

Theosophists also believed in the concepts of karma and reincarnation. Karma is a Hindu concept in which the sins in our past lives result in difficulties in our present life. The community school was to help students to live in such a way as to prepare the soul to progress to a higher state.

Tingley named the community school the Raja Yoga School. The word *yoga* did not refer to the physical exercises we are familiar with today. Instead, it referred to the Sanskrit meaning of the word, which is "union." *Raja* means "royal" or "kingly." Tingley meant her school to foster a union, or balance, of mental, physical, and spiritual traits in the children.

Raja Yoga students, dressed in white and wearing flower garlands in their hair and around their necks at the International Theosophical Headquarters, Point Loma, California. (Library of Congress)

The school attempted to shield students from the unhealthy influences of the outside world. They did not read newspapers or magazines from the outside world and only left the community in a group or with an adult.

One unusual aspect of the school, and the community, was its emphasis on silence. A sign in the dining hall stated: "As the body is fed by food, so the soul is sustained by silence" (Greenwalt 1955, 86). Members ate in silence and were discouraged from talking to each other when they passed in the halls or on the grounds of the community. They were permitted to talk at appointed times. Tingley saw excessive talk as a waste of energy. Visitors to the school were struck by the quietness, concentration, and discipline of the students. Physical punishment was not allowed in the school.

Although she discouraged idle chatter, Tingley did plan social evenings for the members. Celebrations were held for the Fourth of July, Christmas, and other occasions. The entire community was also involved in preparing for dramatic performances, which were held in its outdoor Greek theater and in its theater in downtown San Diego. It presented ancient Greek plays and several Shakespeare plays. Tingley felt that these plays embodied Theosophical principles, such as brotherhood, karma, reincarnation, and compassion.

Theosophy embraced the study of all religions. The community held a morning meditation in the Greek theater, followed by readings from the Bhagavad-Gita (a Hindu religious text) or other spiritual works.

Daily Life

The Point Loma community consisted of 330 acres, three large buildings, a number of bungalows for housing, a Greek-style open-air theater (the first in the United States), and gardens, orchards, and forests of eucalyptus trees. Many of the buildings were topped with colored glass domes or glass skylights. Tingley recruited an artist, Reginald Machell, to decorate many of the buildings' walls, doors, and furniture with intricate designs. The community also owned a theater building in downtown San Diego.

Although Point Loma's land and resources were not owned by the members but by a corporation headed by Tingley, the community met the needs of its members in terms of food, clothing, shelter, medical care, and schooling.

The general manager of the community assigned tasks to members. Although Theosophy believed in a "brotherhood" without regard to gender, the jobs at Point Loma were generally segregated by gender. Men were involved with traditionally male occupations such as operating the printing press, blacksmithing, and carpentry, while women were involved in traditionally female tasks such as sewing, dyeing, weaving, and bee-keeping (Kirkley 1997).

Members lived in a communal building called the Homestead or in individual bungalows. Members were also allowed to build their own homes on community land. They ate in one of three common dining rooms (two for adults, one for children).

How They Made Their Living

Point Loma received money from school tuitions, from donations made by wealthy Theosophists, from ticket sales for their dramatic performances, and from sales of Theosophist literature printed by the Point Loma press.

The community attempted to make money through industries. It planted mulberry trees and began raising silkworms to produce silk, but the silkworms proved so delicate that the experiment was abandoned after several years. It had more success with beekeeping and was known locally for the high productivity of its hives. It also sold crafts made by members: decorated china, batik cloth, leatherwork, and so forth.

In addition, the community grew much of its own food. Although the soil was rocky and considered sterile when they bought it, the community gardeners irrigated the land, experimented with crops, and managed—20 years after the founding of the community—to produce hundreds of varieties of fruits. The women of the community sewed almost all the clothing for members. Point Loma also had its own carpenters, blacksmiths, and plumbers.

However, the community was not on sound financial footing. When Tingley died, it was discovered that Point Loma had accumulated a large debt.

Leadership and Decision Making

The Point Loma community was not democratic. Tingley was its leader for life, and she appointed a cabinet of 13 men to manage the community. Tingley did, however, appoint a woman to head the Raja Yoga Academy, and another woman to oversee the Women's Exchange and Mart (the making and selling of craft items).

How New Members Were Recruited or Chosen

Prospective members had to believe in Theosophical principles and pay an admission fee of $500 in order to be admitted on probation. The fee was waived in cases of economic hardship and wealthy members often contributed much more. Members were not required to give up their personal wealth.

Children and Youth

At six months of age, an infant went to live in the communal nursery. Breastfeeding was discouraged because it was considered unhealthy. At age three or four, the children moved to the children's dormitory, where they learned to make their own beds and dress themselves. At this age, the children also began their musical training. Parents saw their children only on Sundays.

School-aged children lived in circular bungalows, with sleeping rooms and a common sitting room. A teacher lived with the children. The students spent two and a half hours per day on academic work, including English, languages, history, arithmetic, and art. They also worked on the community's farm and in the workshops. Girls and boys received the same education until they became teenagers, when they were separated.

Most students at the school did not have parents living in the community but instead were sent to the school as boarding students.

Relationship with the Outside World

The public was intensely curious about the Point Loma community, which received about a hundred visitors a day. The community charged an admission fee and provided a tour.

The outside community also expressed admiration for Point Loma's achievements in drama, music, and agriculture. The local newspaper, the *San Diego Union*, often wrote admiring reviews of the community's plays. Outsiders were impressed with the academic achievements of the students at the community.

Point Loma did not believe in separating itself from the outside world. Instead, members engaged in work to reform the outside world. Tingley and her community led a public campaign to end the death penalty in California. Although they were not successful in California, they did succeed in having the voters abolish the death penalty in Arizona for a few years. As World War I began in Europe, Tingley and the community worked to end all war. She lobbied U.S. president Woodrow Wilson, as well as the nation's governors and mayors, to set aside September 28, 1914, as a "Sacred Peace Day for the Nations." Wilson declined to do so. Tingley organized a "Parliament of Peace" at Point Loma in 1915, and fought for draft exemptions for the men of Point Loma (Greenwalt 1955, 157–169).

Point Loma's relationship with the outside world was also sometimes rocky. In 1901, the *Los Angeles Times* printed negative articles about the community, including accusations that women and children were being starved. Tingley sued the newspaper for libel and won. In 1902, 11 Cuban children on their way to Point Loma were detained in New York because of charges that Point Loma was abusive to children.

After an investigation, the community was cleared and the children were allowed to proceed (Greenwalt 1955, 57–76).

Reasons for Decline of the Community

Tingley did not ensure that the community's finances were sound, but borrowed against the property to run the community. Perhaps she was extravagant in her spending on dramatic productions, music, art, and water for the orchards. However, these were also some of the things that attracted students and members to the community.

After the stock market crash of 1929 and the subsequent Great Depression, the financial situation of the community grew worse until Tingley's successor decided to sell the property.

Influence on the Outside World

Tingley had hoped to set up an international network of Raja Yoga schools. She did help to start three schools in Cuba, starting in 1902, but within 10 years all of them had closed. Tingley bought land in Sweden and started a school there in 1924, which offered only summer sessions and continued until 1937. She also bought land in Germany, but a school was never started there. In the United States, Tingley helped found Raja Yoga schools in San Francisco and San Diego, both of which were short-lived. She bought land in Massachusetts and received a donation of land in Minnesota, but those schools were never built (Greenwalt 1955, 145–156). However, two former Raja Yoga students did run a similar school in Topanga, California, from 1932 to 1948 (Ashcraft 2002, 105).

Although the international network of Raja Yoga schools was never realized, Point Loma did influence the outside world in other ways. Its agricultural experiments benefited Southern California agriculture. Horticulturists from the U.S. Department of Agriculture and from California universities visited the community and obtained plant specimens.

The Point Loma community also introduced Eastern religions such as Hinduism to Southern California and other parts of the United States. For example, Judith Tyberg, who was born and raised at Point Loma, later studied in India. She returned to the United States and set up the East West Cultural Center in Los Angeles to spread the teachings of an Indian saint, Sri Aurobindo. Today, the center is called the Sri Aurobindo Center of Los Angeles (Ashcraft 2002, 106; www.sriaurobindocenter-la.org/).

Other Theosophical Communities

Besides Point Loma, a few other U.S. communities were also founded on Theosophical ideas.

The Temple of the People was founded near Pismo Beach, California, in 1903 by Theosophists who did not agree with Tingley's leadership of the Theosophical Society. One of the founders was a doctor, and he built a sanatorium on the land. In 1905, the Temple of the People formed a cooperative colony called the Temple Home

Association in order to promote land and resource ownership by the people. Upon paying $100, each member received a half acre of land for personal use. Members worked on community land as well. After a few years, 50 people lived at the community. In 1913, the cooperative aspect of the community was ended. However, the Temple of the People continues today as a spiritual organization (Hine 1966, 54–57).

Krotona was also founded by Theosophists who had split from Tingley's original group. It started in 1912 in Hollywood, California. Within a year, the community had 45 members, as well as a printing press, a vegetarian cafe, a temple, a library, and the School of Theosophy, which offered seminars. Unfortunately, the community was beset by debts and in 1924 the land in Hollywood was sold. The Krotona School of Theosophy moved to Ojai, California, where it remains today (Melton 1997, 409–411).

See also: Bellamy, Edward; Great Depression

References

Ashcraft, W. Michael. *The Dawn of a New Cycle: Point Loma Theosophists and American Culture*. Knoxville: University of Tennessee Press, 2002.

Berge, Dennis, ed. "Reminiscences of Lomaland: Madame Tingley and the Theosophical Institute in San Diego," *The Journal of San Diego History*, summer 1974, vol. 20, no. 3, www.sandiegohistory.org/journal/74summer/lomaland.htm (accessed August 2006).

Greenwalt, Emmett A. *The Point Loma Community in California, 1897–1942*. Berkeley: University of California Press, 1955.

Hine, Robert V. *California's Utopian Colonies*. New Haven, CT: Yale University Press, 1966.

Kirkley, Evelyn. "Starved and Treated Like Convicts: Images of Women in Point Loma Theosophy," *The Journal of San Diego History*, winter 1997, vol. 43, no 1, www.sandiego history.org/journal/97winter/theosophical.htm (accessed August 2006).

Melton, J. Gordon. "The Theosophical Communities and Their Ideal of Universal Brotherhood," in *America's Communal Utopias*, edited by Donald Pitzer. Chapel Hill: University of North Carolina Press, 1997, 396–418.

Web sites

Sri Aurobindo Center of Los Angeles: www.sriaurobindocenter-la.org/ (accessed August 16, 2007).

Temple of the People: www.templeofthepeople.org/ (accessed August 16, 2007).

The Theosophical Society in America: www.theosophical.org/ (accessed April 22, 2008).

Rainbow Family of Living Light

At a Glance

Dates of existence in United States: 1972 to present
Locations: nationwide and in Europe
Peak membership: 20,000 (annual U.S. Gathering)
Religious or other belief: eclectic spiritualism, anarchism

History

The Rainbow Family of Living Light is a nomadic, temporary community that welcomes anyone who wants to participate. Members of the Rainbow Family live communally when they come together in "Gatherings." In addition to the annual U.S. Gatherings, which take place over two months, Rainbow Gatherings happen in Europe, and regional Rainbow Gatherings happen around North America. According to Michael Niman, "Today at any given time, there is at least one Rainbow Gathering taking place somewhere in the world" (1997, 33).

The Rainbow Family likes to suggest that it has always been in existence. Its Web site states: "The Rainbow Family of Living Light . . . didn't really begin at any specific time, and has never really existed as a formal organization. In many ways, it is a fundamental human expression, the tendency of people to gather together in a natural place and express themselves in ways that come naturally to them, to live and let live, to do unto others as we would have them do unto us" (http://www.welcomehome.org/rainbow/index.html).

However, historians agree that the Rainbow Gathering did have a concrete beginning: the first one took place in 1972 in Colorado. The general catalyst for the gathering was the hippie atmosphere of the time, in which young people were looking for new and different ways of living. A specific catalyst was a free music festival, the Vortex Festival, held in 1970, near Portland, Oregon. The festival brought together a group of people who later invited others to join them in the wilderness of Colorado. About 20,000 people attended this event, and since then a Gathering has been held in North America every year. In 1983, annual Rainbow Gatherings began in Europe as well (Niman 1997, 32–33).

While up to 20,000 people attended Gatherings in the early 1990s, in 2004 and 2005, the number of people at a U.S. annual Gathering had fallen to about 6,000 due to "massive heavy law enforcement," according to Rob Savoye, who runs a Web site about the Rainbow Family. Savoye estimates that in 2006 attendance was up to 12,000.

Beliefs and Practices

The first Rainbow Gathering invitation encouraged people to gather for the purpose of fostering world peace. This is still one of the main beliefs and goals of the Rainbow Gathering.

Every Rainbow Gathering is noncommercial: money is not used during a Gathering. The Rainbow Family of Living Light does not believe in having designated leaders, and as such its members are anarchists.

Living lightly on the Earth is important, and Rainbow members take pride in how well they care for their site. According to an article in *E Magazine* (an environmental magazine), "A mammoth recycling effort goes into effect to handle the 25 tons of waste generated [by a Gathering]. No private fires are allowed, and water sources are protected as the gathering's lifeblood." During clean-up, "a few hundred Rainbows stay behind, backfill latrines, replant native grasses, break up hardened ground, and attempt to return the site to its natural state" (Rosenfeld 1999, 22).

All religions, spiritual persuasions, and political beliefs are welcome at a Rainbow Gathering. However, there are some spiritual practices that tend to be more prevalent than others. Niman criticizes the Rainbow Family for its use of supposedly Native American spiritual rituals, such as using Native American imagery in its newsletters, wearing loincloths, and holding pipe ceremonies and sacred sweats. "When New Agers and Rainbows embrace a reconstructed native spirituality, even with sincere 'respect,' they are complicit in ethnocide," says Niman (1997, 140).

However, Native Americans can be supportive of the Rainbows and in fact have participated in Gatherings. "Rainbow culture, when not attempting to pass itself off as the spiritual heir apparent of imagined Indian culture, is in fact compatible with many Native American traditions. For this reason, a significant number of Native Americans frequent the Gatherings, which are somewhat akin to powwows" (Niman 1997, 144).

Daily Life

While each Gathering is officially about a week long—generally from July 1 to 7—the process of getting ready for the Gathering and cleaning up afterwards extends the time into about two months.

Gatherings take place on public land, usually in a national forest. Members strive to find a site that has a meadow for a central gathering spot, easily treatable water on site, access to fallen wood for firewood, and a place that can withstand the impact of thousands of people living on it for several weeks.

Alcohol and hard drugs are not allowed at a Rainbow Gathering, although an "alcohol camp" is generally set up at the entrance to the camp, where alcohol is allowed. Also not allowed are weapons and nonrecyclable trash. Gatherers are asked to bring their own tents, sleeping bags, cup and bowl, and other personal necessities, as well as food and items to donate.

Volunteers to set up the camp arrive at the chosen location about a month in advance. They dig latrines, set up kitchens, and create trails. "Taco Mike," a popular Rainbow cook, describes how he sets up his kitchen: "All of it just comes together at the Gathering. I can't haul nothing with me because I live by my back-pack. . . . Every year

Members of the Rainbow Family, hippies who meet every year at a giant campsite, attend a wedding of a young couple, held within a circle of Rainbow Family members. (Corbis)

I show up and I only have me and my back-pack and maybe a crew. Then we scrounge everything." Nevertheless, Taco Mike has managed at times to construct a two-story kitchen structure out of fallen timber, rope, and some nails (Niman 1997, 75).

A Gathering might have almost 100 separate camping areas, each with its own name, as well as various kitchens catering to different cuisines, from meat-eaters to vegans. A map of these camps is posted in the central gathering area. "Unlike other maps . . . the Rainbow map is fluid, always changing as new camps and trails are added by the hour. People passing through the Info area use pens and markers to update the map with their conception of where the newly named area should be. The result is a map completely out of scale, bearing no resemblance to the actual geography of the area. . . . Using the map, people could find their way to most camps. They can't, however, judge just how far, or over what type of terrain, they have to hike to get there" (Niman 1997, 16).

Each Gathering has a medical area called "CALM" (Center for Alternative Living Medicine), which provides first-aid treatment, dispenses homeopathic and herbal remedies, and offers massage, acupuncture, and any other treatment a Gatherer may offer.

How They Make Their Living

All money, goods, and labor are donated at a Rainbow Gathering. Participants are asked to donate money into the "Magic Hat," which is used to buy supplies that have not been donated. Participants also donate food, extra tents or other camping supplies, and anything they think someone else might need.

A section of each Gathering is generally earmarked for bartering. Sometimes an internal currency develops: for example, candy bars or crystals might emerge as something that can be traded for almost any other item in the bartering area (Niman 1997, 71–72).

Leadership and Decision Making

There are no officially recognized leaders of the Rainbow Family. Decisions are made during "councils," or open meetings, and everyone who might be affected by the decisions must be invited to attend the council. Decisions are made by a process of consensus: everyone present at the council must agree that they can live with the decision. Even one person can block consensus. The main governing body of the Rainbow Family is the Main Council, in which any interested person can participate. Its meetings take place during the annual Rainbow Gatherings. In addition to the Main Council, numerous specialized councils exist: for example, a regional council is set up to select the exact site and plan for the next Gathering, and an individual kitchen at a Gathering might hold a council to decide on the day's menu.

No voting takes place in the Rainbow councils. A member describes the decision-making process: "Consensus groups do not vote. To vote is like admitting failure because consensus is not happening. There is usually a long discussion before the group reaches a consensus. This drives newcomers up a wall. But consensus groups believe that at least one solution that satisfies everyone is out there. We just have to find it" (Niman 1997, 39).

Niman points out that, although the Main Council is open to everyone, the vast majority of Gatherers do not participate. "Most participants at the large North American Gatherings forgo attending Council. Their apathy leaves the Gatherings governed by an activist minority. This minority often consists of 'elders' who have attended many Gatherings, a ruling class whose existence the Family members often deny. Full participation by thousands of Gatherers would make the Council unwieldy and chaotic. Rainbows aim for a middle ground with most camps or kitchens, and all ideological viewpoints, represented at Councils" (1997, 40).

Although the consensus process often results in acceptable decisions, sometimes the process deadlocks. In 1992 and 1993, two annual Gatherings were held at two different sites because the Main Council could not come to a decision on where to hold the next year's Gathering (Niman 1997, 57).

Another important leadership body of the Rainbow Gatherings is the Shanti Sena, or peacekeeping force. In theory, any member of any Gathering is a member of this peacekeeping force and therefore can attempt to solve conflicts. In reality, there is an actual group, almost all of whom are men, who act to keep the peace at Gatherings. One common Rainbow way of defusing tension is to form a circle of Gatherers around people in conflict and begin chanting "Om" loudly. The Shanti Sena also interact with local law enforcement by greeting them at the Rainbow Gathering gate. They might, for instance, help a local store owner who complains about shoplifting Gatherers by posting a Gatherer outside the store (Niman 1997, 117–125).

An article in *Rolling Stone* magazine, covering the 1993 Gathering in Alabama, described how the Shanti Sena process works. A man at the Gathering was accused of molesting and making unwelcome sexual advances toward women. A Shanti Sena member brought the man to the "Cooperations" teepee, which was the Shanti Sena headquarters. The women spoke to him and decided that, instead of throwing him into the outside world to continue his misbehavior, they would allow him to stay for 24 hours for the purpose of "healing." He would be constantly observed and counseled. Before the 24 hours were over, the man decided to leave the Gathering on his own (MacAdams 1994).

How New Members Are Recruited or Chosen

Anyone is welcome to participate in a Rainbow Gathering. In fact, some people consider that all living things are already members of the Rainbow Family (Niman 1997, 32).

Children and Youth

Children are welcome at Rainbow Gatherings. Families generally set up camp in "Kid's Village," a section of the Gathering that caters to the needs of children, infants, and pregnant women. Children are also welcome to participate in decision making by voicing their needs and opinions at council meetings.

Relationship with the Outside World

The Rainbow Family terms the outside world *Babylon*. Although this is a derogatory term, the fact is that most Rainbow members live in Babylon for much of the year—although some Rainbow members follow the "Rainbow Trail," traveling from one Gathering to the next. Rainbow members see the Gathering as "home" and in fact, greet each other with the phrase, "Welcome home."

As a community, the Rainbow Family interacts with the outside world in three main ways: through the local community surrounding their Gathering site, the local and national media; and the U.S. Forest Service.

The Rainbow Family typically has good relations with the local community. While small local communities are initially apprehensive about thousands of "hippies" descending upon their area, they generally enjoy the increased business, and often find the Rainbow members to be polite and helpful. The Rainbow Family asks those at the Gathering not to go to the local community for health care or other services, but to make use of the services at the Gathering. Even conservative communities have been impressed with the hard-working Rainbow Family (Niman 1997, 175–182).

On some occasions, however, the local community is unhappy with the Gathering. For example, at the 1996 Gathering in Missouri, the Rainbows apparently received (and never paid for) $60,000 worth of medical treatment at Missouri hospitals after a bacterial infection broke out at the Gathering. After the 1998 Gathering in Oregon, 100 dogs were apparently left behind (Rosenfeld 1999).

Major national media, including the *New York Times* and *Rolling Stone*, covered the first Rainbow Gathering in 1972. However, there seems to be very little major media interest in the Rainbow Gathering nowadays.

Because the Rainbow Gatherings generally take place in national forests, the U.S. Forest Service is involved, and its relationship with the Rainbow Family is sometimes rocky. The Rainbow Family has no recognized leaders and refuses to sign permits to use national forest land. At first, the Rainbow Family tried to work with the permit system, but the Forest Service demanded too much: "We were faced with . . . demands covering lighted parking lots, flush toilets, gigantic insurance premiums, performance bonds, hired policepeople . . . enclosed kitchens, state certified parking attendants, and so on," according to a Rainbow publication (Niman 1997, 187).

The Rainbow Family believes that it does not need anyone's permission to gather on public land. Since 1981, the group has not signed permits. In 1987, the Forest Service harassed the people at the North Carolina Gathering, preventing vehicles from carrying fresh water and latrine covers to the Gathering site, and arresting the clean-up crew, so that the clean-up could not be finished. In 1988, a federal judge ruled that the Forest Service was unfairly singling out the Rainbow Family for harassment through the permit process, and awarded the Rainbow Family over $13,000 (Niman 1997 186, 188–189).

Despite this harassment, some members of the Forest Service are sympathetic to the Rainbow Family and enjoy the friendly, accepting atmosphere. A regional Rainbow Gathering in Vermont had a waiting list for Forest Service employees who wanted to be assigned to work there (Niman 1997, 199).

Influence on the Outside World

Since most Gatherers live in the outside world for most of their lives, and since perhaps hundreds of thousands of people have at one time or another attended a Rainbow Gathering, the Rainbow Family of Living Light undoubtedly has some sort of impact on the outside world—however much that world would like to pretend the Rainbows do not exist. "For twenty-five years the Gatherings have demonstrated that a predominantly nonviolent and nonhierarchical society can successfully operate on a large scale," Niman points out. "Their goal is unwavering. Eventually, they hope, everyone everywhere will always be at a Rainbow Gathering" (1997, 215).

Other communal groups participate in the Rainbow Gathering, including the International Society for Krishna Consciousness (Hare Krishnas) and the Love Family.

See also: Anarchism; Hippies; International Society for Krishna Consciousness (Hare Krishna Movement); Love Family

References

MacAdams, Lewis. "A Gathering of Tribes." *Rolling Stone*, December 23, 1993–January 6, 1994, nos. 672/673, 118.

Niman, Michael. *People of the Rainbow*. Knoxville: University of Tennessee Press, 1997.

Rosenfeld, Hank. "Inside the Rainbow." *E Magazine*, May/June 1999, vol. 10, no. 3, 21–22.

Savoye, Rob. E-mail exchange with author, January 29, 2007.

WEB SITE
Rainbow Family of Living Light: www.welcomehome.org/rainbow/index.html (accessed January 2007).

Rajneeshpuram

At a Glance

Dates of existence in United States: 1981 to 1987 (1974 to present in India and elsewhere)
Location: Oregon
Peak membership: 15,000
Religious or other belief: disciples of Bhagwan Shree Rajneesh

History

Although short-lived, Rajneeshpuram was one of the most ambitious attempts at building a utopian community in the United States. It was also one of the most controversial communities: its leaders pleaded guilty to myriad crimes, including poisonings and attempted murder.

Rajneeshpuram was designed to be the headquarters of a large worldwide movement that had its roots in India. A middle-class college student named Mohan Chandra Rajneesh experienced enlightenment in 1953 and felt that he was reborn. He went on to earn his B.A. and M.A. in philosophy and became a professor of philosophy. During this time, he was also experimenting with meditation. He established his first meditation camp in 1964, and other camps followed.

In 1966, he resigned his teaching position and traveled around India speaking and setting up meditation camps. In 1970, he moved to Bombay and began receiving spiritual seekers (some of whom came from Western countries) in his apartment. He and his followers began to dress in shades of orange and red (orange is the traditional color worn by Hindu holy men). In 1971, Rajneesh took on the name "Bhagwan," which means "the enlightened one." Rajneesh asked some of his foreign-born followers to go back to their home countries and establish meditation centers there.

In 1974, Rajneesh and seven disciples moved to Poona, India, and began the first long-term experiment in communal living: the Shree Rajneesh Ashram. At this time, there were apparently 22 Rajneesh meditation centers outside of India, including six in the United States. Two years later, the Poona ashram had as many as 5,000 residents and up to 35,000 visitors a year (Carter 1990, 56, 58).

In 1975, the Rajneesh ashram and meditation centers began offering "therapy" in addition to meditation. These therapies were often violent, resulting in broken bones in some cases, and included nudity and rape. A German movie made about the ashram, which showed scenes of violence and nudity, prompted the Indian government to ban the movie in India and to cancel the ashram's tax-exempt status. In response, Rajneesh stopped some of the more controversial therapies (Carter 1990, 57, 61–65).

Rajneesh and his followers developed elaborate plans for a community of *sannyasins*—or disciples—that would include a temple, meditation halls, therapy rooms, a university, a hotel, a cinema, stores, and factories. However, none of the state governments in India would give permission for this community to be built, and the Indian government was denying visas to foreigners who wished to visit the Rajneesh ashram in Poona.

The community decided to relocate its headquarters to the United States, and in 1981, it bought over 64,000 acres of land and leased another 17,000 in rural Oregon. Shortly before the move, Rajneesh began a period of silence, during which he gave no public talks for many years. Sannyasins from India and other centers around the world began moving to this new ashram, which was named "Rajneeshpuram."

Local leaders in Oregon became alarmed at the number of building permits being requested by Rajneeshpuram, and at the vague information provided by Rajneeshpuram's leaders. The county officials stopped issuing more building permits to Rajneeshpuram.

In response, Rajneeshpuram attempted to incorporate its land as a new city and also bought property in the nearest town, Antelope, which had a population of just 39 people in 1980. In late 1982, a number of sannyasins moved there and voted their own supporters into most of the official posts. By 1983, they had also taken over the local public school for use by community children, because the only children in town were Rajneeshpuram children. Meanwhile, the local environmental group and residents in other nearby towns continued to ask state and federal officials to help control the growth of Rajneeshpuram or eject the commune from the area.

Also at this time, immigration officials were looking into the visas issued to Rajneesh and many of his followers, and into claims of marriages arranged for the purpose of allowing foreign sannyasins to remain in the United States. The state of Oregon was also challenging the idea of Rajneeshpuram as a city, because it was in essence controlled by one religion.

In 1983, Sheela (the manager of the community) began asking the Rajneesh meditation centers around the world to consolidate into communes along the lines of Rajneeshpuram. Many members objected to this and left the movement. Several communes were formed, although none as large as Rajneeshpuram.

After 1983, the movement worldwide began to decline. Contributions went down and fewer clients were coming for therapy. Sheela apparently began to feel desperate, with challenges coming from within and from outside the movement. In 1984, Rajneeshpuram leaders began wiretapping and bugging the entire commune. That same year the commune bought semiautomatic weapons and assault rifles (Carter 1990, 197).

At about this time, the poisonings began. Although no one was killed, several were hospitalized. The Bhagwan's personal physician, Deveraj, was poisoned (Sheela was jealous of him). Later, two other county officials were poisoned with salmonella after visiting the commune and drinking some water.

In September 1984, the commune apparently attempted to take over the Wasco County elections by bringing in 4,000 homeless people—potential voters—from around the country in what it called its "Share-a-Home" program. Also in September, Sheela and her supporters poisoned salad bars in local restaurants with salmonella. About 750 people became ill as a result. This was supposed to be a "trial run" that was to culminate in a poisoning before the election, in order to disable enough voters so that the Rajneeshees could win the election (Carter 1990, 211–226).

Sheela began to fear that she and other commune leaders would be arrested. It also became apparent that Rajneeshpuram would not be allowed to exist as a closed, religious city. In September 1985, Sheela fled to Europe along with several other commune leaders.

In October, the immigration charges against Rajneesh caught up with him. Rajneeshees attempted to smuggle Rajneesh out of the country, but Rajneesh and his companions were arrested when his plane stopped in Charlotte, North Carolina. Sheela and other leaders were brought back from Germany. Sheela was fined over $400,000 and ordered to serve up to 20 years in prison. She served two and a half years and was released for good behavior. A few other commune leaders also served one or two years in prison.

Rajneesh was ordered to leave the country. He eventually returned to Poona, took on the name "Osho," and died in 1990. The Osho movement continues with about 20 meditation centers worldwide, in addition to the Poona ashram.

Meanwhile, the land and buildings of Rajneeshpuram were sold. According to the Center for Land Use Interpretation (2006), the area that was Rajneeshpuram is now owned by a Christian youth camp called Young Life.

Beliefs and Practices

The movement was purposely inconsistent in its beliefs and practices. According to Rajneesh, "I am a man who is consistently inconsistent. . . . I live in the moment and whatsoever I am saying right now is true only for this moment" (quoted in Carter 1990, 38).

However, Lewis Carter notes that many members believed that Bhagwan Shree Rajneesh was a "returned spiritual master. " Rajneesh claimed that he was the reincarnation of a spiritual master who was born in the 12th century CE and died in the 13th century. He decided to come back to Earth because he wanted to create "a synthesis between East and West, body and soul, materialism and spiritualism . . . creating a new man" (1990, 41).

Carter explains that Rajneesh believed that "people must be shocked to 'awaken them.'" Rajneesh shocked Indian audiences by calling for sexual freedom, by criticizing all organized religion, and by attacking revered figures such as Mahatma Gandhi and Mother Theresa (1990, 44–45). However, while these attacks may have shocked Indians, they apparently attracted Westerners, as Frances FitzGerald notes. "Westerners had poured in and laughed at his anti-Catholic jokes, his anti-Semitic jokes, his anti-Hindu jokes, and his dirty jokes. He made his listeners feel that they belonged to an elite of truly freethinkers who saw beyond the superstitions and pathetic social props of everyone else's existence" (1986, 341).

The ashram in Poona offered visitors and residents up to nine different types of meditation, as well as classes in yoga, acupuncture, Sufi dancing, and shiatsu massage. Nearly 60 different types of therapies were also offered. Rajneesh thought that traditional methods to reach enlightenment would not work for modern people. FitzGerald explains that "for this reason he turned the Poona ashram into a kind of spiritual garage for anyone with a method, and at the same time into a laboratory for experimentation of all sorts. His test of legitimacy was merely what worked—or what seemed to work" (1986, 292, 297–298). One type of meditation, "Dynamic Meditation," was common to many Rajneesh centers. It involved deep breathing, jumping, screaming, and dancing.

The disciples of Rajneesh were called *sannyasins,* which is a word to refer to Hindus who renounce the world. Rajneesh's followers were given new Sanskrit or Hindi names to indicate that they were "born again" and were asked to wear shades of orange or red. However, Rajneesh preached that his sannyasins did not need to renounce anything at all (FitzGerald 1986, 292).

Because renunciation was not a part of the belief, Rajneesh welcomed expensive gifts. In Oregon, at one point, he owned 80 or more Rolls Royce automobiles, in addition to many expensive watches and pieces of jewelry.

Daily Life

Rajneeshpuram was planned to be a self-sufficient community of up to 3,500 residents and 15,000 guests, including housing, therapy centers, a shopping mall, an air terminal, transportation, and businesses to serve the residents and guests. Rajneeshpuram was built with remarkable speed. Sannyasins constructed roads, water and sewage services, wells, houses, therapy centers, and a huge meditation hall. During 1983, the community completed the Meditation University, a hotel, cabins, and cottages (Carter 1990, 158–159, 166).

Unlike life at the Poona ashram, which was described as "a madhouse-carnival atmosphere," Rajneeshpuram was fairly regimented. Sannyasins worked 12 to 16 hours per day building the community. When Frances FitzGerald visited in 1983, she noted the "expensive, well-cared for look" of the greenhouses, cows in a concrete-floored milking shed, a poultry farm, and a market garden. The sannyasins had breakfast between 6 and 7 in the morning, and then went to work, with breaks for lunch and dinner, as well as for a mid-morning and mid-afternoon snack. At two in the afternoon the sannyasins would line up along the road to watch Rajneesh drive by in one of his Rolls Royces. They worked six days a week and had meetings on Sundays (1986, 256, 268–269, 293).

The sannyasins wore any style of clothing they liked, but in shades of orange or red. They also wore a "mala," a necklace of beads with a photo of Rajneesh attached. The food was vegetarian and plentiful.

How They Made Their Living

In Oregon, India, and around the world, the Rajneeshees made money from a variety of businesses as well as through donations from wealthy supporters. Rajneeshees believed that "work is worship," and almost any kind of work was acceptable.

Clients paid the Rajneesh ashrams and meditation centers for therapies and meditation training. The communities also provided unrelated services to outsiders such as travel agency services, credit services, and cleaning and laundry services (Carter 1990, 73).

Rajneeshpuram held annual "worldwide festivals" for sannyasins in other parts of the world, and for the public. These festivals brought millions in registration fees and payments for food and lodging (Carter 1990, 156, 166).

Leadership and Decision Making

Rajneesh appointed his own top managers. The two main managers were two Indian-born women. Laxmi, Rajneesh's first disciple, managed the efforts in India, and Sheela, a longtime member, was in charge in Oregon. In Rajneeshpuram, a group of "coordinators" overseen by Sheela managed different aspects of the ranch (Carter 1990, 160).

Although Rajneesh gave no public talks during most of his time in Oregon, the sannyasins believed that Sheela was taking her direction from him and realized that they had to obey Sheela or leave the commune.

How New Members Were Recruited or Chosen

The Rajneesh movement was already huge worldwide by the time Rajneeshpuram was set up. Members generally moved to Rajneeshpuram from one of the other centers around the world.

There were no restrictions on who could become a sannyasin. Any interested person could be dubbed a "sannyasin" even through the mail and receive a new name and mala with photo of Rajneesh attached.

Carter notes that "taking sannyas gave no one special privileges or entree into any commune. Such association depended on the consent of the commune leaders or members—in the case of Rajneeshpuram, Sheela" (1990, 186).

Children and Youth

No children were born during the six years of Rajneeshpuram's existence. Although there was apparently no rule against having babies, those who were pregnant or had babies found it difficult to get into and stay in the commune, because Sheela and the other leaders wanted people who could work hard to build the community. Birth control and abortions were preferred (FitzGerald 1986, 301).

Around the world, children of Rajneesh members were sometimes sent to schools on Rajneesh communes and at other times to local schools. Tim Guest, who lived in a number of Rajneesh communes around the world while growing up, describes a system that essentially ignored children and their needs. While the children were generally not mistreated, there was no particular philosophy about child rearing or education, and the children were often left to play or wander on their own. Rajneesh did not want the children to be taught any of his beliefs. "We were to discover the world for ourselves," Guest remarks (2004, 35).

In Rajneeshpuram, the 53 school-aged children were sent to the public school in the nearest town, Antelope. However, this was basically a Rajneesh school, since the commune had taken over the town, including the school, and no non-Rajneesh children attended the school (Carter 1990, 182).

Relationship with the Outside World

From almost the beginning, Rajneeshpuram was characterized by bitter relations with the local community. The Rajneeshees often used a confrontational style when dealing with the outside world. For example, Sheela, the main leader in Rajneeshpuram, declared on local television that the children of Antelope ranchers "looked retarded." When a local land-use planner and an environmental lawyer went to Rajneeshpuram to inspect the buildings and land-use permits, they were harassed by Rajneeshees who shouted anti-Semitic remarks and chanted slogans so loudly that the men could not do their work (FitzGerald 1986, 335).

Outsider scholars were often puzzled as to why the Rajneeshees seemed to deliberately attack and provoke people. FitzGerald found that this hostile behavior was a deliberate attempt to wake up the outside world. One member explained, "Being here [in Rajneeshpuram], you see the phoniness of all politics. . . . So it's better to offend people to the point where they say what they mean" (quoted in FitzGerald 1986, 336).

Others have suggested that the Rajneeshee leaders' provocative behavior was designed to make enemies of the outside world, in order to downplay the dissension within Rajneeshpuram and give members a reason to stick together against an outside enemy. "Isolated as they were, it was easy to persuade sannyasins to believe that they lived in the midst of a wilderness populated only by rednecks with guns" (FitzGerald 1986, 340).

Residents of Rajneeshpuram were shielded from the outside world. For example, there was only one TV on the ranch, which was controlled by Sheela. Outside newspapers and magazines were not easy to come by. The commune provided almost everything residents could need, including food, medical services, and education, so there was little need to leave it (Carter 1990, 148, 158, 198).

Especially after 1983, when a bomb was set off in a Rajneeshee-owned hotel in Portland, Oregon, Rajneeshpuram became more and more closed off to outsiders. Visitors had to go through checkpoints and searches in order to enter, sign a release form, and wear an armband. Once inside, visitors were restricted to certain areas of the commune. Additionally, sannyasins were increasingly confined to the commune, and were asked not to travel outside alone (Carter 1990, 187–188, 198).

Reasons for Decline of the Community

The community in the United States, and the movement worldwide, imploded due to the ineptness and crimes committed by its top leaders.

References

Carter, Lewis. *Charisma and Control in Rajneeshpuram*. Cambridge, U.K.: Cambridge University Press, 1990.

Center for Land Use Interpretation, http://ludb.clui.org/ex/i/OR3126/ (accessed December 2006).

FitzGerald, Frances. *Cities on a Hill: A Journey through Contemporary American Cultures*. New York: Simon and Schuster, 1986.

Guest, Tim. *My Life in Orange: Growing Up with the Guru*. Orlando, FL: Harcourt, 2004.

Web site

Religious Tolerance: www.religioustolerance.org/rajneesh.htm (accessed December 2006).

Renaissance
Community/Brotherhood
of the Spirit

At a Glance

Dates of existence in United States: 1968 to 1988
Location: Massachusetts
Peak membership: 400
Religious or other belief: New Age spiritualism

History

The Brotherhood of the Spirit—renamed the Renaissance Community in 1974—was one of the few hippie communities that survived beyond a few years.

The group was started by Michael Metelica, who was born in 1950 in Massachusetts. From a young age, he had psychic and out-of-body experiences. He talked about his experiences with a friend's mother, Beth Hapgood, who was a psychology professor. Hapgood took Metelica to see Elwood Babbitt, a local farmer who was well known as a "trance medium" (someone who goes into a trance and then communicates with spirits, including those who have died). Babbitt started helping Metelica try to understand his spiritual, psychic experiences.

At the age of 16, Metelica read about the Brotherhood of Hell's Angels, a motorcycle gang. He dropped out of high school and went to Florida to meet the Hell's Angels, but after seeing them fight with each other, he was put off.

Next he traveled to California and found himself participating in the 1967 "Summer of Love" in the Haight-Ashbury district of San Francisco, one of the first major gatherings of the hippie youth movement. "The hippie movement was the beginning of my life," Metelica said in an interview included in the movie *Free Spirits*. "The vision of people living together, working together, loving each other—that's what I wanted to pursue" (2007).

Metelica returned to his hometown—a small, depressed factory town. He built a tree house in the woods and lived there, worked for local farmers in exchange for part of their crop, and meditated in the evenings. He was joined in the tree house by several friends. In 1968, while Metelica and his friends were at work, the tree house was burned by suspicious local people.

The group began a stressful two-year period of moving numerous times within Massachusetts and Vermont. In the fall of 1969, they rented a 680-square foot bunk house at a summer camp in Massachusetts, and by the middle of winter, up to 80 people lived there or visited on the weekends.

By 1970, the group had named itself the Brotherhood of the Spirit. People from all over the country arrived to check out and join the group, bringing with them money and skills. In March 1970, the group bought an old inn on 25 acres in Warwick, Massachusetts. The community instituted rules banning drugs (including cigarettes and alcohol). As its membership grew to 150 people, it tore down old barns on its land and used the lumber to build a three-story dormitory. By the end of the year, Beth Hapgood turned her home in Northfield, Massachusetts, over to the community.

Membership had expanded to almost 300 in 1972, and the community bought property in nearby towns to house its members. It also bought a block of buildings in Turners Falls, Massachusetts, and started a number of businesses in these buildings. Some of these businesses did well; others did not.

Around 1973, Metelica began to demand unlimited power to run the community and to be in charge of all the money. Members had to turn over their paychecks to Metelica, who, in an effort to change the image of the community, bought expensive clothes, cars, and even an airplane. Those who questioned Metelica were accused of being "negative." Some members began to leave at this time.

In 1974, the group changed its name to Renaissance Community and formally organized itself as the "Renaissance Church." Metelica changed his last name to "Rapunzel." At about this time, Metelica and other members also began smoking, drinking alcohol, and using cocaine.

The next year the group decided that all of its members should live together and so bought an old inn on 80 acres in Gill, Massachusetts. It started the "2001 Center," which was to become a self-sufficient homestead for all members. In 1980, it sold its buildings in Turners Falls. At about this time, the group began contacting and learning about other communal groups, such as Findhorn in Scotland and the Love Family in Washington State.

By the early 1980s, the group had declined to about 60 adults and 45 children. There were not enough members to carry out the ambitious goals of the 2001 Center. Daniel Brown, a former member, attributes this decline to the fact that Metelica was using community money to feed his own drug and alcohol addictions. Metelica also set up a rifle range on community land, which angered people, since they had assumed the community was pacifist.

The community's successful bus touring business went bankrupt. In 1988, the remaining members (about a dozen) offered Metelica $10,000 to leave the community, and he agreed. After his departure, the community sold off much of its property. This marked the formal end of the Renaissance Community, although former members continue to live on the property and run businesses in the area. Metelica died of colon cancer in 2003.

Beliefs and Practices

According to Brown, who was a former member of the community and has written a short history of the group, the community's spiritual belief system "was based on aspects of Buddhism and New Age thinking mixed with an enlightened, almost Gnostic form of Christianity. Reincarnation, meditation, and the power of positive thought were considered to be major doctrines" (Brown, "History of the Brotherhood").

Metelica was the spiritual leader of the group. He was advised by Elwood Babbitt, who introduced Metelica and his group to a book called *The Aquarian Gospel of Jesus the Christ*, first published in the early 1900s. This was a popular book among hippies and describes Jesus traveling to India, Tibet, Persia, Greece, and Egypt, and learning mystical insights from spiritual masters in those countries. This book became an important spiritual text for the group (Popenoe and Popenoe, 1984, 53).

Babbitt received information from his spirit guides warning that humanity's greed and selfishness would cause "Earth Changes" that would bring death and destruction, and afterwards, an age of spiritual enlightenment called the Aquarian Age. Babbitt believed that Metelica and his group were teachers to lead others to the higher wisdom of the Aquarian Age. Babbitt would go into a trance and give lectures to the community.

The community banned "promiscuity," but its definition of promiscuity was different from that of the outside world. Sex was supposed to take place in a spiritual context. In practice, anyone could have sexual relations with a member of the opposite sex as long as the two were in love or were experiencing some sort of deep connection.

For many years, the community banned alcohol, drugs, and cigarettes. It wanted to pursue druglike states using natural techniques such as meditation. Singing was also important: the group would learn the same songs and sing them together.

In the mid-1970s, when Metelica began to use alcohol, cigarettes, and drugs, Babbitt distanced himself from Metelica and the community. Babbitt felt that Metelica was going in the wrong direction.

Their 2001 Center was designed to be a self-sufficient community, "where people from different backgrounds can live together and learn about each other: where members can unfold the creative energies within themselves in an atmosphere of love, joy and wisdom," according to a hand-out for visitors (Popenoe and Popenoe, 1984, 58).

Religious services were held on Sunday afternoons featuring music, meditation, and a talk by Metelica. The services were open to the public.

Daily Life

The community painted the outside of the Warwick hotel purple with blue and green swirls. The ceiling of the dining room featured calligraphy of the "Seven Immutable Laws" from Babbitt's trance lectures. One unusual aspect of the Warwick property was "toilet city"—seven toilets in one room, arranged in a circle, so members could talk to each other while attending to the call of nature. This arrangement was supposed to help members release previous hang-ups.

In Warwick, members built their own homes and grew and processed their own food. Members were organized into teams that took charge of areas such as business management, child care, car maintenance, farming, and food production. They were poor—at times they had little to eat besides rice, potatoes, and squash.

At the 2001 Center in Gill, the community used alternative energy technology, including passive solar design, wind power, and wood heat. Members worked six days per week and spent Saturdays on group projects. They planted an orchard and an organic garden.

The group had no strict rules about food. Some were vegetarians, but most ate meat when it was available.

How They Made Their Living

At first, members worked for local farmers. In the 1970s, members formed several musical groups and performed throughout the northeastern United States. One such group, "Spirit in Flesh," aimed to introduce people to spirituality through rock and roll.

Several community businesses grew out of the music groups. The community founded its own recording studio to produce its music. It built its own sound equipment and formed a business to rent this equipment to other groups. The group bought buses and installed bunk beds, kitchenettes, and bathrooms, and rented the buses and drivers to bands that needed to travel at night in order to play at new locales each day.

About 50 members were employed by a nearby state institution for people with mental retardation, working in all departments from janitorial to administration.

The group started a number of businesses in the block of buildings it owned in Turners Falls, Massachusetts, including a plumbing and refrigeration company, a grocery store, restaurants, and a youth center. Unfortunately, most of these businesses did not make a profit, partly because many community members did not have experience running a business, and partly because they did not have enough local customers for such businesses as the restaurants.

The businesses that did not depend only on local customers did well. For example, the Renaissance Greeting Card Company received orders from all over the country, as well as from other English-speaking countries, and grew to employ a dozen people. In early 1981, the people who ran the greeting card company split with the Renaissance Community and moved to Springvale, Maine, where the company continues to operate.

Leadership and Decision Making

Michael Metelica was the spiritual and administrative leader of the community. At first, when the community was small and most members had known each other since before its founding, there was very little need for any sort of management, and Metelica was seen as mostly the spiritual leader. Starting in 1973, though, Metelica began exercising more authority, including controlling the community's finances.

A former member of the community, Daniel Brown, states that Metelica used community money to feed his own drug and alcohol addictions and that this misuse of money caused community members to leave—including the members who ran successful community businesses, such as the greeting card company and the silkscreen company.

Children and Youth

By 1975, there were about 70 children in the community. There did not seem to have been any formal, community schooling system, although community women did take turns caring for groups of children.

How New Members Were Recruited or Chosen

In the early 1970s, the community received publicity in national magazines, which brought hundreds of potential members who wanted to check things out.

At first, anyone who wanted could join the community. By the time of the 2001 Center in the late 1970s, potential members were interviewed to make sure they understood the purpose of the community and were willing to follow the rules. Members were expected to turn over all personal assets to the group, and sign a vow of poverty.

Relationship with the Outside World

In the 1970s, the outside world was curious about the Renaissance Community, which was covered in large national publications such as *The Wall Street Journal, Family Circle*, and *Mademoiselle,* and featured on national television shows such as *60 Minutes.*

To reach the outside world with its spiritual message, the community had a weekly radio show that was distributed nationally. It also printed a magazine called *The Free Spirit Press.*

At times the local community in Massachusetts was hostile to or suspicious about the community. The group's tree house was burned down. It had a difficult time buying the property in Warwick because the owners did not want to sell to a bunch of hippies. The members were at times run off the road and shot at. One of its members, Peter Luban, was killed, and the community believed he was murdered. The mystery of his death was never solved.

At other times, the local community was welcoming, patronizing Renaissance businesses and participating in Renaissance events. The community invited outsiders to its church services, held a street festival that attracted 3,000 people, and hired local young people to work in its businesses.

Reasons for Decline of the Community

Many members left because they disagreed with Metelica's leadership. After Metelica's departure, the community had dwindled so much that it could not recover.

See also: Hippies; Love Family

References

Brown, Daniel. "The History of the Brotherhood of the Spirit/Renaissance Community: 1968–1988," http://acornproductions.net/history.php (accessed July 2007).

Dowling, Levi. *The Aquarian Gospel of Jesus the Christ.* London: L. N. Fowler and Company, 1920, www.sacred-texts.com/chr/agjc/index.htm (accessed July 2007).

Free Spirits: The Birth, Life & Loss of a New-Age Dream (documentary). Directed by Bruce Geisler. Acorn Productions, 2007.

Popenoe, Cris, and Oliver Popenoe. *Seeds of Tomorrow: New Age Communities That Work.* San Francisco: Harper and Row, 1984.

Rugby

History

Rugby was started by a British man who was very famous in his time. Backed by large sums of money, Rugby was meant to provide a cooperative community, based on farming and crafts, for the "younger sons" of British aristocracy, who under British social custom could not inherit their father's wealth and could only pursue a livelihood in a few socially acceptable occupations.

Rugby's founder, Thomas Hughes, was the author of the popular novel *Tom Brown's School Days*. He was also a lawyer, a former member of Parliament, and a social reformer. The son of a middle-class clergyman, Hughes had attended the prestigious Rugby School under a headmaster who believed that such schools should not be open only to the upper class. While working as a lawyer in London, he became interested in the cooperative movement promoted by Robert Owen.

Hughes was concerned for the welfare of the well-educated young English gentlemen who could not find employment as doctors, lawyers, or priests. What these young men needed, he decided, was the freedom to pursue a livelihood in farming or crafts. He decided that the United States was the place to put this experiment into action. "The success of Americans," Hughes noted, "lies in starting anew and accepting agriculture as a good profession, for farming is the basis of subsistence" (quoted in Stagg 1973, 3).

In 1879, Hughes met some capitalists in Boston who happened to own land in Tennessee. The Bostonians suggested that Hughes could use this land for his community. Hughes agreed, and together they formed the Board of Aid to Land Ownership, which would own the land, finance the community, and eventually, they hoped, make a profit from the venture.

The community began in 1880. Although the members suffered during an extremely cold first winter, by the summer of 1881, they had 300 residents and more than a dozen buildings completed or being constructed. One of their first buildings was a hotel they named the Tabard Inn, after the hotel in Geoffrey Chaucer's famous 14th-century English collection, *The Canterbury Tales*. The community itself was named Rugby after Hughes's school.

In August and September 1881, seven members died of typhoid, traced to tainted water from the Tabard Inn. The Tabard Inn's well was sealed, and the hotel was closed and remodeled, but the damage had been done: almost all Rugby settlers left, and the population dropped to 60.

Hughes, determined to save his venture, appointed a new manager for the community. New members began arriving and by 1883 the population was up to 150. The Tabard Inn was open again, and tourists were frequenting the establishment. By 1884, Rugby had over 400 members. The school for community children opened.

That same year, however, the Tabard Inn was destroyed by fire. Although the hotel was rebuilt by 1887, the number of tourists declined. After 1887, the number of people living at Rugby began decreasing. By the early 1900s, it was no longer a viable community (Stagg 1973, 14–15).

Today, Rugby is listed on the National Register of Historic Places.

Beliefs and Practices

Hughes did not believe in government socialism and communism. The community was founded on the principle of voluntary cooperation. Individuals and families bought land and built homes, or they rented living space. The community was open not just to the English, but "to all who like our principals and our ways. . . . Englishmen and Americans can stand shoulder to shoulder, and work with one mind and one heart for the same great end." Hughes believed in individual liberty, so Rugby members were free to worship in their own way. The community church was to be used for all Christian denominations (Egerton 1977, 47, 50–51).

Hughes hoped, in Rugby, to produce people who were hard working, humble, and yet highly cultured. "Our aim and hope are to plant on these highlands a community of gentlemen and ladies; not that artificial class which goes by those grand names, both in Europe and here, the joint product of feudalism and wealth, but a society in which the humblest members, who live by the labour of their own hands, will be of such strain and culture that they will be able to meet princes at the gate, should any such strange person ever present themselves before the gate tower of Rugby in the New World" (Egerton 1977, 52).

Daily Life

Rugby was located in east Tennessee, on a high, wooded plain between two river gorges and gained a reputation as a health resort. At first the land had only one house, a barn, and an acre of cleared land. By 1884, the community had built 65 buildings, including a three-story schoolhouse, a hotel, a public library with 7,000 volumes, a boarding house, an office building that housed the printing press and telegraph office, public stables, the commissary, a drug store, and several private homes (Stagg 1973, 4, 12, 22–33; Egerton 1977, 42).

According to the Historic Rugby Web site, the settlers enjoyed literary and drama clubs, lawn tennis, rugby football, horseback riding, croquet, and swimming in the nearby rivers (www.historicrugby.org/).

How They Made Their Living

Rugby's residents were engaged in private enterprise as well as cooperative owner-ship. For example, residents could farm their own land for their own private profit or could participate in the collective farm. The community owned a canning com-pany for a short time, as well as a sawmill, a commissary (grocery and supply store), the Tabard Inn, and a cafe (Egerton 1977, 42).

The community was not financially successful. The United States as a whole was suffering from an economic depression, and prices for farm products were down. Rugby also suffered a long drought in 1887. After the first two years, the community was not able to sell much land to new settlers. John Egerton notes that "the motives of idealism and philanthropy and profit-making were constantly in conflict; and while some people sought to make it a farming community or a trading center, others wanted it to be a health resort or a tourist haven, and still others envisioned it as a utopia for young Englishmen or a leisurely retreat for the upper class" (1977, 58).

Leadership and Decision Making

The Board to Aid Land Ownership ran the community. Egerton points out that Rugby was, in essence, "a company town, a benevolent oligarchy in which Hughes and a few others made all of the major decisions" (1977, 52). Hughes seemed to have no plan to transition the community to any sort of democratic leadership structure.

How New Members Were Recruited or Chosen

Because Hughes was the well-known author of *Tom Brown's School Days*, his com-munity received extensive publicity in the United States and England. Hughes wrote magazine articles and made speeches to young, well-educated British men, urging them to go to Rugby. Although Hughes meant to found the community for the younger sons of British aristocracy, in reality the majority of its members were Amer-ican (although Britons were a significant minority, maybe 40 percent). About half of its members were female. While the community was almost entirely white, there was at least one black family (Egerton 1977, 54).

Children and Youth

Hughes hoped to start a university at Rugby. Although this never happened, a preparatory school was started with six students and operated for several years. It never grew as large as was intended (Stagg 1973, 14).

Relationship with the Outside World

Rugby was covered extensively in British and American newspapers during its time. Rugby also printed its own weekly newspaper. According to the Historic Rugby Web site, two trains per day ran from Rugby to Cincinnati, Ohio (www.historicrugby.org/).

Reasons for Decline of the Community

Rugby was never able to become financially successful. The reasons for this include a countrywide economic depression; the burning of the Tabard Inn; the drought in 1887; and perhaps the fact that some of the educated young men from England were not hard working, but instead were "naive and uninitiated idealists and adventurers, grumblers, loafers, snobs, gilded playboy pioneers with too much money from home and too little understanding of their surroundings to be anything more than a hindrance to their fellow colonists" (Egerton 1977, 59).

Influence on the Outside World

Historic Rugby receives 65,000 visitors per year, according to its Web site. Its library of 7,000 volumes continues to be one of the best collections of Victorian books in the United States (www.historicrugby.org/).

See also: Owen, Robert

References

Egerton, John. *Visions of Utopia: Nashoba, Rugby, Ruskin and the "New Communities" of Tennessee's Past.* Knoxville: University of Tennessee Press, 1977.
Stagg, Brian. *The Distant Eden: Tennessee's Rugby Colony.* Paylor Publications, 1973.

WEB SITE
Historic Rugby: www.historicrugby.org/ (accessed March 2007).

Ruskin

At a Glance

Dates of existence in United States: 1894 to 1901
Locations: Tennessee, Georgia
Peak membership: 250
Religious or other belief: socialism

History

Ruskin was founded by Julius Augustus Wayland, a poor boy from Indiana who became a moderately successful capitalist, who then converted to socialism.

Wayland worked as a printer, a newspaper owner, and a real estate speculator, moving from Indiana to Missouri to Colorado. He thought very little about how the economic system impacted his and others' ability to get ahead, until he realized that he was ignorant of how the system worked. As he sought to learn more, a friend gave him socialist reading material, including Laurence Gronlund's book *Cooperative Commonwealth*. According to Wayland, he "saw a new light" as a result of reading Gronlund's book (quoted in Shore 1988, 23).

He also read Edward Bellamy's novel, *Looking Backward 2000–1887*. Wayland was especially influenced by the writings of John Ruskin, an English philosopher, art critic, and social critic. Because Ruskin believed that healthy social conditions were necessary to produce good art, he criticized the capitalist system.

In the early 1890s, Wayland became convinced that the country was about to head into a depression. He sold most of his property in Colorado and in 1893 returned to Indiana to start a socialist newspaper that he called *The Coming Nation*. By 1894, he was asking his readers to help him raise money in order to buy land on which to form a socialist community. He bought land in Tennessee, where land was cheap, and the community began in the summer of 1894, with a dozen members living in tents. Wayland named the community the Ruskin Cooperative Association in honor of his favorite author, John Ruskin.

The first construction project was a building for the printing press, because Wayland's socialist newspaper was to be a main source of income. By the fall of 1894, the community had 100 residents.

In 1895, community members began attacking Wayland because he continued to control the newspaper, which was a major source of income for Ruskin. Some members accused him of making a private profit from its publication. In the summer of 1895, Wayland resigned from the newspaper and left for Kansas City, where he started another socialist newspaper. The community appointed another editor for *The Coming Nation*.

Because of a lack of water and the fact that the land proved unsuitable for farming, in late 1895 the community moved to a site nearby. Things went well until about 1897, when internal dissension began to build. Members accused other members of not being socialist enough, or of being capitalist, anarchist, individualistic, and so forth. Members leaving the community began suing to recover the $500 they paid for shares. The population of Ruskin stopped growing and *The Coming Nation* had fewer subscribers.

In May 1899, the majority of the stockholders held a secret meeting and voted to abolish the Ruskin Cooperative Association and re-form as the Ruskin Commonwealth. The stockholders who were left out of the secret meeting found out about these plans and asked a judge to sell the community's assets at an auction. This forced sale brought little money to the community.

About 240 members re-formed as the Ruskin Commonwealth, and moved to Waycross, Georgia, where they continued to publish their newspaper. This community ended 18 months later, due to infertile land, declining subscribers to *The Coming Nation*, food shortages, fire, and sickness (Brundage 1996, 150–160).

About a dozen Ruskin members moved to Alabama to join the Fairhope single-tax community there (Egerton 1977, 84).

Beliefs and Practices

Wayland's socialism was an eclectic blend of ideas he had drawn from other socialist authors. He did not believe in dividing socialists into different camps, but wanted all who identified as socialists to live and work together toward a world that would provide opportunities for everyone. He argued that competition and monopolistic capitalism were imports from Europe, and that cooperation was truly American. The goal of Ruskin was to provide good homes, jobs, schools, and wages to all members (Brundage 1996, 23–24, 98).

Wayland believed in economic equality above all. Each adult member of Ruskin—women and men—would earn the same wage per hour, no matter what the job. Everyone was to enjoy leisure time and opportunities for culture and education. Wayland envisioned that the center of community life would be its library and meeting hall (Brundage 1996, 32–33).

Ruskin members were allowed to worship in any way they liked, but were not to use community money for this purpose (Brundage 1996, 46–47).

Daily Life

Ruskin's first site was in Dickson County, 50 miles west of Nashville, Tennessee. As it turned out, water was difficult to find on this land, so members built their homes wherever they could strike water for a well, resulting in a haphazard layout. They moved to a new site nearby in 1895, dismantling and moving their buildings over the course of several months.

Two large caves were located on this land. The largest contained a deep pool of water and was cool all year round. This cave was used as a storage facility for produce and as a cool community gathering place.

By 1898, residents had constructed 70 homes. The center of the community was the Commonwealth House, which housed the print shop, communal dining room, 700-seat auditorium, lodging for visitors, nursery, bookstore, and library. The group had also built a flour mill, steam laundry, machine shop, coffee house, bakery, photo gallery, school, store, tin shop, hen house, stable, and livestock pen. Apparently the community was seen as shabby by the outside world: the houses were small and unpainted, and visitors slept in rooms formed by curtains (Egerton 1977, 74–75; Brundage 1996, 100–101, 114–115).

Ruskin members woke up at 5:30 a.m. to the sound of a whistle, which blew several times per day to announce meals and work shifts. They breakfasted at 6:00 a.m., started work at 7:00 a.m., and had lunch at noon before returning to work at 1:00 p.m. At 5:00 p.m., they had dinner, and in the evening, they held meetings or other activities (Brundage 1996, 109).

Although women received the same wage as men for each hour of their labor, and although according to Ruskin bylaws they were allowed to choose any work they liked, women tended to perform work traditional to their gender, such as cleaning, child care, and teaching the younger children. Some men performed heavy household chores such as washing floors, hauling water, and cleaning the huge cooking pots.

Men were required to work nine hours per day, and women without children, eight. Women with older children worked five hours per day within the community, and women with young children earned wages for caring for their own children and performing their own household chores. Pregnant women were excused from community work for the last three months of pregnancy, and then for a year after the baby was born.

Community members were paid at first with cash, and then with labor notes that could be used at the community store, or redeemed for cash. They could use these labor notes or cash to buy whatever they liked (Brundage 1996, 70, 82–85, 111).

Ruskin members sometimes complained that their food was badly prepared, spartan, and monotonous. The kitchen served eggs, bread, some meat, beans, vegetables, fruits, milk, tea, and a "cereal" coffee manufactured at Ruskin. Community members organized clubs, concerts, and plays; held parties and dances; and attended evening classes in a variety of subjects (Brundage 1996, 88, 113–114, 123–125).

How They Made Their Living

The community's socialist newspaper, *The Coming Nation*, was a major source of income. The print shop also printed 26 other labor union newspapers and published books and pamphlets. The community also made money from stock purchases by new members, and contributions from outside supporters.

Ruskin members tried to be self-sufficient by growing their own vegetables, raising their own meat, sawing their own lumber, and so forth. The community's sawmill provided lumber for railroad ties to the Nashville, Chattanooga and St. Louis Railroad. Ruskin members also made and sold a diversity of products, such as chewing gum, leather suspenders and belts, pants, and a cure-all medicine that they called Ruskin Ready Remedy (Brundage 1996, 101–103, 115).

Leadership and Decision Making

Ruskin was run by a seven-member elected Board of Directors. Colony members who had purchased stock for $500 were allowed to vote for the Board of Directors. Although women could purchase stock, and some did, about 80 percent of stockholders were men (Brundage 1996, 91–92).

Each work department had a manager who was elected by the workers. By 1898 the community had 26 different departments (Brundage 1996, 87, 108).

How New Members Were Recruited or Chosen

Wayland publicized Ruskin through his newspaper, which had a circulation of over 50,000 by 1894. Members paid $500 to join and received one share of stock in return, which entitled them to a vote. Wives of male stockholders could also pay $500 and receive a share of stock, or they could receive the benefits of the community in exchange for their labor. The community was open to all white people who believed in cooperation and who could pay the fee. Although Wayland supported the freeing of the slaves, he did not want any black members in his community. Almost all members of Ruskin were American born (Brundage 1996, 35, 41–44).

Children and Youth

Ruskin ran a school for its children with help from the county and state school boards, which gave Ruskin money to operate a public school for its children. Ruskin provided the building and teachers. The aim of the school was to teach children the value of manual labor, as well as academic subjects. Girls were to be provided the same education as boys. Subjects included the usual academics, as well as drawing, painting, chemistry, botany, speech, and music. Ruskin members, influenced by the educational philosophies of Friedrich Froebel and Johann Pestalozzi, did not believe in memorization or competition, which were prevalent in outside schools. They did not give students grades and believed students learned best by doing. In addition to classroom schooling, the children were organized into work groups and received labor credit for their work (Brundage 1996, 117–119).

Relationship with the Outside World

Ruskin members aimed to have a good relationship with their local neighbors. They paid their taxes and voted in elections.

The community was proud of its library, which offered a variety of newspapers and magazines from around the country, as well as hundreds of books (Brundage 1996, 124).

Ruskin members invited their outside neighbors to attend their lectures, concerts, plays, and dances. In 1896, they held a Fourth of July celebration at which they served a free barbecue to 2,000 people in their large cave. In 1899, when Ruskin was preparing to sell its assets, they invited the local neighbors to another barbecue and sale. The Ruskin members were overwhelmed by the generosity of their neighbors, who bought 5,000 barbecue tickets at 25 cents apiece, bought the goods Ruskin offered for sale, and threw extra money into a hat (Egerton 1977, 78, 80; Brundage 1996, 127).

Reasons for Ending the Community

Although Ruskin seemed to have prospered economically in Tennessee, its members found it difficult to get along with each other. Perhaps the liberal admissions policy was to blame. Community members were from a variety of social classes and did not share an ideology or religion that could help them bond as a community. In Georgia, they were not able to grow enough food for themselves or to make enough money to support themselves (Brundage 1996, 50, 150–160).

Influence on the Outside World

Like other socialist utopian communities, Ruskin hoped to be an example to the outside world of an alternative way of living. Although it failed at this, W. Fitzhugh Brundage points out that "Ruskinites grappled with timeless questions about how to free this world of the evils of poverty, depravity and injustice. . . . However eccentric and misguided, the good life the Ruskinites sought to create was a bold act of imagination" (1996, 200).

> *See also:* Bellamy, Edward; Fairhope and Single-Tax Communities; Gronlund, Laurence; Socialism

References

Brundage, W. Fitzhugh. *A Socialist Utopia in the New South: The Ruskin Colonies in Tennessee and Georgia, 1894–1901*. Urbana: University of Illinois Press, 1996.

Egerton, John. *Visions of Utopia: Nashoba, Rugby, Ruskin and the "New Communities" in Tennessee's Past*. Knoxville: University of Tennessee Press, 1977.

Shore, Elliott. *Talkin' Socialism: J. A. Wayland and the Role of the Press in American Radicalism, 1890–1912*. Lawrence: University Press of Kansas, 1988.

Shakers

At a Glance

Dates of existence in United States: 1774 to early 1900s, although there
are still a few adherents

Locations: 24 communities in New York, New England, Ohio, Indiana,
Kentucky, Georgia, and Florida

Peak membership: over 5,000

Religious or other belief: Christianity, United Society of Believers in
Christ's Second Coming

History

The Shakers are among the longest-lived and best-known American utopian communities. The movement began in the 18th century in England, with a few people who broke away from a religious group called the Quakers. Like the Quakers, the Shakers were against war and believed in dressing in a simple manner. Unlike the Quakers, who held almost silent religious services, the Shakers included shouting, singing, and a type of dance known as "shaking" in their services. They began to be called the "Shaking Quakers," or the "Shakers." The Shakers believed that the second coming of Christ would happen soon and that Christ would come to Earth in the form of a woman.

A blacksmith's daughter named Ann Lee was part of this group. Lee's four children all died in infancy, and this suffering caused Ann to believe that marriage and sexual intercourse were sinful, since they led to such tragedy. Lee began preaching her views to the Shakers, who came to agree with her.

The Shakers were not welcome in England because of their noisy worship services and because their religious views were considered unusual. Lee was imprisoned several times. During her time in prison she had visions, including one that revealed to her that Christ was inhabiting her body and speaking through her.

When she came out of prison in 1770, many Shakers believed that Christ had come back to Earth in the form of Ann Lee. They accepted her leadership and began calling her "Mother Ann." In 1774, Mother Ann led eight of her followers to New York. For a few years, she and other followers worked to support themselves. Mother Ann found a job as a laundress and maid. Then, in 1776, they all settled in a log cabin on land bought by one of the Shakers, about eight miles north of Albany. This was the beginning of the Shaker communities. Influenced by Mother Ann's preaching and the Shakers' hospitality, other people joined them and agreed to live a life involving no personal property, separation of the sexes, manual labor, cleanliness, the confession of sins, and religious services on Sundays that included fervent dancing and singing.

From this time until 1826, 19 different Shaker communities were founded around the eastern part of the United States. By the time of the start of the Civil War (1861), the Shakers had reached their largest total membership of over 5,000. Shakers formed a total of 24 communities in New York, Massachusetts, Connecticut, New Hampshire, Maine, Ohio, Kentucky, Indiana, Georgia, and Florida.

After the Civil War, their membership began to decline until the early 1900s, when most Shaker groups had dissolved. Today, a handful of members still live together in the Sabbathday Lake community in New Gloucester, Maine.

Beliefs and Practices

The Shakers believed that God was both male and female and that Jesus Christ was a spirit who appeared first in a male body and later in the female body of Ann Lee. While they read and followed the Bible, they also believed that people could receive communications from God in the present day. They followed principles that they considered to be true to the original Christianity: community property, pacifism, simple living, and celibacy.

Shaker worship services were designed to help members come into direct communication with God or spirits. During the early years when Ann Lee was alive, the group's services were not very structured: members sang, danced, and shouted as they felt called to do so, and some fell into trances during which they received visions or communications. In the late 18th century, Shakers began creating more formal dances and composing their own hymns (Andrews 1963, 138–141).

An eyewitness who spent four months with the Shakers in 1842 and 1843 reported that an elder would lead the dance, calling out instructions while several members sang. The dancing might take the form of marching in square or circular patterns. The dancers then formed a circle to see if anyone had received a "gift," or an inspiration from God to do something. Some members might whirl in response to a gift, and others might speak (Noyes 1961, 597; 603–604).

By the late 19th century, the Shakers were forced to stop the dances, because the members were becoming old. However, music continued to be important (Shaker FAQs 2008).

The Shakers believed they could communicate with the dead, and frequently reported communications from dead persons such as Ann Lee, Napoleon, Benjamin Franklin, and George Washington. Another important part of the Shaker religion was the confession of sins. Members were expected to confess their sins to an elder or eldress several times a year. Confession was encouraged but voluntary and could be done whenever a member felt the need (Andrews 1963, 154–155; Brewer 1986, 50–51).

The Shakers believed in the equality of all humans. Women and men were considered equal, although they worked, ate, and lived in separate areas. Women could and did serve as leaders within the Shaker community. The Shakers were against slavery and welcomed blacks and former slaves as members (Andrews 1963, 60, 214).

Order and cleanliness were important parts of Shaker belief. Their houses and furniture were designed to plainly reveal any dirt and to allow for easy cleaning. There were no rugs, no pictures, and no ornamentation to their houses, because those things were believed to catch the dirt. The walls of the rooms held pegs that were used to hang up the chairs so that sweeping would be easier and more efficient.

In addition to cleanliness, the Shakers loved orderliness. Cabinets and drawers were often built into the walls, and the Shakers created many different kinds of drawers and boxes to hold various supplies.

Orderliness extended to the way they behaved, as well. For example, rules at mealtime were written out. Shakers were to sit upright, to allow elders to serve themselves first, to clean their plates, and to cross knife and fork on the plate after a meal (Andrews 1963, 182–184).

Because of this order and cleanliness, visitors were often struck by the quietness, unhurriedness, and tranquility of the Shaker way of life.

Daily Life

The members of each Shaker community were divided into "families" of 30 to 100 people, governed by two elders and two eldresses. At each Shaker settlement there might be three or more such families. Each family lived and worked separately from the others. The men were called "brothers" and the women, "sisters" (Brewer 1997, 43; Kephart 1982, 213–214).

The Shakers believed that the women and men of one family should live under one roof. The men lived in one part of a house and the women in the other. Even though the Shakers considered women and men to be equal in the eyes of God, the two genders engaged in different work, with the women doing the cooking, cleaning, spinning, sewing, laundry, and other tasks traditionally done by women, while the men farmed, built buildings, made furniture, and performed other jobs traditionally done by men.

The daily schedule consisted of waking up between 4:00 and 5:30 a.m., depending on the season. The brothers went to their morning chores and the sisters made all the beds, put the rooms in order, and cooked breakfast. Before breakfast the sisters and brothers would pray in separate groups for 15 minutes. Meals were eaten silently for much of Shaker history. After breakfast everyone went to work until lunchtime, when they gathered again and prayed before the meal. After lunch, more work until supper, after which evening chores were performed. In the evenings, members met to pray, talk, dance, or sing. Bedtime was between 9:00 and 9:30 p.m. (Andrews 1963, 181–185; Kephart 1982, 217–219).

Although the men and women lived, worked, and ate separately, they did talk with each other several times a week at "union meetings." Four to 10 members of each gender met in one of the men's rooms, where they sat facing each other, about five feet apart. Each sister was matched with a brother of a similar age, with whom she could converse. Sometimes the meetings turned into singing sessions. The members joked with each other, ate fruits and nuts, drank cider, and even smoked pipes (Andrews 1963, 179).

Shaker food was plain but nourishing. At first food was scarce. Early members speak of not having butter, bread, milk, or cheese. The main foods during this time were porridges made of beans or rice. Later on, however, the Shaker farms and industries were productive and prosperous. Members ate a variety of vegetables, fruits, dairy products, and bread. Pork was forbidden at all Shaker communities, and some communities forbade all meat (Shaker FAQs 2008).

The Shakers wore simple, uniform clothes that did not reveal much about the body underneath. The men wore baggy pants and the women, long dresses with high collars, and caps on their heads.

How They Made Their Living

"Put your hands to work and your hearts to God," Mother Ann often said. "You must not lose one minute of time, for you have none to spare."

Work was very important to the Shakers. Their work was a form of worship, and although they did not get paid for doing their jobs, they believed in doing excellent work. Their products gained a good reputation for their high quality.

The Shakers farmed for their own needs and sold products to the outside world as well, including garden seeds, herbs, and some food, such as dried apples, dried sweet corn, fruit jellies, wine, canned vegetables, butter, cheese, and eggs. Leather goods, such as shoes and saddles, were made for use within the community and to sell to outsiders. The group also made and sold tin ware (cups, candlesticks, oil cans); shingles and bricks; brooms; wooden pails, bowls, boxes, and furniture; baskets; clothes; and hats.

Leadership and Decision Making

The Shakers did not believe in democracy when it came to choosing their own leaders. They felt people ought to be concerned with doing God's will and not with following their own wills.

When Mother Ann died in 1784, James Whittaker took over Shaker leadership. He was one of Mother Ann's followers from England, and apparently the other Shakers accepted him as their leader without any fight or fuss. He lived only three years more, and when he died, the new leader was chosen by an "assembly." The Shakers prayed and waited for a sign from God as to who their new leader should be. Several people felt called to mention Joseph Meacham, a preacher and someone whom Mother Ann had spoken of as "the wisest man that has been born of a woman for six hundred years" (Brewer 1986, 17). Meacham took over the leadership and appointed Lucy Wright to be the leader of the women. After Meacham died in 1796, Wright became the sole leader of the Shakers until 1821.

Each settlement (the Shaker community in a particular town) had its leaders, and each family within the settlement had its leaders. There were also people appointed to be in charge of the farm work, food production, money, child care, and so forth. The topmost leaders appointed or approved of the others, although new leaders were often selected by the previous leader. Leaders were chosen for qualities such as humility, kindness, and meekness. Even though the leaders were not elected by the people, they seem to have been trusted and followed without any conflict.

How New Members Were Recruited or Chosen

The Shakers held religious revival meetings in order to attract new converts to their way of life. Once someone decided to join the Shakers, she or he went through three stages. The first stage was that of a novitiate, who accepted the Shaker faith but continued to live a private life. Second was the Junior Order: people who had joined a Shaker community but who had not yet donated their private property to the community. The final stage, the Senior Order, was made up of those who had handed over all property, cut off all external family ties, and committed completely to the community (Oved 1988, 45).

Children and Youth

Although the community believed in celibacy and no children were born to people who were already Shakers, children often came into the community when their parents joined. The girls and boys were separated, and girls were raised by the women and boys by the men. The Shakers also taught the children within the community. At first, the children learned only reading and writing at noontime, and penmanship in the evenings. The youngsters were taught values such as honesty, punctuality, diligence, cleanliness, and respect. Gradually, as the communities expanded and grew, more academic subjects—mathematics, geography, astronomy, chemistry, and music, among them—were added, and the school day and school sessions were expanded (Kephart 1982, 216–217; Oved 1988, 53–54).

The Shaker schools were so well run that people from outside the community sometimes chose to send their children there. Despite the high quality of their schools, the Shakers were not interested in scholarly pursuits. They wanted their children to learn a trade instead of going on to college. The children were treated gently and fed well. At the age of 21, each young person could decide whether to join the Shakers or to go out into the world. To the Shakers' disappointment, most young people chose to go out into the world. Apparently, despite the good care they received with the Shakers, most young women and men did not wish to continue this simple life with no higher education, no marriage, and no children of their own (Oved 1988, 53–54; Kephart 1982, 221–223).

Relationship with the Outside World

Shakers were encouraged to keep separate from the outside world. The elders sometimes made it difficult for Shakers to contact or visit with members of their own family who were not Shakers. However, Shakers could not completely isolate themselves from the outside. They sold their products to the outside world. Their religious services were always open to the public, and they educated non-Shaker children in their schools. They gave away food and clothing to needy people who happened by. They welcomed writers and politicians who wanted to see what Shaker life was like. And they held religious meetings in order to attract more members to their faith.

While the Shakers lived peacefully for the most part with the outside world, there were occasional conflicts. Differences sometimes arose when members of a Shaker community decided to leave the community. Occasionally, such people demanded the return of the property they had originally given to the community, or demanded to be paid for their labor while living in the community. The Shakers felt that the property and labor that had been freely given belonged to the Shakers as a whole and not to any individual member. Former members were usually given some money, clothes, and tools with which to start their new life.

However, sometimes former members sued the Shakers in court to regain the property or wages they felt they were due. None of these cases was successful. In every case, the courts found that the Shakers had not coerced or forced anyone to join, to give up property, or to agree to work within the community. The courts agreed that the Shakers could hold their property in common and not return portions of it to members who left.

Another conflict arose when a parent took children into the community against the wishes of the other parent. One of the most famous cases concerned Mary and Joseph Dyer, who had both joined the Shaker community in Enfield, New Hampshire, in 1810, with their five children. Mary left the community about a year later. She wanted to take her two youngest children with her but was not allowed. In fact, her husband and the Shaker elders, fearing that she would flee with the children, did not allow her to even see her children before she left. In her distress, she sued the Shakers several times and also wrote books and pamphlets charging the Shakers with indecency and misconduct, including the abuse of children. Her claims were mostly fabricated. A court case determined that the Shakers were, in fact, appropriate guardians for children (Brewer 1986, 91–92).

The Shakers also refused to engage in military service, which caused some conflict with the outside world. For example, in 1780, the Shakers began preaching against war. Four men and two women, including Mother Ann, were arrested for trying to persuade others not to take up arms. Mother Ann was kept in prison for five months (Brock 1968, 274).

For many years the Shakers paid fines instead of allowing their young men to be conscripted into the army. However, later they came to see even these payments as aiding war efforts. For many years the Shakers were involved in legal battles on this issue, and as a result many states did pass laws exempting Shaker men from military duty and fines. By the time of the Civil War, the Shakers were instructing their young men to both refuse service and fines. Some Shakers were arrested and imprisoned for their antimilitary views (Brock 1968, 430–431, 828–829).

Reasons for Decline of the Community

The Shakers reached their peak membership around 1860. After that, membership declined, until by 1925, most Shaker communities were no longer in existence.

One reason for this decline was that, as more and more goods were being produced by factories, the Shakers could not compete economically with their handmade furniture and goods. Another reason may have been that, with the railroad and automobile, it was more and more difficult for the Shakers to remain isolated from the rest of the world. Younger Shakers may have been too tempted by the outside world to remain within this closed, restricted society. Many Shaker communities also lost money due to mismanagement, lawsuits, and stealing from within. In the past, many members joined the Shakers for the security the community provided: even those who were too young, sick, or old to work were cared for among the Shakers. But increasingly, the government began to provide assistance for people who could not provide for themselves (Oved 1988, 60; Kephart 1982, 226–228).

Influence on the Outside World

The Shakers' successful, long-lived communal way of life influenced many other communities. Shakers visited and were visited by members of other communities, including the Harmony Society, the Amana Colonies, and the Zoar Society.

The Shakers believed that, through celibacy and living in community, they could make their lives a "heaven on Earth"—a perfect society of peace, brotherhood, and purity. Along with these high ideals, they were also interested in making their work easier and invented a number of time- and labor-saving devices that reached the outside world.

For example, Shakers are credited with inventing the circular saw, the clothespin, the flat broom, a threshing machine, an improved washing machine, a fire engine and hose cart, a dough-kneading machine, a pea-shelling machine, and a cream separator, among many other things. They even invented hair caps for brethren who were bald. At first, Shakers did not believe in obtaining patents on their inventions. However, in later years they did apply for and receive several patents (Andrews and Andrews 1974, 152–159).

Probably the Shakers' greatest influence is in the area of furniture. Shakers developed their style of furniture because they believed in simplicity and a lack of unnecessary ornamentation. Also, simple furniture is easier and faster to make, which became important as the Shaker population expanded during the first half of the 19th century. Despite a lack of ornamentation, Shaker furniture is often strikingly beautiful. For Shakers, beauty was expressed through a harmony of shapes and an orderly, balanced design. Furniture originally made by Shakers is today in high demand and extremely expensive.

Like their furniture, Shaker buildings were also simple and without ornamentation, yet they could be beautifully balanced and harmonious. Several Shaker villages in New York, New England, and Kentucky are now preserved as historic sites.

A former Shaker village, New Lebanon, in New York, is now home to a Sufi community called Abode of the Message.

See also: Millennialism

References

Andrews, Edward Deming. *The People Called the Shakers: A Search for the Perfect Society*. New York: Dover Publications, 1963.

Andrews, Edward Deming, and Faith Andrews. *Work and Worship: The Economic Order of the Shakers*. Greenwich, CT: New York Graphic Society, 1974.

Brewer, Priscilla. *Shaker Communities, Shaker Lives*. Hanover, NH: University of New England Press, 1986.

Brewer, Priscilla. "The Shakers of Mother Ann Lee," in *America's Communal Utopias*, edited by Donald Pitzer. Chapel Hill: University of North Carolina Press, 1997, 37–56.

Brock, Peter. *Pacifism in the United States, from the Colonial Era to the First World War*. Princeton, NJ: Princeton University Press, 1968.

Holloway, Mark. *Heavens on Earth: Utopian Communities in America, 1680 to 1880*. New York: Library Publishers, 1951.

Kephart, William. *Extraordinary Groups: The Sociology of Unconventional Life-Styles,* 2nd ed. New York: St. Martin's Press, 1982.

Kirk, John. *The Shaker World: Art, Life, Belief*. New York: Harry N. Abrams, 1997.

Noyes, John Humphrey. *History of American Socialisms*. New York: Hillary House Publishers, 1961 (reprint of 1870 edition).

Oved, Yaacov. *Two Hundred Years of American Communes*. New Brunswick, NJ: Transaction Books, 1988.

Shaker FAQs, http://www.shakers.org/index.php?option=com_content&task=view&id=17 &Itemid=32 (accessed May 2008)

Web sites

Abode of the Message: www.theabode.net/ (accessed April 2006).

Canterbury Shaker Village, Canterbury, NH: www.shakers.org/ (accessed April 2006).

Sabbathday Lake Shaker Village, New Gloucester, ME: www.shaker.lib.me.us/ (accessed April 2006).

Skinner, B. F.

B. F. Skinner (1904–1990) was a psychologist who was involved in a field of study called "behaviorism." His theories inspired the formation of a few utopian communities, including Twin Oaks in Virginia.

Skinner built a box, called the "Skinner box," to study the behavior of rats and other small animals. He experimented to discover how to encourage the animals to perform certain behaviors, such as pushing a bar, by providing positive reinforcement—a pellet of food, for example.

Psychologist B. F. Skinner studied human and animal behavior in ingenious experiments that profoundly affected educational methods and theories. (AP/Wide World Photos)

In his novel *Walden Two* (first published in 1948), he showed how one might apply his animal experiments to human behavior. The novel describes a utopian community in which negative behaviors and emotions are limited through behavioral conditioning. For example, children are encouraged to develop self-control by hanging lollipops around their necks that they are not permitted to eat until later. The members of this community share work and income equally and have much time for leisure and the pursuit of the arts.

Skinner acknowledged that at the time he wrote *Walden Two*, the idea of applying behaviorism to humans was "little more than science fiction" (Skinner 1976, vi). The novel was controversial. However, since its publication, behavioral modification techniques have been shown to work successfully in mental institutions, workplaces, prisons, and even family settings.

Another controversial idea of Skinner's is the "air crib." In response to his wife's comment that baby care was difficult for the first two years, Skinner created an enclosed crib with a regulated temperature and a plastic sheet. The baby could sleep comfortably without any clothes on but a diaper. The crib helped cut down on laundry and was used only while the baby was sleeping. However, some people confused the air crib with the "Skinner box" and thought the baby was kept in it constantly.

See also: Literary Utopias; Twin Oaks Community

References

Nye, Robert. *What Is B. F. Skinner Really Saying?* Englewood Cliffs, NJ: Prentice-Hall, 1979.

Skinner, B. F. *Walden Two*. New York: Macmillan, 1948, reprinted with an introduction by the author, 1976.

Socialism

Socialism is the idea that the public, or the community, should own productive property, such as land and factories. At the basis of socialism is the idea that every human is equal to every other human and that everyone's basic needs should be met. Socialists disagree with the idea that some individuals can accumulate great wealth while the vast majority of people remain poor.

According to William Ebenstein and Edwin Fogelman, the idea of a group of people sharing wealth and property is an ancient one. For example, the New Testament's Book of Acts describes the early Christians as living without personal property or wealth, and sharing everything with each other, so everyone's basic needs were met. Christians throughout the centuries have formed monasteries and nunneries, where monks and nuns had no private property but shared whatever they needed. In 1516, an English statesman, Thomas More, wrote a fictional work called *Utopia*, which described an ideal society where people took turns farming and cooking food for each other and did not accumulate private wealth (1980, 207–208).

Modern socialist ideas arose in response to the poverty created by the Industrial Revolution, during which a few business owners became very wealthy while many workers were desperately poor. Socialist ideas led to the formation of a number of utopian communities based on the idea of community ownership and values of cooperation and sharing of wealth.

Socialism is a contrast to capitalism, and especially to British philosopher Adam Smith's idea that markets should not be controlled or regulated by the government, but should be allowed to operate freely. Smith, who wrote his influential book *The Wealth of Nations* in 1776, before the start of the Industrial Revolution, provided a rationale for government to stay out of business operations. Smith felt that the natural market forces of supply and demand would automatically ensure that workers received fair wages and that consumers had access to the goods and services they wanted.

However, the Industrial Revolution created factory owners who were so powerful that they could pay workers next to nothing and force them to work in dangerous, unsanitary conditions.

The word *socialism* was first used in the 1830s, but became common in the 1840s. Some of the first socialist writers were Henri de Saint-Simon, Francois-Marie-Charles Fourier, and Etienne Cabet in France, and Robert Owen in the United Kingdom.

Saint-Simon (1760–1825) and his followers felt that everyone should have an equal opportunity to get ahead. They disagreed with the reality that some people became wealthy and powerful just because they were born into wealthy, powerful families.

Fourier (1772–1837), a salesman, developed a hatred for competition and commerce. He created plans for model communities called "phalanges" (phalanxes) in which humans could choose a variety of work in line with their personalities and inclinations. His work inspired the creation of a series of communal utopias in the United States.

Cabet (1788–1856), a lawyer and political activist, wrote a novel, *Voyages en Icarie* (*Travels in Icaria*), which described an ideal society without money or private property. He formed a community in the United States called Icaria.

Owen (1771–1858) was an owner of a textile mill in Scotland. He felt that competition was at the root of the evils of industrialism, and he tried a number of different ways to insert cooperation into industry, such as by forming utopian communities in the United States and Great Britain and inspiring the trade union movement.

One of the most famous and influential socialists was German-born philosopher Karl Marx (1818–1883). With German journalist Friedrich Engels, he wrote *The Communist Manifesto* in 1848. He called his brand of socialism "scientific socialism." Marx looked down on many earlier socialists, calling them "utopian socialists." He said that his views were based not just on the wish to create a more just, equitable society, but on a scientific study of history.

Based on his study of history, Marx predicted that the oppressed workers of the Industrial Revolution would stage a violent revolt against the factory owners, take over the factories, and then rule as a "dictatorship of the proletariat." Eventually, Marx predicted, there would be no need for government at all and it would wither away.

Marx and other socialists later wrote that violent revolution was not the only way for workers to take charge; countries might also follow a peaceful path toward socialism.

Marx's brand of socialism was popular in Europe, and eventually, through the interpretation of Russian political activist Vladimir Lenin, led to the Communist governments of the Union of Soviet Socialist Republics (USSR—a federation of Russia and a number of nearby countries), some Eastern European countries, China, Cuba, North Korea, and Vietnam. This form of socialism relied on government ownership and control of factories, land, and other means of production. While the Communist governments often did achieve a more equitable distribution of wealth, they also suppressed individual freedom, imprisoning people who disagreed with the Communist Party. Instead of withering away, as Marx predicted, these Communist governments became all-powerful, controlling most aspects of people's lives. Most Communist governments ended in the 1990s.

Marx's form of socialism was never popular in the United States. Instead, the utopian socialists such as Albert Brisbane (a follower of Fourier), Cabet, and Owen were active in forming communities during the 1800s.

Socialists in the United States formed the Brotherhood of the Cooperative Commonwealths in 1895 with the idea of solving unemployment by starting colonies in western states. However, this idea was dismissed at a Socialist Party convention in 1898, because many socialists believed that starting communities would hinder them from their political work of transforming the entire culture (Oved 1988, 12–13). In the early 1900s, socialist political parties gained some power in the United States, especially under the leadership of Eugene V. Debs, who ran for U.S. president several times.

Despite the fact that the main American socialist organizations were not in favor of forming communities, in the late 1800s and early 1900s two American socialists

Karl Marx was an important figure in 19th-century Europe, but his status as the founder of modern communism has placed him among the most influential people in the history of the modern world. (Library of Congress)

and authors, Laurence Gronlund and Edward Bellamy, influenced the formation of utopian communities. Gronlund's book *Cooperative Commonwealth* inspired the founders of the Kaweah Cooperative Commonwealth and Ruskin. Bellamy's novel, *Looking Backwards 2000–1887*, advocated for government control of all industry, and inspired communities such as Llano del Rio and Point Loma.

While socialist political parties were never strong in the United States, socialist ideas have influenced the American government to pass laws regulating the behavior of business (child labor and minimum wage laws, for example) and laws providing help for those in need (such as Social Security and Medicare).

An important socialist holiday is May 1, also called International Workers Day or Labor Day in some countries. Some socialist communities chose to begin on this day, such as the Catholic Worker Movement and Llano del Rio.

See also: Anarchism; Bellamy, Edward; Bible Communism; Brook Farm and Fourierist Phalanxes; Capitalism; Catholic Worker Movement; Gronlund, Laurence; Icarian Movement; Industrial Revolution; Kaweah Cooperative Commonwealth; Llano del Rio and New Llano; New Harmony and Owenite Movement; Owen, Robert; Point Loma and Theosophical Communities; Ruskin; Twin Oaks Community; Valley of the Swans

References

Ebenstein, William, and Edwin Fogelman. *Today's Isms: Communism, Fascism, Capitalism, Socialism.* Englewood Cliffs, NJ: Prentice-Hall, 1980.

Jarnow, Jesse. *Socialism: A Primary Source Analysis.* New York: Rosen Publishing Group, 2005.

Oved, Yaacov. *Two Hundred Years of American Communes.* New Brunswick, NJ: Transaction Books, 1988.

"Socio-Economic Doctrines and Reform Movements." *The New Encyclopedia Britannica,* 2005 ed., vol. 27, 393–401.

Society of the Woman in the Wilderness

```
┌─────────────────────────────────────────────────────────────┐
│                        At a Glance                           │
│                                                              │
│  Dates of existence in United States: 1694 to 1708          │
│  Location: Pennsylvania                                       │
│  Peak membership: 40                                         │
│  Religious or other belief: Christianity, millennialism     │
└─────────────────────────────────────────────────────────────┘
```

The Society of the Woman in the Wilderness was one of the earliest communal ventures started in the New World. Despite its name, the community had no women; it was made up of men who lived in small cells. In this way it resembled a monastery.

The community had originally come together in Germany under the leadership of Jakob Zimmerman, who spoke out against the corruption within the Protestant Church. Zimmerman was persecuted for his views. He predicted that the millennium would begin in 1694. (The millennium refers to a period of 1,000 years of peace, to be preceded or followed by the return of Christ to Earth.) Zimmerman asked his followers to travel with him to the North American wilderness to await this event. Before they could sail for the New World, Zimmerman died, and a 20-year-old follower, Johann Kelpius, was named the new leader. The group decided to pool its resources in order to pay for the trip.

The group landed in Philadelphia in June 1694 and bought land along Wissahickon Creek. At first they lived in caves. Later, they built a large community building, which they called the "Tabernacle." The number 40 was a sacred number to them and symbolized perfection. Thus the Tabernacle was 40 feet square and contained 40 sleeping cells for members. The house also had a meeting hall and study rooms.

The members were pleased with the freedom offered in the New World. One member commented that in this new land "one can be peasant, scholar, priest and nobleman all at the same time without interference" (quoted in Durnbaugh 1997, 21).

Members studied and meditated together, awaiting the arrival of the millennium. Members engaged in the study of astronomy and spent hours on the roof of their building, examining the sky for signs of the final days of humanity. When 1694 passed with no sign, they continued to hope and to watch for signs (Sachse 1970, 107; Oved 1988, 21).

Kelpius hoped to unite all the Christian sects in Pennsylvania. The community invited the public to attend its religious services, held twice a day in the Tabernacle. Kelpius exhorted the worshippers to repent, because the millennium was drawing near. He made reference to a section of the New Testament Book of Revelation, which describes a woman who gives birth to a male child who is taken up by God.

The woman then flees to the desert to be taken care of by God. Kelpius taught that this "woman in the wilderness" was a sign for the approach of the millennium. Outsiders named the community the Society of the Woman in the Wilderness after this passage from the Book of Revelation. According to Julius Sachse, the community never called itself by this name. The members did not give themselves a name at all, but "desired to live in comparative seclusion, without name and . . . in love and religious harmony with all men" (Sachse 1970, 78–80).

Despite their preoccupation with the end of the world and their desire for seclusion, the members did engage with the outside world: they started a school for neighborhood children and sometimes attended other Christian services.

Kelpius and his followers also made contact with Native Americans. They wanted to ascertain whether the Native Americans were descendants of the 10 lost tribes of Israel, as was widely believed at that time. The community tried to find out whether the Native Americans kept a Sabbath day and attempted to learn about the philosophy and religious rites they practiced. Kelpius and his community also worked on converting the Native Americans to Christianity (Sachse 1970, 82–83).

In 1697, one prominent member, Heinrich Bernhard Koster, left the community and started his own—Irenia, or the True Church of Brotherly Love. Koster returned to Germany in 1699.

Over the years, members of the Society of the Woman in the Wilderness began to leave, and even though new members joined, the population of the community dwindled. Kelpius died in 1708, and no leader took his place. By this time the community had mostly disintegrated, although a few members continued to live there until their death.

In 1720, the fading community received a visit from Conrad Beissel, a Christian dissident who had traveled to Pennsylvania from Germany, hoping to join them. He was disappointed to find that it was no longer a viable community. Beissel went on to found his own community, the Ephrata Cloister. In 1741, the land and buildings belonging to Society of the Woman in the Wilderness were sold.

Sachse visited the site of the community in 1894, hoping to find some signs of the Tabernacle. He found "no trace whatever," although he did find a sort of cave or cell built into the side of a hill, which may have been a solitary retreat for Kelpius or another member of the community (1970, 211–213).

See also: Ephrata Cloister; Millennialism

References

Durnbaugh, Donald. "Communitarian Societies in Colonial America," in *America's Communal Utopias*, edited by Donald Pitzer. Chapel Hill: University of North Carolina Press, 1997, 19–22.

Oved, Yaacov. *Two Hundred Years of American Communes*. New Brunswick, NJ: Transaction Books, 1988.

Sachse, Julius Friedrich. *The German Pietists of Provincial Pennsylvania*. New York: AMS Press, 1970 (reprint of 1895 edition).

Steiner, Rudolf

Rudolf Steiner (1861–1925) developed a philosophy called "Anthroposophy" that influenced the formation of utopian communities, including the Camphill movement.

Steiner was born in a section of Austria that is now part of Croatia. As a child, he sensed that the spiritual world was just as valid and real as the physical world, yet he saw that the outside society did not justify his perception. During and after his university studies, he continued to search for a way to talk about and perceive the reality of the spiritual world (Wilson 1970, vii-viii).

He found that Theosophists shared many of his views. The Theosophical Society was founded in 1875 in New York City and spread worldwide. Theosophy is based on the idea that a spiritual reality exists, and that this spiritual reality can be directly experienced through meditation, studying sacred texts of many religions, and awakening one's psychic powers.

Steiner began lecturing at the German branch of the Theosophical Society. In 1902, he became the head of the society's German branch. In about 1912, he left the Theosophical Society over internal disagreements and formed the Anthroposophical Society. While the word *Theosophy* means *divine wisdom, Anthroposophy* means "wisdom of the human being," stressing Steiner's idea that humans have the innate capacity for spirituality within themselves.

It is not easy to define what Anthroposophy is, or how to practice it. Steiner said: "Anthroposophy is a path of knowledge, to guide the Spiritual in the human being to the Spiritual in the universe. It arises in man as a need of the heart, of the life of feeling; and it can be justified only inasmuch as it can satisfy this inner need" (Steiner 1973, 13). In other words, it is a way for humans to find their own spiritual nature and connect with the spirituality of the universe. In order to connect with one's own spiritual nature, Steiner advocated such practices as meditation and involvement with nature and the arts.

People from many different disciplines have used Steiner's philosophy to create institutions, programs, and movements. For example, Waldorf Schools help children develop by emphasizing the arts, nature, and handicrafts. The Biodynamic Farming and Gardening movement seeks not only to avoid the use of artificial chemicals, but actually to heal and nurture the Earth and plants. Anthroposophical medicine looks at the patient holistically, including the patient's spirituality.

See also: Camphill Movement; Point Loma and Theosophical Communities

References

Steiner, Rudolf. *Knowledge of the Higher Worlds and Its Attainment.* New York: Anthroposophy Press, 1947.

Steiner, Rudolf. *Anthroposophical Leading Thoughts.* London: Rudolf Steiner Press, 1973.

Wilson, Michael. "Introduction," in *The Philosophy of Freedom* by Rudolf Steiner. London: Rudolf Steiner Press, 1970.

WEB SITES

Biodynamic Farming and Gardening Association: www.biodynamics.com/biodynamics.html (accessed April 22, 2008).

Physician's Association for Anthroposophic Medicine: http://www.paam.net/ (accessed April 22, 2008).

Why Waldorf Works: www.awsna.org/ (accessed April 22, 2008).

Synanon

```
┌─────────────────────────────────────────────────────────────┐
│                        At a Glance                          │
│                                                             │
│  Dates of existence in United States: 1958 to 1991          │
│  Locations: California, New York, Michigan                  │
│  Peak membership: 2,000                                     │
│  Religious or other belief: drug addiction rehabilitation,  │
│  personal growth                                            │
└─────────────────────────────────────────────────────────────┘
```

History

Synanon made a name for itself as a successful residential community to treat drug addiction, morphed into a community that aimed to use powerful tools for personal growth to change the world, and ended up spiraling down into a void of alcoholism and violence.

The community was started by Chuck Dederich, a recovering alcoholic and an inspirational speaker at Alcoholics Anonymous (AA) meetings, who decided to do something to help drug addicts. At that time, AA did not allow people with addictions to nonalcoholic drugs to attend their self-help meetings. Drug-addicted individuals looking for help were generally sent to mental hospitals, where they were subjected to such treatments as solitary confinement and straitjackets; few were cured. Dederich, however, believed that a self-help approach could also be successful with people addicted to nonalcoholic drugs.

In 1958, Dederich rented a building in Venice, California, for his new organization and started with about 40 members. The name *Synanon* may have come from a member's mispronunciation of "symposium" or "seminar," or it may have been a play on the word *sinners* (Janzen 2001, 11).

A year later, Dederich moved the organization to Santa Monica and developed one of the most characteristic aspects of Synanon, known as "The Game." People gathered in a circle and players were asked to be brutally honest with each other. The goal was to prevent drug addicts from secretly using drugs by sniffing out lies and hypocrisy and to develop personal integrity and a sense of responsibility.

During the 1960s, Synanon opened communities in San Diego, San Francisco, New York City, and Detroit. Synanon claimed to have a cure rate of up to 80 percent. However, this could not be confirmed because the group refused to allow drug testing, and because most addicts who joined Synanon left within a few days or months. Nevertheless, there were enough success stories to attract the attention of the outside world. Celebrities and musicians with drug problems joined Synanon. Politicians such as California governor Jerry Brown took a great interest in Synanon. By the end of 1967, Synanon had 823 members (Janzen 2001, 24–25).

The community bought the Del Mar Club in Santa Monica in 1967 for $5 million. Santa Monica residents were suspicious of this racially integrated community of drug users. The city leaders claimed that they owned part of the property and ordered the police department to bulldoze part of the facility. That same year, Dederich moved the headquarters of the movement from Santa Monica to a rural area in Marin County, California (Janzen 2001, 27, 50–51).

In the late 1960s, with the advent of the hippie youth movement, more nonaddicts became interested in living at Synanon. Called "squares," these nonaddicts were expected to adhere to the same rules as the addicts, including playing The Game, being cheerful and hard working, and abiding by the rules of no alcohol, drugs, or violence. This marked the transition of Synanon from a community almost exclusively devoted to the rehabilitation of drug addicts to a community that hoped to use The Game and other personal growth tools to transform the world. The end of the 1960s and the beginning of the 1970s was also the period of the largest Synanon membership.

Starting in the 1970s, violence began to creep into Synanon life. In the mid-1970s, the community accepted a number of juvenile delinquents in an attempt to reform them. Leaders of this "punk squad," as it was called, began using physical violence at times to control the youth. Around the same time, Synanon began purchasing guns and established an armed security system. Dederich and other community members claimed they needed the weapons in order to protect themselves from outside persecution (Janzen 2001, 122–123).

In 1977, Dederich's wife, Betty, died. Dederich began drinking again. Some observers speculate that he may also have been suffering from manic-depressive disorder. In addition, a former member, Phil Ritter, was attacked by Synanon members that year and almost killed, because he sought custody of his daughter, who was still in the community. A lawyer, Paul Morantz, had sued Synanon on behalf of people who claimed their family members were wrongfully held in the community. In 1978, Morantz was attacked by a rattlesnake—with its rattles cut off—that had been placed in his mailbox. Two Synanon members were eventually sent to prison for this crime, and Dederich was fined $10,000 (Janzen 2001, 135–136, 182–184).

After the death of his wife, Dederich remarried and then called for all Synanon members to leave their current spouses or partners and choose new ones. He also announced that members should not have biological children and asked all male members to get vasectomies. These new rules caused many members to leave Synanon. Dederich moved away from a communal lifestyle when he began paying himself and other top leaders large salaries; in the past, everyone had lived on very modest monthly allowances. By 1982, Synanon membership had dropped to 700, and then to 370 by 1988 (Janzen 2001, 141–153, 180).

The final blow came when the federal government decided that Synanon was no longer a tax-exempt charity, because the community had strayed from the original purpose of drug rehabilitation and had become a profitable business. The government asked Synanon to pay $17 million in back taxes. This caused Synanon to declare bankruptcy, and the community was dissolved in 1991 (Janzen 2001, 214).

Beliefs and Practices

Dederich believed that drug addiction was not an illness, but a behavioral problem that could be addressed with the right social atmosphere. The Synanon philosophy is explained in a three-paragraph statement that emphasizes that people must accept themselves, work hard, do their best, and continue learning (Janzen 2001, 247).

Dederich coined the phrase, "Today is the first day of the rest of your life."

One of the most important aspects of Synanon life was The Game. Residents were required to play this three times per week. For many years, no physical violence or the threat of violence was allowed in The Game, but players were allowed to say anything they liked to others, including using profanity. Spectators as well as participants were allowed in the room, and in later years, The Game was taped.

A visitor described one game, in 1969, as beginning with Dederich introducing a subject: his concern about how a Synanon leader, visiting from another branch, had allowed this branch to deteriorate into sullenness, arguing, and whining. Next, other members took turns "backing the play" of Dederich, adding their own observations about the deterioration of the Synanon branch. In response, other people started criticizing the people who were criticizing the branch leader, and from there on, anyone could say anything to anyone else. The Game went on for over five hours, with people leaving and arriving at all times (Gerstel 1982, 9–20).

Outside of The Game, members of Synanon were to remain relentlessly cheerful, upbeat and gung ho about their work and life. The idea was that by expressing anger and other negative emotions within the controlled atmosphere of The Game, these emotions would not creep up in day-to-day life.

Some people found playing The Game exhilarating and effective at helping them live a sober life. "By identifying with others as well as ripping into them, participants tapped deep psychological resources, one addict assisting another," explains Rod Janzen (2001, 14).

Other people found The Game to be harsh and cruel. One player, who was not a drug addict and was new to The Game, said she was "emotionally raped," and that 11 years later she still felt traumatized (Janzen 2001, 209).

From the beginning, Synanon was committed to integration: not only racial integration, but also integrating people of different ages, social classes, skills and accomplishments, and viewpoints. Dederich's wife and an important community leader, Betty Dederich, was black. About 12 percent of the Synanon population was African American, and 10 percent was Latino. Members were encouraged to get to know other members with different backgrounds and to do jobs for which they had no experience. Women were encouraged to operate heavy construction equipment, for example (Janzen 2001, 57–59, 95–96).

Daily Life

Residents lived together in dorm-like rooms. Synanon buildings had the reputation for being sparkling clean and orderly. A visitor in 1969 describes seeing bunks with taut covers, glistening bathrooms, waxed floors, shiny machinery, and no litter or debris on the ground, even at construction sites (Gerstel 1982, 4–5).

More than 500 women from Synanon communities throughout California shaved their heads in a demonstration of women's liberation. The shaved heads symbolize Synanon women's acceptance of an equal responsibility with Synanon men for the management and operation of the foundation, which re-educated drug addicts, juvenile delinquents, and other character-disordered people. (Bettman/Corbis)

Dress was casual, and often members wore donated clothes. Many members wore overalls. Newcomers were allowed few personal possessions. Members with higher status—those who had been promoted to important jobs, for example—enjoyed more material benefits. For example, a dormitory manager might have a private room with a television or record player.

Members who broke community rules had their hair cut very short—including women. At one point in the mid-1970s, all the members, including women, decided voluntarily to shave their heads, and this became community policy. When they went out in public, Synanon members were conspicuous with their overalls and shaved heads (Janzen 2001, 21, 126).

Residents lived on donated food. At first, such food consisted of dishes like home-made stew made from stale sandwiches donated by a catering company. Members ate meals together at round tables with lazy Susans built into the middle, so everyone could help themselves. "Grazing tables" provided donated food to members 24 hours per day (Janzen 2001, 12, 23, 104).

One unusual way of structuring life was called the "Cube," which was started in 1968. The Cube consisted of a cycle of 28 days: 14 days involved 10- to 14-hour work-days, followed by 14 days of self-reflection and relaxation. Synanon experimented with various configurations of The cube, as well as other unusual cycles.

Synanon members enjoyed getting involved in all sorts of activities in their free time, such as theatrical performances, music, dancing, crafts, sports, and martial arts. Daily aerobic exercises were required of all members for many years. A number of addicted musicians joined Synanon, and jazz music was an important part of Synanon life (Janzen 2001, 98–103).

How They Made Their Living

Synanon members and outside supporters were encouraged to donate generous amounts of money to the community.

Synanon members engaged in what they called "hustling," which meant asking local and national businesses for donations. Synanon, in turn, gave away excess hustled products to other worthy causes, such as the United Farm Workers, a union of mainly Mexican American farm laborers. Because companies could get tax deductions for donating items, Synanon received millions of dollars worth of donations, including furniture, lumber, food, clothing, and medical supplies. Eventually, Synanon had to rent warehouse space to store these donations (Janzen 2001, 28–30).

The community also ran businesses such as gas stations. One successful business was called AdGap, which imprinted products such as coffee mugs, pencils, and clothing with company names and logos. Its customers were major corporations. AdGap continued to be a successful company as of 2007 (Janzen 2001, 49–50).

Leadership and Decision Making

Chuck Dederich was in charge of Synanon, and the community was not democratic. Dederich appointed a board of directors to serve under him. Under the board were department heads, facilities directors, and general managers. Each Synanon branch had its own local leadership cabinet for local decisions.

For many years, members were allowed to express new ideas and criticize Synanon policies during games. Dederich and other leaders could be "gamed" and criticized for their personal and leadership flaws. However, after Dederich's wife, Betty, died in 1977, he no longer allowed anyone to game him or to criticize leadership decisions (Janzen 2001, 15, 31–32).

How New Members Were Recruited or Chosen

Synanon sent recovered drug addicts to give public talks across the country. Synanon communities also held Saturday night open houses for nonmembers and operated "Game Clubs," in which nonmembers played The Game.

Potential members were interviewed to determine whether they were willing to engage in radical personal change. If the person was a drug addict, he or she was then placed on a couch in a public area to undergo withdrawal from the drugs while being cared for by other Synanon members. New members were given the most menial jobs in the community, such as washing dishes. With time, they could move up to better jobs.

Children and Youth

In the middle to late 1960s, when nonaddicts began joining Synanon with their children, Synanon set up communal child care arrangements and community schools.

The Synanon communal child care system was influenced by communal child care at Israeli kibbutzim, which Synanon members read about. Infants remained with their parents for the first six months, after which time they were cared for communally. Parents sometimes lived in different branches of Synanon than their children.

Children under two lived in the "hatchery." From two to four, they were in the lower school. The goal was to allow the children to initiate play without much adult interference. From the age of three, the children were expected to make their own beds and do simple chores. They began doing academic work at four and continued until the age of 13. The teachers were called "demonstrators," and there was one demonstrator for every three or four students.

Youths over 13 spent 12 hours per week doing a series of apprenticeships within the community, such as work in the kitchen, in the auto shop, or caring for animals. They also learned the usual high school academic subjects.

The Synanon school system was eclectic and open to experimenting with different ideologies. According to Rod Janzen, one school might operate with free-form learning centers, and another school might feature marching and drilling. Often, the students learned by doing: they might figure out how to build a water supply system, or go on a field trip to Sacramento to learn California history (2001, 73–77).

Deborah Swisher, who was raised at Synanon from the age of 7 to 18, comments that she refused to learn to read in conventional school, but upon coming to Synanon she learned to read in two weeks. "Synanon was like summer school, it seemed too fun" (quoted in Morgan 1999).

Synanon also started a college called the Academy. This was formed partly because Dederich wanted Academy students to plan and design an ideal "Synanon City." The Academy "was to be the place where the best and the brightest, the most self-actualized, would search together for the soul of the universe," as Janzen puts it (2001, 81).

Dederich hoped that the future Synanon City would be a "beacon to the world. . . . We're going to build a city that will demonstrate just how high the quality of life can be pushed if people are willing to make that little step to trusting and cooperating with each other" (quoted in Gerstel 1982, 32).

One controversial aspect of child rearing at Synanon was the fact that children as young as three participated in the Synanon game. Children were allowed to critique each other as well as their teachers and other adults. Some outside observers noted that, outside The Game, the children rarely argued or fought, and that The Game taught them to speak assertively. However, former members and teachers later felt that The Game might have been emotionally damaging to the children, who were not ready to deal with such harsh criticism (Janzen 2001, 78–80).

Relationship with the Outside World

On the one hand, medical professionals, politicians, and other outsiders were often impressed with Synanon's work with drug addicts. On the other, outsider neighbors were sometimes suspicious of the interracial, bald-headed, overall-wearing community members. A Synanon bus was shot at in the 1960s. Teenagers in automobiles reportedly tried to hit Synanon children, and members reported bomb threats (Janzen 2001, 131).

Reasons for Decline of the Community

Synanon declined and finally ended in 1991 for a number of reasons. Dederich began drinking and perhaps suffered from a mental illness. Because Synanon was not democratic and depended heavily on his leadership, changes in his personality affected the entire community. Members became disillusioned by new rules (no childbirth, new marriage partners) and by the acceptance of violence within the community. The Internal Revenue Service ruling that Synanon owed millions in back taxes was the final nail in the coffin.

Influence on the Outside World

Synanon pioneered a new way to treat drug addicts. Synanon members were influential in the "therapeutic communities" movement—residential treatment centers that employ a group-based, communal approach to treatment. After leaving Synanon, many members worked as counselors in the therapeutic communities movement (Janzen 2001, 2).

See also: Hippies

References

Gerstel, David. *Paradise, Incorporated: Synanon.* Novato, CA: Presidio Press, 1982.

Janzen, Rod. *The Rise and Fall of Synanon, a California Utopia.* Baltimore, MD: The Johns Hopkins University Press, 2001.

Morgan, Fiona. "One Big Dysfunctional Family: A Former Member of the Synanon Cult Recalls the 'Alternative Lifestyle' That Shaped Her, for Better and Worse." *Salon,* March 29, 1999, www.salon.com/mwt/feature/1999/03/29feature.html (accessed August 2007).

WEB SITES

AdGap—Integrated Marketing Solutions: www.adgap.com/ (accessed August 2007).

Association of Therapeutic Communities: www.therapeuticcommunities.org/ (accessed August 2007).

Synanon Museum: www.synanon.org/Synanon/Museum/ (accessed August 2007).

Transcendentalism

The American philosophy of Transcendentalism gave rise to two utopian communities: Brook Farm, which is profiled elsewhere in this book, and Fruitlands, described below.

The first and most famous American Transcendentalist was Ralph Waldo Emerson, the son of a Unitarian minister who, after his father's early death, grew up in poverty and hardship. Emerson went on to study at Harvard Divinity School, where he learned about the ideas of the German philosopher Immanuel Kant from a friend who had traveled in Germany. Kant concluded that the mind, through intuition, could transcend the experiences of the senses, and so called his philosophy "transcendental."

Emerson became a Unitarian pastor of the Second Church in Boston in 1829. However, he grew more and more dissatisfied with the traditional rituals of the church, including communion, in which the wine and bread were said to be the blood and body of Christ. He came to believe that it was better for humans to approach God directly, rather than through ancient writings (the Bible) and ancient rituals. He gave up his lucrative job and turned to lecturing to support himself. In addition, with the death of his first wife, he received an inheritance from her estate that enabled him to be somewhat financially independent.

In 1836, he wrote a poetic essay called *Nature* and had it published anonymously. This was the first written exploration of the new philosophy that would come to be called "American Transcendentalism." *Nature* praises the beauty and wonder of nature, and exhorts readers to see God in nature, instead of looking for God in old texts and histories.

After the publication of this book, Emerson gathered interested people together for the "Transcendental Club," named after Kant's philosophy. The club members, who included a number of Unitarian ministers, met periodically to discuss topics such as educational reform, religion versus morality, and why American society has not produced genius. Emerson invited women to participate in the Transcendental Club. He also began a magazine, *The Dial*, to publish writing that reflected their views.

Although Transcendentalists did not share a common belief system—they believed in freedom of thought more than anything else—in general, Transcendentalists opposed slavery, war, and class distinctions and were in favor of challenging the male domination in society. Emerson lectured against the evils of slavery, and *The Dial* published an article about women's rights by Margaret Fuller. In one of his most famous essays, "Resistance to Civil Government," Henry David Thoreau argued that individual conscience was more important than the laws of the land. The Transcendentalists were also some of the first Americans to become interested in Eastern religions such as Buddhism and Hinduism.

Ralph Waldo Emerson, the leader of the Transcendentalism movement, was one of the foremost American writers and thinkers of the 19th century. (Library of Congress)

One member of the Transcendental Club was a Unitarian minister named George Ripley. He wanted to bring these ideas to life in a utopian community, so he started a community called Brook Farm in 1841. Few of the other members of the Transcendental Club joined him, although he attracted many outsiders. Nathaniel Hawthorne, an early member of Brook Farm, was not formally a member of the Transcendental Club—he was extremely shy and avoided gatherings—but he was a friend of club members.

Another Transcendental Club member, Bronson Alcott, started a community in 1843 that he called "Fruitlands." Alcott was the father of Louisa May Alcott, who would later become famous as the author of the children's classic *Little Women*.

Bronson Alcott was an educational reformer who had experimented with teaching methods and started schools in the 1820s and 1830s. He was influenced by Swiss educational reformer Johann Pestalozzi. Louisa May Alcott explains: "My father taught in the wise way which unfolds what lies in the child's nature, as a flower blooms, rather than crammed it, like a Strasbourg goose, with more than it could digest." Bronson Alcott himself told the students that "all truth is within. My business is to lead you to find it in your own Souls." Alcott did not believe in physically punishing the students (quoted in Schreiner 2006, 37, 39–40).

Alcott and his assistant, Elizabeth Peabody, held conversations with the students to bring forth their innate wisdom. Some of these conversations were collected into a book. Unfortunately, when the book came out in 1836, the public was shocked because some of the discussions involved talking, in an oblique way, about birth. Many parents withdrew their children from the school. At this point, Alcott admitted a black child to the school, and the rest of the parents withdrew their children (Schreiner 2006, 50–51).

Although the school folded, Alcott's philosophy inspired the formation of a school in England called Alcott House. Alcott visited the school in 1842. Two men involved with the school, Charles Lane and Henry Wright, became so inspired by Alcott's speeches that they returned to the United States with him, for the purpose of forming a community based on Alcott's ideas.

Alcott's ideas were influenced by Brook Farm, but he intended his community to observe another principle: not exploiting animals. Members would be strict vegetarians, eating no animal products and avoiding even root vegetables. Animals would not be used for plowing the land, and even animal manure would not be used for fertilizer. Members were not to wear wool or leather, or even cotton, which was produced by slave labor. In addition, members were not to consume tea, coffee, alcohol, or tobacco.

With money provided by Lane, Alcott bought a farmhouse and a 90-acre farm in Harvard, Massachusetts. In June 1843, Alcott, his wife, and four daughters moved in, along with Charles Lane and his son, and a few others. Alcott compromised his principles enough to hire a man and a team of animals to plough the land and even to plant root vegetables.

The daily schedule at Fruitlands consisted of waking up early, taking a cold bath, and then eating breakfast after a musical interlude. Members worked or pursued their own interests until after lunch, when they gathered for conversation. Afternoons were dedicated to work, followed by an evening meal and more conversation (Gutek and Gutek 1998, 147).

The vegetables did not do well, though, because the ground had not been fertilized. Furthermore, Lane and Alcott were often away from the community on speaking engagements. An early frost destroyed most of the crops. The members were at risk of starvation. In December, Alcott's wife, Abba, persuaded him to move in with a nearby farm family who had offered them shelter. Charles Lane and his son left the community to join the Shakers. By January 1844, the Fruitlands experiment was over (Schreiner 2006, 117–118).

Fruitlands failed because of too many principles and not enough practical application. Although the community was extremely short-lived, the building that housed the Fruitlands members was restored in 1914 by Clara Endicott Sears, who was inspired by Alcott's vision. The house also contains collections of Shaker artifacts, a Native American collection, and a picture gallery of Hudson River School landscapes, all collected by Sears.

American Transcendentalism, and the two communities inspired by it, had a great influence on American culture, despite the small numbers of people involved. The movement gave rise to some of the most influential writers of our country, including Emerson, Thoreau, Hawthorne, Fuller, and Louisa May Alcott.

American reformer Bronson Alcott pioneered child-centered education and is considered a forerunner of John Dewey in his new educational philosophy. As a Transcendentalist, he joined many reform efforts of the time and started the experimental Temple School and a utopian community called Fruitlands during the early 19th century. (Library of Congress)

See also: Brook Farm and Fourierist Phalanxes; Shakers

References

Francis, Richard. *Transcendental Utopias*. Ithaca, NY: Cornell University Press, 1997.

Gutek, Gerald, and Patricia Gutek. *Visiting Utopian Communities: A Guide to the Shakers, Moravians, and Others*. Columbia: University of South Carolina Press, 1998.

Schreiner, Samuel A., Jr. *The Concord Quartet: Alcott, Emerson, Hawthorne, Thoreau, and the Friendship That Freed the American Mind*. Hoboken, NJ: John Wiley and Sons, 2006.

WEB SITE
Fruitlands Museum: www.fruitlands.org/ (accessed May 2007).

Twin Oaks Community

At a Glance

Dates of existence in United States: 1967 to present
Location: Virginia
Peak membership: 100
Religious or other belief: socialism, equalitarianism

History

Although Twin Oaks is small by historic standards (only 100 members), it is one of the longest-lived and most successful of the secular utopian communities.

In 1966, a conference was held in Michigan with the idea of launching a real community based on the novel *Walden Two* by B. F. Skinner, which describes a utopian community in which members share work and income, enjoy much leisure time, and people's negative emotions and behaviors are limited through behavioral modification training. While the conference organizers did not produce a community, several of the participants decided to form a community themselves (Kuhlmann 2005, 48–50).

One of these people used his own money to buy a farm for the group. Twin Oaks began in June 1967 on a farm in rural Virginia (Louisa County), with eight members. During their first two years, they put into place a labor credit system, began making rope hammocks to sell, constructed a few buildings, and struggled with leadership issues, personality clashes, unsuitable members, and lack of money.

One of the biggest problems was community members leaving. Things were so difficult at times that in November and December 1969, one of the founders was afraid that the community would fold. There were only 10 members at that point, down from a high of 22. The community decided to dispense with the entrance fee (which was $200 at the time) and to open the membership to anyone who wished to join, with the idea that they could expel people who refused to work. New members began to arrive, and the community began pulling itself out of debt (Kinkade 1973, 267). Since then, the community has prospered and grown to 100 members.

Beliefs and Practices

One might expect that a community founded on the principles of *Walden Two* would try to incorporate behavioral modification and scientific child rearing into its beliefs and practices. However, one of the founders, Kat Kinkade, admits that she did not at first realize that Skinner's ideas, as applied to humans, were fiction. Also, at the Michigan conference, Kinkade was disillusioned by the psychologists present, who were apparently planning a "psychologist-king" role for themselves in the proposed community, whereas Kinkade saw their role as "technical consultants" (Komar 1983, 10–11). Kinkade was more interested in the happy, harmonious community depicted in *Walden Two* than in the behavioral engineering aspect of the work (Kuhlmann 2005, 83–84).

Nevertheless, the Twin Oakers did make some attempt at integrating Skinner's ideas. Early on, they built an "air crib," as described in *Walden Two,* for a community baby. It had Plexiglas sides so the baby could be seen from all sides, a built-in humidifier and thermostat, and an intercom to the mother's room. The baby was able to sleep in its crib with no clothes but a diaper and be warm and comfortable. The baby and mother in question left soon after, and the crib was dismantled and put away. The community also held a psychology class to teach its members about behavioral modification techniques. Some members used these techniques to cure themselves of fears or bad habits, but participation was voluntary (Kinkade 1973, 258–265).

Today, Twin Oaks does not claim to have any connection with the theories in *Walden Two*. However, the community still uses a leadership system and labor-credit system based on those described in the book. "In general our approach to systems has been to take first the ones described in *Walden Two* and stick to them as long as they work well," Kinkade wrote. "As we find fault with them, we then make changes to correct the faults and make the systems fit our situation better" (Kinkade 1973, 57–58).

The firmest and most enduring belief at Twin Oaks is economic and social equality. As described on the Twin Oaks Web site (www.twinoaks.org/):

> Each member here has equal access to our decision-making process; we all have a voice in making decisions, unlike hierarchical communities where a sub-group of the community or a single individual makes decisions for the whole. This value also plays out in how we share our resources. We all have an equal opportunity to access our resources; there is no individual or group here that has access to community resources that others don't. We have no structured inequality as can be found in the mainstream (one example: there is no disparity here between what women and men or new members and long-term members receive as compensation for their labor). However, we also balance this with our creed "From everyone according to co's abilities, to everyone according to co's needs" ("co" is our gender-neutral pronoun that means "s/he").

Twin Oaks is a member of the Federation of Egalitarian Communities and abides by its standards, which include holding land and resources in common; assuming responsibility for the needs of members; nonviolence; allowing members an equal opportunity to participate in decision making; working toward equality and not allowing discrimination based on race, ethnicity, age, gender, or sexual orientation; and conserving natural resources.

Twin Oaks is a secular community and members adhere to a variety of spiritual persuasions. The community as a whole celebrates the solstices and equinoxes, its founding day (June 16), Halloween, and Thanksgiving. It has an official "holiday manager" to organize celebrations. Other members might hold pagan rituals, Quaker meetings, Friday night Shabbat services, or meditation groups, or they might attend church nearby.

Daily Life

As of 2008 the community owned 465 acres, seven group residences, a children's building, a community center with communal kitchen, industrial buildings and workshops, and other structures. Most buildings are heated by solar or wood heat. Much of the Twin Oaks property is wooded, with tree-shaded paths between buildings.

Every adult member has a single room in one of the residence buildings. Bathrooms and living areas are shared, and each residence hall has its own kitchen for snacks. Members generally eat meals in the central dining hall.

All Twin Oaks members must work an equal amount of time. The number of required work hours has varied with the economic health of the community. As of 2008, members were required to work 42 hours per week. This "work" includes not just income-generating activities, but also tasks such as child care, cleaning, cooking, laundry, lawn maintenance, household repairs, and community meetings.

For some years, Twin Oaks experimented with a system in which more desirable jobs were awarded a lower labor credit than less desirable jobs. Such a system was recommended in *Walden Two* and in Edward Bellamy's novel *Looking Backward 2000–1887*. However, members soon found out that almost any job is attractive to someone. Today, all work earns one labor credit per hour. Members are assigned to work of their choice as much as possible, and most people work at a variety of different tasks during a given week. Twin Oakers earn vacation time by working extra hours and earning more labor credits. Members take about eight weeks of vacation per year.

The community takes care of all members' needs, such as food, clothing, housing, and health care. Members also receive a small pocket-money allowance for such things as candy and gifts. But members do not share absolutely everything. They are allowed to keep personal belongings that they brought into the community; they may earn personal money by working while on vacation; and they are allowed to accept gifts of cash from parents or others in the outside world. This extra money is meant to be spent away from the community.

The Twin Oaks kitchen tries to cook food to satisfy all members' dietary inclinations, including those of meat eaters, vegans, and those with allergies. Recreational drugs are not allowed in Twin Oaks. Depending on the community's income, coffee may or may not be available. Candy, alcohol, and other nonessentials are generally not provided but can be bought with personal allowance money.

How They Make Their Living

When the community was first founded, members had to work outside the community in order to bring in income.

By 1975, the community became completely self-supporting when it was awarded a large contract by Pier One Imports (a retail store) for its rope hammocks. In addition to making and selling hammocks and hammock chairs, Twin Oaks also earns money by making tofu and other soy products and through indexing books.

In general, Twin Oaks members must turn over to the community any income they derive from outside sources, such as Social Security payments, child support payments, or interest from a bank account. The only exception to this is money earned while on vacation, to be spent on vacation.

Twin Oaks produces much of its own food, such as vegetables, dairy products, and meat. Members build their own buildings. Because the per-capita income of Twin Oakers is low, members generally qualify for government-subsidized health care.

Leadership and Decision Making

The government of Twin Oaks is based on one described in the novel *Walden Two*. The leaders are called planners and managers.

The community has three planners who serve 18-month staggered terms. They make long-range policy decisions and control the resources of the community. Planner candidates are selected by the other planners and then must be voted in by at least 80 percent of the community members.

There are about 75 managers in the community, in charge of such things as the businesses, the residences, the vehicles, and the gardens. Any member can volunteer to be a manager. Potential managers are then interviewed and "hired" by a group of other managers in related areas, called a "council." Since the manager job is not a full-time job, a person can be a manager in one area and a worker in another area.

If a member disapproves of a decision made by a planner or manager, that member can appeal the decision to a higher governmental body: managerial decisions are appealed to the council; council decisions are appealed to the planners; and planner decisions are appealed to a vote by all the members.

Members can also voice their opinion by talking personally to leaders; at public meetings; through a bulletin board, called the "'O and I' Board," on which members can post papers on any subject and ask for feedback; and through the "Trade-Off Game," in which each member is asked to allocate money to the various departments and balance the budget for the coming year. The planners take everyone's Trade-Off Game into account when distributing the money.

A founder of the community, Kat Kinkade, compares the Twin Oaks governance to two other common forms of secular community governance: consensus decision making (members discussing issues until they can all come to a common agreement) and direct democracy (members voting on every issue). "Like consensus procedures (but unlike direct democracy), our system enables us to make compromises that include minority interests. Unlike consensus, it doesn't always leave everyone feeling satisfied. But it takes much, much less time than consensus, and that time is precious to us" (Kinkade 1994, 22).

How New Members Are Recruited or Chosen

Those who want to join Twin Oaks are asked to visit for three weeks. After this period, they are asked to leave while the community decides whether to accept them. In the interim, prospective members must get physical check-ups and deal with any outstanding medical or dental problems. If accepted, they become "provisional members" for six months. Provisional members are not allowed to vote and also must pay for their own care related to pre-existing medical conditions. After six months, they are accepted as full members, or are voted out. Full members must sign a membership agreement stating their willingness to abide by community rules.

Children and Youth

At first, the founders of Twin Oaks decided that children would be raised by the community as a whole and not by their parents. For many years (from the early 1970s to the mid-1990s), Twin Oaks children lived separately from their parents in a special children's house. Nevertheless, they did often sleep and eat with their parents. Starting at about age 10, children got their own private room in a residence hall where at least one of their parents lived.

The communal child care system began to unravel because parents wanted more responsibility for and contact with their children. Today, each child is allotted a certain number of labor credits for child care. These labor credits can be performed by parents and/or by other community caregivers.

Children at Twin Oaks are educated in different ways. For years, many attended a Twin Oaks cooperative school called Oakley. Today, some children are home schooled by members of the community and others are sent to the local public school.

Because child care is a community responsibility, Twin Oaks is careful about how many children are accepted or born into the community. It attempts to have a limit of 15 children at a time.

Relationship with the Outside World

The Twin Oaks Web site states: "Although we are interested in creating a culture that is distinct from the mainstream, we are not interested in isolating ourselves from the mainstream" (www.twinoaks.org/). Twin Oakers read newspapers, listen to the radio, and are connected to the Internet. They interact with the outside world when shopping or volunteering in the nearest town and when selling their products or services. Twin Oakers often visit nearby cities—Richmond, Charlottesville, and Washington, D.C. They host an annual Women's Gathering, open to all women and girls, and an annual Communities Gathering, open to the interested public. They welcome visitors for tours on Saturdays.

Influence on the Outside World

In the 1970s, interest in Twin Oaks was widespread. The community was covered in *Time* magazine as a real-life example of B. F. Skinner's theories. Sections of a book about Twin Oaks, *A Walden Two Experiment*, were excerpted in the magazine *Psychology Today*, and in 1979, Skinner's visit to the community was covered on the television program *60 Minutes*. Around the same time, a German movie about Twin Oaks sparked about a thousand German visitors to the community (www.twinoaks.org/; Kuhlmann 2005, 196; Komar 1983, 72–74).

Gradually, outside interest in Twin Oaks has faded, although it is still famous among those interested in utopian communities.

The Twin Oaks governance system and labor-credit system have been adopted by other communities. Twin Oaks has also helped to found other communities such as East Wind (in Missouri) and Acorn (in Virginia).

East Wind has about 75 members and was founded in 1973. It rivals Twin Oaks as one of the longest-lived of the secular utopian communities. The community's beliefs and structure are similar to those at Twin Oaks. East Wind helps produce Twin Oaks hammocks and also produces its own line of nut butters and crafts.

The Future of the Community

Kinkade speculated as to why Twin Oaks has survived for so long when so many other secular communities have failed. Here are her reasons: "We get the work done, and we have enough work equality so that members don't feel badly ripped off by each other. . . . We keep enough money coming in. . . . We maintain a communal economy and hold a rein on personal consumption. . . . We keep the door open [to new members]. . . . We leave people's minds alone. . . . We have systems. . . . We have freedom. . . . We're big enough to survive upheavals and turnover" (Kinkade 1994, 5).

Originally, Twin Oaks was meant to replicate the community described in *Walden Two*. It was meant to grow and then split in two, with one of the groups going off to form a new community (Kinkade 1973, 271).

Members resisted this kind of growth. Today, Twin Oaks is a stable community that is not growing. However, it is thriving, and it has succeeded in figuring out how to make a secular, income-sharing community work. Its time-tested governance and labor systems are an example to other communities.

See also: Bellamy, Edward; Literary Utopias; Skinner, B. F.; Socialism

References

Jones, Tamara. "The Other American Dream." *Washington Post Magazine*, November 15, 1998, W12, www.twinoaks.org/community/media/articles/washington-post.html (accessed September 2006).

Kinkade, Kat. *A Walden Two Experiment*. New York: Quill, 1973.

Kinkade, Kat. *Is It Utopia Yet? An Insider's View of Twin Oaks Community in Its 26th Year*. Louisa, VA: Twin Oaks Publishing, 1994.

Komar, Ingrid. *Living the Dream: A Documentary Study of Twin Oaks Community*. Louisa, VA: Twin Oaks Publishing, 1983.

Kuhlmann, Hilke. *Living Walden Two: B. F. Skinner's Behaviorist Utopia and Experimental Communities*. Urbana: University of Illinois Press, 2005.

Skinner, B. F. *Walden Two*. New York: Macmillan, 1948, reprinted with an introduction by the author, 1976.

WEB SITES
East Wind Community: www.eastwind.org/ (accessed September 2006).
Federation of Egalitarian Communities: http://thefec.org/ (accessed September 2006).
Twin Oaks Intentional Community: www.twinoaks.org/ (accessed May 2008).

Valley of the Swans

At a Glance

Dates of existence in United States: 1663 to 1664
Location: Delaware
Peak membership: about 41
Religious or other belief: Christianity, "Collegiant"

The Valley of the Swans is considered to be the first utopian community in what was to become the United States. It was surprisingly liberal in its philosophy and far ahead of its time.

The community was founded by Pieter Cornelius Plockhoy of Holland. He was a leader of a group of "Collegiants" in Amsterdam. Collegiants were liberal Christians from a number of different churches. They stood for freedom of religion, speech, and thought. They also believed in the separation of church and state. Although they did not consider themselves members of a religion, Collegiants held meetings on Sundays, during which they read from the Bible, prayed, and listened to a lecture on the implications of their reading for the world. The only requirement to attend a Collegiant meeting was a belief in the Bible. "They insisted on the complete toleration for divergent ideas," according to Leland Harder. They were also concerned with social justice (1952, 10, 14–16).

Plockhoy was interested in helping poor people and wrote a tract called *A Way Propounded to Make the Poor in These and Other Nations Happy*. His plan called for self-supporting cooperative societies, similar to those proposed much later by socialists such as Charles Fourier in the 19th century. Plockhoy traveled to England and attracted the interest of powerful figures, including Oliver Cromwell, who was the ruler of England during the "interregnum"—the time between kings, after Parliament had defeated King Charles I.

Cooperative societies were attempted in England and Ireland. Plockhoy proposed that these societies should tolerate diverse opinions and beliefs. His societies were to be divided into four classes: farmers, craftsmen, mariners, and masters of arts and sciences. Each class was to elect an overseer, and the overseer was to work the same number of hours as the others. Women were not included in this structure: they were to work at keeping house. Boys and girls were to attend school for three hours per day and spend three hours learning a trade. Although the members of these societies were to pool their labor, they were not to own all property in common (Harder 1952, 19, 33–35).

After the death of Cromwell and the Restoration of King Charles II to the throne in 1660, the societies were not able to be realized in England or Ireland.

Plockhoy returned to Holland and looked to the New World for a site for his community. The Dutch government controlled part of the New World colonies, including a section along the South River (today called the Delaware River). In order to encourage Dutch people to settle there, the government offered free land. Plockhoy petitioned for some of this land. He intended for his community to be based on equality, with an elected government of three branches (similar to the executive, legislative, and judicial branches of the current U.S. government). The people were to work for six hours per day and were to be free to pursue whatever activities they liked during their leisure time. Property would be owned communally for a time, and later divided among the members. Most significantly, Plockhoy intended to forbid slavery in his community, even though the Dutch government was involved in the slave trade (Harder 1952, 49–61).

Although Plockhoy tried to attract at least 100 settlers for his new community, apparently only 41 arrived in the New World in July 1663. Almost nothing is known about the workings of this group, known as the Valley of the Swans, except that it was destroyed in August 1664 by English forces. Plockhoy settled in a cabin in the town of Lewes (later part of Delaware) and apparently made no further attempt to form a community.

According to Harder, Plockhoy intended the Valley of the Swans to "grow to be the ideal commonwealth of love and equality" (1952, 1), and perhaps it would have, had bad luck not intervened.

Although Plockhoy's communal society was destroyed, his writings indirectly influenced the thinking, generations later, of socialists such as Karl Marx and Robert Owen (Harder 1952, 72).

See also: Owen, Robert; Socialism

References

Durnbaugh, Donald. "Communitarian Societies in Colonial America," in *America's Communal Utopias*, edited by Donald Pitzer. Chapel Hill: University of North Carolina Press, 1997, 15–17.

Durnbaugh, Donald, ed. *Every Need Supplied: Mutual Aid and Christian Community in the Free Churches, 1525–1675*. Philadelphia, PA: Temple University Press, 1974.

Harder, Leland. *Plockhoy from Zurik-zee*. Newton, KS: Board of Education and Publication, 1952.

Women, Status of

The status of women in utopian communities varies depending on the community. However, the fact that utopian communities often value women's work equally to men's work, and the fact that women are often relieved of responsibility for child care and housework in community, means that women's status within utopian communities tends to be higher than in the outside world—even within communities that explicitly state that men are to rule over women.

Sociologist Rosabeth Moss Kanter points out that, in utopian communities, "there is less differentiation between types of jobs on the basis of whether or not they are considered 'work,' worthy of reward. There is less differentiation between places of work, between locales for women and men. There is less differentiation between rewards for work. And there is less differentiation with respect to access to knowledge, to gossip, and to influence over decisions" (1973, 301).

Some communities are based upon gender equality. The Shakers were founded by a woman and believed that God was both male and female. Women and men were accorded equal status within Shaker communities, and women often became leaders within the communities. Although women generally worked in traditionally female areas (such as cooking, cleaning, and sewing), men were involved with child care—they took care of boys who lived with the Shakers, since the community kept the genders separated. Shakers also developed time-saving techniques and machines to make domestic work easier, such as the clothespin, the flat broom, a washing machine, a dough-kneading machine, a pea-shelling machine, and a cream separator.

The Koreshan Unity also believed that God was female and male. The leader of this community, Cyrus Reed Teed, chose a woman to lead with him and set up committees of women and men leaders. He also supported votes and equal wages for women.

Socialist communities generally believed in gender equality. The first socialist community in the United States, New Harmony, drew up a constitution giving women and men equal rights. Unfortunately, this constitution was never implemented because the community was in chaos and ended soon after.

In the Ruskin socialist community, women and men were paid the same wage per hour, regardless of the work they did, and mothers of young children were paid a wage for taking care of their own children.

The Icarian socialist communities believed in gender equality, but did not always practice it. Girls and boys were provided with the same education, but for many years, women were not allowed to vote on community matters. This changed when a new group of people joined and demanded the vote for women.

The Fourierist socialist communities believed that women should not be economically dependent upon men and that gender should not influence the course of

Shakers believed that God was both man and woman, therefore their roles within the community were equal; however, men and women remained strictly separated during worship. (Shaker Community, Inc.)

a child's education. At Brook Farm, one of the most well-known of the Fourierist phalanxes, although many of the chores were often divided along traditional gender lines, a man did all the community's baking, and both genders taught in the school.

Fairhope—based on both socialist and single-tax principles—believed in equality for all people. Members formed a women's suffrage association.

Twin Oaks, a modern socialist community, believes in the equality of all humans. Members have even developed a gender-neutral pronoun, "co," to use instead of "he" and "she." Women and men share leadership within the community, and jobs are not segregated by gender.

Anarchist communities also valued women's freedom. Several women members of Home Colony published articles and magazines about the concept of "free love." They believed that marriage was a threat to a woman's freedom and control of her body.

Point Loma was a Theosophical community that believed in the equality of all humans. Although its founder was a woman, the community's members did not put much emphasis on gender equality. Some leaders were women, but most were men. Work was segregated by gender, with women performing traditionally female tasks. The community did provide communal child care from the age of six months, allowing women to return to work after giving birth. The community's main interests were spirituality and peace, not gender equality.

Ramona Christopherson works in the deli at The Farm. The role of women on The Farm is considered just as important, if not more so, than that of males. (Douglas Stevenson/Village Media)

Some communities did not believe in the equality of women and men, but they instituted practices that helped women to function in equality with men. The founder of the Oneida community, John Humphrey Noyes, preached that males were superior to females. However, women attended all community meetings and voiced their opinions as men did. (The final leadership rested with Noyes.) Women and men both performed a variety of work within the community, and women were selected for leadership roles. Women were encouraged to cut their hair short and to wear bloomers, in order to save time and make movement easier. Childbearing was discouraged, because Noyes felt it put a great health burden on females. Children were cared for in a communal nursery, freeing women for other work.

The Moravians did not believe in gender equality, but because they believed in separation of the sexes, women led and helped other women, and men led and helped other men. For example, Moravians sent husband-and-wife teams on missionary postings so the wife could minister to women and the husband to men.

For many years, the spiritual leader of The Farm, Stephen Gaskin, preached that women and men had different "energies." Women were encouraged to embrace traditional female roles such as motherhood and homemaking. However, at The Farm, "women's work" was considered just as important as, if not more important than, traditional "men's work," and men were encouraged to support women in their role.

Jesus People USA, a modern Christian community, believes that women and men are equal before Christ. Women are allowed to hold leadership positions within the community. However, the community rejects feminism (the movement for equal social and economic rights for women) and abortion rights (which feminists consider central to women's freedom).

Some communities prevent women from holding many leadership positions. Within the Hutterites, the Bruderhof, and the Amana Colonies, women are considered spiritually equal to men. However, women were supposed to submit to male authority. Women were and are only allowed to be leaders in traditionally female jobs, such as that of kitchen manager, kindergarten teacher, or housemother; yet, even in these communities, women's work is respected and valued. The Amana community provided a two-year maternity leave to new mothers, during which time they did not have to perform any community work but still received community benefits. The Bruderhof communities provide nurseries for babies six weeks and older, allowing mothers to return to work. The Hutterites have communal nursery schools. In all these communities, families eat in the communal dining hall or bring food home from a communal kitchen, relieving women of the burden of cooking every meal.

In some communities, women seem to be treated like second-class citizens. In the Love Family, a modern Christian community with a strongly hierarchical structure, women were considered of lower rank than men. Most leaders were men—the women leaders were generally partners of high-ranking men.

The International Society for Krishna Consciousness (Hare Krishnas) believed that, although women and men were equal spiritually, women should submit to men's leadership. At the age of 12, girls and boys were given a different education: girls were taught to cook and sew, while boys continued to study religious texts. Girls were often married as teenagers. A former woman member of the Hare Krishnas remembers that women received the worst accommodations and had to stand at the end of the line during meals.

See also: Amana Colonies; Anarchism; Brook Farm and Fourierist Phalanxes; Bruderhof; Fairhope and Single-Tax Communities; The Farm; Hutterites; Icarian Movement; International Society for Krishna Consciousness (Hare Krishna Movement); Jesus People USA; Koreshan Unity; Love Family; Moravian Movement; New Harmony and Owenite Movement; Oneida Community; Point Loma and Theosophical Communities; Ruskin; Shakers, Twin Oaks Community

Reference

Kanter, Rosabeth Moss, ed. *Communes: Creating and Managing the Collective Life*. New York: Harper and Row, 1973.

Zoar Society

At a Glance

Dates of existence in United States: 1817 to 1898
Location: Ohio
Peak membership: 500
Religious or other belief: Christianity, Pietism, Separatism

History

The Zoar Society originated from the same area of Germany as the Harmony Society's group of Separatists. However, they had different leaders: the German spiritual leader of the group that would become the Zoar Society was Barbara Gruberman.

Like the Harmonists, the German immigrants who founded the Zoar Society fled their country because of religious persecution. In Germany, they were imprisoned and sometimes had their children taken from them because they refused to submit to the authority of the Lutheran or Catholic churches of that time.

About 200 members of this Separatist group traveled to the United States in 1817. Gruberman had died by this time; their new leader was Joseph Bimeler. Upon landing in the United States, they were given housing by American Quakers and provided with money sent by English Quakers. With the help of the Quakers, Bimeler bought land near present-day Canton, Ohio, and the members moved there starting in November 1817. They named their village "Zoar" after an ancient Dead Sea town. They survived their first winter with the help of neighbors who gave them flour and potatoes.

The Zoarites did not at first intend to live communally. The idea was that each family would eventually buy whatever land it needed from Bimeler. However, some members were too old or sick to farm the land, so the community members all began working to help each other. They also were inspired by the communal life of the early Christian church. In 1819, Bimeler and the Zoarites signed a declaration that the land and property belonged to the entire community.

Women constituted about two-thirds of the Zoar community, and their work was invaluable. Therefore, when women were burdened with young children, the society suffered. Starting in 1822, marriage and sexual relations were banned in order to allow all the women to work for the community. Married members were required to live separately. The marriage ban was lifted in 1830, when Bimeler fell in love with and married a young woman who worked in his household. By this time, the society had repaid its debts and did not depend so heavily on the work of all the women.

Zoar Hotel was built in 1833 by enterprising Zoarites to make money on the tourist trade. The Hotel is a building that represents the changed commercial emphasis of the community. (Library of Congress)

The society prospered for many years. In 1834, however, an outbreak of cholera brought by a visitor caused the deaths of about a third of the community's members. In the 1840s and 1850s, the society dealt with a series of lawsuits brought by a number of former members. All the courts ruled in favor of the Zoar Society.

Joseph Bimeler died in 1853. The society was not able to find an equivalent leader. Instead, several men took his place, reading sermons and taking charge of administrative duties.

After the Civil War, industrialization made it difficult for the Zoar businesses to keep up. They closed a number of their businesses because they found it was cheaper to buy consumer goods from the outside.

In 1884, a railroad station opened at Zoar, resulting in many more visitors who came to enjoy the tranquil little town. At this time, Zoar incorporated as a village and chose its own mayor and council members.

By 1892, Zoar had expanded its hotel and some visitors stayed for weeks at a time. However, the society was not doing well financially. Society leaders made some unfortunate investments, resulting in heavy losses. There were not enough willing and able workers within the community, and they had to hire outside laborers. The Zoar Society slipped into debt. In 1898, the members voted to disband the community and distribute the property among the remaining 222 members.

Beliefs and Practices

Like the Harmony Separatists, the Zoar Separatists rejected the ceremonies of the established church, such as baptism, confirmation, and even weddings. Two people could get married by mutual consent before witnesses. Priests and preachers played no part in the wedding. While they allowed sexual relations for the purpose of reproduction, they believed celibacy was a better choice.

The group's main religious leaders—Barbara Gruberman in Germany, and Joseph Bimeler in the United States—both preached through inspiration from the Holy Ghost. Bimeler felt that because the community's spiritual needs changed over time, a fixed, written message would not meet their needs. Only the inspiration of God would suffice.

Although Bimeler did not believe in writing down his words, one member began transcribing the sermons so his deaf father could read them. Later, other members continued this tradition. When Bimeler died in 1853, the Zoarites were not able to replace him as their spiritual leader. They printed and bound his preachings into three volumes and often read from them during Sunday services.

Bimeler preached repentance of sins, moderation in eating and drinking, and an orderly and clean lifestyle. He did not believe in celebrating any of the Christian holidays, nor did he believe that Sunday was a particularly special day. Work could be done on Sunday if necessary.

The Zoar Society was pacifist, but during the Civil War about a dozen Zoar men enlisted to fight against slavery.

Daily Life

In the center of the Zoar village was a beautiful flower garden occupying an entire block. The gardener lived in a house adjacent to it and kept the garden in top shape with the help of a crew of teenage boys. In the center of the garden was a Norway spruce, representing Jesus Christ and heaven, and around this were 12 bushes representing the 12 apostles. Several straight paths led from the outside of the garden to the center, representing the "straight and narrow path" that devotees must follow to reach heaven. Another path, which encircled heaven but did not reach it, represented the path of sin.

Surrounding this garden were about 75 buildings along eight or nine streets, including Bimeler's large two-story house, which was sometimes called "the palace" by visitors. After the ban on marriage was lifted in 1830, families lived together, but sometimes two or three families shared one home. Each family maintained its own vegetable and flower gardens, and kept its own poultry. Families did their own cooking and housework.

Unlike other communities, the Zoarists had no communal dining room. Each household sent someone to the communal storehouse, dairy, and bakery to get supplies as needed.

The village also had workshops for sewing, baking, weaving, printing, cider making, and blacksmithing; a church; an assembly house in which the leaders would meet; a schoolhouse; dormitories for the children; a hotel; and a store. On the banks of the Tuscarawas River, the community built water-powered sawmills and flourmills.

Apparently the village did not measure up in esthetics to some of the other communities of the day. Charles Nordhoff, who visited the community in the 1870s, commented that "the little town of Zoar, though founded fifty-six years ago, has yet no foot pavements; it remains without regularity of design; the houses are for the most part in need of paint; and there is about the place a general air of neglect and lack of order, a shabbiness . . . which shocks one who has but lately visited the Shakers and the Rappites" (Nordhoff reprinted 1960, 109).

Because women made up a majority of the Zoar Society, women's labor was very important. They worked in the fields, raised the sheep, raised and spun flax, and tended the dairy, in addition to the traditional tasks of sewing, cooking, tending home gardens, and looking after children.

To emphasize the equality of all members, they dressed in similar clothing. Women wore long dresses, aprons, and bonnets. Men wore overalls, similar to other farmers of the day.

Music was important to the Zoar Society. It had its own brass band, and its members sang as they worked. However, dancing was prohibited. The members ate a variety of foods, but pork was not allowed. As was common with other German communities, they ate three meals and two snacks.

How They Made Their Living

Members of the Zoar Society made their living from agriculture and industry. They raised grain, fruits, vegetables, cattle, sheep, horses, hogs, and poultry. Zoar community industries included blacksmithing, cabinet making, a shoe shop, carpentry, a tin shop, a wagon shop, a sawmill, and a flourmill. They also made and sold maple sugar and syrup, as well as beer, wine, and cider.

Between 1825 and 1833, the community earned money by constructing a portion of the Ohio and Erie Canal, which passed through it. Men and women worked on this project. Once the canal was built, the Zoarists operated four canal boats.

The society had access to iron ore and coal on its land. In the 1830s, members built two blast furnaces on their land to make pig iron and castings.

Zoar also earned money by attracting visitors to their area. Its members built a hotel and general store.

Leadership and Decision Making

The Zoar Society elected three directors to manage the property and businesses. The directors were also in charge of resolving disputes among the members. Each director served for three years. In addition to these three directors, its spiritual leader, Joseph Bimeler, acted as the general manager of the society. Women were allowed to vote in the Zoar Society. While there was no prohibition against women serving as directors, none ever did.

How New Members Were Recruited or Chosen

Those who wished to join the Zoarists had to present letters of reference. People who had a skill or trade that was needed by the community were more likely to be admitted, as were those of German origin and single people. The community rejected applicants who did not understand its religious mission; most people who joined were relatives or friends of members.

Prospective members lived in the community as novices for one year. After that, if the directors approved and the membership had no objections, the novices could join as full members by giving all their property to the community. They also had to pledge to obey the directors. People who had debts were not allowed to join.

Children of Zoar Society members also went through this process when they were adults and wished to join as full members.

Members who decided to leave the community were not entitled to wages or property, unless a majority of members approved.

Children and Youth

Children between the ages of 3 and 14 lived separately from their parents in the community nursery. The children rarely saw their parents. The food and living conditions in the nursery were so poor that in 1840 one of the leaders of the community refused to send his daughter there. Beginning in 1845, children lived with their families.

The Zoar Society constructed a school, but it was part of the county school system, which chose and paid for the teacher. Children from outside of Zoar could attend this school. The children learned reading, writing, geography, arithmetic, English, and German. The boys also worked in the community flower garden and in the fields. The girls worked in the dairy industry, tended sheep, and helped with harvesting. They did not have much time for leisure activities, but they enjoyed singing, sailing, ice skating, and sledding.

At age 14, young people finished their schooling and returned to live with their parents.

Relationship with the Outside World

The Zoar Society interacted extensively with the outside world through the canal and canal boats that passed through its land. It also operated its own boats, hauling supplies north to Cleveland, and south to the Ohio River.

The society seems to have gotten along well with the outsiders. However, they had problems with former members. The case of John and Anna Maria Goesele made it all the way to the U.S. Supreme Court. The Goeseles and other former members claimed that Bimeler lived in luxury while providing only the barest necessities to the rest of the members. They demanded to be given a portion of the society's wealth. In an 1853 decision, the Supreme Court disagreed, ruling that because the society's members had agreed to hold all property in common, former members had no claim to it.

The Court's decision also included praise for Bimeler and Zoar: "That Bimeler is a man of great energy and of high capacity for business, cannot be doubted. The present prosperity of Zoar is evidence of this. There are few men to be found any where, who, under similar circumstances, would have been equally successful. The people of his charge are proved to be moral and religious. It is said that, although the society has lived at Zoar for more than thirty years, no criminal prosecution has been instituted against any one of its members. The most respectable men who live near the village say, that the industry and enterprise of the people of Zoar have advanced property in the vicinity ten per cent" (*Goesele v. Bimeler*, www.churchstatelaw.com/cases/goeselevbimeler.asp).

Reasons for Decline of the Community

With the death of Joseph Bimeler in 1853, the Zoar Society lost a capable spiritual and practical leader. When it disbanded in 1898, the community cited a number of reasons, including economic difficulties, declining religious faith, and members who were not following the society's rules.

Influence on the Outside World

The peaceful village of Zoar served as a retreat for people from nearby Ohio cities. A group of artists from Cleveland stayed at Zoar during the summers and used the village as the subject of their artwork.

The Zoar Society was an inspiration to other utopian groups. The leader of the group that eventually became the Amana Colonies, Christian Metz, visited Zoar when he and his followers were trying to decide whether or not to live communally. In addition, two of the founders of Brook Farm, Sophia and George Ripley, visited Zoar and found it very attractive.

The Village of Zoar is today a tourist attraction.

> *See also:* Amana Colonies; Bible Communism; Brook Farm and Fourierist Phalanxes; Harmony Society

References

Goesele v. Bimeler, 55 U.S. 589 (1852): The RJ&L Religious Liberty Archive, www.church statelaw.com/cases/goeselevbimeler.asp (accessed May 2006).

Holloway, Mark. *Heavens on Earth: Utopian Communities in America, 1680 to 1880.* New York: Library Publishers, 1951.

Nordhoff, Charles. *The Communistic Societies of the United States: From Personal Visit and Observation.* New York: Hillary House Publishers, 1960 (first published 1875).

Randall, E. O. *History of the Zoar Society from Its Commencement to Its Conclusion.* Columbus, OH: Press of Fred J. Heer, 1904.

Rokicky, Catherine. *Creating a Perfect World: Religious and Secular Utopias in Nineteenth-Century Ohio.* Athens: Ohio University Press, 2002.

Sutton, Robert. *Communal Utopias and the American Experience: Religious Communities, 1732–2000.* Westport, CT: Praeger, 2003.

WEB SITES
Ohio Historical Society—Zoar Village: www.ohiohistory.org/places/zoar/ (accessed May 2006).

Zoar Community Association: www.zca.org/ (accessed May 2006).

Index

Note: italic page numbers indicate pictures.

About the Author

Jyotsna Sreenivasan is a writer living in Moscow, Idaho. She has an MA in English literature from the University of Michigan. While studying there, she lived in student owned and operated cooperative housing, which sparked her interest in communal and cooperative living. She is the author of a biography for young people, *Ela Bhatt: Uniting Women in India* (Feminist Press, 2000), as well as two novels for young people: *The Moon over Crete* (Smooth Stone Press, 1996) and *Aruna's Journeys* (Smooth Stone Press, 1997). Her short stories have been published in many literary magazines.